Reforming Public Health in Occupied Japan, 1945–52

While most facets of the Occupation of Japan have attracted much scholarly debate in recent decades, this is not the case with reforms relating to public health. The few studies of this subject largely follow the celebratory account of US-inspired advances, strongly associated with Crawford Sams, the key figure in the Occupation charged with carrying them out. This book tests the validity of this dominant narrative, interrogating its chief claims, exploring the influences acting on it, and critically examining the reform's broader significance for the Occupation. The book argues that rather than presiding over a revolution in public health, the Public Health and Welfare Section, headed by Sams, recommended methods of epidemic disease control and prevention that were already established in Japan and were not the innovations they were often claimed to be. Where high incidence of such endemic diseases as dysentery and tuberculosis reflected serious socio-economic problems or deficiencies in sanitary infrastructure, little was done in practice to tackle the fundamental problems of poor water quality, the continued use of night soil as fertilizer and pervasive malnutrition. Improvements in these areas followed the trajectory of recovery, growth and rising prosperity in the 1950s and 1960s.

This book will be important reading for anyone studying Japanese History, the History of Medicine, Public Health in Asia and Asian Social Policy.

Christopher Aldous is a Principal Lecturer in Modern History at the University of Winchester, UK.

Akihito Suzuki is a Professor of History at Keio University, Japan.

Routledge studies in the modern history of Asia

Reforming Public Health in Occupied Japan, 1945–52

Alien prescriptions?

Christopher Aldous and Akihito Suzuki

Routledge
Taylor & Francis Group

LONDON AND NEW YORK

First published 2012
by Routledge
2 Park Square, Milton Park, Abingdon, Oxon OX14 4RN

Simultaneously published in the USA and Canada
by Routledge
711 Third Avenue, New York, NY 10017

Routledge is an imprint of the Taylor & Francis Group, an informa business

British Library Cataloguing in Publication Data
A catalogue record for this book is available from the British Library

Library of Congress Cataloging in Publication Data
Aldous, Christopher.
   Reforming public health in occupied Japan, 1945–52 : alien
   prescriptions? / Christopher Aldous and Akihito Suzuki.
   p. cm. – (Routledge studies in the modern history of Asia ; 73)
   Includes bibliographical references and index.
   1. Public health–Japan–History–20th century. 2. Japan–History–Allied
   occupation, 1945–1952. I. Suzuki, Akihito, 1963– II. Title.
   RA321.A43 2012
   362.10952'09044–dc23
                                                                    2011027461

ISBN: 978-0-415-68149-0 (hbk)
ISBN: 978-0-203-14282-0 (ebk)

Typeset in Times
by Wearset Ltd, Boldon, Tyne and Wear

Printed and bound in Great Britain by
TJI Digital, Padstow, Cornwall

For Thomas and Nicholas (CA)
To my parents, who lived through the Japan discussed in this
book (AS)

Contents

Figures

Acknowledgements

Rather like some cases of tuberculosis infection, this book incubated for several years before it entered its active phase. Bringing it to fruition was made possible by a year of research leave (February 2010–January 2011) and associated research expenses, awarded by the Wellcome Trust (Grant number 090658/Z/09/Z). This represented the culmination of a lengthy period of study that began in 2004 and included several research sallies to the National Diet Library in Tokyo, focusing on such topics as Japan's typhus epidemic of 1946, environmental hygiene and enteric diseases, the intractable problem of tuberculosis, and the much-contested issue of Japanese nutrition. These short bursts of research were funded in large part by the Research and Knowledge Transfer Centre and the Department of History at the University of Winchester, as were trips to libraries and archives in London and Sheffield. The efforts of library staff and archivists to locate materials and assist with enquiries were much appreciated. Special thanks are due to the staff of the *kensei shiryōshitsu* in the National Diet Library and those at the Hoover Institution Archives (Stanford University).

One of the benefits of co-authorship is the chance to discuss ideas and contentions about a subject with a colleague similarly committed to illuminating it, and this project has been no different in that respect. Others, too, have assisted with encouragement or thoughtful criticism of arguments as they evolved, most notably Gordon Daniels, Hirata Yōko, Janet Hunter, Kunii Osamu and Watanabe Mikio. Also helpful and appreciated were the comments of the anonymous referees of the original application to the Wellcome Trust and those of the book proposal and sample chapters for Routledge. Most academics have to juggle research with heavy teaching commitments, and this project certainly benefited from the support of my colleagues in the History Department at the University of Winchester, and the questions and comments of several years' of undergraduates on my third-year depth study. I am particularly grateful to Michael Hicks (Head of Department) for his unflagging support, Neil Curtin (BA Programme Leader) for helpful discussions in the pub, Natalya Chernyshova for urging me on, and Dayna Barnes for teaching my modules so well in my absence.

Finally, family members are the ones who lose out when academics are immersed in their research, particularly when the writing falters and domestic matters are neglected as a result. I would like to thank my parents for regularly enquiring after my progress, Simon for letting me fish in his lake, Rob and Jackie for all those Sunday lunches, Yōko for holding the fort during my research trips abroad, and, most important, Thomas and Nicholas for their general good humour and for knowing when to drag me away from my computer. Fishing trips together were an enjoyable escape from the world of microbes, vaccines and vector control.

Chris Aldous

I would like to thank Chiemi Iwamoto, whose secretarial efficiency made this work possible. Conversations with Nagashima Takeshi, Wakimura Kohei, Iijima Wataru, Ichinokawa Yasutaka, Akinobu Takabayashi, Sato Masahiro and Hogetsu Rie have been inspirational.

Akihito Suzuki

Notes on the text

Japanese words are romanized according to the modified Hepburn system. While long vowels are indicated by macrons, these do not appear in such well-known place names as Hokkaido, Kyoto, Kyushu, Osaka, Tohoku and Tokyo.

The usual conventions concerning Japanese names are observed throughout the book – the family name followed by the given name. However, the order is reversed for Japanese scholars writing in English.

Abbreviations

ACJ	Allied Council for Japan
AFPAC	Armed Forces Pacific
ATIS	Allied Translator and Interpreter Service
CAH	*Civil Affairs Handbook*
CSB	Central Sanitary Board
ESS	Economic and Scientific Section
FEC	Far Eastern Commission
GHQ	General Headquarters
HIA	Hoover Institution Archives
HNMA	*History of Non-Military Activities*
LNHO	League of Nations Health Organisation
NCTS	*Nihon Chōki Tōkei Sōran* (*Historical Statistics of Japan*)
NDL	National Diet Library
NRS	Natural Resources Section
PH&W/PHW	Public Health and Welfare Section
RAA	Recreation Amusement Association
RTC	rapid treatment centre
SCAP	Supreme Commander for the Allied Powers
USSBS	*United States Strategic Bombing Survey*

Introduction

In early 2010, when the authors began writing this book, public health issues were at the forefront of people's minds in the UK. There was great relief that some of the more dire warnings of the disruptive effects of the 'swine flu' pandemic had not come to pass and the H1N1 virus had not been as deadly, at least in the UK, as some had feared at its outset. In April 2009, television viewers had nervously watched presenters trace the spread of the disease as it fanned out from Mexico, and had listened carefully as they questioned public health experts about the virus' epidemiology. It was not long before a leaflet dropped through everyone's door, expressing a simple message, not of prevention but of containment: 'Catch it (cough or sneeze into a tissue), bin it (as soon as you can), kill it (kill the germs with soap and water or use a sanitiser gel).' Here was an example of a government organizing and mobilizing its citizens against an infectious disease. It dramatized the importance of public health interventions at a time when most discussions of public health at the national or community level are preoccupied with such chronic problems as obesity, alcohol consumption and smoking.

The flu pandemic takes us back to a time, during the nineteenth and early twentieth century in the UK, when the chief province of public health was communicable diseases, generating the twin challenges of preventing their outbreak and containing their spread. Typical responses were quarantining or isolating those who were infected and vaccinating contacts. The current exhortations about the importance of hand hygiene and the need to stay at home once infected with swine flu, together with the rush to manufacture a vaccine, remind us of these fundamentals of public health. They capture the joint response to disease threats required of both government and citizens, mediated by a variety of actors at the community level. Existing at the interface between state and society, public health can be viewed from multiple perspectives, ranging from national government, through local agencies to communities and families. Moreover, the flu pandemic serves as a warning to those in the developed world that generally high living standards and sophisticated infrastructures and systems of public health have not and cannot eliminate the threat of epidemic diseases in a world constantly contending with rapid environmental change, unstable microbes, stark social inequalities and swift movement of people across continents.

Wretched social conditions conducive to the spread of disease, a dilapidated public health infrastructure and the movement of people from one country to another (through repatriation) combined to make Japan in 1945 a public health challenge on a par with such recent natural disasters as the 2010 earthquake in Haiti. In his diary entry for 5 December 1945, the American journalist Mark Gayn vividly captured the devastation and social privation he encountered as he approached Yokohama:

> Before us, as far as we could see, lay miles of rubble. The people looked ragged and distraught. They dug into the debris to clear space for new shacks. They pushed and dragged carts piled high with brick and lumber. But, so vast was the destruction that all this effort seemed unproductive.[1]

Just over five years later, in April 1951, one year before the end of the Allied Occupation of Japan, there seems to have been general agreement that public health was a field in which the Occupation had excelled. James S. Simmons, Dean of the Harvard School of Public Health from 1946 to 1954, was unstinting in his praise of its achievements. In a letter to the head of the Occupation's Public Health and Welfare Section (PH&W), Crawford F. Sams, he remarked that the 'civilian health program organized by you in Japan has never been dupli-cated in the history of the world'.[2] This judgement that Sams and his section were responsible for extraordinary successes in public health has not been sub-jected to the rigorous critical scrutiny that it merits, and that has characterized other areas of Occupation policy, particularly those relating to political and eco-nomic reforms. Far from there being a debate about this triumphalist narrative of public health advances, there is pervasive neglect of the subject. A welcome and rare exception to this is Takemae's detailed and wide-ranging study of the Occu-pation, *Inside GHQ*, which devotes more than half a chapter to 'welfare reforms'. Nonetheless, despite acknowledgement of 'darker undercurrents' in relation to the use of Japanese scientists complicit in war crimes, the treatment of atomic bomb victims and eugenics legislation,[3] his assessment of public health reforms does little to temper the celebratory account associated with Simmons and Sams. Indeed, Takemae's characterization of these reforms as 'fundamentally apolitical in nature'[4] goes some way to explain the extraordinary neglect of this vital aspect of any military occupation – the measures taken to prevent epidemics and to improve the health of the subject population, motivated first and foremost by the need to prevent disruptive and destabilizing outbreaks of disease and unrest.

This book seeks to address this lacuna in the historiography of the Occupa-tion, to illuminate the public health challenges faced by the Occupation and the Japanese authorities, to consider how they were framed and the origins and effi-cacy of measures taken against them. It interrogates claims made by the PH&W that many of the solutions adopted were novel and 'modern', and alien to the Japanese experience. In short, the extent to which the Occupation's reforms rep-resented 'alien prescriptions' rather than familiar and practised remedies for the serious health problems Japan faced in the wake of defeat is the principal question addressed in this book.

This approach reflects the historian's fascination with the tension between continuity and change and the assumptions, influences and motivations underlying an emphasis on one rather than the other. It follows a trend in the historiography of the Occupation of Japan that has been pronounced since the 1980s, namely a tendency to highlight the limitations of its reforms and the degree to which pre-war/wartime Japanese forms and patterns persisted across the divide of Allied rule.[5] This reflected a much greater willingness to properly contextualize the Occupation, to view it 'as an integral segment that connected two eras of Japanese history, rather than as a period of timely changes that triggered a new beginning for Japan'.[6] This more nuanced approach owed much to the pioneering studies of such historians as Takemae and Dower, made possible during the 1970s by the opening of the massive US Occupation archive.

Access to these source materials enabled Japanese scholars to resist the ideological approaches adopted by their forebears during the 1950s and 1960s. Rather, they preferred to immerse themselves in detailed studies of the formulation and implementation of particular policies. At the same time, American academics, animated by concerns arising from the war in Vietnam, shifted their attention from the Occupation's political and social reforms to broader frames of Cold War foreign relations, security and international capitalism. These positions represented interesting twists on the first wave of post-Occupation historiography of the 1950s and 1960s, when most American commentators, some of whom had participated in the Occupation, emphasized the lasting democratic reforms of the early years. In contrast, the majority of their Japanese peers, smarting at later policy shifts or reversals that benefited the Japanese establishment, expressed a sense of betrayal and frustration at what was seen as incomplete democratization.[7] This unresolved tension between excitement and disappointment, between praise and disdain, is captured in John Dower's remark that the Occupation 'simultaneously represented a great epoch of reform and one of history's impressive holding operations'.[8] Written principally in the scripts of political, economic and diplomatic history, the historiographical disputes of these years masked a common perspective, namely policy formation and the domestic and international influences informing it. Much attention was paid to the manoeuvres of the Japanese government and bureaucracy in the face of Allied demands or pressure, the power struggles that occurred within General Headquarters (GHQ) Supreme Commander for the Allied Powers (SCAP) and the shifting balance of power between General MacArthur and his staff in Tokyo and the US administration in Washington.

With very few exceptions, there was no mention, let alone sustained analysis, of public health reform and its meaning and significance in these accounts. On the very few occasions it was discussed, it was dealt with cursorily and was usually presented as an unqualified success. Its absence from the historiography is demonstrated by the failure of all eight volumes of the MacArthur Memorial symposia on the Occupation, published between 1975 and 1992, to meaningfully engage with it.[9] Only two of them touch on issues germane to the subject of this book: a short section on welfare is included in the fourth volume on educational and social reform, and some mention is made of the public health implications of poor sanitation and repatriation in the last volume.[10] The latter acknowledges in its introduction that it is the first to illuminate 'the implementation, conduct, local initiatives, and the efficacy of the attempted reforms', eschewing the policy focus of the other volumes.

Interestingly, it was shortly before this last symposium that Gordon Daniels, a British historian of the Occupation, suggested in a short piece on the social history of the period that the flood of international research of the previous 15 years represented 'an escape *from* as well as an encounter *with* historical reality'.[11] Both Japanese and American historians, he contended, had been viewing the Occupation through the prisms of the American–Japanese Alliance and Japan's recent economic prowess, so losing sight of 'many humiliating and painful aspects of the immediate postwar years'. Daniels was absolutely right when he remarked that 'Historians may have gained comfort and esteem by taking a hygienic elevator to the written and oral archives of men in high places but they have forfeited much else in the process.' He wondered aloud about such questions as the nature and gravity of the food supply situation, whether or not it led to starvation, the problems faced by the millions of Japanese repatriated to the home islands, and the changing rates of morbidity and mortality of epidemic diseases. In the same vein, Carol Gluck had observed some years earlier that 'it remains for occupation scholars to depart from examining the policy-making process and strike out into the real social world'.[12]

It seems that this call was answered in the 1990s and 2000s, during which time 'the occupation has been renaturalized into the stream of Japanese history' as scholars have explored 'the social and cultural interactions between victor and vanquished'.[13] At the forefront of these studies has been John Dower's comprehensive and compelling sweep of the Japanese experience of Occupation, *Embracing Defeat: Japan in the wake of World War II.*[14] Despite his rich portrait of a nation suffering 'exhaustion and despair' in the early part of the book, his engagement with the subject of public health is limited to a few succinct paragraphs. Very little attention is paid to the public health emergencies of 1946, when the Occupation and the Japanese authorities struggled to prevent or check such rampant diseases as typhus, smallpox and cholera. Despite his expert treatment of the colonial mentality of many American reformers and the ways in which the Cold War influenced US policy, neither of these crucial influences is discussed in relation to Crawford Sams and his Public Health and Welfare Section. The man and his vehicle for reform are accorded a kind of neutrality. They are implicitly dismissed as peripheral to the great struggles over land reform, civil liberties, the 1947 constitution, unionization of labour and the breakup of big business that dominated earlier accounts and now, it seems, are similarly absent from studies of social and cultural topics.

A recent edited collection on the Occupation, structured around the themes of innovation, continuity and compromise, demonstrated awareness of gaps in the historiography by exploring such neglected topics as food policy, fisheries, crime and health insurance, among others.[15] Here at last was a willingness to examine aspects of the environmental history of the Occupation and to consider issues relating to public health, whether it was malnutrition or health insurance.[16] The dearth of studies in English and Japanese of public health and natural resources cannot be explained by a lack of source material – the archives of the Occupation's PH&W and Natural Resources Section (NRS) are a tremendously rich resource. Rather, it reflects an assumption that these areas were 'less controversial than other occupation tasks, such as drafting a new constitution or purging wartime leaders',[17] and by extension are therefore less engaging as historical topics, less worthy of detailed analysis. However, as will be demonstrated in the next section, there are now a few shafts of light illuminating the controversies around public health and medicine in Occupied Japan, a topic overshadowed for too long by other supposedly more dramatic reforms.

Parameters: public health, welfare and medicine in Occupied Japan

One of those shafts of light comes from the detailed, nuanced study of medical reform during the Occupation by Akiko Sugiyama, published in Japanese in 1995.[18] Divided into three main sections on the character of the Occupation, medical policy and the evolution of medical reform, her work skilfully highlights the reconstruction and reform of the medical infrastructure and the Cold War imperatives informing US policy. While the book's chief focus is medical structures and systems (e.g. hospitals, medical research, education of medical students, nurse training, health insurance, pharmaceuticals), together with the domestic and international contexts for reform, some attention is paid in the second and third sections to topics more clearly associated with public health, namely 'preventive medicine' (*yobō igaku*) and 'public hygiene' (*kōshū eisei*). These subsections address policy issues relating to quarantine of repatriates, prevention of epidemic diseases, environmental hygiene, nutrition and venereal diseases.

Here lies the conceptual distinction between public health and clinical medicine. The former operates at the national or local level and is concerned with protecting the health of communities, whereas the latter focuses chiefly on the needs of individual patients and is structured around the doctor–patient relationship, diagnosis and treatment (including surgery). While public health strategies are concerned with preventing or limiting the incidence of acute and chronic health problems, medical services focus on treatment of disease and the resources required to carry this out. Still, the distinction should not be drawn too sharply, given that the benefits of treating an individual with an infectious disease (e.g. tuberculosis) may reach beyond him/her to the community at large by preventing its spread. Indeed, as Bernard Turnock explains, 'the demarcations between public health and medical practice are neither clear nor absolute', although the blurring between the two is now greater than it was in the 1940s.

Medical practice, conducted or supervised by a doctor, operates at three levels, the second and third of which lie outside the bounds of public health – it is at the level of primary medical care, concerned with the basic health needs of individuals and families, that some overlap between public health and medicine is evident.[19] Indeed, Winslow defined public health in 1920 as necessarily including a clinical dimension:

> the science and art of preventing disease, prolonging life and promoting physical health and efficiency through organized community efforts for the sanitation of the environment, the control of community infections, the education of the individual in principles of personal hygiene, the organization of medical and nursing services for the early diagnosis and preventive treatment of disease, and the development of the social machinery which will ensure to every individual a standard of living adequate for the maintenance of health.[20]

Along with its acknowledgement of medical inputs, Winslow's definition usefully draws attention to the collective effort required to tackle the fundamental problems of poor environmental sanitation and communicable diseases. Moreover, its reference to 'the development of the social machinery' to ensure a satisfactory standard of living highlights the importance of confronting social conditions inimical to good health.

The scope and import of public health is immense. Ranging across disciplines, it encompasses a wide range of activities, conducted by epidemiologists, sanitary engineers, statisticians, nutritionists and veterinarians, as well as doctors and nurses, among others. Its chief purpose is to reduce 'a population's *exposure* to disease – for example through assuring food safety and other health regulations; vector control; monitoring waste disposal and water systems; and health education to improve personal health behaviours'.[21] Public health must be viewed from several angles in order to illuminate its *modus operandi* and its effectiveness, from the perspectives of its 'capacity' (i.e. the resources brought to bear on the problems it confronts), its 'practices' or interventions (e.g. programmes of immunization) and its 'outcomes', measurable most obviously according to rates of disease morbidity and mortality.[22]

Just as these three dimensions of public health figure throughout this analysis of the Occupation period, so too did they influence those Japanese responsible for establishing a modern system of public health in the late nineteenth century. Taking its cue chiefly from Germany, the central government took charge of this endeavour. Nagayo Sensai, the architect of this new order of public hygiene (*kōshū eisei*), was a key figure in Meiji Japan's nation-building project. He understood that confronting the challenge of disease and improving the health of its people was one of a number of vital initiatives Japan must take to address its weakness and vulnerability vis-à-vis the Western powers. Only by presiding over this vast apparatus of public hygiene, he argued, could the state hope to 'eliminate threats to life and ... improve the nation's welfare'.[23]

In the same way that the concepts of public health and medicine require clear differentiation, so too do those of public health and welfare, particularly as these functions were explicitly brought together in the Occupation's PH&W Section and the Japanese Ministry of Health and Welfare (*Kōseishō*).[24] Interestingly, the authors of the official history of the period, entitled *History of the Non-Military Activities of the Occupation of Japan*, produced separate volumes on 'public welfare' and 'public health'. The latter includes clinical medicine (with chapters on medical education, hospitals and clinics, dentistry, nursing and midwifery), but the bulk of the text covers the various facets of public health services specified above (e.g. disease control programmes, sanitation, laboratory services, port quarantine, public health statistics, nutrition, veterinary services). Rather like its sister volume, the one on public welfare follows the evolution of Occupation reform by focusing first on emergency measures – in this case emergency relief for millions of indigent Japanese – before considering the development of long-term plans, here concerned with post-war public assistance and social work.[25]

These endeavours are relevant to public health in the sense that they may ameliorate social conditions that produce disease. Indeed, public health is sometimes described as 'social medicine'. Poverty and deprivation obviously provide fertile conditions for the spread of disease, perhaps the best example being tuberculosis. Indeed, this was the most serious public health menace in Japan during the first half of the twentieth century.[26] One indicator of the need to tackle its underlying social causes was the famous study of Japanese textile workers undertaken by Ishihara Osamu during the period 1909–11. This established a strong correlation between high rates of tuberculosis and poor living and working conditions.[27] As George Rosen puts it, 'Historically, the appearance of a concept of social medicine has occurred in response to problems of disease created by industrialism. To a very considerable extent the history of social medicine is also the history of social policy (welfare).'[28]

This book navigates these distinctions and overlapping fields by employing disease as the key analytical construct. In contrast to Sugiyama's study, public health rather than medicine is its primary focus, the analysis structured for the most part around particular disease groups and associated rates of morbidity. The book aims to properly situate the Occupation experience of acute and chronic infectious diseases within its broader historical context; to identify statistical trends associated with the chief notifiable diseases in modern Japan, to examine how this category of diseases was altered during the Occupation, and to interrogate the statistical claims made by the PH&W. Long overdue is critical scrutiny of the assumptions that underlay US policies for reducing or eliminating the incidence of disease, particularly the strong contrast drawn between Japan's 'feudal', outmoded approaches and the US's 'modern' methods. This is encapsulated in Sams' description of Japan as an 'underdeveloped' country[29] – rhetoric perhaps animated by colonial assumptions and Cold War concerns.

The conventional emphasis on American agency and Japanese passivity does not sit well with the exigencies of an indirect Occupation, which necessitated meaningful Japanese engagement with the demands made of them. There is a need to evaluate the role of Japanese participants at the national and community levels, and to investigate the *joint* efforts made by Americans and Japanese charged with confronting public health challenges. One of the ways the Occupation underlined its leadership role was to highlight its technological edge, proclaiming the extraordinary success of such products as DDT, penicillin and streptomycin in tackling epidemic and endemic diseases. These claims merit critical appraisal, as does the official literature on sanitary teams and health centres, both of which were presented as American-inspired innovations.

Above all, this book aims to highlight the pivotal importance of public health for the perceived success of the Occupation. Such was the urgency of some of the problems facing the PH&W, its responses were invariably politically charged. By way of example, controversy swirled around claims of pervasive starvation among Japanese in the early months of the Occupation, vigorously denied by Sams. Likewise, appalling conditions on 'cholera ships' in 1946 attracted much unwelcome attention in the domestic and international press, and unease characterized efforts to tackle malnutrition among Japanese, particularly school children, and to explain the rising incidence of dysentery towards the end of the Occupation. Finally, what of the broader significance of the Occupation's polices concerning public health? To what extent did the strategies adopted for preventing, managing and treating disease represent a break with the past, a list of 'alien prescriptions'?

These aims are reflected in the structure of the book. The first two chapters investigate the historical backcloth to the Occupation's reforms. Chapter 1 explores the origins and evolution of Japan's modern system of public hygiene, from the late nineteenth century until the 1920s, examining the foreign and domestic influences that shaped it, the emphases placed on science and technology, on control and surveillance. Attention is paid to the authorities' record in combating reportable diseases, identified in 1880 as cholera, typhoid, dysentery, diphtheria, epidemic louse-borne typhus and smallpox, to which were added plague and scarlet fever in 1897.

Although the institutions and systems of public health established during the Meiji period generally performed well in relation to the challenge of acute infectious diseases, by the beginning of the Taisho period in 1912 their limitations were increasingly evident from the entrenched nature of a number of chronic infectious diseases, most notably tuberculosis.

Chapter 2 begins by exploring the challenge of these chronic, endemic diseases, rooted in particular socio-economic conditions, and the means by which state and society sought to confront them in the 1920s and 1930s. In contrast to such Western countries as the US and UK, against which Japan increasingly gauged its progress in public health, tuberculosis represented an intractable problem. In addition, nutritional and sanitary deficiencies were a cause for concern, as were comparatively high rates of infant mortality and venereal disease. These were problems that exercised those involved in the 'daily life improvement campaigns' (*seikatsu kaizen undō*) of the interwar years and increasingly preoccupied the Japanese military as it came to dominate Japanese politics in the second half of the 1930s. The public health demands and impact of full-scale hostilities in China from 1937 and war with the US and its allies from 1941 are considered in the second half of Chapter 2. Stubbornly high rates of tuberculosis and their implications for effective military mobilization were key factors in the establishment of the Welfare Ministry in January 1938. Heading the bureau of preventive medicine, Takano Rokurō endeavoured to confront 'the enormity of the tuberculosis problem' with 'public health centres' (*hokenjo*) and new sanatoria for the care of patients.[30] Juxtaposed with these institutional advances was the rising threat of epidemic disease in the face of deteriorating social conditions, caused by the diversion of resources (e.g. doctors and medicines) to the Japanese military, Allied naval blockade and aerial bombardment. The serious social dislocation and deprivation besetting Japan at the time of its surrender in August 1945 represented major challenges for the incoming Occupation, particularly those responsible for public health.

Chapter 3 begins by exploring how public health fitted into the Occupation's broader policy aims for Occupied Japan and how GHQ SCAP's PH&W, in the person of its head, Colonel Crawford Sams, framed the challenges it faced. Sams was scathing about the deficiencies of public health in Japan and apparently chose not to look beyond the devastation and social deprivation of 1945 to earlier decades of the twentieth century, when Japan had demonstrated both commitment and ingenuity in its public health endeavours. These attitudes serve as the backcloth to the public health emergencies that confronted the PH&W in early 1946, the main focus of Chapter 3. The potential for epidemics of smallpox, typhus and cholera to overwhelm the country necessitated an active and effective partnership between American public health officials and their Japanese counterparts, on whose energy and commitment the PH&W undoubtedly depended. Perhaps the most common image of American-inspired public health interventions is the dusting of Japanese with DDT, a chemical insecticide heralded as revolutionary for Japan, and generally regarded as the key to arresting the typhus epidemic of 1946.

Chapter 3 contests the dominant narrative of decisive American leadership, initiative and participation. It highlights the pivotal role of Japanese in typhus control, the manufacture and administering of smallpox vaccine to millions of Japanese, the quarantining of 'cholera ships' and related disinfection and immunization drives, and the production and utilization of diphtheria toxoid. All these activities drew on Japan's proven expertise, evidenced by the elimination, or at least control, of these diseases as public health menaces in the early decades of the twentieth century.

Together with the agents and measures of disease control, Chapter 3 explores the manner in which smallpox, typhus and cholera were framed by Japanese and Americans alike. Both represented them as foreign diseases originating with repatriates returning from the Asian continent or aliens within – Korean workers – who were blamed for infecting others as they travelled legally and illegally between Japan and Korea. Japanese prejudices about Korea and Koreans as diseased folded neatly into American attitudes about Asia more generally – a region associated with varying degrees of primitiveness in public health terms. Thus, it is not surprising that an address by Sams to American colleagues in San Francisco in November 1951 was entitled 'American public health administration meets the problems of the Orient in Japan'. Early on in his presentation he stated that 'since there was only a very primitive health and welfare organization in Japan before termination of the war in 1945', it was necessary for his team of reformers to promote modern, American-style methods and organizations.[31]

This image of 'the Orient' as chronically unhygienic is explored in Chapter 4 in relation to attitudes and responses to more entrenched, enteric diseases, namely typhoid, paratyphoid and dysentery. The high incidence of these diseases was blamed on poor standards of sanitation. Particularly derided was the use of 'night soil' to fertilize fields. The prevailing view among the Occupation authorities that this reflected a lack of hygiene consciousness among ordinary Japanese was strengthened by what was perceived as an indulgent attitude towards such common vectors of disease as rats and flies. The American claim that *they* were 'cleaning up Japan' needs to be viewed with some scepticism in view of the modern (and pre-modern) history of Japanese engagement with issues of environmental cleanliness, the realities of an indirect Occupation and, perhaps most interestingly, the *rising* incidence of dysentery from 1949.

Chapter 5 examines the Occupation's engagement with the issue of nutrition. To begin with it concentrated on measuring caloric consumption so as to convince the US administration in Washington of the urgent need for food aid to avert famine. By 1947, however, the focus was shifting to more fundamental considerations of dietary balance. Sams constantly alluded to 'faulty nutritional patterns', chiefly the disproportionate consumption of carbohydrates and the lack of animal protein in the Japanese diet. Particular concern about the diminished stature of Japanese children acted as the spur for a school lunch programme, which aimed above all to rebalance children's diets in favour of animal protein. As well as addressing the origins and efficacy of this drive to improve children's health through nutrition, the chapter explores its symbolic importance for the Occupation.

Chapter 6 focuses on the intractable problems of tuberculosis and venereal disease. Rooted in particular social conditions and characterized by persistently high rates of morbidity, tuberculosis and venereal disease together represent a major test of the Occupation's claim that it presided over a revolution in public health. In both cases there was an urgent need to identify cases of infection and to treat or isolate them to prevent the diseases spreading. In the case of tuberculosis, Sams endorsed established Japanese strategies, particularly inoculation with BCG vaccine, to bring down its incidence. This was in contrast to the problem of venereal disease, where the PH&W encouraged the Japanese medical authorities to break out of the confines of conventional practice – to view these diseases more broadly as a social problem requiring active community engagement rather than a disease chiefly of prostitutes, subjected to medical checks and detention in special hospitals. Unfortunately, the latter position seems to have been the one advocated by American military commanders, exercised above all by rising incidence of venereal disease among their soldiers. Ultimately, it was pharmaceutical advances in the form of penicillin and streptomycin, both essentially American innovations, that brought swift declines in rates of morbidity and mortality. However, the speed with which the Japanese deployed available expertise and resources to produce stocks of their own casts doubt on American claims of a primitive public health establishment. So too does the extent to which many Japanese doctors and public health nurses embraced the opportunities for advancing public health afforded by the health centres or *hokenjo*, relaunched in 1948 as modern, progressive agencies in the community. The degree to which these were alien to the Japanese in terms of organization, ethos and efficacy is explored in Chapter 7.

The politics of public health: Crawford Sams and the Public Health and Welfare Section

For Mark Metzler, 'the Occupation was above all a political event, and the central focus of occupation historiography, properly, has been on the occupation's political reforms'.[32] Thus, much attention has been paid to the pivotal role of Government Section as the engine of demilitarization and democratization, particularly in relation to the abolition of the Japanese military and the 1947 constitution. The publication in 1949 of *The Political Reorientation of Japan, September 1945–September 1948* celebrated the achievements of Government Section. By comparison, the work of the PH&W seems inconsequential, 'fundamentally apolitical' in Takemae's judgement, but this impression is deceptive.

'Inherently political' and necessitating an active governmental role are just two of the 'unique features of public health' identified by Bernard Turnock, an American authority on the subject.[33] As has already been stated, the public health crises with which Sams and his staff wrestled were politically charged. Both the reputations of the PH&W and, by extension, the US (as the dominant Occupation power) were at stake. Domestic and international critics did not hesitate to capitalize on any perceived failures, exploiting them to the full to advance their own political agendas. For this reason, matters of public health fell under the aegis of what Dower refers to as the Occupation's 'phantom bureaucracy', an elaborate system of censorship operating from 1945 to 1949.[34] Sey Nishimura has researched medical censorship during this period, noting, for example, great sensitivity on the part of the US with regard to associations drawn between the presence of Allied forces and either rising incidence of venereal disease or the birth of illegitimate *konketsu* (mixed-blood) children.[35]

Politics suffused all facets of the Occupation in very obvious ways – it was essentially a military occupation whereby a victor dictates terms to its defeated foe; it was committed to reform, a process that is inherently political, a new order vigorously promoted as the *ancien regime* is discredited. Furthermore, the Occupation was indirect, necessitating delegation of tasks and responsibilities to the Japanese government; its preferred styles of rule ranged from diktat to more consultative, persuasive methods, and Japanese responses likewise varied from keen cooperation to stubborn resistance. Politics operated on several levels and on a number of axes simultaneously. First, there was the internal politics of GHQ SCAP. Its various sections jostled for position, their leaders often unquestionably loyal to MacArthur and keen to impress him with the value of their work. Each section head was an advocate for his staff and their endeavours, and the importance of this role was felt all the more keenly by the heads of what were perceived to be more peripheral sections. Figures I.1 and I.2 illustrate the chain of command and division of labour within GHQ, SCAP and the PH&W, respectively.

As for the politics of indirect Occupation, these operated at both national and local levels. The formal interface between the Japanese government and GHQ SCAP was the Central Liaison Office, through which communications passed. There were many opportunities for Japanese government officials to resist Occupation demands, often manoeuvring skilfully to stymie reform efforts. Determination and persistence were qualities required of American reformers keen to bring their plans to fruition.

At the prefectural level, there were military government teams, whose chief function was to monitor developments at the local level. These teams were assigned a 'secondary mission of local-level surveillance and reporting'; their range of expertise reflected the division of functions (by section) at the level of GHQ.[36] In a rare example of engagement with the local dimension of public health work, Sey Nishimura has examined the activities of the PH&W of Kyoto Military Government Team. His articles explore the section's response to such challenges as tuberculosis, trachoma, sexually transmitted diseases, leprosy, natural disasters and the provision of safe vaccines, highlighting both common efforts on the part of Americans and Japanese with whom they worked, and instances of Japanese resistance.[37]

Beyond the Japanese theatre of operation, there was the Washington-based politics of US Occupation, the various elements of the US administration interacting with MacArthur and GHQ SCAP in a constant dialogue over policy and its implications. This was evident from the early years of the Occupation, when it was reported that Japan was threatened with famine, and the disease and unrest that would inevitably follow in its wake. In this case the US government had to accommodate both the urgent requests of Occupation officials for substantial quantities of food aid and the resentment of its allies, angered by what was perceived to be indulgent treatment of an enemy nation that should be last in the queue for relief during a time of global food shortage.

This last point highlights the politics of *Allied* Occupation that were played out in the Far Eastern Commission (FEC) in Washington and the Allied Council for Japan (ACJ) in Tokyo. Both were institutions designed to placate the US's allies over what was perceived by some of their number as disproportionate American influence over Japan. Eleven countries were represented on the FEC – Australia, Canada, France, India, the Netherlands, New Zealand, the Philippines, the Republic of China, the Soviet Union, the UK and the US.[38] It was formally accorded a policy-making role, but in practice seldom constrained the actions of

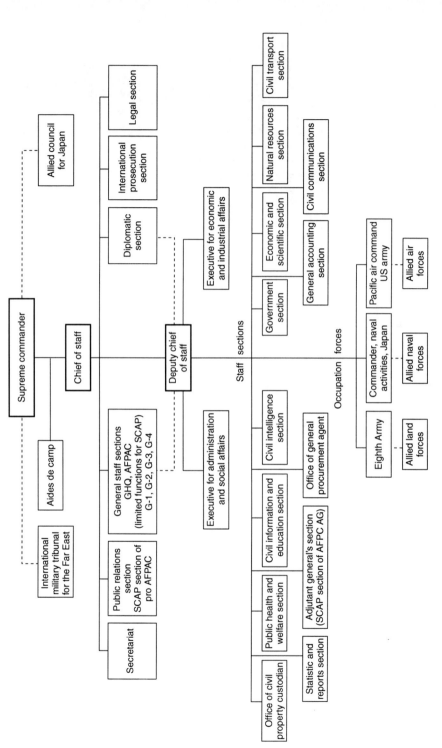

Figure 1.1 Structure of General Headquarters, Supreme Commander for the Allied Powers (GHQ SCAP). Tokyo, 26 August 1946 (source: *HNMA*, vol. 2 (*Administration of the Occupation*), Appendix 4.B, p. 9).

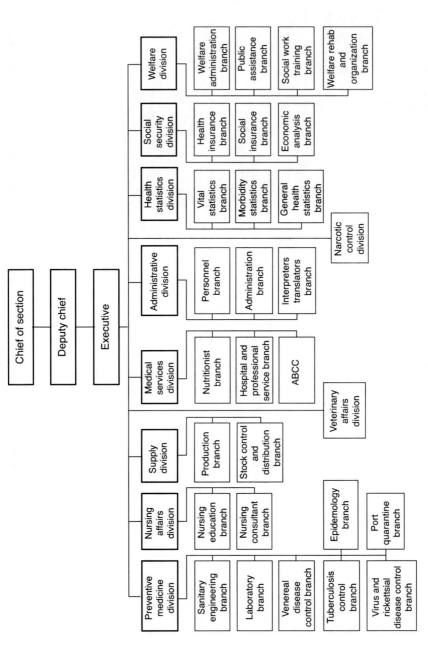

Figure 1.2 Structure of Public Health and Welfare Section of GHQ SCAP (source: GHQ SCAP, PH&W, *Public Health and Welfare in Japan, Summary, 1945–48*, p. 1).

MacArthur and GHQ SCAP. Nonetheless, much energy and time was expended in dealing with its concerns. Likewise, with members representing the British Commonwealth, China, the Soviet Union and the US, the ACJ may have been only an advisory body, but that did not stop it trying to hold the Occupation to account. For example, at the thirty-first meeting of the ACJ on 30 April 1947, the head of PH&W was questioned about American claims of success in tackling disease and its root causes. Sams responded to a number of issues raised by the Soviet representative, General Derevyanko, recalling in his memoir that 'We were able, in our presentation, to refute all of the statements of the Russians; we believe we made a very effective counterattack.'[39] Sams was indeed combative during the proceedings, prone to hyperbole at times. His performance betrayed his political priorities, his determination to present the work of his section, and by extension that of the Occupation, as responsible for great strides of improvement in public health.[40]

An exceptional administrator, exhibiting huge reserves of energy, drive and determination, together with an impressive track record in public health, Crawford Sams indelibly stamped his personality and politics on the PH&W and its perceived significance for the Occupation. The celebratory narrative of striking public health advances during this period is a testament to his great success as an advocate for the work of his section, always adept at protecting and enhancing its image. It was Takemae Eiji who brought Sams' views of public health during the Occupation to a Japanese audience by publishing his memoir in 1986 under the title *C. F. Samusu, DDT kakumei: senryōki no iryō fukushi seisaku o kaisō suru*. Reflecting perhaps the dearth of Japanese sources on this subject, the principal text on public health during the Occupation for the next decade therefore drew principally on Sams' interpretation of post-war developments, despite doubts among Japanese medical historians as to its reliability.[41]

The privileging of Sams' views was reinforced by the publication of his memoir in English, edited by Zabelle Zakarian, in 1998, appearing just four years before Takemae's authoritative survey of the Occupation, *Inside GHQ*. This was an updated and much-expanded version of his original work in Japanese, entitled *GHQ*. As already explained, *Inside GHQ* highlighted areas where medical ethics gave way to political expediency, but did not substantially revise the established narrative of success in disease control and preventive medicine. This may reflect what Stephen Large refers to as Takemae's '"progressive" Japanese interpretation of the occupation and its historical significance'.[42] Born in 1930 and growing up during a period of rising militarism and authoritarianism, Takemae's endorsement of the positive effects of American influence in public health is perhaps the natural corollary of his rejection of Japan's 'Old Order'. Likewise, Nishimura's positive view of the work of the PH&W may owe something to his survival during this period of national trauma, a sense captured by his remark that 'the provision of inoculations in 1948 saved 48,672 Kyoto infants from contracting diphtheria that year – including me'.[43]

Interestingly, soon after the Occupation ended, Sams expressed some misgivings about those who think that the work in Japan constitutes one of the so-called 'monumental' pieces of work in medical history ... such an evaluation is one for historians to make in a better perspective than we have at this early date.

And yet, when he finished his memoir in 1958, he had no hesitation in declaring that 'a major revolution was accomplished in Japan from a medical and welfare standpoint'.

Keen to capture the broader significance of the reforms for which he was responsible, he argued that they were central to the Occupation's programme of democratization: 'We think we sold democracy – not our form of democracy, but the principle of democracy – that is, the worth of the individual, to the Japanese people.' He was also willing to admit that public health had generated its share of controversy, and that this was one of the reasons that he had delayed writing his memoir. Acknowledging that 'the interpretation of events is my own and is, therefore, biased by my own background, my own experience, and my own professional interests', Sams nevertheless insisted that 'all of the factual statements included in it can be documented from my own files [surely a rather circular exercise] or from other sources'.[44] Those 'other sources', now considerably more numerous than when Sams completed his memoir in 1958, provide the raw material for this book.

Methodology and sources

Contained in 189 boxes in the US National Archives, the records of the PH&W represent an extraordinarily rich resource for defining policy and, more importantly, highlighting the gap between confident statements of rapid progress made by Sams, among others, and the more dejected tenor of many reports from the field. These documents are available also on microfiche (fiche) in the National Diet Library (NDL), Tokyo, where a computerized catalogue and search engine has enabled the authors to locate documents on particular diseases and the associated debates about their epidemiology, impact and the efficacy of recommended responses. The archive consists of a great variety of types of document, namely radios to and from Washington, lengthy reports written by Occupation officials and missions from the US, memoranda for the record, Japanese government communications, reports from the field, press translations and circulars and statistics submitted by the Japanese Welfare Ministry. Close scrutiny and interrogation of these sources reveals a much more nuanced, finely balanced narrative of public health endeavours – one that revises the triumphalist orthodoxy associated with Sams and captures the mutual dependence of American reformers concerned with public health and their Japanese colleagues. The lower-level dialogue and discussion that took place in the field between visiting American officials and Japanese doctors actually reveals much more about the nature and dynamic of the Occupation's campaign against disease than high-level statements concerned with protecting and enhancing the image of the PH&W against its detractors.

Its achievements are celebrated in the relevant volume of the official history of the Occupation, but again a willingness to read between the lines reveals as much about the enterprise's shortcomings as it does its triumphs. Similarly, the annual summaries of the PH&W published from 1949, together with a volume that covers the period 1945–48, are motivated in large part by the section's desire to burnish its successes. Nevertheless, the mass of data in tables and graphs that accompany the text include figures that do not sit well with some of the claims made. Another source produced by the Occupation, and one less susceptible to the limitations of retrospective history, is the *Summations of Non-Military Activities in* Japan (September/October 1945–August 1948). These monthly accounts of the Occupation cover matters relating to public health and provide fascinating snapshots of crises and responses as they occurred. There is little room for analysis or assessment – rather, the emphasis is on quantitative indicators (e.g. number of repatriates, available supplies of medicines, etc.). As the series progresses the presentation of data supplied by the Welfare Ministry becomes increasingly sophisticated, exemplified by graphs illustrating morbidity and mortality rates for eight communicable diseases and maps from mid-1947 detailing the spatial/prefectural distribution of 11 communicable diseases (dysentery, typhoid fever, diphtheria, paratyphoid fever, scarlet fever, epidemic meningitis, typhus, smallpox, malaria, cholera and Japanese B encephalitis). With regard to nutrition, there is a wealth of data covering average daily caloric intake, average daily per capita consumption of vegetable proteins, animal proteins, fats, carbohydrates, minerals and vitamins, together with graphs showing symptoms associated with nutritional deficiencies and the proportion of the population classified as underweight.

Similarly detailed is the report produced by the Medical Division of the US Strategic Bombing Survey in June 1947.[45] Its length, at around 250 pages, demonstrates the thoroughness of its authors, who liaised closely with the PH&W, and questioned officials of the Japanese Welfare Ministry, local health authorities, food officials, police authorities, and both public and private hospitals. The report's scope was considerably broader than its title suggests. Its specified aims were to 'describe the system of public health and medical care in Japan, and to analyze the direct and indirect changes therein caused by the war, particularly by bombing'. There is therefore much material of a historical and contextual nature, and particularly useful for this study are the chapters on food supply and nutrition, environmental sanitation, notifiable diseases, general morbidity, tuberculosis, venereal disease and medical supplies. Also helpful for providing a social backdrop to the Occupation's efforts in the field of public health are relevant reports in Japanese newspapers and the records of the Allied Translator and Interpreter Service (ATIS), which translated and summarized an enormous number of national and local newspaper articles. While Japanese journalists were subject to censorship and were, for example, warned against 'overplaying starvation', their articles capture common anxieties, local and national, about hunger, suffering and disease.

Finally, the papers of Crawford F. Sams, extending to the late 1970s, reveal much about the character, motivation and politics of the chief architect of public health reform in Japan. His correspondence reveals an ambitious man, who defined himself according to the values of science, medicine and the US military. He regarded his achievements during the Occupation of Japan as the pinnacle of his career and was bitterly disappointed not to be appointed Surgeon General of the Army in May 1951. Indeed, Sams declared that President Truman had nominated him for the post, only to reverse his decision due to his close association with MacArthur, now relieved of his command. This experience served as a dividing line between a period of great accomplishment and one of despondency as the Assistant Commandant at the Medical Field Service School in Fort Sam Houston, Texas. The frustrations that came with this position and the army's refusal to accede to his request to retire, until August 1955, served to heighten his sense of pride in what he had achieved in Japan.

Drawing on this impressive array of documentary materials, this study views the subject of public health from multiple perspectives – international, national, prefectural, local – principally, but not exclusively, through the eyes of the Occupation authorities. While the indirect nature of US control necessitated full and meaningful engagement on the part of American officials with Japanese perspectives, official and otherwise, the responses of those on the receiving end of Allied policy are nevertheless mediated by those same officials. This is not a social history of the Japanese experience of public health crises and reforms, a book that would draw on a very different selection of sources. Rather, it is a critique of the dominant narrative of public health reform *from within*. It uses the records of the very engine of reform, the PH&W, to demonstrate that the advances made were mostly in step with Japanese expectations and did not represent a significant departure from Japan's historical trajectory as established since the late nineteenth century.

This is the first study of public health during the Occupation to make extensive use of the relevant Occupation records, to focus sharply on public health rather than medical care, and to subject the Sams version of events to sustained critical scrutiny. By interrogating the rich variety of sources available, ranging from Japanese newspapers and academic articles to a diverse selection of US records, this book seeks to dislodge the Occupation's reform of public health from the historiographical rut in which it has been stuck for too long. In short, this subject belongs in the thick of the historiography of the Occupation, not on its periphery, where it has languished for the most part since the 1950s.

1 Confronting epidemics

One of the most insistent claims made by the Occupation's Public Health and Welfare Section (PH&W) related to its instrumental role in modernizing and democratizing Japan's system of public health. And yet those who looked beyond the wreckage of defeat and the health crises that came in its wake and explored the evolution of public health in Japan since the Meiji period (1868–1912) would have been struck by the strong emphasis on the 'modern' and 'scientific', terms inevitably defined according to Western criteria, that animated hygiene and social improvement campaigns from the late nineteenth century onwards. Indeed, there are striking parallels *in practical terms* between the reforming ambitions of Sams and his staff and the endeavours of such key figures as Nagayo Sensai, Gotō Shinpei, Mori Ōgai and Kitasato Shibasaburō during the Meiji period (1868–1912). The two groups were united in their determination to strengthen immunity to disease by means of vaccination, prevent the incursion of alien infections by strict quarantine regulations, reduce rates of morbidity by cleaning up local environments, and protect the health of Japanese through better nutrition.

Both groups of reformers embraced science and technology as the core components of a modern public health system, the essential difference between them best described as an *ideological* one: whereas the starting point for Nagayo and his contemporaries, born of the immediate challenges that Japan faced, tended to be nation building, a predominantly statist perspective, the declared point of departure for Sams was the health of the individual, the essential social foundation for a robust democracy. Sams contrasted this American paradigm of public health with the 'German model' of state hygiene that had held sway in Japan since the late nineteenth century and that had largely failed, he argued, to safeguard the health of the Japanese people. Indeed, Sams complained in February 1946 of Japanese ineptitude in relation to the control of communicable diseases, blaming it on 'a blind following of the theories and system of Germany'.[1]

This chapter critically examines this claim. It explores the origins and defining principles of Japan's public health system from the late Tokugawa period (1600–1868) through to 1931, when Japanese aggression in Manchuria heralded the beginning of what some historians call the 'fifteen-year war'. It first examines the architects of modern hygiene in Japan, and their keen appreciation of developments throughout Europe, particularly in Britain and Germany. Interestingly, the origins of Japanese public health coincided with the lively, sometimes acrimonious, debate over the 'germ theory' of disease – the attribution of diseases to particular bacteria – and the bacteriological triumphs of its chief advocate, Robert Koch, with whom Kitasato came to have a close professional relationship. This was one of a number of partnerships that demonstrated Japanese engagement with international developments in public health, the implications and ramifications of which seem to have captured the attention of Japanese scientists as much as those of other nations.

Following this book's predominant approach, the chapter then focuses on key diseases, most notably smallpox (a disease with a long history in Japan) and cholera and plague (both apparently alien infections), and the origins and efficacy of measures taken at both national and local levels to prevent or check them. Judgements about the degree to which the Meiji and Taisho (1912–26) authorities succeeded in building and maintaining a modern public health infrastructure can best be made with reference to rates of disease morbidity and mortality. These data sets shed some light on the seriousness with which the Japanese government sought to identify and monitor health problems. The focus here is on acute infectious diseases, cases of which had to be swiftly reported and dealt with due to their potential for generating epidemics. It seems that the challenge represented by some of these diseases, most notably dysentery, typhoid and diphtheria, was greater than that posed by smallpox, cholera, plague and typhus. The latter were apparently more susceptible to public health interventions that included immunization, quarantine, isolation and disinfection. Of course, the methods of control adopted by the authorities is just one vantage point from which the rising, steady or declining profile of a disease can be viewed – others include the behaviour of society at large and the virulence of the disease itself, which may decline due to subtle changes in its ecology. The chapter concludes with a brief appraisal of the impact of the influenza pandemic of 1918–19 on Japan, a useful gauge by which to measure the efficacy of public health systems and organizations set up to meet the challenge of a major epidemic.

Learning from Europe

By the time Japan was 'forced open' by Commodore Perry in 1853, there was already much interest and some expertise among Japanese in Western medicine. This was due to the Dutch trading post on the island of Dejima at Nagasaki, representing a single, narrow window on the Western world from 1641. Here, contact with a number of European doctors, most notably Germans, fostered a private network of *ranpō* – Japanese doctors who gravitated towards the 'Dutch style' of medicine, regarding it as superior to the traditional Japanese approaches of *kanpō*, deriving originally from China. Several studies of this period have illuminated the advances in medical understanding, particularly anatomy, made by such Japanese pioneers as Sugita Genpaku (1733–1817) and Ogata Kōan

(1810–63). Ogata founded the famous Teki juku, which trained Japan's future 'father of public health', Nagayo Sensai, in the 1850s.

Alongside such Japanese students of Dutch learning (*rangaku*) stand a number of dedicated German doctors, most notably Philipp von Siebold, who resided in Japan twice – during 1823–29 and 1859–61 – and whose energy and commitment to promoting medical science in Japan did much to recommend German medicine to Japanese advocates of modernization. What concerns us here, however, is not the decline and eclipse of *kanpō* by Western, scientific medicine, nor the Meiji government's apparent preference for research-focused German medicine over the clinical education-based British model.[2] Rather, it is the emergence of public health as a central governmental concern and a strategic priority. In the face of devastating cholera epidemics, the Meiji oligarchy saw it as fundamental to the process of *fukoku kyōhei* (enrich the country, strengthen the military).

The history of public health in Japan really begins in 1872, with Nagayo Sensai's participation in the Iwakura Mission (1871–73), his original brief being medical education. The chief purpose of this mission was revision of the 'unequal treaties' imposed on Japan by Western nations in 1858. However, largely due to failure in that regard, it is remembered more as a wide-ranging exercise in learning from the West. A trip to London provided an opportunity to consider the outlines of a national structure of sanitary districts and health officers, in advance of the third Public Health Act of 1875.[3] Nevertheless, it was in Berlin that Nagayo's interest decisively shifted away from medical education to something much broader and more significant in terms of the Meiji project of nation building. Hugely impressed by the research laboratories he visited in Berlin and inspired by the political importance of German medical experts, Nagayo began to broaden his horizons. He started to grapple with problems and issues that transcended those of medical education and practice, demonstrating a rising awareness of the young discipline of public hygiene or sanitary science. Later, Nagayo recalled his realization of the crucial role of the state as guardian of the people's health:

> I heard the words 'sanitary' and 'health' everywhere and, in Berlin, 'Gesundheitpflege'.... Eventually I came to understand that these words meant not only protection of the citizens' health, but referred to the entire administrative system that was being organized to safeguard citizens' health.

He identified the chief features of a sophisticated administrative order that encompassed sanitary engineering. This included the provision of clean water and the effective disposal of human waste, the dissemination of information about hygiene among the public by local governments, the policing of hygiene regulations and the careful recording of morbidity and mortality rates for infectious diseases, together with those of vaccination. According to Ann Jannetta, 'This vision of a way to build a healthy and strong Japan through the offices of the state appealed to him enormously. He could see an entirely new field of operations in which he could play a formative role.'[4]

Before he could set about playing that decisive role, however, he had to define it. The fundamental problem for Nagayo at the outset was how to capture the meaning of an enterprise which was largely alien to Japanese experience, and for which there was no recognized terminology. In her fascinating study of 'hygienic modernity', Ruth Rogaski explores the rather round-about route by which Nagayo sought to encapsulate the novelty and import of what he had encountered in Europe. Rejecting 'plain' terms like *kenkō* or *hoken* (meaning 'health'), Nagayo chose the term *eisei* from a Chinese Daoist classic. He was swayed by the elegance of the characters and their apparent suitability for the grand undertaking he was describing.[5] Ironically, the term *eisei* already had some currency in Japan but described an individual's regimen rather than a collective enterprise.[6] Indeed, Nagayo found it necessary to caution Japanese in 1883 that *eisei* was essentially a public endeavour (as captured by the phrase *kōshū eisei* or 'public hygiene'), and that it should be understood in terms of 'social benefits rather than ... individual pleasures'.[7] As William Johnston puts it, 'Nagayo used *eisei* to connote community health policed with state authority, but in common usage *eisei* was synonymous with "nurturing life" (*yōjō*)', attributing this discrepancy to his 'near absolute faith in the powers of the state'.[8]

This sense of an overwhelmingly top-down approach to improving the public's health for the sake of the nation caused Kajiwara Saburō of Osaka University to characterize Japanese hygiene before the Second World War as 'a hygiene of authority (the government), a non-democratic hygiene'.[9] This was in contrast to the situation in Europe, particularly Britain, where there was a real tension between local autonomy and central control and where civic engagement lay at the heart of public health reform. Indeed, Susan Burns argues that 'even in the German states ... the nineteenth century saw the rise of civil reformers, many of them physicians, who worked to take power over medical matters away from government bureaucrats'. In stark contrast, the emergence of public hygiene in Japan 'predated industrialization and its attendant health problems and ... emanated not from civil society but from the new central government'.[10]

Hence Johnston contends that Nagayo found the term *eisei* particularly appealing, because it could readily be translated as 'police' (*ei*) 'life' (*sei*), so drawing on ideas that he had encountered in Germany relating to the concept of 'medical police'. This envisaged an extensive system of public regulation of people's lives 'from the womb to tomb', defined in Professor Johann Peter Frank's multi-volume *System of Complete Medical Police*, published during the period 1779–1817. According to Rosen

> the exposition serves not so much for the instruction of the people, or even of physicians, as for the guidance of the officials who are supposed to regulate and supervise for the benefit of society all the spheres of human activity, even those most personal.[11]

At the heart of this new ideology was the conviction that a large and healthy population was the *sine qua non* of a powerful state. For Johnston, this conviction impelled the architects of modern hygiene in Japan: 'Medical police maintained public health not because individuals had the right to a healthy life but for the good of the state.'[12]

However, there is some debate among historians concerning Nagayo's preferred model of public health. Kasahara Hidehiko argues, for example, that he was keen to promote an 'autonomous' hygiene policy (*jichi eisei*) along British lines.[13] Of course, there was no sense at this time of a stark division between a German centralized model of state intervention and a British localized one of community engagement, a dichotomy that has perhaps been overdrawn in the historiography of this subject.[14] Indeed, Rogaski contends that 'Nagayo's vision for *eisei* hoped to combine the best of the British and German systems. It was not only laboratories and quarantines: It also included education, welfare, and popular participation.'[15] This was made clear when Nagayo underlined the importance of local initiative in public hygiene in an address to the Great Japan Private Hygiene Society (*Dai Nihon Shiritsu Eiseikai*) in 1888, praising Britain's achievements in this respect, and noting that they had influenced developments in Germany from the 1870s.[16] Lee pushes this argument even further, arguing against the historical grain that 'the Meiji government considered the British administrative system of public hygiene to be most suitable for enhancing Japan's national strength'.[17] However, its fragmented nature surely ran counter to the Meiji oligarchy's determination to control policy and administration from the centre. Perhaps more persuasively, Marui Eiji maintains that 'Japanese "eisei" had never been a progeny of Edwin Chadwick, but one of the most honest children of Pettenkofer or Grotjahn', and that 'human-oriented activity in the community was apt to be neglected...'.[18] As will become clear from the next section, Nagayo's philosophy of *jichi eisei* gave way to one of police control, an approach apparently favoured in particular by Gotō Shinpei.

Hygiene police, hygiene associations and military hygiene

Perhaps the best way to test some of these assertions is to trace the development, both at the centre and in the localities, of an administrative and regulatory framework for public hygiene. On his return from Europe, Nagayo took charge in June 1873 of the new Bureau of Medical Affairs (*Imu Kyoku*), located within the Education Ministry, and set about designing a nation-wide system of public hygiene, presenting his ideas in a 76-article 'medical policy' (*Isei*). In addition to urging the licensing of doctors, midwives and pharmacists, the establishment of medical schools and public hospitals, and the control of pharmaceutical products, this foundational document called for the establishment of a Bureau of Hygiene. This would serve as the core of a network of seven public health districts, each equipped with an organization charged with ensuring that local authorities acted on the central government's hygiene directives.[19]

Effective policies of public health, particularly for a country unfamiliar with its precepts, necessitated central control and coordination. Thus, the new Bureau of Hygiene (*Eisei Kyoku*), which supplanted the Bureau of Medical Affairs, was transferred in 1875 to the Ministry of Home Affairs (*Naimushō*), the key engine of administrative centralization and enforcement. Nagayo headed this bureau from its inception until 1891, working above all to combat epidemics by means of quarantine, vaccination and improved sanitation.[20] In 1876, for example, the bureau issued Regulations for Smallpox Prevention, which specified a schedule of vaccination from birth, and sent instructions to prefectural authorities in 1879 to increase rates of vaccination among the public. The following year the Regulations for the Prevention of Infectious Diseases outlined strategies for the prevention of cholera, typhoid, dysentery, diphtheria, epidemic typhus and smallpox, together responsible for 150,771 (16 per cent) of the total deaths in 1886.[21] Monitoring these developments closely was the Central Sanitary Board (*Chūō Eiseikai*), a body that rapidly grew in importance as the challenges of public hygiene mounted.

Established within the Ministry of Home Affairs in July 1879 as a cholera epidemic raged, the Central Sanitary Board was charged with developing strategies to contain it and to advise the Sanitary Bureau accordingly. Once again Nagayo was at the forefront of policy-making, chairing the Board from 1885 to 1902. Although it was originally conceived as a temporary body, the Central Sanitary Board soon became indispensable. A long-term perspective and firmness of purpose were clearly evident from the Board's first annual report: 'Where hygiene (*eisei*) is lacking, it must be imposed; where it is poor, it must be improved. No region must be deprived of its appropriate hygienic techniques.' By 1900 the Board's membership reflected the broad purview of public hygiene in terms of expertise and enforcement. It included doctors, chemists, engineers and representatives of the Ministries of Home Affairs and Agriculture and Commerce, the police, the army and navy, and the House of Peers. The Board's membership, characterized by Johnston as 'a web of influence that entwined all parts of the government', highlights the central importance of *eisei* for the Meiji modernization project.[22]

The success of the Board's endeavours depended on extending the reach of public hygiene into the prefectures and localities, a priority that produced a rather fitful process of centralization in the 1880s and 1890s. It began in 1879 with orders for the establishment of prefectural hygiene departments, together with elected local hygiene committees (*eisei ka*) and the designation of sanitary officials (*eisei in*) in each town.[23] It may be that elected committees were seen by Nagayo as a device for energizing communities to address problems of public hygiene based on the British model, but their abandonment in 1885 due to a dearth of suitable candidates demonstrated the limits of a bottom-up approach.[24] Administrative adjustments were made in 1886, 1890 and 1893, culminating in the permanent transfer of jurisdiction for public hygiene to the police. By 1899 the prominence of disease as a threat to social order was evidenced by the majority of prefectural police departments having a separate hygiene section. Fukuda maintains that the increasing involvement of the police 'unfortunately meant that more emphasis was placed upon administration and strict regulation than on implementing the effective measures of prevention and treatment'. In his view, the 'oppressive attitude of the medical police did more harm than good especially in 1882 when Tokyo was attacked severely by a cholera epidemic'.[25]

According to Joseph Wicentowski, the modern Japanese police system, formed in the early 1870s, was involved in public hygiene from its inception. Indeed, he contends that 'nowhere were the sanitary police [*eisei keisatsu*] instituted earlier or more comprehensively than in imperial Japan (1868–1945)'.[26] Japanese historian of the police, Obinata Sumio, outlines the police's breadth of responsibilities in relation to *eisei*. These were identified in the 1885 Fundamentals of Police (*keisatsu yōsho*) as enforcement of regulations concerning port quarantine, food, drinking water, swimming, dyes, medicines, farm animals, slaughterhouses, cemeteries, crematoria and disposal of refuse. From 1886, with the development of hygiene sections in prefectural police organizations, they were assigned additional responsibilities, namely epidemic prevention, disinfection, quarantine and smallpox vaccination.[27] Wicentowski observes that the comprehensive role afforded the Japanese police in public hygiene was reflected in the thick 'sanitary police' textbooks and manuals published for their guidance.[28] The Police Bureau stood alongside the Bureau of Hygiene within the Ministry of Home Affairs. Their formal parity masked the tension between a system of public hygiene centred on local doctors and hygiene officials, favoured by Nagayo, and one dependent on police enforcement of government regulations.

The urgent need to improve local engagement with issues of public hygiene was highlighted again in 1886 by another serious cholera epidemic, the crisis prompting the Japanese emperor to donate funds for the creation of 'hygiene associations' (*eisei kumiai*). These were first piloted in Tokyo and Saitama prefecture and then identified by the Central Sanitary Board as an essential adjunct to the work of the police throughout Japan in ensuring the observance of hygiene regulations, promoting smallpox vaccination and, perhaps most importantly, urging rapid disclosure of any cases of infectious disease.[29] The potential seriousness of concealing victims of epidemic disease or resisting police controls had been underlined by Nagayo in his speech to the opening meeting of the Great Japan Private Hygiene Society, of which he was a founding member, in May 1883:

> People evaded not only cholera prevention activities, but also avoided all things concerning hygiene, so the popularization and promotion of hygiene was adversely affected.... Then I thought that it was necessary to establish a society which ... should aim to reconcile the people with the government'.[30]

Although this was ostensibly a private (*shiritsu*) society, its governmental steer was evident from the participation of such prominent political figures as Ishiguro Tadanori, the Surgeon General of the Army, Nagayo Sensai, and Gotō Shinpei, all of whom used it as an alternative instrument for the achievement of their aims. Initially, the society focused on the urgent need to prevent and check acute infectious diseases, namely cholera, by means of disseminating information among local groups for the adoption of effective hygienic measures. Later, when the threat of raging epidemics had passed, it focused its energies on tackling the entrenched problems of tuberculosis and venereal disease.[31] The society was an important agent of 'hygienic modernity', publishing its own journal, the *Dai Nihon Shiritsu Eiseikai Zasshi* (*The Magazine of the Great Japan Private Hygiene Society*) from 1883 to 1920, even composing a 'hygiene anthem' (*eisei shōka*) for schools in 1900, which conveyed the message that 'body and mind must be healthy in order to express loyalty to the emperor and respect for ancestors'.[32] Thus, the society was 'deeply involved with the state'. It assisted in the licensing of doctors for practice, and fully supported the government's endeavours to control epidemics and to improve standards of public hygiene throughout the country.[33]

In light of these developments at both national and local levels, Nagayo Sensai could justifiably argue by the early 1890s that, acting on the spur provided by his contact with European exemplars of public health, he had met the challenge of introducing modern hygiene to Japan. In this endeavour he was assisted by other vocal advocates of change along European lines, namely Gotō Shinpei (1857–1929), who would play an important role in Japan's imperial administration, and Mori Rintarō (1862–1922), whose primary responsibility was army hygiene. Gotō is generally associated with the promotion of *eisei keisatsu* as the key instrument of state hygiene, seeing its improvement as dependent on active intervention on the part of the authorities. These ideas were shaped by his readings of German works on the subject and his own experiences vis-à-vis the development of *eisei* policy. When he assisted Ishiguro Tadanori with the care of the new army's casualties in the civil war (*seinan sensō*) or Satsuma Rebellion of 1877, Gotō was impressed by the 'coercive measures' employed and 'the efficiency of military medicine'.[34] Increasingly struck by the potential of modern hygiene administration to improve standards of health, Gotō undertook local hygiene surveys (*eisei chōsa*) in Aichi prefecture, where he worked as a doctor, and implemented a system of sanitary police in Nagoya, the prefectural capital. These were approaches he continued to endorse as a member of the Bureau of Hygiene from 1883, succeeding Nagayo as its head in 1892.[35]

Again, however, it would be over-simplistic to view Gotō as an advocate of hygiene police in place of local semi-official health boards and Nagayo as an advocate of the opposite; rather, it was a question of balance. Official regulation was necessary in any case, whether by hygiene officials and doctors or by the police, and both figures obviously favoured fuller popular engagement with the meaning and application of *kōshū eisei*. Visiting London in 1891 to attend the seventh International Congress of Hygiene and Demography, Gotō admired the balance struck in Britain between local autonomy and state control in public health, noting that the former's strength worked to enhance genuine social commitment in a way seldom achieved by central diktat.[36] Philosophical differences aside, both Nagayo and Gotō presumably understood that such were the challenges facing their country in the shadow of Western imperialism that it could not wait for the emergence of a hygiene consciousness among the masses. Kasa-hara maintains that what transpired in the 1890s was a hybrid system of public health, combining 'local autonomy' with 'centralized policing'. This begs the question of whether or not they were mixed in equal parts. The emphasis on hygiene police and the degree to which they intruded into ordinary people's lives strongly suggests that the balance was skewed towards the state rather than society.

As head of the Bureau of Hygiene in 1897, Gotō presided over the Law for the Prevention of Infectious and Contagious Diseases, identified now as cholera, dysentery, typhoid fever, smallpox, typhus, scarlet fever, diphtheria and plague.

The law required physicians to react quickly to any diagnosis of cases of these diseases. Stringent rules on disinfection of the premises, burial or incinera-tion of corpses, removal of the patient to an 'epidemic hospital or isolation house', quarantine of the house or neighbourhood and restrictions on public gatherings demonstrate the degree to which the Bureau of Hygiene had embraced modern, intrusive methods of infectious disease control. The 36 articles of the law contain frequent references to actions taken under 'the direction of the pre-fectural governor', 'the physician' or 'the authorities concerned', usually the police, highlighting the top-down, command approach that both Nagayo and Ishiguro had reservations about.

Likewise, Mori Rintarō (Ōgai) argued that the development of a modern, effective system of public hygiene depended on genuine popular support for the required measures. Capturing the tension between state intervention and social engagement, he called on people to 'grasp authority over hygiene' but acknow-ledged that 'public health is one important aim of government'. The challenge was to 'define that part which belongs to government and that part which should be carried out by the people'. Mori was a prolific writer, now best known for his fiction. When it came to his writings on hygiene, he always favoured a rational approach, arguing, for example, that Japanese housing, footwear and diet suited Japanese conditions and therefore should not be considered inferior to their Western counterparts. Adopting a thoughtful, analytical approach towards medi-cine and public health, however, led him to the conclusion that 'In the world of today there is only one medicine: modern medicine', resting on the sure founda-tion of the scientific method.[37]

Mori's scientific mind was much exercised by the military demands of the Sino-Japanese War of 1894–95, during which standards of army hygiene were found wanting. Of 170,000 soldiers hospitalized during the war, around 4,500 had battle injuries. The rest were suffering from dysentery, malaria, cholera and beriberi.[38] Winning this 'war against disease', Mori realized, necessitated improvements in such areas as nutrition, sanitation and isolation of soldiers with contagious diseases. Thus, he lost no time in recommending changes. His *Eisei Shinpen* [*A New Guide to Hygiene*], published in 1897, ranged across an extra-ordinary variety of subjects, from epidemic prevention, sanitation and nutrition to gases, climate and acclimatization.[39] According to Jong-Chan Lee, Mori's book was widely read in civil and military circles, and 'caused hygiene to be popularized in the name of military medicine'.[40] Certainly, it seems to have produced more stringent hygienic controls for the Japanese military, Japan's civil population and the subjects of Japan's first colony, Taiwan, where Gotō served as head of the Civil Administration Bureau from 1898.

Identifying microbes

As this process of entrenching *eisei* unfolded in Japan during the 1880s and 1890s, a divisive debate was raging in Europe about the nature of disease, a question fundamental to conceptions of modern hygiene. On one side of the argument were 'sanitarians', who deferred to the prevailing view that disease arose from filthy local conditions, putrescence and foul odours (miasmas). On the other were those who embraced the new science of bacteriology, which attributed diseases to specific microbes. This acrimonious debate was played out in Japan too, due to the close ties fostered between German and Japanese scientists. Battle lines formed between proponents of the germ theory of disease, most notably Kitasato Shibasaburō, who had cut his research teeth in Berlin under Robert Koch, and Japanese colleagues more influenced by the sanitarian or environmental approach, championed by Max Pettenkofer in Munich, the 'founder of modern hygienic science'.[41] Interestingly, Pettenkofer acknowledged that germs were partly responsible for causing infectious diseases but more important were particular environmental conditions.

The great promise offered by advances in microbiology, namely the identification and isolation of particular pathogens and associated advances in the production of vaccines and antitoxins, had profound implications for the future course of public hygiene in Japan. It provided a *scientific* justification for the state's active promotion of diagnostic laboratories, preventive vaccination, quarantine of ships and isolation of victims of infectious disease in homes or hospitals. However, while the discovery of bacteria was crucial to the implementation of effective strategies for combating acute infectious diseases, its impact was much less impressive in relation to chronic ones like tuberculosis and dysentery. And so, in Japan, as Paul Weindling notes in relation to Germany, 'bacteriology did not displace environmental reform'.[42] The voices of those who declared that the challenge of disease was best met by public hygiene campaigns that targeted sanitary infrastructure, lifestyle and nutrition could still be heard amidst the loud acclaim that greeted the discovery of bacterium after bacterium in the 1880s and 1890s.

Reflecting Japan's close ties with Germany, Kitasato was at the forefront of these discoveries. Indeed, James Bartholomew states that in the early 1890s he was 'not only the top bacteriologist in Japan, he was among the top three or four in the world and had helped to create the discipline of serology on which any effective bacteriological campaign would necessarily have to depend'.[43] Employed by the Bureau of Public Health from 1883, Kitasato first worked under Ogata Masanori, recently back from Pettenkofer's Hygiene Institute in Munich. Kitasato's impressive research on cholera in chickens led to his being awarded, on Nagayo's recommendation, a fellowship to work at Robert Koch's laboratory in Berlin. There he undertook research for nearly six years (1886–91), developing such a high regard for Koch and his advocacy of the germ theory that he refused to act on Nagayo's instruction to transfer to Pettenkofer's Hygiene Institute in 1887. Both workaholics, the two men developed a high regard for one another. Kitasato worked extremely hard to demonstrate the *tetanus bacillus* in pure culture in 1889, largely in response to a German challenge to his mentor's position.[44] The following year, 'he shared, in collaboration with Emil von Behring, the fame of the discovery of the principle of serotherapy in their joint discovery of tetanus antitoxin'.[45] And just as Robert Koch had travelled to India to identify the pathogen of cholera in 1884, so too did Kitasato succeed in isolating the plague bacillus in Hong Kong ten years later (simultaneously with a rival scientific mission led by Alexandre Yersin).

Following his return from Germany in 1891, Kitasato quickly emerged as the pre-eminent authority in Japan on matters of public hygiene. His prominence reflected the excitement generated by his scientific discoveries in association with those of Koch, not least because of the rising mortality rate of tuberculosis in Japan and the high death toll from epidemic diseases in the closing decades of the nineteenth century. In relation to tuberculosis, the rate more than doubled from 99 per 100,000 in 1888 to 206 in 1905.[46] As for the impact of epidemics, 108,405 Japanese had died from cholera in 1886, and 41,284 from dysentery in 1893.[47] In response to such elevated rates of mortality and the excitement surrounding recent bacteriological developments, most notably the (misplaced) optimism invested in tuberculin as a cure for tuberculosis,[48] Japan's first institute for the study of infectious diseases was established in September 1892 with Kitasato as its director. With a hygiene laboratory already operating at Tokyo University under Ogata, Japan's first Professor of Hygiene, the new institute generated its share of controversy, arising chiefly from bureaucratic rivalry between the Education Ministry and the Home Ministry. This was resolved only by securing private funds for the institute (principally from the Great Japan Private Hygiene Society), and a government commitment to subsidize it. Largely as a result of a number of striking successes, exemplified by Shiga Kiyoshi's identification of the bacillus of dysentery in 1897, the Institute of Infectious Diseases was nationalized in 1899. Its activities expanded in advance of and during the Russo-Japanese War of 1904–5.[49] The great strides that Japan had taken in terms of improving its standards of public hygiene, not least in relation to advances in microbiology, were thrown into sharp relief by that war.

In his book, *The Real Triumph of Japan: The conquest of the silent foe*, Louis L. Seaman commended Japan for its achievements in its war with Russia. An American medic much concerned by poor standards of hygiene among US forces, Seaman regarded Japan's record as 'unparalleled and unapproachable in the annals of war'. Employing the motto 'prevention not treatment', the 'sons of Nippon' had reversed the usual ratio of deaths from disease to those from combat: now it was 'four men killed by bullets to one who dies from disease!' He attributed this remarkable success largely to 'the most elaborate and effective system of sanitation that has ever been practised in war'. This was exemplified by universal compliance with the stipulation that water for drinking was boiled and the diligence of sanitary officials who tested sources of water for advancing troops, placing on the well a placard stating whether or not the water was contaminated. Moreover, Seaman highlighted Japan's embrace of modern, scientific medicine by referring to the prominence of 'the bacteriological laboratory', found in 'every base and field hospital in Manchuria'. Indeed, he praised Japan for being the first country to recognize that 'microscopes were as important as 11-inch guns' and for deploying them in 'every place where extended stay was made, and wherever bacteria were likely to be found'. Microscopes, he contended, were used effectively to forestall epidemics and to save individual lives by prompt diagnosis. Summarizing the lessons of the war for his home country, Seaman noted that pioneering advances had been made in sanitary science and dietetics rather than in surgery or the care of the wounded and sick.[50]

Despite the 'simple, non-irritating, and easily digested rations of the Japanese troops', the incidence of beriberi (*kakke*) remained high. This was a disease caused by a deficiency of thiamine (vitamin B1) but regarded by most scientists at this time as infectious. In a fascinating article that suggests that the rise of Western 'scientific medicine' actually impeded the implementation of practical measures to reduce the incidence of beriberi, Christian Oberlander maintains that Japan's victory against Russia was 'tarnished by the fact that more than 200,000 Japanese army soldiers or almost 20 per cent of total army personnel in the field in Japan and Asia fell sick with beriberi, many of them dying from the disease'.[51] Aoki Kunio states that deaths from the disease amounted to 27,800, 3 per cent of the total number of troops.[52] This was in spite of the highly suggestive epidemiological studies of beriberi conducted by Takaki Kanehiro, a naval medical officer, who rather than receiving his training in Germany had studied at St Thomas' Hospital in London (1875–80).

On the basis of rigorous epidemiological surveys, Takaki identified dietary deficiency as the cause of beriberi, although he was not able to correctly identify the nature of the deficit. In any case, he set out to improve sailors' rations, first switching from polished rice to a Western-style ration, then later – for reasons of affordability – to a barley–rice mixture. As a result of these innovations, morbidity rates among sailors fell from up to 41 per cent between 1878 and 1883 to just 13 per cent in 1884. Despite this startling record of success, there was much resistance to Takaki's findings among his peers, many of whom were convinced that the disease was an infectious one. Army hygienists like Mori and Ishiguro, for example, had no truck with Takaki's theories. Thus, they welcomed the claim made by Ogata Masanori in 1885 that he had discovered the germ that causes beriberi, and had demonstrated such according to Robert Koch's rigorous methods.[53] Still, it was not long before the more expert microbiologist, Kitasato, at Koch's prompting, identified flaws in Ogata's research, finding it insufficiently rigorous rather than wrong it principle – Kitasato likewise believed in beriberi's bacterial etiology.[54] Apart from the divisions between the Japanese army and navy that it reveals, the controversy over beriberi highlights the degree to which the exacting standards of modern medicine and bacteriology were preferred to the more speculative epidemiological studies of Takaki. This was in spite of the proven efficacy of his reforms. Interesting and revealing as this controversy was, however, beriberi was atypical of the disease challenges faced by the Japanese government in the late nineteenth and early twentieth centuries – it was a disease with a low profile in Europe and it was non-infectious. Divisions among Japanese medical officials over beriberi stand in marked contrast to the much greater unity of purpose that characterized public health campaigns against such major challenges as smallpox, cholera, plague and typhus.

Battling microbes: acute infectious diseases

Nothing spurred on the advocates of public hygiene in Meiji Japan more than the threat posed by acute infectious diseases, distinguished by their potential to spread very rapidly among the population and so prove particularly disruptive for state and society. As demonstrated by the onslaught of cholera in the 1870s and 1880s, these outbreaks of disease could be truly devastating, producing serious social discord when the government resorted to coercive measures against households and neighbourhoods. They also presented tremendous political challenges to the new government, determined to master effective systems of disease prevention and control and yet unable to operate a system of strict quarantine until 1899, when the terms of the unequal treaties of 1858 were finally revoked. The chief disease menaces were identified by the Law for the Prevention of Infectious and Contagious Diseases (1897) as cholera, dysentery, typhoid fever, smallpox, typhus, scarlet fever, diphtheria and plague. Some, like smallpox, were indigenous to Japan; others, like typhus and plague, were alien invaders. As 'legally designated infectious diseases' (*hōtei densen byō*), requiring swift and decisive countermeasures, immediate disclosure of any case was required of the attending Japanese doctor, who would lose his licence to practise if found to be negligent in this regard.

This section explores the extent to which the Japanese authorities successfully met the challenge posed by these diseases, the approaches they adopted to prevent outbreaks and to check them when they occurred, and the degree to which their record demonstrated proper engagement with the latest advances in public health internationally. The official statistics that enumerate cases and deaths from the principal communicable diseases are the chief factor by which that success is measured in this necessarily broad survey of Japan's disease profile from the late nineteenth century to the 1930s. Clearly these statistics are problematic, particularly during the Meiji period when new procedures for reporting and recording disease incidence were introduced as part of a larger process of rapid, sometimes fitful, centralization. It can be assumed that there was under-reporting and misdiagnosis of illness, and the complex epidemiology of these infectious diseases caution against too hasty an assumption of reduced incidence being a consequence of public health interventions. Nevertheless, when examined alongside the strong commitment of the Meiji and Taisho authorities to strengthen the nation by improving the public's health, the majority of data sets discussed here are suggestive of a strong correlation between rigorous public health measures and reduced disease incidence.

The story of effective intervention to control acute infectious diseases really begins with the introduction of Jennerian vaccination against smallpox in 1849 and its rapid transmission throughout Japan in the early years of Meiji. These developments evidence the solid foundation on which the Meiji drive for hygienic modernization rested. Particularly significant was the network of *ranpō* doctors who smoothed the way for innovation by disseminating knowledge of Western medical practice and – as successful vaccinators – by recommending modern forms of prophylaxis. Once the obstacles preventing the transfer of live cowpox virus (*Variolae vaccinae*) from Dutch Batavia to Japan had been overcome with the successful import of crusts of cowpox (rather than lymph), the web of contacts among *ranpō* doctors that had been developing over several decades served to facilitate swift uptake of the practice throughout Japan. Its success led in 1860 to the Tokugawa shogunate belatedly endorsing it.[55] This change from private to public support for vaccination enabled Nagayo, as director of the Bureau of Hygiene, to move quickly to promote this safe and effective preventive measure as a strong support for the modern, nation-wide system of public health he envisaged.[56] Tackling the leading cause of death among Japanese children at this time would surely recommend Western approaches to public hygiene to ordinary Japanese.

Nagayo therefore lost no time in issuing a 'Vaccination Proclamation that made Jennerian vaccination the only legal way to protect against smallpox. Variolation (inoculation with smallpox virus) was declared illegal.'[57] However, Nagayo understood that vaccination on the scale required to eradicate the disease required ample supplies of vaccine and a commitment on the part of doctors throughout the country to carrying out the procedure, and careful monitoring and recording of it. By the early 1880s, the effective use of calves for vaccine production ensured an increasing supply of vaccine for distribution to the prefectures, the quality of which impressed visitors from Korea and Russia. As for the introduction of effective systems for reporting and recording information, Jannetta states that the systematic collection of public health statistics began with the diffusion of vaccination. This is evidenced by the Hygiene Bureau's publication of records of smallpox incidence, mortality and vaccination for the period 1874–79, detailing in its report prefectural success rates for first vaccinations and re-vaccinations. By the mid-1880s, doctors were expected to produce monthly reports, specifying the names and addresses of those they had issued with certificates of vaccination, and the police charged with monitoring rates of vaccination in their neighbourhoods and actively intervening where cases of disease occurred. By the turn of the century, therefore, the Meiji authorities had succeeded in extending their reach into neighbourhoods and households, ensuring levels of compliance with vaccination and hygiene regulations that produced a marked decline of smallpox incidence and mortality.[58] Whereas the smallpox epidemic of 1886 had generated 73,337 cases of the disease and 18,791 deaths, the figures for the last major epidemic of 1908 were 18,075 and 4,274, respectively.[59] According to Yamamoto, the success of vaccination caused 'the concept of immunization ... to be accepted by the public', so advancing public understanding of modern techniques of disease prevention.[60]

However, this proved of little consequence in the case of cholera. Faced with an alien, virulent disease, and with no vaccine to deploy against it until one was developed in 1902, the Meiji authorities were forced to resort to alternative methods of control. In contrast to advances made against smallpox during the Tokugawa period, the Hygiene Bureau had to devise strategies for combating this disease *de novo*. Cholera came to Japan in successive waves, first through the port of Nagasaki in 1822, towards the end of a pandemic that began in Bengal in 1817. This outbreak chiefly affected the western part of Japan, spreading to Osaka but not as far as Edo (Tokyo). The next wave of cholera came during the pandemic of 1846–63, brought to Nagasaki by the US warship *Mississippi* in 1858. This was the year the Tokugawa shogunate felt compelled to sign humiliating 'unequal treaties' with the Western powers. And so, as Susan Burns remarks, 'the creation of the treaty ports in Japan brought not only political and economic turmoil but also an epidemiological crisis'.[61] This time the disease spread throughout Japan, causing 10,000 deaths in Osaka and 30,000 in Edo during September and October, and provoking little response from the Tokugawa authorities.[62] According to Yamamoto Shun'ichi, this epidemic had run its course by 1863.[63] The third wave of cholera, arriving in 1877, proved to be much more protracted, marking the start of a period of around four decades when the disease was semi-endemic in Japan.

The nature and effectiveness of the Meiji government's response to the cholera emergency illuminate the purposefulness of the new regime in the face of some insurmountable obstacles. In 1877, for example, the government was hamstrung by foreign resistance to quarantine of vessels at Japanese ports, the British conveniently objecting to 'the theory that cholera would be propagated through maritime traffic'.[64] Moreover, the government had to contend with an internal challenge to its authority from southern Japan in 1877, when the spread of cholera was accelerated by the movement of troops northwards following the suppression of the Satsuma Rebellion. A much more serious epidemic occurred in 1879, strengthening the government's resolve to combat the disease by surveillance, isolation of patients and compulsory disinfection. Enforced by the new centralized police force, these intrusive measures provoked angry resistance, particularly the removal of patients to isolation hospitals where they invariably died.

> The high death rate of the patients sent there and the wretched conditions of the cheap and makeshift buildings [caused the] isolation hospitals to be feared and hated, with rumours running that doctors disembowelled the patients alive and sold the livers as medicine.[65]

As a result of these anxieties, around 50 eruptions of popular anger occurred in 1879. These 'cholera riots' capture for some historians the clash between the isolation hospital as a symbol of the elite's embrace of modernity and the culture of the masses, trusting in religious rituals to protect them against the disease. However, perhaps more striking than the violence with which some Japanese responded to rigorous control measures was the apparent willingness on the part of both the authorities and much of the public to work together to deal with the crisis. The adoption of a softer policy on isolation, permitting patients to remain at home, suggested greater sensitivity towards popular disquiet, and public donations of money and disinfectant evidenced widespread support for government policy. These developments demonstrate the government's balancing act between policing and educating the public in relation to disease control, a dichotomy discussed earlier in the chapter.[66]

Modern science figured prominently in efforts to combat cholera and treat its patients. Once again, Japanese leaders looked to Germany for answers, dispatching the Surgeon General of the Army, Ishiguro Tadanori, to Berlin in 1888 to consult with Robert Koch about how best to control the disease.[67] In 1895 Kitasato, four years back from Germany, developed a cholera serum that 'saved two-thirds of the victims in a Tokyo epidemic'.[68] Furthermore, by the late 1890s, bacteriological research into cholera in Japan was paying dividends in terms of the identification of different strains of the disease and the development of an effective vaccine. The latter was produced in 1902 and by the following year had been adopted for public use, despite its proving much less effective than smallpox vaccine.[69] Presumably as a result of its limitations, the Institute of Infectious Diseases, transferred to the Education Ministry in 1914, and the breakaway Kitasato Institute – formed in protest to the transfer – competed to produce an advanced cholera vaccine.[70] According to a League of Nations Health Organisation (LNHO) report on cholera in Japan, published in 1926, the choice was between a heated vaccine and a sensitized one,[71] promoted by the Kitasato Institute. The report states that

> This sensitized vaccine, which has been in use since 1916, has been more readily accepted by the general public and, in spite of heated discussion as to its relative effectiveness, even the opponents of its use must admit that it has done much to popularise prophylactic inoculations.[72]

The same report begins with the statement that

> Cholera in Japan is always an exotic disease.... The homes of cholera, where enormous numbers of lives are lost yearly, are near our door [India and China], so constant watch has to be kept against the invasion of the disease.[73]

That vigilance could be fully justified once the bacterial transmission of cholera was firmly established and, more importantly, it could be properly exercised by means of 'an autonomous "quarantine law of seaports" ... as soon as Japan was freed from the fetter of unfair treaties with foreign powers' in 1899.[74] It can be assumed that the twin devices of mass immunization and an effective quarantine regime together account for the disease's declining profile from 1900 and its very low incidence from 1920, when it passed from its epidemic phase to what Yamamoto refers to as its 'age of intermittent occurrence (1921–45)'.[75] Between 1921 and 1945, the highest annual incidence of the disease was in 1922 and 1925, when there were 743 and 624 cases, respectively; otherwise there was only one year when the number of cases exceeded 200 (205 in 1929) and plenty of years with no recorded cases at all (1924, 1930, 1931, 1933–36, 1939–44).[76]

Just as modern science provided the main solutions to smallpox and cholera, so too were Japanese microbiologists at the forefront of campaigns to tackle the other notifiable diseases (typhoid, dysentery, typhus, plague, diphtheria and scarlet fever).

By far the most serious of these in terms of their rates of morbidity and mortality were the enteric diseases of dysentery and typhoid. The statement made in the LNHO study of cholera (cited above) that 'Experiences with sensitised typhoid vaccine suggested a sensitised cholera vaccine'[77] demonstrates that typhoid prophylaxis was a research priority. This was certainly justified by the number of cases and deaths produced by the disease – a peak of 66,224 cases and 14,002 deaths in 1886, and despite falls thereafter a rise to 58,404 cases and 14,063 deaths in 1924.[78] Sams would later claim that the Japanese had 'turned their backs on typhoid vaccine as a means of protecting their people against a hazard that, before the war, caused 40,000 to 50,000 cases per year and 6,000 to 12,000 deaths'.[79] However, recent research by Nagashima Takeshi highlights the introduction of a 'voluntary vaccination program' following the Great Kantō Earthquake of 1923, drawing on Tokyo Metropolitan Police data to estimate that around 20 per cent of the capital's population received the vaccine every year in the late 1920s and 1930s.[80] From 1927 to 1937, the incidence of the disease remained fairly constant at around 40,000 cases per year, with a death rate of around 20 per cent, suggesting an increasingly endemic profile.[81]

Those wrestling with the intractable problem of enteric diseases in Japan and elsewhere tended to focus their efforts more on measures to reduce *exposure* to the disease rather than trusting in vaccines that proved difficult or – in the case of bacillary dysentery – impossible to develop. Indeed, 'voluntary vaccination' was just one of 16 'preventive measures' recommended in the wake of the Great Kantō Earthquake. Others related to 'supervision of the infected', 'food hygiene', 'water and sewage' and 'other'. The first of these called for speedy diagnosis, notification and isolation of those who were infected, together with 'supervision of "carriers"'. Under the 'food hygiene' heading were provisions calling for the eradication of flies (as vectors of the disease) and control of food outlets/markets and their products. 'Water and sewage' stated a need to safeguard the quality of well water by disinfecting it, to improve standards of sewage disposal and to promote flush toilets. The final group of measures included special efforts to assist those living in temporary shelters, close cooperation between relief organizations and education of the general public about domestic hygiene.[82] Such a broadly conceived plan of action rather than straightforward, targeted interventions was required for enteric diseases, because of the 'major role' played by 'environmental factors and living standards ... in both the[ir] propagation and transmission'.[83] No less an authority than Shiga Kiyoshi, who discovered one type of the dysentery bacillus in 1898, remarked in a lecture at Harvard in 1935 that 'practical application is more difficult to attain than the search for the causes of disease'. He contended that 'the suppression of intestinal infectious diseases like typhoid and dysentery must rely upon the progress of modern public health practices' rather than 'medical science'. Two discussants at the lecture, Professor F. F. Russell of Harvard Medical School and Colonel James Simmons of the US Army Medical Corps, identified 'improved personal hygiene and improved sanitary engineering' (a clean water supply, effective treatment of sewage and disposal of waste) as the key factors in curbing dysentery.[84]

In his address at Harvard, Shiga highlighted the progress made against the disease in Japan but expressed disappointment at its recent upward trend. In 1898 the case rate for dysentery was 20.81/10,000 population, rising to the peak of 24.59 in 1899, before dropping to 10.35 in 1900, after which it 'gradually decreased with narrow fluctuations until 1920, when it reached the lowest level of 2.27 cases'. From then, it showed an upward trend, reaching 7.07 cases/10,000 population in 1935.[85] Shiga's survey did not go further back than 1898, and so omitted the explosive rise in dysentery cases from 1,098 in 1878 to 167,305 in 1893. Jannetta maintains that the Meiji authorities were quick to respond to the challenge of diarrhoeal infections. Indeed, she praises their response to a dysentery epidemic in Okayama in 1877:

> The residents were ordered to pour sterilized liquid over a person's waste material and to dispose of it in an isolated place far from houses and wells. Contaminated clothing was to be sterilized or burned. Similar public health measures were not adopted in the US until much later.[86]

Presumably, the spread of increasingly rigorous environmental controls, coinciding with those deployed against cholera and typhoid, helped bring dysentery under control by the early 1900s.

In the absence of a strict quarantine regime until 1899, environmental controls were likewise important in checking any outbreaks of bubonic plague or epidemic typhus, both of which were apparently new to Japan.[87] There are no reliable statistics for plague until 1897, because only then did it become a notifiable disease, but its very limited incidence thereafter (a peak of 646 cases in 1907) suggests either that public health controls, including quarantine of foreign ships, were exercised effectively or – somewhat improbably – that conditions were inimical to its spread.

In the case of epidemic typhus, a rickettsial disease spread by body lice,[88] there were 2,341 cases in 1879, the first year for which there are reliable records, rising to 3,459 in 1884 and reaching 8,225 and 7,317 in 1886 and 1914, respectively. The mortality rate was around 25 per cent. In the intervening years there were seldom more than 1,000 cases and from 1896 recorded incidence dropped below 100 until 1914.[89] Research conducted by Nagashima and Watanabe Mikio into the 1914 epidemic, its epidemiology and the measures taken against it provide some insight into not only the origins and transmission of the disease, but also its broader social and economic implications. Both agree that the likely origin of the epidemic, focused chiefly in Tokyo and the Kantō region, was the northeast, a predominantly agrarian area, where there is evidence to suggest that typhus cases had been misdiagnosed as typhoid in Yamagata and Aomori prefectures for some years. The movement of migrant labourers (*dekasegi*), increased by poor harvests in the northeast in 1913, facilitated 'the transmission of typhus from its hiding places in the north-east to Tokyo', from which it was re-exported to other regions.[90] Aware that typhus thrived amidst the cramped, unsanitary living conditions endured by casual labourers, Kitasato counselled that these be improved to prevent a recurrence of the epidemic. However, the authorities ignored his advice, preferring the reactive devices of isolation of patients and disinfection of households to more expensive, proactive measures that tackled the underlying causes of the disease.[91] The national incidence of typhus dropped to 615 in 1916 and swiftly declined thereafter.

As in the case of typhus, it seems that the chief measures adopted to check the spread of diphtheria and scarlet fever were isolation and disinfection. A major cause of deaths among children in the early twentieth century, diphtheria is an acute respiratory disease, spread by droplet infection and close contact. It seems that the forces of modernization, industrialization, urbanization and nation building unleashed the infection among the Japanese; cramped living conditions and compulsory education fostered its spread. Hays maintains that 'the spread of systems of universal state education … created more opportunities for such a crowd disease of children',[92] and certainly its growing incidence during the early years of the twentieth century in Japan correlates with the rising attendance of children at primary schools, reaching nearly 100 per cent by 1910.[93] The official Japanese statistics suggest a trend of increasing incidence from 1,838 cases in 1880 to a peak of 20,094 in 1911, after which it oscillated between 13,000 and 19,000 cases, until it started rising again, reaching a pre-war peak of 28,234 cases in 1936. Mortality rates ranged between 20 and 30 per cent until the mid-1930s, when they started to drop to around 15 per cent.[94]

Japan's limited success in tackling the diphtheria menace is all the more surprising given Kitasato's involvement in the development of serology or serum therapy. While he had worked to identify tetanus toxin (produced by the bacilli) and its pathological effects, his colleague, Emile Behring, had researched diphtheria toxin. Together they had contributed to the discovery that injections of carefully graduated doses into animals could produce a curative serum or 'antitoxin', which could then be used to neutralize the disease in human patients. Japan lost little time in developing this diphtheria antitoxin, producing 'a highly effective serum that Kitasato called "superior to any in Europe or America"', so much so that Germany and other countries began importing it.[95] Exciting a development though it was, the use of antitoxin was limited to treating those already suffering from diphtheria and their immediate contacts. The real challenge was to find a means of preventing the disease, of active immunization. Efforts were made with some success to combine toxin with antitoxin to bring about immunity, but more effective was Gaston Ramon's discovery of anatoxin or toxoid (toxin treated with formalin) in 1923.[96] Mass immunization drives followed in Canada, where 10,000 people were immunized with toxoid between 1 July 1926 and 1 February 1927. A steep drop in diphtheria mortality apparently occurred as a result. Similar results followed an immunization drive in New York City.[97] At a time when official statistics indicate that diphtheria morbidity was rising in Japan, Shiga observed in his Harvard lecture of 1935 that 'Diphtheria serum stands as the queen of all the serum treatments. But it did not reduce the diphtheria incidence very materially until antitoxin and toxin or anatoxin [toxoid] or the like were used for prophylactic purposes'.[98] Japanese school children were immunized against diphtheria at this time, but coverage did not extend to preschool children or adults due perhaps to inadequate supplies of toxoid.[99] This may have been due to caution about the treatment and concerns about its cost, both of which were factors that inhibited the mass immunization of school children in Britain until 1940.[100]

It may be that some of the scepticism about the toxoid was partly justified. There were a great variety of types and brands of toxoid, not all of them equally reliable, and some fatal accidents had resulted from its use.[101] Perhaps most interesting, the trend of diphtheria morbidity and mortality was downward 'before diphtheria antitoxin began to be used generally, and continued progressively even before preventive immunization became widespread'.[102] In other words, the disease was on the wane before the introduction of therapeutic and prophylactic countermeasures, therefore making their effectiveness difficult to measure. Ann Hardy makes a similar point about scarlet fever in Britain in the late nineteenth century, noting that despite it being seen as 'a great triumph of preventive medicine', its incidence remained high and the measures adopted to combat it 'were largely irrelevant to the declining fatality of the disease after 1870'.[103] Declining rates of mortality for scarlet fever were evident in Japan during the 1930s (from 5.02 per cent in 1930 to 2.012 per cent in 1940), despite the incidence of the disease rising from 6,025 cases in 1930 to 19,327 in 1940, perhaps indicating a milder form of the disease.[104]

While diphtheria and scarlet fever represented perennial, manageable problems for the Central Sanitary Board (CSB) of the Home Ministry, the influenza pandemic of 1918–19 was a national emergency that severely tested Japan's public health provision as it did that of other affected countries. A study of the epidemic by Rice and Palmer states that there were 21,168,398 cases and 257,363 deaths, a case fatality rate of 1.22 per cent. Drawing on the annual reports of the CSB and the official report on the epidemic (1922), their work reveals the degree to which Japan had developed systems of public hygiene that were certainly comparable with, in some respects superior to, those operating in other modern, developed nations. Much evidence is provided to demonstrate that the CSB and prefectural authorities responded with alacrity to the 1918–19 epidemic and those that followed in 1920 and 1921. According to Rice and Palmer, 'the advice sent out by the Central Sanitary Bureau was sound and appropriate.

The three main precautions recommended – masks, gargling and inoculation – are now recognized to be the most effective medical responses available in any country at that time.'[105] Information was disseminated by means of leaflets distributed through primary schools and by well-designed posters, supplied by the CSB and visible in such public places as cinemas, public baths, transport facilities, schools, offices, factories, etc. All these attest to effective systems of communication and information exchange. Likewise, the establishment of gargling facilities in schools and inoculation stations throughout cities indicated high levels of community involvement and engagement, as did the efforts of local sanitation associations to disinfect schools and kindergartens. Rice and Palmer remark that disinfection was such a 'common practical response in an era that thought in terms of dirt and "germs" as the cause of infectious diseases' that it did not merit a mention in the official report or indeed in most newspapers.

Public fear of germs and a keen appreciation of the need to limit the spread of this air-borne infection accounted for the ubiquity of face masks. Indeed, Rice and Palmer contend that 'In their willingness to use masks, Japanese people ... showed themselves far more alert to the dangers of droplet infection than most European people in 1918.'[106] Moreover, they seem to have embraced the merits of inoculation. By the time mass inoculation campaigns were properly up and running – during the 1919–20 and 1920–21 epidemics – demand outstripped supply. Interestingly, inoculation targeted secondary infections, principally respiratory diseases such as pneumonia, as it was not possible to identify and isolate the influenza virus (this would have to wait until 1933). Nevertheless, the Kitasato Institute produced an influenza vaccine that the CSB rapidly approved for mass production in November 1918.

Finally, Rice and Palmer highlight the absence of any discussion of hospital care in the official report, noting in connection to this that 'Japan had only 1,237 registered hospitals in 1918, with 50,853 doctors and 33,534 nurses, for a population of at least 57 million.' Noting this deficit, they attribute the comparatively low fatality rate to the 'quality of home nursing' – compliance with official guidance, recommending bed rest, isolation and generous provision of fluids. Interestingly, they argue on the basis of limited evidence that 'traditional herbal medicine may have had an important effect alongside public health measures and Western-based medical responses'.[107] Still, the latter stand out most forcefully from their account. The efforts of Dr Gomibuchi Ijirō, who apparently managed to cure 99 patients by injecting them with diphtheria serum, testified to the resourcefulness of Japanese doctors in the face of the pandemic.

Conclusion

The official and public responses to the influenza pandemic – the emphasis on germs, face masks, vaccines and disinfection – highlight the degree to which Japan succeeded in organizing modern forms and systems of public hygiene that drew support from the Japanese people and reflected the latest developments in Western science regarding infectious diseases. Indeed, Japan's integration with international science from the concluding decades of the nineteenth century is captured in the extraordinary figure of Kitasato, whose research endeavours in Germany were at the forefront of the bacteriological revolution chiefly associated with Louis Pasteur and Robert Koch. On his return to Japan, Kitasato presided over an institute that confronted the challenge of infectious diseases by producing vaccines and anti-toxins – advances that attracted much interest in both military and civilian circles. Whether or not Seaman was justified in his ringing endorsement of Japanese military hygiene during the Russo-Japanese War, there is no doubt that the military authorities now fully appreciated the importance of microscopes and water-testing kits for preventing and checking disease among their troops.

By investigating Japan's record in relation to the chief infectious diseases, this chapter has illuminated the strengths and limitations of the drive to improve public health from the 1870s. The foundations for an effective campaign against smallpox had been laid in the late Tokugawa period and so the Meiji government was able to make relatively rapid progress with vaccination. Unable to institute strict quarantine of foreign vessels at its ports until 1899 and without a vaccine until 1902, cholera proved much more problematic and disruptive. While quarantine, isolation and disinfection of local environments seem to have worked to limit the impact of plague and typhus, this was not the case with typhoid and dysentery, which proved to be persistent, endemic problems. Rooted in particular environmental and social circumstances, these enteric diseases, together with tuberculosis and syphilis, will be explored in Chapter 2 as chronic problems that increasingly exercised the authorities as the 1920s gave way to the 1930s. The interwar 'lifestyle improvement movement', also discussed in Chapter 2, was animated by the need to tackle these problems through educational campaigns.

The importance of education had been understood by Japan's pioneer in this field, Nagayo Sensai himself. On his return from the Iwakura Mission, he designed the nation-wide administrative structures and systems required to ensure Japan met high standards of public hygiene as soon as possible. He deployed the term *eisei* to convey novel, modern ideas about community health that were pivotal to the Meiji effort to build a robust, healthy nation, capable of holding its own in the world. Although the German variant of modern medicine was the preferred model for Japan, and this affinity was strengthened by Germany's achievements in the research laboratory, Nagayo and the other advocates of modern hygiene were fully aware of Britain's pioneering role in public health. They sought to strike a balance between central control and local initiative, between rigorous enforcement of regulations and increasing hygiene consciousness among the Japanese public by means of education. The new Japanese police force, again modelled along European lines, was afforded an extraordinarily wide ambit of control that included *eisei*, but that did not necessarily exclude voluntary local initiative and hygiene awareness among ordinary Japanese. Sams' claim, quoted at the beginning of this chapter, that Japan slavishly followed the German example in public health was more a retrospective judgement born of wartime propaganda than an accurate portrayal of the origins and progress of *kōshū eisei* in Japan.

2 The limits of disease prevention

The main aim of this chapter is to explore those public health problems that emerged as major social issues once the threat of acute infectious diseases had passed or at least diminished. Narita Ryūichi identifies a period from around 1900 to 1935 'when health care discussions began to focus on ways to fight chronic infectious disease rather than merely acute disease'.[1] After 1935 he sees the various issues surrounding endemic diseases and the social conditions that fostered them coalescing into clear positions on improving hygiene. Such chronic diseases as tuberculosis, syphilis, trachoma and enteric or parasitical diseases proved to be intractable problems that increasingly plagued the Japanese authorities as the country drifted towards war with China and the West after 1931. All seen as sapping the nation's strength, these diseases and the contributory factors of poverty and malnutrition became all the more urgent as preparations for war gathered pace. Thus, the army's call for a separate welfare ministry was heeded in 1937. This and other public health advances necessitated by the demands of the Asia-Pacific War (1937–45) served as solid foundations for Allied reform efforts during the Occupation.

The first part of this chapter explores the pre-war history of endemic diseases, most notably tuberculosis, which thrived amidst the conditions of early capitalism, rapid urbanization and rural hardship. Reflecting more fundamental problems of overcrowded housing, inadequate sanitation, unsatisfactory working conditions and poor nutrition, these chronic medical conditions, together with high infant mortality, demanded much more than the kind of public health interventions (disinfection, quarantine and inoculation) that had seen off the scourges of smallpox and cholera. Moreover, as the Meiji period gave way to the Taisho era (1912–26), so the emphasis on building and securing the nation state competed with concerns about 'the structure and justice of society',[2] producing a social ferment largely couched in the language of modernization. A commitment to scientific progress alongside traditional values animated the interwar campaigns to improve daily life, which, Garon contends, successfully married local, middle-class activism with the authority of the state.[3] The government's anxieties about social problems, unhealthy factory workers, syphilitic soldiers and malnourished children only grew as its preparations for 'total war' mounted.

The second section of this chapter investigates the impact of total war on public health. It juxtaposes institutional advances in the form of the Welfare Ministry and local health centres with the deterioration of standards of public hygiene. The latter was occasioned by an Allied naval blockade that strangled imports of crucial foodstuffs, and a strategic bombing offensive that reduced Japan's main cities to 'burned fields'. As the pressures of war mounted and its tide turned against Japan, so the incidence of tuberculosis and enteric diseases increased, as did case rates of some acute infectious diseases. This is the crucial backcloth to the Occupation. August 1945 was not a watershed in public health terms. Undoubtedly the emperor's surrender broadcast of 15 August 1945 administered a severe psychological jolt to the Japanese people, but once the shock of defeat and imminent Occupation had passed, most Japanese continued in their daily struggle to eke out an existence and ward off the rising threat of disease amid dire conditions of social deprivation.

Meeting the challenge of chronic infectious diseases

The previous chapter explored the Japanese commitment, born of a rising faith in modern science, to identifying and battling against microbes. While this produced striking advances against acute infectious diseases, less progress was made against their chronic counterparts. This deficit highlighted the limitations of focusing chiefly on the pathogen itself, just one part of the disease equation. Also relevant was the health of the human host (the individual's resistance to infection) and his/her living conditions and working environment, which obviously affected the degree of exposure and susceptibility to infection. Such factors as excessive working hours, gruelling factory conditions and inadequate standards of nutrition made individuals vulnerable to infections they might otherwise have been able to ward off. The speed of Japan's industrialization, urbanization and military development, the heavy demands made of a predominantly rural population to support these processes, brought about conditions that favoured the spread and entrenchment of chronic infectious diseases. As fundamental reordering of social and economic relations was thus required to tackle these problems, it was not surprising that progressive forces for reform struggled against vested interests in government and industry during the 1910s and 1920s.

Such strains were evident in the case of tuberculosis. On the one hand, its high rates of morbidity and mortality were viewed as the necessary human cost of Japan's headlong rush to 'catch up' with the West; on the other, they were seen as undermining Japan's ability to succeed in that venture. Hence, there was an apparent ambivalence on the part of the Japanese government towards this 'disease of civilization'. A clarity of purpose only really emerged when Japan's military establishment became increasingly alarmed at the toll that tuberculosis was taking on its pool of conscripts. Their sense of urgency about actively and effectively combating the disease grew in proportion to the scale of the army's commitments overseas. While tuberculosis was not the only health problem that troubled the military authorities in the late 1930s, it was undoubtedly the most prominent one and remained so during the Occupation period. It therefore merits detailed attention, and before examining other challenges to public health, it is first necessary to explain the nature and scale of the tuberculosis problem and the Japanese government's fitful response to it before the 1930s.

As William Johnston has shown in his detailed and wide-ranging study of the 'tuberculosis epidemic' in Japan from the late 1890s until 1950, the incidence of tuberculosis was growing from the onset of Japan's drive to modernize along Western lines in contrast to its declining profile from the mid-nineteenth century in those very countries that Japan was emulating.[4] In the absence of any public health interventions that can explain that decline, it is usually correlated with rising living standards in the US and the nations of Western Europe.[5] This divergence of trends is evident from a Japanese statistical comparison for 1930, when Japan's death rate (per 10,000 population) from tuberculosis was 18.6, compared with 9 in the UK, 7.9 in Germany and 7.2 in the US.[6] Johnston traces the epidemic in Japan through several stages. The key ones here are a 'take-off stage' (late 1880s until around 1900) chiefly associated with a steep rise in the incidence of tuberculosis amid slum conditions in swelling cities, together with a slight increase in the countryside; an early-twentieth-century phase (c.1900–c.1919) when the disease spread among downtrodden female textile workers, who subsequently propagated it further on return to their home villages; and a period from 1919 to around 1935, marked by 'stagnation' when incidence declined mainly in urban areas due to improved living standards, but rose in socially deprived rural areas.[7]

Unlike cholera, which burst onto the scene loudly and dramatically, grabbing the attention of its audience, tuberculosis was easy to miss, emerging from the shadows quietly and insidiously. The disease took years to develop and was very difficult for doctors to diagnose,[8] both in terms of its symptoms and the social impact of the diagnosis on the patient's family. Despite solid scientific evidence to the contrary by the late nineteenth century, the Japanese public, together with many of its doctors, remained convinced that rather than being infectious the disease was hereditary, bringing shame to the families of those identified as harbouring it. For all these reasons, it did not attract much attention until the early years of the twentieth century, when it was causing considerably more deaths in 1902 (82,559) than the eight legally designated infectious diseases combined (26,570).[9] Even more striking is the figure for 1920 (125,165), which exceeded the peak number of deaths from the influenza pandemic that year (108,428).[10] Moreover, the tendency of those suffering from tuberculosis to conceal their condition and the willingness of many doctors to opt for alternative diagnoses (pneumonia or bronchitis) as camouflage must mean that recorded mortality figures significantly underestimate the true number of deaths from tuberculosis.

Recorded mortality from tuberculosis very nearly doubled between 1900 (71,771) and 1918 (140,747),[11] after which it fell to 132,565 in 1919, dropping to 113,045 in 1926, before rising again to 132,151 in 1935. From then on it climbed steeply in line with the pressures and demands of war.[12] Mortality rates

increased from 187 per 100,000 in 1926 to 207 in 1936, reaching the unprecedented figure of 225 per 100,000 in 1943.[13] Focusing first on Johnston's second
phase of the epidemic during the first two decades of the twentieth century, there
was much evidence accumulated at the time by Japanese researchers to demonstrate the link between very poor working conditions in factories and high incidence of tuberculosis. This was particularly the case among young women who
worked in the textile mills, the mainstay of Japanese industrialization during this
period.

Most definitive in this regard was the research undertaken by Ishihara Osamu
for the Ministry of Agriculture and Commerce between 1909 and 1911. Ishihara
calculated that 'one out of every six to seven mill girls returning to the countryside did so with serious illness (13,000 out of 80,000 surveyed in 1910). Of those
workers discharged because of serious illness, around one-quarter (3,000) had
tuberculosis.'[14] He thus demonstrated how migrant (*dekasegi*) workers were suc-
cumbing to infection due to very poor working and living conditions and how
they were then spreading the disease throughout rural communities. Factory
managers were criticized for their neglect of the labour force, who were overworked, often exhausted and suffered a cramped, dusty and poorly ventilated
factory environment. Workers also had to endure crowded, unsanitary living
conditions in company dormitories. Poor standards of nutrition, particularly a
deficit of animal protein, may also have contributed to workers' lack of resistance to infection.[15] As for the spread of tuberculosis to the villages, Johnston
attributes this to returning factory workers and army conscripts.[16]

How, then, did the Japanese government react and respond to this incipient
crisis? Until the 1930s its efforts to control tuberculosis can best be described as
lacking in force and impact. Discounting the Cattle Tuberculosis Prevention Law
of 1901 as more precautionary than necessary in a country that consumed so
little milk, the government began in earnest with the Pulmonary Tuberculosis
Prevention Ordinance or 'spittoon law' of 1904. This took its cue from ideas in
the West, linking the spread of tuberculosis with the habit of spitting in public.
The ordinance therefore required that spittoons containing disinfectant (carbolic
acid) be available in public places to alert Japanese to the problem. In addition,
tuberculosis patients were to be isolated from others in hospitals, and patients'
homes and property were to be disinfected, further underlining the infectious
nature of the disease. While this ordinance may have increased public awareness
of tuberculosis, there is no evidence to suggest that it significantly slowed the
spread of the disease.[17]

In contrast to this rather limited measure aimed at restricting the transmission
of the bacillus in phlegm, the Factory Law, passed in March 1911, seemed to
signal a much broader assault on the breeding ground of the disease. It was
inspired by numerous studies and reports of the kind conducted by Ishihara
Osamu, and was sponsored by 'progressive bureaucrats' concerned about the
implications of harsh treatment of workers for industrial output and labour mili-
tancy. Nevertheless, it turned out to be a weak instrument, affecting less than 5
per cent of the labour force and doing little to improve unhealthy or dangerous

working practices. Moreover, its implementation was delayed until 1916 and the ban on night work for women and children postponed until 1929, further demonstrating effective resistance on the part of factory owners and their political supporters.[18] The power of vested interests, disingenuously reiterating common views of tuberculosis as hereditary rather than infectious, largely nullified the Factory Law as an effective response to the problem.

In the absence of a medical cure, any attempt to significantly reduce mortality from the disease had to tackle its root causes. As Johnston puts it, 'as long as industrial living and working conditions demanded more of factory workers than they contributed to improving their lives, high tuberculosis mortality remained inevitable'.[19] The difficulty of reversing this equation caused all involved to invest their hopes and limited funds in the search for a cure. This was demonstrated by a reluctance to give up on Koch's tuberculin therapy until around 1910, by which time attention was shifting to the construction of sanatoria for the care and isolation of tuberculosis patients in line with developments in Europe and the US. Although Shiga introduced a vaccine developed by Leon Calmette and Camille Guerin (BCG) to Japan in the mid-1920s, and the government funded research into its efficacy, it was not adopted until after 1940. Thus, those Japanese endeavouring to combat tuberculosis were constrained by the limits of science as well as prevailing socio-economic circumstances. Even when tuberculosis *mortality* dropped steeply in the final years of the Occupation due to the use of effective antibiotics, continuing high rates of *morbidity* reflected the persistence of socio-economic problems.

In the meantime, the issue of tuberculosis increasingly attracted public attention in Japan. The *Asahi Shimbun* highlighted the human suffering involved in a series of articles in 1911 and the government's perceived passivity provoked censure in the House of Representatives in March 1912. In response, the Japanese authorities tried to engage with the problem without committing much in the way of scarce resources to resolving it (just one-tenth of what the US was willing to spend in 1912). This approach meant trusting in the efforts of the Japan Anti-Tuberculosis League, established in February 1913 at the behest of the Great Japan Private Hygiene Society (introduced in Chapter 1). A quasi-official organization like its sponsor, the League worked alongside more genuinely private groups like the White Cross Society (*Haku Jūji Kai*), set up by Japanese doctors in Tokyo, and other prefectural anti-tuberculosis associations. Facing rising public discord and largely defeated by the scale of the problem, the authorities judged that, in the absence of a cure, the most cost-effective strategy was to devolve responsibility for education and prevention to semi-official organizations operating outside the constraints of government.

Those constraints arose from the involvement of several ministries in tuberculosis control, the need to consult various interested parties, the resulting protracted negotiations and endless redrafting of legislation. They were typified by the Tuberculosis Prevention Law of 28 March 1919, which had been under discussion for around ten years. The new law widened and strengthened the provisions of the 'spittoon law' of 1904, introducing fines if its provisions were infringed. The bodies and property of the deceased were to be disinfected; those with active disease were barred from employment; and where conditions were viewed as conducive to the spread of the disease, officials were required to take action. Moreover, the legislation strengthened the provisions of a 1914 law on the construction of pulmonary tuberculosis sanatoria. Cities with a population of more than 50,000 were now required to develop these facilities and were empowered to enforce attendance. The law also specified a financial commitment on the part of the government to subsidize their construction and running costs.[20]

During the 1920s, however, neither the sanatoria nor the educational efforts of the Anti-Tuberculosis League met with much success. As well as isolating the patient from others they might otherwise infect, sanatoria provided a 'change of air' and the prospect of medical treatment. However, private sanatoria were beyond the financial means of all but the most wealthy, and the limited number of public ones (14 in 1931) catered to the needs only of the terminally ill. Despite annual mortality figures for tuberculosis well in excess of 100,000 in the early 1930s and a level of morbidity perhaps ten times greater, there were just 13,334 beds for such patients in 1934.[21]

As for the efforts of the Anti-Tuberculosis League to foster a modern, scientific view of the disease – essential if it was to be properly controlled – these made little headway against popular notions of the disease as hereditary and shameful. Such ingrained attitudes towards the disease, together with the knowledge that patients went there to die, meant that public sanatoria were seldom full. Likewise, tuberculosis consultation centres (*kekkaku sōdan jo*), established to diagnose and support patients, were shunned, their numbers shrinking from 1,208 in 1926 to 615 in 1930. Interestingly, the response of the Anti-Tuberculosis League was to disguise the nature of these facilities, establishing 'health consultation centres' (*kenkō sōdan jo*) in 1931 that carefully avoided any direct reference to tuberculosis.[22]

Such problems demonstrated that the strategies adopted by organizations like the Anti-Tuberculosis League were beset with problems as fundamental as those faced by advocates of more radical social and economic reform. Nevertheless, both approaches contributed to a more unified policy, centrally directed and properly resourced, that began to emerge in the wake of the Manchuria Incident of September 1931. The driving force behind this belated commitment to confront the scourge of tuberculosis was the Japanese army, which had discovered a rising trend of tuberculosis in its ranks.[23] Indeed, a Western observer remarked in 1936 that 'almost unbelievable numbers of soldiers have been invalided back with tuberculosis from Manchukuo (Manchuria)' and that 'the number of conscripts being rejected for physical defects is increasing annually'.[24] According to the army's medical bureau, the percentage of conscripts deemed unfit for service had risen from 25 per cent for the period 1922–26 to 35 per cent for 1927–32 and 40 per cent in 1935.[25]

Later, the Occupation would attribute such pervasive ill health among Japanese to poor standards of community hygiene and nutrition. It paid little heed to

Japan's past endeavours to improve nutrition, evidenced by the establishment of the Imperial Government Institute for Nutrition in the wake of the rice riots of 1918. One of the first of its kind in the world, the new institute signalled 'the increasing involvement of the Japanese state in the diet of its citizens'.[26] Instrumental in its creation was Saiki Tadasu, recipient of a PhD from Yale University and a nutritionist of international renown. In 1926 the Health Organisation of the League of Nations (HOLN) published *Progress of the Science of Nutrition in Japan*, edited by Saiki.[27] Here, Saiki highlighted the challenges Japan faced as a 'relatively small and poor' country, her food supplies always 'an agonising problem for statesmen and hygienists alike'. His aim was to draw up a 'food code', which would serve to correct some of the deficiencies of the Japanese diet, its over-reliance on starchy foods like rice, barley and potatoes at the expense of animal protein and fat intake. Particular concern with child nutrition caused the Education Ministry to fund primary-school canteens, numbering 12,000 by 1940, and to sponsor the Secondary School Law of 1943, which aimed to foster greater nutritional awareness.[28]

Saiki referred in his volume to the contributions made by Mori Ōgai and Takaki Kanehiro to improving the food supply of the army and navy. Indeed, it was the demands of war and military expansionism, best met by healthy, well-fed soldiers and sailors, that necessitated a more eclectic mix of foods, including Japanese, Chinese and Western ingredients. According to Cwiertka, the military diet was far superior to that of most civilians, with a soldier consuming 13 kg of beef per annum by the 1910s compared to the average civilian per capita consumption of around only 1 kg. A similar discrepancy was evident in the case of fish, where the military advantage increased during the 1920s in the wake of economic recession in Japan. By 1929 a Japanese soldier's daily energy requirement was estimated to be 4,000 calories, more if he was engaged in combat, and there was no way that this could be supplied by traditional fare alone. Cwiertka estimates that around 2,600 calories could be provided by rice, the remainder best met – in terms of cost and nourishment – by 'large-scale adoption of foreign cooking techniques, such as deep-frying, pan-frying and stewing, and foreign ingredients, such as meat, lard and potatoes'.[29]

Interestingly, it seems that these changes in military cuisine had a progressive effect on civil society. Susan Hanley argues that alterations made in the wake of Japan's involvement in foreign wars, chiefly the Russo-Japanese War of 1904–05 and the First World War, broadened dietary horizons and began to change food habits, as conscripts took new ideas about food and cooking methods back to their villages. This trend, she argues, accelerated in the 1920s with the increasing popularity of such dishes as curry rice and pork cutlets and greater consumption of meat, milk and bread.[30] Greater awareness of nutritional issues, together with generally rising income levels, may explain the 75 per cent drop in mortality from beriberi between 1925 and 1945.[31] Bruce Johnston, who was actively involved in food policy during the Occupation,[32] likewise maintains that there was some dietary rebalancing during the interwar period in line with perceived deficiencies. He noted a tendency for some foods which are relatively expensive per 1,000 calories to rise in per capita consumption (fish, meat, eggs, fruits, visible fats and oils); and for some foods relatively inexpensive per 1,000 calories to fall (barley, naked barley, white and sweet potatoes).

Still, Johnston recognized that compared to Western countries Japanese consumption of animal protein was low, and that this concerned the Japanese authorities.[33]

The need for more protein-rich diets was just one of the rallying cries of those middle-class activists associated with the interwar 'daily life improvement campaigns' (*seikatsu kaizen undō*). Working in tandem with the state, participants mobilized to improve standards of health, hygiene and sanitation, among other priorities and activities.[34] This provides a useful vantage point from which to view community-level initiatives against lifestyles and environments conducive to the spread of endemic diseases like trachoma and dysentery. Narita highlights the degree to which women were expected to shoulder the burden of improving hygiene in their families and communities. As one magazine article put it in 1902, since 'laundry, sewing, and cooking are all under the supervision of women, surely we should expect women to be responsible for the development of hygiene as well'.[35] In the same year no less an authority than Kitasato Shibasaburō maintained that

> It will be extremely difficult to attain our goal of individual hygiene unless we truly have the efforts of women [particularly given] the government cannot be expected to solve the problem quickly only by means of regulations for combating chronic infectious disease.[36]

The Daily Life Improvement Campaign, launched by the Education Ministry in 1920 and supported by the Home Ministry, likewise afforded women the role of 'the state's prime agents in improving "daily life"'.[37] Established in the wake of the 'rice riots' and the economic recession of 1919–20 and drawing on the science of home economics, the movement was initially concentrated in the cities and principally concerned with urban life. Partner contends that 'Only with the creation in 1925 of the rural magazine *Ie no hikari* did male and female educators, commentators, activists, and local elites find a voice capable of reaching significant numbers of rural homes.'[38] As in the case of tuberculosis, while most efforts were directed at preventing disease by changing attitudes and behaviour in relation to hygiene, there were those who attacked the root causes of rural poverty, most notably the landlord system and rising rates of tenancy. Such pluralism during the 1920s, however, surrendered to firm government control by the mid-1930s, when 'military-industrial mobilization demanded healthy recruits and workers'.[39]

In the meantime, local activists worked through such organizational vehicles as *eisei kumiai* (sanitary associations), focusing on the toilet and kitchen as the key sites of hygienic modernization. Dark, dirty, cramped and ill-equipped kitchens, devoid of running water, were inimical to proper standards of nutrition and food hygiene. Such unsanitary conditions were conducive to the spread of enteric infections like typhoid and dysentery and intestinal parasites (e.g. round-worm and hookworm). Likewise, unsanitary toilets and careless storage of 'night soil' for fertilizer encouraged flies – key agents of bacterial transmission. On the face of it, the use of human waste as fertilizer was an obvious cause of high rates of enteric disease, but such assumptions ignored the trend away from night soil towards an increasingly intensive use of chemical fertilizers in the interwar period.

Moreover, Japanese scientists had long been engaged in research concerned with eliminating or debilitating pathogenic organisms in night soil by means of effective storage or treatment. For example, a study published in the *Journal of the Public Health Association of Japan* in December 1927 outlined an elaborate night soil receptacle, made of concrete, divided into five compartments and with a capacity of around 1,000 litres. Its design rested on the positive effects of the flow of the liquefied night soil through the compartments, which would cause the eggs of parasites and bacteria to sink to the bottom and remain there. More-over, it was argued, 'It is not difficult to suppose that the muddy substance that grows and accumulates at the bottom of the first compartment will more or less serve as a filter for the bacilli and parasite eggs.'[40] The Bureau of Hygiene worked hard to promote this standard 'sanitary privy' to facilitate the elimination of pathogens by natural putrefaction over a period of three months. According to a report by the League of Nations in 1937, the bureau's efforts in this regard resulted in the alteration of 45,000 installations with good effect.[41]

Nevertheless, these successes did little to mitigate what was a poorly developed sanitary infrastructure. Only large cities boasted modern, water-borne sewerage systems, in contrast to the ubiquity of open drains. In 1938, 49 cities and towns were so equipped, the figure jumping to over 70 in 1940 due to a greater willingness by the government to subsidize construction costs. The expected return on this investment was presumably lower incidence of water-borne infections. Sewage treatment facilities were very scarce, benefiting just Gifu, Nagoya, Kyoto, Osaka and Tokyo, although others were planned for Kawasaki, Kure and Wakayama in 1940. In the absence of such plant, cities and towns were apt to discharge surplus, untreated sewage into canals, rivers, bays and oceans.[42]

As regards the other part of the sanitary infrastructure – the provision of piped, clean water – the Japanese trailed Western Europe badly, due to the scale of the financial commitment required. Only around one-quarter of Japanese households received treated water by 1935, compared to around 80 per cent of their English counterparts.[43] With the bulk of modern waterworks predictably located in large industrial cities, the great majority of Japanese consumed untreated water from wells and streams, providing routes for transmission of diarrhoeal diseases. This assumption is borne out by the clear correlation from around 1960 between a steady decline of water-borne infectious diseases and the rise of the 'water supply penetration rate'.[44] Although such generalizations –

such single-factor explanations – do not sit well with the complex aetiology of diseases like dysentery, they nevertheless highlight the degree to which chronic infectious diseases are rooted in particular environmental conditions.

This was certainly true of trachoma, also known as granular conjunctivitis, which 'generally requires prolonged contact in filthy and overcrowded conditions for transmission'.[45] Like tuberculosis, therefore, the incidence of trachoma serves as a useful index of social conditions. Narita notes that by the turn of the twentieth century, school health programmes targeted tuberculosis and trachoma, the latter reaching epidemic proportions after the Sino-Japanese War of 1894–95. Struggling in the face of a case rate of 15 per cent among pupils, school nurses moved quickly to educate the children in disease prevention, instructing them, for example, not to share towels and handkerchiefs. Greater awareness of hygiene thus 'passed from children to the home, and from mothers to women in general'.[46] Apparently, this was of little benefit to female textile workers, who were experiencing dire working and living conditions in the late nineteenth and early twentieth centuries. Their plight was captured by a health survey of 1,300 workers in a cotton-spinning mill in 1911, which revealed that 42 per cent (546) were suffering from trachoma, 200 of whom had caught it since joining the factory.[47] In parallel with the development of organizational forms and legal instruments to combat tuberculosis, an association for the prevention of trachoma was formed in 1916, essentially engaged in educating the public about the disease itself and the various sources of infection within the family and community. This was followed by the enactment of the Trachoma Prevention Law in 1919, which testified to the government's determination to combat and eradicate the disease.

Addressing the meeting of the International Organisation against Trachoma on 5 April 1935, Professor Miyashita judged the 1919 law to have been a success. Its provisions required any doctor diagnosing the condition to clearly instruct the household concerned about disinfection and preventive measures and to ensure that the patient received immediate treatment (this was free of charge in districts with a high trachoma index). In schools, workshops, hotels, lodging houses and hairdressers' shops, the onus was on those in charge to comply with necessary precautions to prevent epidemics. Anyone involved in an occupation that involved close contact with the public was licensed by the police and 'if found to be trachomatous ... submitted to compulsory treatment until certified to be non-infective'. Such surveillance was commonplace: men were twice checked for trachoma, first by a local doctor when they had preliminary military training aged 19, and then by the army medical corps when they were formally recruited at the age of 20; school teachers and pupils were examined annually for the condition; general eye examinations were undertaken in districts with a high incidence of trachoma; and immigrants were checked for active disease. According to Miyashita, ten million Japanese were examined every year for trachoma, and strict enforcement of the law had produced 'a decline in the trachoma index in all classes of the population and among all professions'.[48]

In the case of trachoma, as in others, Japan was integrated into an international network of public health organizations, demonstrating both an openness to foreign influences and a willingness to contribute to collaborative research efforts. Particularly interesting in this regard, not least because it prefigured the Occupation's reform of public health, was the decision of the International Health Board of the Rockefeller Foundation to sponsor the establishment of a school of public hygiene in Tokyo. In response to a wave of international sympathy that followed the devastating Great Kantō Earthquake of September 1923, the foundation had originally intended to rebuild the Imperial Medical School, hoping that by such means American ideas on medical education would supplant those of Germany. The inauguration of a fellowship programme was likewise intended to educate Japanese about American approaches to public health and so foster closer ties between the two countries. While this was approved in 1925, it was not until 1930 that agreement was reached on the establishment of the National Institute of Public Health. By this time, it was argued, Japanese had finally embraced the American paradigm by shifting their primary focus from combating disease to protecting the health of the Japanese people. The fellowship programme had been helpful in this regard, providing a conduit for American ideas about public health to flow into Japan. Lauding the project as 'a major governmental activity which had not yet been provided for efficiently in Japan', Japanese officials involved in the agreement seemed to acknowledge American criticisms of their contradictory record in public health. On the one hand, they boasted superb laboratory facilities and excellent standards of public health education; on the other, they faced an infant mortality rate far higher than the figures for the US and Britain.[49]

Regarding the latter, a study by the Rockefeller Foundation in 1924 revealed infant mortality (the death rate during the first year of life) in Japan to be 'a startling 163.3/1,000 live births'.[50] Some headway had been made by 1930, but the rate was still high – 12.4 per cent, compared to 6 per cent in England and Wales, 7.8 per cent in France, 10.6 per cent in Italy, 8.4 per cent in Germany, 6.5 per cent in the US, 9.3 per cent in Belgium and 5.1 per cent in the Netherlands.[51] The Hygiene Bureau of the Home Ministry had recorded an upward trend in infant mortality from the 1880s to the 1920s.[52] This was attributed by health officials to 'chronic infectious diseases and what some of them perceived as the general deterioration of social life, which was, in Japan and elsewhere, associated with urbanization and industrialisation'.[53] The establishment of the Health and Hygiene Research Committee (*Hoken Eisei Chōsakai*) by the Home Ministry in 1916 demonstrated a determination to clarify and tackle the tightly entwined issues of chronic disease, malnutrition, social deprivation and unsatisfactory levels of hygiene and sanitation. The committee conducted research principally into the following subjects: the health of infants and children; tuberculosis; food, clothing and housing; sanitation in rural villages; statistics; leprosy (Hansen's disease); mental illness; and sexually transmitted diseases. Its findings underlined the need to grapple with such problems as tuberculosis, infant mortality and the poor physiques of many Japanese, all of which were markedly more serious than in other modern countries with which Japan identified. Serious intent was reflected in the legislation that followed – the Tuberculosis Prevention Law and the Trachoma

Prevention Law, both passed in 1919, the Parasitic Disease Prevention Law of 1932 and the Venereal Disease Prevention Law of 1927.

Venereal disease (syphilis, gonorrhoea and chancroid) had been identified as a problem by the military authorities as early as the 1880s, when it was found to have infected around two-thirds of conscripts.[54] Very quickly a strong association was forged between licensed (and unlicensed) prostitution and the prevalence of venereal disease. Syphilis, for example, was commonly referred to as the 'disease of the pleasure quarters' (*karyūbyō*). By 1890, this representation of the prostitute as the source of disease was fixed, justifying the compulsory examination of prostitutes for syphilis and their confinement and treatment in 'prostitute hospitals' if infected.[55] The number of these institutions swiftly grew from 57 in 1880 to 158 in 1910 as the rigour of control increased. In 1900 the Home Ministry issued rules defining the legal basis of licensed prostitution, and afforded the police powers to arrest unlicensed prostitutes and force them to submit to medical examination.[56]

The state regarded the system of licensed prostitution within segregated 'pleasure quarters' as the most effective means by which to facilitate 'the regulation of public morals and public hygiene'.[57] Weekly medical inspection of prostitutes was regarded as an effective instrument of surveillance and control. This strategy of containment was presented as the main justification for registering prostitutes in the face of opposition from 'abolitionists', who opposed the system of licensed prostitution on the grounds that it was oppressive, exploited women and fostered complacency about the spread of venereal disease. In response to this critique, the Home Ministry produced data to demonstrate that venereal disease was far less common among licensed prostitutes than among their unlicensed counterparts – case rates of 2 per cent and 32 per cent respectively were recorded by doctors carrying out medical checks of both groups in 1927.[58] The Japanese authorities were confident about the efficacy of their approach. As Narita explains,

> Unlicensed prostitutes were specifically identified with sexually transmitted diseases in part to justify the existence of licensed prostitutes, as well as to argue for the continued necessity of testing licensed prostitutes for venereal disease. Such testing ... was loudly rationalized from a hygienic viewpoint as the only means to cut the spread of sexual diseases.[59]

With the rise of café culture in the late 1920s and early 1930s, however, the number of café waitresses, associated with promiscuous and hedonistic lifestyles, rocketed from 51,000 in 1929 to 112,000 in 1936. This was more than twice the number of licensed prostitutes, so throwing the strategy of containment into disarray.[60] Moreover, the assumption that what were often cursory medical examinations of prostitutes were sufficiently rigorous to detect venereal disease may well have been wrong. In short, venereal disease control was undermined by an overemphasis on monitoring the sexual health of licensed prostitutes and, where possible, clandestine ones, an over-confidence in the efficacy of the checks themselves, and arguably the failure to legally designate syphilis, gonor-rhoea and chancroid as infectious diseases.

The absence of national statistics as opposed to figures for incidence among conscripts and prostitutes makes it difficult to assess the scale of the problem. For obvious reasons, the army was particularly concerned about venereal disease due to its implications for operational effectiveness. Rates of morbidity among conscripts were recorded at around 26.57 per 1,000 conscripts in 1914, falling to just over 21.87/1,000 in 1920, 14.27 in 1925, 12.69 in 1930 and 11 in 1938.[61] Associated treatment was required for around 5,000 soldiers annually between 1912 and 1925. Anxious to get to grips with the problem, the army pioneered antibiotics for the treatment of these diseases (Salvarsan) as well as devices for their prevention. Condoms, the use of prophylactic solution and authorized brothels, subjecting both prostitutes and soldiers to military control, followed the failure of hygiene education and such punitive methods as beating and demotion.[62]

The assumptions behind the decision to permit soldiers to use army-sanctioned brothels were much the same as those justifying licensed prostitution quarters in civil society. Control of prostitutes and perceived suppression of sexual diseases lay at the heart of both approaches. Signalling perhaps a broader social perspective on the problem, the Venereal Disease Prevention Law of 1927 cast its net wider than licensed prostitutes, targeting 'other vulnerable groups of people like geisha girls'. It required local authorities to establish treatment clinics, subsidized by government, and brought in punitive measures against prostitutes who knowingly spread venereal disease.[63] Later, Crawford Sams would be scathing about Japanese attitudes towards venereal disease, dismissing the law of 1927 as too 'loosely drawn' and 'unenforced'. Nevertheless, incidence of disease among conscripts seems to have been falling during the 1920s and 1930s.[64] This apparently reflected growing awareness of venereal disease as a public health problem rather than merely a disease of prostitutes.[65] That much is captured by changes in nomenclature: the Japanese Association for the Prevention of Venereal Disease, established in 1905 as *Nihon Karyūbyō yobō kyōkai*, was renamed *Nihon seibyō yobō kyōkai* in 1921, the disease of the pleasure quarters (*Karyū*) giving way to the broader conception of sexually transmitted disease (*seibyō*).

The exigencies of war

The period of uninterrupted conflict in Asia and the Pacific from 1937 to 1945 brought reform and innovation to Japan, causing John Dower to characterize it as the 'useful war'. There were important legacies for the post-war years, 'in continuities of personnel and institutions, in technological and economic legacies, in bureaucratic and technocratic activities, and in the permutations and transformations of consciousness and ideology at both elite and popular levels'.[66] As regards public health and welfare, the demands of war focused minds and swept away impediments to change, the urgent need for effective social mobilization trumping the power of vested interests. The most striking advances in this respect perhaps were the establishment of the Welfare Ministry in January 1938, the formal creation of public health centres (*hokenjo*) and the expansion of medical insurance. All occurred around the time of the outbreak of full-scale hostilities in China in July 1937.

These institutional advances are analysed in the first part of this section; the second part assesses the impact of the war on the incidence of communicable diseases. As the tide of war turned against Japan, and the enemy's naval blockade reduced the flow of imports, so the country found itself increasingly vulnerable to food shortages and related health problems. Most significant, however, for standards of public health was the strategic air offensive that began in June 1944 and escalated significantly in March 1945. Bombing of urban housing and sanitary infrastructure caused a mass exodus of people from the cities to the countryside. It was the consequent breakdown in standards of public hygiene – the relaxation of inoculation schedules, the accumulation of untreated night soil and the press of unwashed bodies on the move – that foreshadowed the resurgence of such acute infectious diseases as smallpox and typhus. Although the outbreak of serious epidemics was averted until the early months of Occupation, the conditions that gave rise to them are examined in the final part of this chapter. The epidemics themselves are explored in Chapter 3.

The crystallization of concerns about poor standards of health occurred in the mid-1930s as part of the movement for a 'national defence state' (*kokubō kokka*), a design promoted by reform-minded bureaucrats and military leaders.[67] It was argued by the army in particular that effective mobilization for total war presupposed healthy, fit workers and servicemen, and yet a survey of recruits undertaken by the army in 1936 'revealed a shockingly high percentage of males who were unfit for military service because of malnutrition, communicable diseases or job-caused disabilities'. These problems, it was lamented, caused Japanese to be in much poorer physical shape than their American or European equivalents.[68] The resultant drive to redress this imbalance involved strengthening existing legislation concerning public health (discussed below). Much more significant, however, was the creation in January 1938 of the Welfare Ministry (*Kōseishō*), a device by which to ensure purposeful, decisive action in place of the disjointed endeavours that arose from the competing interests of various ministries. Campaigning hard for such an outcome from 1934, Koizumi Chikahiko, the Army Surgeon General, addressed the House of Peers in November 1936 on 'the condition of the nation's physical strength'. His speech called for much greater attention to public health rather than medical treatment, improving poor physiques and preventing chronic diseases.[69] It was less than a year later, on 9 July 1937, just two days after the beginning of the 'China Incident', that the cabinet approved plans for the new ministry. Koizumi's priorities were reflected in the prominence given to the physical fitness bureau (*tairyoku kyoku*), the first one to be established.[70] Robust soldiers and factory workers were indispensable for effective mobilization for total war. Motivated by the same considerations, the National Health Insurance Law of 1938 nevertheless represented another progressive advance, benefiting about 60 per cent of the population. Particular stress was placed on the inhabitants of rural areas, who 'had become so physically weak that many were unable to pass the basic health checkup required of conscripts'.[71] Overall, wartime imperatives enabled the new ministry to exercise greater control over public health and medicine, wresting power from the Japan Medical Association by effectively replacing it with its own Pharmaceutical and Medical Investigation Council.[72] Kasza makes the point succinctly when he observes that 'The state could not have humbled the medical association, which had long opposed national health insurance, without the authority that wartime conditions provided.'[73]

Just as the physical capability of Japanese was foremost in the minds of those calling for a dedicated Welfare Ministry and a system of universal health insurance, so too did it figure prominently in the justification for health centres, formally launched in 1937. Indeed, the first article of the Public Health Centre Law of April 1937 identified the new organizations as providers of health guidance to improve physical fitness for war, encapsulated in the slogan 'healthy soldiers, healthy people' (*kenpei-kenmin*).

Health centres were to focus their energies on improving disease prevention and management, sanitation and nutrition, and to carry out physical examinations (X-rays, etc.) where necessary. New centres, established at Kyōbashi in Tokyo (1935) and Tokorozawa in Saitama (1938) as part of the Rockefeller's sponsorship of the new National Institute of Public Health, provided sites for practical training and prototypes for the projected organizations in urban and rural settings. There was to be one centre for every 200,000 Japanese in the six largest cities and one for every 123,000 elsewhere, with the facility to set up branches where required. Two doctors, one pharmacist and three public health nurses made up the core staff team, supported by five administrators. By April 1938, 49 public health centres were in operation, the number rising to 133 in 1941 and 770 by 1944, when all public health organizations were stamped accordingly (see Chapter 7 for comment on their variable quality). With 155 centres reportedly destroyed in the war, it seems there were a substantial number still in existence at the onset of the Occupation.[74]

Indicative of the greater emphasis on proactive approaches to health protection and disease prevention was the growing role of the public health nurse (*hokenfu*) in the 1920s and 1930s. With this came a stronger emphasis on combating chronic infectious diseases, improving maternity and infant care and engaging with the health needs of children through school nursing. The Public Health Centre Law formalized their role without providing proper professional standards for accreditation. These were specified in the Public Health Nurse Regulations of 1941, by which time '18,000 nurses, midwives and even "lay women" with no clinical qualifications were already known to be working as *hokenfus* with mothers, babies and children, as well as with the prevention of tuberculosis'.[75] Havens rates the health centre and its public health nurses quite highly, particularly in relation to rural areas, where 'doctors were scarce and health care spotty'. For example, he praises the Fukui public health centre for making headway against malaria and tuberculosis from the moment of its inception in 1938.[76]

As made clear in the first section of this chapter, tuberculosis figured more prominently than any other public health menace in the 1920s and 1930s. In large part the establishment of public health centres in 1937 and the Welfare Ministry in 1938 can be attributed to tuberculosis' implications for effective war preparedness. This provided the necessary stimulus for far-reaching measures against the disease. A report by the Health and Sanitation Committee in 1934 ('The Fundamental Policy for Tuberculosis Control') provided the basis for the revised Tuberculosis Prevention Law of April 1937. This sought to end the practice of doctors concealing cases of the disease by demanding that they register patients who might infect others. However, the low number reported in the first year (just 2 per cent of the estimated total) suggests that this made little difference, and that entrenched attitudes were to blame.[77] This was in spite of efforts to recommend the public sanatoria to those with some prospect of recovery, and to strengthen provision in the countryside.[78]

As Japan's military commitments deepened in China and relations with the US and Britain deteriorated, so greater efforts were made to improve coordination and effectiveness of tuberculosis control. These led, in April 1939, to the formation of a dedicated tuberculosis section within the Welfare Ministry's Prevention Bureau. Moreover, the establishment of the Foundation for the Prevention of Tuberculosis, absorbing the ostensibly private Japan Anti-Tuberculosis League, reflected the government's determination to stamp its own authority on anti-tuberculosis initiatives.[79] The following year the National Physical Fitness Law introduced comprehensive procedures for detection and treatment of disease by subjecting all those between 15 and 19 years of age (15–25 from 1942) to annual physical medicals that included X-rays, tuberculin testing, percussion and auscultation. BCG vaccine was given to those shown not to be infected, the rate of inoculation rising steeply after 1941 to reach 540,000 Japanese in 1943. Following successful efforts to produce much larger quantities of BCG, mass inoculation began in 1944, reaching ten million people before the end of the war. This level of commitment was consonant with the cabinet's 'Essential Tuberculosis Policy' of August 1942, which underlined the urgency of the problem, provided more guidance about prevention and the care of patients according to the seriousness of their condition, and injected funds into rapid expansion of sanatorium facilities. While the aim was to supply 35,000 additional beds by 1943, it had only managed 6,800 by 1945. Johnston views these developments as evidence of the government finally confronting the disease's aetiology, and belatedly trying to tackle poor working and living conditions. War provided the government with the power and justification to take on those very vested interests that had resisted such improvements in the past.[80]

Despite some real successes against the disease – in Ishikawa prefecture, for example, where the problem was particularly serious – the pressures of war and increasingly defeat brought about conditions that cancelled out the benefits arising from the government's new initiatives. Thus, after a slight drop in mortality from 216.3 per 100,000 in 1939 to 212.9 the following year, the rate rose constantly thereafter – to 215.3 in 1941, 223.1 in 1942 and 235.3 in 1943, after which there is no reliable statistical evidence until 1947.[81] As Japan's prospects seriously deteriorated from 1944, signalled by the resignation of Prime Minister Tojo Hideki in July of that year, so the strains of war in terms of hunger and exhaustion became more telling. Large-scale incendiary bombing began in February 1945. Just one raid on Tokyo on 9 March killed 84,000 inhabitants, destroying 25 per cent of the city and causing more than three million people to flee to the countryside.[82] The social dislocation that resulted from such aerial assaults, combined with inadequate supplies of food, onerous workloads and anxiety about family, produced conditions ripe for the spread of tuberculosis. Japanese health officials interviewed by members of the US Strategic Bombing Survey stressed that 'The tuberculosis problem had been greatly aggravated by the air raids because of increased malnutrition, overcrowding, dispersal of infectious cases and a break-down in the tuberculosis control program.' The head of the tuberculosis section in the Welfare Ministry singled out malnutrition as a key factor in the spread of the disease.[83] While it is impossible to disentangle nutrition from the other factors contributing to tuberculosis' rising incidence, it is nonetheless important to consider the impact of the war on caloric intake and dietary balance.

Consuming sufficient calories rather than a healthy diet was the case for most Japanese during the war, particularly after 1941. Rationing and hunger pangs are powerful leitmotifs for the social history of this period. A selection of wartime accounts, edited by Samuel Hideo Yamashita, leaves the reader with the strong impression that food – for adults and children alike – was foremost in people's minds for much of the war, particularly from 1944. For example, the diary entries of Tamura Tsunejirō (9 July 1944–15 May 1945), aged 74 and living in Kyoto, constantly refer to shortages of food. On 18 July 1944 he complained of 'no fish distribution for some time' and the following year on 18 March moaned about 'a distribution of vegetables fit for a sparrow'.[84] Another diary, this time of an 11-year-old schoolboy, describes in great detail what was served at meal times, suggesting that food was a major preoccupation. Its author, Manabe Ichirō, was evacuated from Tokyo in August 1944 to Yumoto (Fukushima prefecture). This precocious schoolboy regularly records the contents of his 'rice gruel' – 'tofu, wheat gluten, pumpkin squash and eggplant' on 17 July 1944, potatoes but no *tōfu* (bean curd) on 20 July, and 'nothing good in it' on 7 August 1944. On 3 December 1944, he remarked that 'sweet potatoes disappeared from our rice bowls, and [white] potatoes have replaced them. It appears that this was done to keep us from getting tired of sweet potatoes.'[85] Rich in vitamin A and high in calories, sweet potatoes were introduced to Japan in the early seventeenth century. According to Hanley, this may help to explain 'the maintenance of a dense population in the eighteenth and nineteenth centuries'.[86]

As Japan's situation deteriorated from 1943, it was only supplies of sweet potatoes and white potatoes, together with those of beans and soybeans, that were increasing. Everything else was becoming scarcer, particularly fruit, meat, eggs, oils and fats, fish, milk products and sugar. Availability of dairy products was affected by falling imports and the use of domestic fodder crops for human consumption. The steady decline in supplies of fish – as the key source of animal protein – was particularly serious. Supplies of white and sweet potatoes were not vulnerable – as were many other foodstuffs – to naval blockade as Japanese consumers could depend on local farmers or their own 'victory gardens' for provision of these versatile foods. This was not the case with soybeans, nearly three-quarters of which came from abroad, chiefly from Manchuria. Supplies increased towards the end of the war as the Japanese government worked to offset declining supplies of rice with soybeans.[87]

As the key staple food, accounting for more than 50 per cent of calories, the bulk of carbohydrate content and a substantial proportion of protein intake, rice was obviously the government's priority, and this is reflected in comparatively small swings in its supply compared with other foodstuffs. Indeed, the US Strategic Bombing Survey concluded that the fundamental balance – or rather imbalance – of Japanese diets was not significantly altered by the war. While in Britain carbohydrates contributed only 52 per cent of total calories in 1943 (in 2009 the UK Food Standards Agency recommends a proportion of one-third), on average rice, other grains and potatoes continued to provide more than three-quarters of calories for Japanese during the Pacific War.[88]

Fully aware of the vital importance of rice as the mainstay of the Japanese diet, the Japanese government moved quickly to control its supply. As non-food producers, the residents of Japan's six major cities (Tokyo, Yokohama, Nagoya, Osaka, Kyoto, Kobe) were the first to experience rice rationing in April 1941; the system expanded to include the whole country in February 1942, affecting even farmers or 'self-suppliers'.[89] The priority for the authorities was to meet the requirements of the 'staple ration', namely 2.3 *go* (1 *go*=0.18 litres) of rice per person per day. Of course, this quantity was adjusted upwards or downwards according to age, physiological need (e.g. pregnant women) and degree of activity. According to Havens, the government's efforts paid off, because 'the state somehow managed to meet this basic ration through thick and thin until the last months of the war'.[90] However, in order to achieve this it resorted to the expedient of 'adulteration', that is to say, the substitution of other grains or potatoes for rice. Whereas Cwiertka contends that the levels of adulteration ranged from 10 to 30 per cent from 1943, Havens maintains that as late as May 1945 only 13 per cent of the staple ration in Tokyo was made up of substitutes, the proportion then jumping to around 50 per cent in June, July and August.[91] The diversion of these foods into the staple ration made them scarcer on the open market or the 'free list', so squeezing supplies of supplements to the rice ration.[92] In any case, the depth of the staple food supply crisis, compounded by a poor crop in 1944, was grave enough in July 1945 to force the government to reduce the staple food ration by 10 per cent to 2.1 *go* – effective from 11 July 1945 for Japanese outside the six major cities and from 11 August for those city dwellers.

By comparison, the distribution of so-called 'supplementary foods' (fruits, vegetables, fish and soybean products) was looser and more haphazard, and became increasingly ineffective as the war situation deteriorated. Perishable foods necessitated proper storage or rapid transit to deficit areas. Both proved difficult amidst an increasingly dislocated economy and dysfunctional transport network, particularly in the closing months of the war. Still, the main obstacle to fair distribution was the growing black market, which 'expanded with each new level of control, gradually becoming a structure where protest against wartime sacrifice intertwined with nutritional necessity'.[93] Indeed, it is estimated that 80 per cent of perishable foods ended up in black market channels.[94]

The government's determination to safeguard the staple ration meant that as imports declined so it had to demand higher quotas of rice and rice substitutes from its farmers. Farmers often responded by withholding and hoarding produce to feed themselves and to profit from any surplus by selling directly on the black market, so reducing supplies in legitimate channels and strengthening demand elsewhere. As a result, the status of so-called 'self-suppliers' was greatly enhanced at the expense of city dwellers, the great majority of whom increasingly found themselves engaged in the practice of *kaidashi* – journeying to rural areas to buy food directly from farmers. One witness to this, Takahashi Aiko, who lived in Tokyo, captured the developing urban–rural divide in her diary entry of 4 January 1944:

> In the past the daily lives of farmers were not blessed in any sense, but now they suddenly hold the key to our lives – food – and sit in the kingly position of lords of production. By selling on the black market, they are enjoying extraordinary prosperity.[95]

The advantageous position of many of those in the countryside underlines the difficulty of generalizing about hunger and malnutrition in wartime Japan. So much depended on local availability of foods and, of course, disposable income that many of those with low or fixed incomes found the black market beyond their reach. It can be assumed that their share of nutrients fell below the national average.

Available food supplies in 1945 provided an average of only 1,680 calories per capita per day – even if evenly distributed this amounted to 86 per cent of the restricted wartime requirements specified by the Japanese Nutritional Efficiency Committee. Japanese health officials informed members of the Medical Division of the US Strategic Bombing Survey that by the end of the war, weight loss was prevalent among urban Japanese. The survey's report contended that despite 'considerable progress ... made during the 10 years prior to 1938 in improving the nutritional status of the people, particularly of those in urban areas', the period 1943–45 witnessed serious reductions in caloric intake and protein from animal sources. It was noted that from 1943 many Japanese were consuming much less than per capita figures for the whole country indicated due to 'the failure of farmers to market their produce and to the rapid growth of the black market'. While famine was averted and the incidence of vitamin deficiency diseases (beriberi, scurvy, rickets) remained low, the dearth of food particularly affected vulnerable sections of the population, most notably pregnant and nursing mothers, infants and children. It was reported that infant mortality in the six large cities increased from 67.6 per 1,000 births in 1940 to 75.4 in 1943, and that 12.53 per cent of all children up to two years old in 1943 were 'ill-nourished or poorly developed'.[96] The final diary entry (15 December 1944) of Manabe Ichirō, the 11-year-old schoolboy mentioned earlier, reveals how his constant hunger pangs translated into developmental problems for children of his age: 'In the third period, they measured our height at the infirmary ... most of us had shrunk. I was 136.6 centimetres and had shrunk four centimetres.'[97]

This sketch of the wartime food situation may appear as a digression from the main theme of the war's impact on public health. Its importance lies, however, in its cumulative effects on the ability of people to fight off infection and ward off disease. Nutritional deficiencies, compounded by a disastrous harvest in the autumn of 1945, foreshadowed the outbreak of epidemics during the first year of the Occupation, as did the decline of sanitary standards. The latter must at least partly explain the steep rise in the incidence of typhoid and paratyphoid in 1943 and 1944, and that of dysentery in 1945.[98] It seems that the exigencies of war caused people to apply raw sewage to fields and 'war gardens'.[99] Later, during the Occupation, the American official with chief responsibility for sanitary engineering maintained that 'regulations were completely relaxed ... night soil was used indiscriminately on all types of vegetables without undergoing proper digestion processes before being used'.[100] As explained by Havens, these irregular practices also reflected the breakdown of systems of sewage disposal:

> private contractors ran short of manpower to haul the accumulation to nearby farms ... and by 1944 the head of sanitation of Tokyo told the *Asahi* newspaper that broken-down trucks, aging equipment, and gasoline shortages meant that city workers could not handle more than 70 per cent of the sewage that was produced each day.[101]

These problems became crises following bombing raids, causing the systems of night soil collection and disposal to cease. The consequent build-up of human waste provided a reservoir for enteric diseases that could then be transmitted to people by flies. Dumping it into watercourses carried similar risks of disease transmission. Contamination of drinking water may also have occurred due to breaks in water supply pipes due to bombing. This was identified by the Strategic Bombing Survey as a likely contributory factor in the dysentery epidemic of 1945 in Nagoya, where the case rate was 637.4/100,000, compared with a rate for all Japan of 134.[102]

Mass bombing raids on Japan's six largest cities (Tokyo, Nagoya, Kobe, Osaka, Yokohama and Kawasaki) and 58 others with populations over 100,000, together with the atomic bombing of Hiroshima and Nagasaki, caused devastation. They destroyed 40 per cent of Osaka and Nagoya, 50 per cent of Tokyo, Kobe and Yokohama, 90 per cent of the prefectural capital of Aomori, and almost 100 per cent of Hiroshima.[103] Between 500,000 and 900,000 Japanese were killed and more than one million injured. The social dislocation occasioned by these catastrophic bombing raids produced conditions ideal for the outbreak of acute epidemic diseases. Perhaps the most notorious was epidemic typhus, which Anne Hardy describes as 'above all an environmental fever, which cannot survive in conditions of personal and household cleanliness'.[104] Personal hygiene was inevitably neglected amidst makeshift dwellings, the breakdown of organized sanitation, disruption to the water supply, and the absence of fuel. Careful examination of available statistics indicates that case incidence of diseases of the typhus fever group increased more than ten-fold between 1942 and 1943 – from 100 to 1,374 – only to jump again the following year to 3,941. The degree to which these higher numbers for 1942 and 1943 were still small in absolute terms and represented a relatively minor problem for public health is underlined by the apparent drop in case incidence to 2,461 in 1945.[105] Although there may have been no epidemic of typhus during these years, Havens' point that 'Typhus was a threat near the end of the war because lice were so common' is well made. Likewise, there was no epidemic of smallpox during the war, just a slight jump of cases in 1940–41 and 1943, both of which seem to have rapidly subsided.[106] The aetiology of the typhus and smallpox epidemics that erupted during the first year of the Occupation will be discussed in the next chapter.

Perhaps the most serious epidemic in 1943 and 1944 was that of diphtheria. Its incidence jumped from 44,629 in 1942 to 63,863 in 1943 and 94,274 in 1944 (there is no reliable figure for 1945). In 1944 the Welfare Ministry gave clear instructions to the cities of Tokyo, Yokohama, Yokosuka, Kawasaki, Sapporo, Nagoya, Kyoto, Osaka and Kobe to immunize infants and children with anatoxin, but the degree to which this was carried out was not effectively monitored. Moreover, there were concerns about the variable quality of diphtheria anatoxin and the adequacy of supplies in the face of declining production due to the war. Additional difficulties with separating the product into the required smaller doses, packaging it, distributing it and finding sufficient doctors to administer it all conspired against an effective immunization campaign. On 20 October 1944 the Welfare Ministry issued a warning about the rapid spread of the disease, cautioning doctors that misdiagnoses and delays in carrying out tests were exacerbating the problem.[107] Interestingly, our 11-year-old diarist, Manabe Ichirō, records 'typhoid and diphtheria shots for those going off on the collective evacuation' on 9 August 1944, stating the 'second diphtheria shot will be on the twelfth and the second typhoid shot on the sixteenth' (further details were given about the needle and how much it hurt on the days in question).[108] While this demonstrates that systems were in place to implement disease prophylaxis, the rapid growth in diphtheria's incidence suggests that they were not sufficiently robust to offset the deterioration of living conditions that eased its spread.

Conclusion

This chapter has highlighted the limits of Japan's modern public health system that developed from the early Meiji period and proved so adept at applying scientific solutions to such acute infectious diseases as smallpox and cholera. Where it proved much less effective, however, was in its response to such chronic infectious diseases as tuberculosis, dysentery and trachoma, all of which were rooted in particular social conditions. These were created or exacerbated by Japan's headlong rush to 'catch up' with the West, its determination to industrialize rapidly and to build a modern military to protect and promote its national interests. Social diseases like tuberculosis thrived amid the oppressive conditions of early capitalist development, spreading among female mill workers who then infected others when they returned to their villages. These were communities highly susceptible to infection due to their lack of previous exposure. The problem was so inextricably bound up with the processes of economic development and modernization promoted by the establishment that it was no surprise that they neglected to confront its root causes. Likewise, the fundamental nature of other social problems like high infant mortality and poor nutrition militated against meaningful, effective responses.

It was only really in the 1920s that the social dimension of public health came to the fore, challenging the view that public health was first and foremost the province of the state. This tension is captured in the lifestyle improvement movement of the 1920s, when middle-class activists pushed progressive agendas for the reform of domestic hygiene, nutrition and sanitation. At the same time, major cities like Tokyo and Osaka pioneered advances in maternal and child health and greater efforts were made to combat tuberculosis and trachoma in line with new legislation. It is interesting that by 1930 the International Health Board of the Rockefeller Foundation judged that Japan had finally embraced the American conception of public health, so justifying its sponsorship of the new National Institute of Public Health. Running parallel with the evolution of this project during the 1930s, however, was the rise of the Japanese military in line with Japan's increasing international isolation following the Manchuria Incident of 1931. Some credit is undoubtedly due to the military for major advances in public health, represented by the establishment of nation-wide public health centres, the creation of a dedicated ministry of health, and revisions to legislation to strengthen disease prevention. However, such gains were soon offset by the decline of Japan's military prospects from 1943 and the rapid deterioration of social conditions, culminating in widespread destruction and deprivation in 1945. When the emperor broadcast the government's decision to surrender on 15 August 1945, most Japanese were confronting the twin perils of hunger and disease. In a matter of weeks Crawford Sams and his staff in the PH&W would be similarly faced by these menaces.

3   'Controlling wildfire diseases'

The primary function of the Public Health and Welfare Section (PH&W) of GHQ SCAP, formally set up on 2 October 1945, was to prevent 'widespread disease and unrest'.[1] For understandable reasons, the welfare of the Occupation forces was paramount and, at least according to early policy documents, the suffering of the Japanese was only relevant insofar as it might engender social disruption inimical to the safety and successful operation of the Occupation. Indicative of this set of priorities was an article in the *Nippon Times* on 9 October 1945 with the heading 'U.S. soldiers here in excellent health' and a subheading that captured the main threat to their wellbeing – 'All Japanese returning troops, repatriates examined to check diseases'. Anxiety about epidemics and such key contributory factors as large-scale repatriation, malnutrition and unsanitary conditions dominated the thinking of key members of the PH&W for at least two years. Colonel Crawford F. Sams and his staff had little time to adjust to the very difficult environment of defeated Japan before they were forced to confront the challenge of 'wildfire diseases',[2] namely smallpox, typhus, cholera and diphtheria.

These challenges are reminiscent of the origins of Japan's modern system of public health in the Meiji (1868–1912) and Taisho (1912–26) periods (see Chapter 1), when Japan routinely suffered epidemics of these diseases and devised methods of successfully combating them. This chapter explores the aetiology of these epidemics, the efficacy of measures taken to confront them during the Occupation, their parallels with earlier initiatives, their familiarity to Japanese implementing them and subjected to them and the relative contributions of Japanese and American medical personnel involved in carrying them out. Important considerations are the degree to which Japanese personnel required training and who provided it when needed, the existence or adequacy of supplies of vaccine and the willingness of the Japanese people to comply with schedules for vaccination and re-vaccination. Before examining these issues, however, it is first necessary to consider the public health reform agenda as defined in initial Occupation planning documents, together with the assumptions and prejudices that informed preliminary policy statements.

Framing the challenge

The purpose of the Allied Occupation of Japan, as defined in the Potsdam Declaration, was to establish 'in accordance with the freely expressed will of the Japanese people a peacefully inclined and responsible government'. Its 'ultimate objectives', declared the United States Initial Post-Surrender Policy for Japan of 29 August 1945, were complete disarmament and demilitarization and the formation of democratic and representative organizations. Not surprisingly, these rather broad statements of intent stressed political and economic goals. They were largely silent on such social topics as public health and welfare, except in the negative sense that the Japanese government was 'expected to provide goods and services to meet the needs of the occupying forces', provided this did not cause 'starvation, widespread disease and acute physical distress'.[3]

In the much more detailed Basic Initial Post-Surrender Directive to Supreme Commander for the Allied Powers for the Occupation and Control of Japan (JCS 1380/15), sent to General MacArthur on 3 November 1945, the implications of indirect occupation for civilian supply and relief were spelled out. MacArthur was charged with ensuring that the Japanese authorities fully utilized 'essential Japanese resources in order that imports into Japan may be strictly limited' – resort to imported supplies would only be justified in the event that they were 'needed to prevent such widespread disease and civil unrest as would endanger the occupying forces or interfere with military operations'. Such imports, the directive declared, would be 'confined to minimum quantities of food, fuel, medical and sanitary supplies'. It was the responsibility of the relevant Japanese agencies to distribute these supplies fairly and equitably.[4]

Above all, the official line was that there was no obligation on the part of the US to ameliorate the harsh conditions of defeat. The US Initial Post-Surrender Policy for Japan put it rather starkly: 'The plight of Japan is the direct outcome of its own behaviour, and the Allies will not undertake the burden of repairing the damage.' The Japanese could not expect the guarantee of any 'particular standard of living in Japan',[5] the meaning of which was that they should expect to suffer for the foreseeable future. Only in exceptional circumstances of social breakdown, occasioned by disease and civil strife, would the US actively intervene to assist the Japanese people. Otherwise they would have to depend on their own efforts and resources to improve their lives. In practice, of course, this policy of restraint quickly proved unworkable, particularly in the face of a grave dearth of food supplies (Chapter 5), when MacArthur himself made representations to Washington for food aid.

As far as public health was concerned, however, Japan was expected to produce its own supplies of medicines and vaccines for the most part, and MacArthur was happy to let Sams' PH&W direct and monitor the work of its counterpart in the Japanese government, the Welfare Ministry (*Kōseishō*). There were no great controversies, long since debated by historians, like those that faced Government Section, for example, in relation to the 1947 constitution or police reform. Although public health was mentioned in the new constitution in article 25, where the state was charged with promoting and extending it, it lies outside the dominant narrative of Occupation reform, receiving a few lines of comment here and there, and only recently commanding more detailed attention by a limited number of historians. Largely peripheral to the great debates about democratization and economic deconcentration, the work of PH&W seems to have attracted much less attention than its chief, Crawford F. Sams, would have liked. He worked hard to publicize the achievements of his section, to stress its importance for the overall success of the Occupation. A less prominent profile, however, brought with it some benefits, not least of which was a tendency among observers to accept the word of Sams perhaps less critically than they would claims made by more well-known figures like MacArthur himself, Courtney Whitney or Charles Willoughby.

This meant that Sams, more than anybody else, was able to frame the challenge of public health reform in Occupied Japan as he saw fit, contrasting what he claimed were Japan's past failings in this field with the striking successes he attributed to the endeavours of American reformers. An extraordinarily able and experienced public health administrator, Sams had an impressive career history. He was top of his class when he graduated in 1931 from Walter Reed Army Medical School. Here he met Major James S. Simmons, considered by Sams to be his mentor in preventive medicine. Sams went on to serve in Panama from 1937 to 1939, where he gained invaluable experience in malaria control, and in a wartime capacity in North Africa and the Middle East, engaging with public health issues in Tunisia, Libya and Sicily. According to Zabelle Zakarian, who edited and published his memoir in 1998, he gained much from his time in the Middle East, learning 'methods of prevention through immunization and environmental controls, which he later applied to the control of smallpox, typhus fever, cholera, diphtheria, typhoid, tuberculosis, and dysenteries in Japan and Korea'. After a brief stint in Washington as Chief of the Programme Branch in the War Department's Logistics Division (February–June 1945), Sams was put in charge of the Public Health and Welfare Division of Military Government Section of GHQ/AFPAC (Armed Forces Pacific) in Manila.[6]

Sams arrived in Japan with a strong sense of mission – to modernize Japanese public health according to the standards pertaining in the US – and in common with other American reformers a tremendous self-confidence that at times bordered on arrogance. He had no previous experience of East Asia and tended to lump Japan in with the other countries of 'the Orient'. In an article on 'Japan's new public health program' for the *Military Government Journal* he remarked that 'prior to the termination of the war such health and welfare activities as existed in Japan were primitive in nature and ineffective in practice'.[7] Interviewed much later in his life by Reiko Ryder-Shimazaki, whose principal interest was nursing reform during the Occupation, Sams reiterated the central premise of his memoir – that his PH&W was 'giving modern concepts to Japan', which he characterized as an 'underdeveloped country'.[8] With reference to the model public health centre sponsored by the Rockefeller Foundation (see Chapter 2), he claimed that 'the Japanese did not know what to do with it as it far exceeded their needs or capabilities at the time'. This begs the question of why the Foundation had committed funds to such an apparently lost cause.[9] Sams' attitude was typical of the bearing of the higher echelons of GHQ SCAP. Indeed, one of MacArthur's aides, Faubion Bowers, admitted that 'I and nearly all the Occupation people I knew were extremely conceited and extremely arrogant and used our power every inch of the way.'[10] John Dower develops this theme in *Embracing Defeat*, referring to MacArthur's underlings as 'petty viceroys', Occupied Japan as a 'colonial enclave' and highlighting the prevailing 'assumption that, virtually without exception, Western culture and its values were superior to those of "the Orient"'.[11]

What also emerges from the exchange of letters between Ms Ryder-Shimazaki and Sams, and a lengthy interview she conducted with him on 22 May 1982, is a hard political edge to his character, a strident anti-communism that chimes well with the Cold War colouring of much of his memoir. Takemae notes that Sams was 'fiercely loyal to MacArthur',[12] resigning when the Supreme Commander was dismissed by President Truman on 11 April 1951, and a great fan of Willoughby, affectionately described by MacArthur as his 'lovable fascist'.[13] Like Willoughby, Sams saw communist conspiracies everywhere. In his view, 'communist New Dealers in Washington' and President Roosevelt's 'New Deal' represented 'an attempt to destroy the US as a Federal Republic with a Capitalist Economy and replace it with a Socialist Communist Dictatorship'.[14] He had no compunction about labelling Theodore Cohen, head of the Labour Division of the Economic and Scientific Section, a communist. Typical was his claim that he had 'numerous Communists sent to infiltrate my staff and a few were able to do great harm',[15] the nature of which is not disclosed. All this is important because it reveals the lens through which Sams viewed Japan, one very much tinted by colonialism and anti-communism. His vision of the world in the mid-to-late 1940s ensured that he never lost an opportunity to underline the huge challenge facing his section in Japan, the contribution the US could make to meeting that challenge as the world's leader in public health and the benefits that would accrue to Japan if it followed the US's example. Developing close ties in this field would form one of many strands of a solid, anti-communist alliance.

Like other section chiefs, Sams could present his views to the media in the happy knowledge that they could not be publicly contested due to the existence of a system of censorship. While this 'phantom bureaucracy', in Dower's memorable phrase, was perfectly understandable in the context of a military occupation, it ran counter to the Occupation's commitment to freedom of speech. There could be no public acknowledgement of the existence of this apparatus of control, nor could there be any criticism of SCAP or the US. Any mention of potentially unsettling topics – like mixed-race children, starvation, black market activities – was likely to be censored.[16]

Thus, when Sams tempted fate by declaring in early January 1946 that 'there has been a steady decline in various common communicable diseases since the start of the Allied Occupation' or when he refuted claims of starvation among Japanese the previous month,[17] he knew that these positions would not be publicly challenged. These kinds of privileges, together with his background and political convictions, ensured that Sams' avowed views of Japanese public health would remain fixed for the duration of the Occupation. They would seldom acknowledge the more positive portrayal of Japan's accomplishments in public health, interestingly expressed in the *US Army Civil Affairs Handbook on Public Health and Sanitation in Japan*, dated 10 February 1945. 'The Public Health Service and Sanitary Bureau of Japan', it declared, 'are modern, efficient and compare favourably with those of the Western Hemisphere.'[18]

Civil affairs handbooks were written by academics with relevant expertise, and were designed as tools of military government for those administering territory subdued by US military forces. Drawing on a number of official Japanese sources, the *handbook on public health* reads as a thoughtful, balanced and sober appraisal of its subject, identifying the merits and flaws of the institutions and systems with which American personnel would have to contend. It is therefore surprising that its generally positive assessment of Japan's record on public health and sanitation should be so at odds with the views of the chief of SCAP's PH&W.

A final consideration when weighing up the challenge that Sams describes in relation to modernizing public health in Japan, together with the immense achievements he attributes to his team in PH&W, is the resources in terms of manpower and expertise he could draw upon. According to Takemae, his section was 'overworked and understaffed', its membership never more than 150 people, and consisting of 92 in February 1948. That number was made up of 12 officers, two enlisted men, 56 civilian personnel and 22 Japanese.[19] Of course, they were not all working on preventive health – their scope of activity ranged from medical and veterinary matters to welfare and social security. Although the section included individuals with high levels of expertise in such areas as medicine, public health and nutrition, its small size highlights the degree to which it depended on an enormous number of Japanese doctors and public officials, often policemen, to implement its directives or SCAPINs (SCAP instructions). Indeed, we can deduce from the section's impressive range of activities and reform agendas that there cannot have been more than a handful of individuals able to focus their minds fully on combating epidemics in 1946.

In terms of keeping in touch with developments in the field, PH&W officials undertook survey trips to monitor the implementation of public health measures, and liaised with American doctors serving in a public health capacity in the prefectural military government teams. The latter's official reporting channels were through 8th Army (regional and corps) and GHQ AFPAC, based in Yokohama, to GHQ SCAP in Tokyo. According to Sey Nishimura, who has researched the work of the Public Health Section of Kyoto Military Government Team, the team member responsible for public health was expected to compile monthly reports for PH&W. In addition to the military government teams, there were tactical troops, including some with expertise in public health, who represented the potential enforcement arm of GHQ SCAP. These were to be actively employed in the event of social breakdown occasioned by an epidemic, natural disaster or an insurgency. In August 1947, the ratio of tactical troops to military government officials was roughly 30:1.[20]

Even allowing for these tactical reserves, the scale of the endeavour – as regards combating epidemics alone – far exceeded the capabilities of the PH&W, and necessitated an active and perhaps decisive role for what Takemae refers to as 'Japan's public health establishment'.[21] As explained, the motive forces behind Sams' reluctance to acknowledge this relate to his background, status and politics, his determination to present US-sponsored public health reform as transformative for Japan. All of this provides the crucial backcloth to the public health emergencies of late 1945 and 1946, the way they were represented by Sams and the resulting disproportionate credit apportioned to the Occupation authorities. The latter were presented as expert and dynamic, in contrast to the Japanese, too often characterized as indolent and incompetent – classic colonial descriptors.

Confronting smallpox and typhus

On 7 January 1946 Sams was quoted in the press denying that communicable diseases were on the rise in Japan and that in fact the Occupation had contained an outbreak of typhus in Hokkaido and had presided over a decline in the incidence of diphtheria, typhoid, paratyphoid, scarlet fever and smallpox.[22] Very soon, however, it was clear that both smallpox and typhus were spreading rapidly among the Japanese population, and that well-coordinated and very energetic measures were required to bring these epidemics under control. Indeed, less than ten days after Sams' optimistic appraisal of the situation, the Occupation issued SCAPIN 610, dated 16 January 1946. This stated that the 'increasing prevalence of smallpox among Japanese civilians requires more concerted action than is now being taken by responsible Japanese public health officials'. Moreover, it demanded the 'reinstatement of the pre-war *compulsory* vaccination program throughout Japan' (my italics).[23] Nearly 18,000 cases (17,954) would be recorded before the epidemic had run its course, and, occurring almost simultaneously with it, an outbreak of louse-borne typhus would register a staggering total of 32,366 cases.[24] While the smallpox epidemic had a higher rate of mortality (16.87 per cent) than the typhus one (10.35 per cent), the latter was by far the more serious of the two, given that the scale of it was unprecedented in Japan. Indeed, typhus had hardly figured as a significant disease threat since the Meiji period, the epidemic of 1914 (7,317 cases) seeming mild by comparison with the 1946 outbreak. As a result, the Occupation authorities would have to play a much more active role in terms of instructing the Japanese in the manufacture of typhus vaccine, and, more importantly, the deployment of DDT – the chief means of checking the disease's spread by eliminating its vector, the body louse. These measures were relatively unfamiliar to the Japanese, though they had proved themselves adept in the past at combating the threat of smallpox.

The spread of smallpox in January, February and March 1946 seems to reflect the difficult social conditions besetting Japan during the early months of the

Occupation, and the rather confused division of responsibility between the Japanese government and its prefectural administrations on the one hand and the Occupation authorities on the other. In a sense, this fuzziness, which diminished as time passed, was beneficial to the PH&W as it could take the credit for successes and blame the Japanese authorities for failures. This much is clear from the dominant narrative of the anti-smallpox campaign, which attributes delays in bringing the disease under control to Japanese passivity and incompetence, but tends to present the overall achievement of mass vaccination of the Japanese population as a triumph of American drive and initiative. Before exploring the efficacy of measures taken against the disease and the balance of credit due, it is first necessary to explore popular and official perceptions of the aetiology and spread of the epidemic.

According to the Occupation's monthly summation for January 1946, there were smallpox cases in northern, central and southern Japan. Hokkaido was identified as one of the 'principal epidemic foci', as were 'Hyogo, Aichi and Nagasaki prefectures, and to a lesser extent Shimane prefecture'.[25] Provincial and national newspaper coverage (as filtered by the Allied Translator and Interpreter Service – ATIS) tended to focus on the southern half of Japan as the principal breeding ground of the disease. On 15 January it was reported that there were 'signs of smallpox spreading rapidly in Yamaguchi-ken with the coming of the new year',[26] and on 22 January the *Kobe Shimbun* (Hyōgo) noted that the 'smallpox epidemic is not yet stamped out' and that 'the number of victims since 1 January has risen to 257'.[27]

Later on, in mid-March 1946, the *Mainichi Shimbun* would implicitly identify Kobe as the source of the epidemic, declaring that 'smallpox suddenly occurred around Kobe in December, last year'. The article went on to observe that 'at present, there are no prefectures where smallpox has not been witnessed'.[28] Newspaper accounts revealed cases of the disease on the outskirts of Tokyo, and in Akita, Tokushima, Miyagi, Miyazaki, Kagawa and Ehime prefectures in the last ten days of January.[29] On 5 February 1946 the *Nagasaki Shimbun* stated that 'smallpox was rampant' there and three days later the *Tokyo Shimbun* cautioned that as smallpox was 'now raging in Nagoya, Osaka and Kobe' Tokyo must take steps to prevent such an epidemic.[30] Despite this call for vigilance, the first case in the centre of Tokyo was reported on 19 February 1946, a development that was 'considered seriously'. Such concern appeared well founded, when the *Asahi Shimbun* revealed just two days later that there had been a sudden increase of cases in the capital, with smallpox being 'reported in more than twenty wards'.[31] By the end of February the provincial newspaper, *Hokkoku Mainichi Shimbun*, based in Kanazawa (Ishikawa prefecture), claimed that 'smallpox is rampant throughout the country', and that it had made its way to Ishikawa prefecture from the Chūkyō region (centred on Nagoya) and Kansai.[32] Likewise, when a case of smallpox arose in Niigata prefecture (just along the Japan Sea coast from Ishikawa), it was disclosed that the patient was infected during a visit to Nagoya, and that three people had subsequently caught the disease from him.[33] By 12 March, according to the *Nippon Times*, some 25 cases nation-wide were being reported every day, and Hyōgo prefecture had been the 'worst hit with 1,487 [out of 6,512] cases so far'. It seems that the chief focus of the epidemic was Kansai, and that the disease spread from cities there, principally Kobe, Osaka and Kyoto, to Nagoya and Tokyo, and subsequently from urban to agrarian areas.[34] By April the epidemic of typhus had largely eclipsed that of smallpox and by early May the latter was definitely on the wane. Its peak, according to Sams, had been reached on 30 March, when the daily rate for all of Japan was 102 cases per 100,000, a figure that had declined to 65 by 20 April.[35]

As well as tracking the epidemic's routes of infection, newspaper commentaries were often at pains to stress that smallpox was a disease foreign to Japan, one that had long ceased to have an endemic profile within the country. While some Americans framed the disease as a reflection of the Orient's unhygienic conditions and poor public health provision, Japanese commentators posited a division between its former colonies as diseased and itself as relatively healthy. In this vein, Dr Yahagi Hideo of the Infectious Diseases Investigation Laboratory warned that the destructive potential of the epidemic was all the greater as 'smallpox is a foreign pestilence'. The *Tokyo Shimbun*, which quoted his view on 8 February, claimed that the virus had been introduced from Korea, Manchuria and China.[36] Likewise, when the *Nippon Times* summarized a report on infectious diseases compiled by the director of the relevant bureau, it noted that the smallpox epidemic was due principally to 'the import of labourers from the Asian continent' and so 'prevailed in localities where there was a big influx ... such as Hokkaido, Fukushima, Nagano, Yamaguchi, Shizuoka, Osaka and Hyogo'. Concentrations of typhus were likewise blamed on foreigners.[37] On 26 February 1946 the *Asahi Shimbun* explained that the virus had 'entered our country from the continent around April, May and June of last year when the traffic was busy between them'.[38] Seldom was any attempt made to back up these assertions with evidence beyond the merely circumstantial. Indeed, these claims reveal much more about Japanese denial of the ill-effects of war and defeat on their standards of public health than they do about the complex aetiology of these epidemics.

Sometimes this strong association between epidemic disease and diseased Koreans or Chinese blurred into more general, less racially charged, statements about destitute urban residents, some of them repatriates, struggling to rebuild lives in the cities. For example, the *Asahi Shimbun* asserted that outbreaks of typhus and smallpox in Tokyo in early March 1946 centred on the districts of Ueno and Asakusa, where 'vagrants swarm'.[39] It was not long before the failure to bring the epidemics quickly under control was blamed on these unfortunate victims of the war. The *Nippon Times* stated on 9 April 1946 that the increasing incidence of disease in Tokyo, Nagoya and Osaka was due to 'the unemployed and vagrants who have no definite shelters ... spreading germs'. This tendency to scapegoat particular groups was subjected to critical scrutiny by the *Asahi Shimbun* on 10 April 1946, when it examined a survey conducted by the People's Welfare Bureau of the Tokyo metropolitan government. This revealed that of 1,704 cases of typhus on 5 April, 'only one vagrant was stricken with the disease'. As for the 1,269 smallpox cases, around one-third were infants aged 1–5, 392 patients were people with no fixed occupation, 156 were salaried employees, 78 were craftsmen, 50 day labourers, 48 factory workers, 32 were held in custody in police stations and 23 ran market stalls. Only 86 were classified as vagrants.[40]

Those charged with halting the spread of the disease, American and Japanese alike, fully appreciated that all sections of Japanese society must be vaccinated with cowpox vaccine, a practice with a long history in Japan (see Chapter 1). The challenge was to produce enough potent vaccine quickly to combat the emerging epidemic. Also important was rapid disclosure of cases by doctors and swift isolation of patients to reduce the likelihood of others catching the virus. Close reading of the sources reveals that the Japanese government, working through its prefectural administrations, was expected to produce sufficient vaccine and proceed with effective vaccination schedules as soon as possible. SCAPIN 610 of 16 January 1946 required the Japanese authorities first to vaccinate employees of the Occupation forces or those likely to come into contact with them such as hotel staff,[41] before vaccinating populations in areas where smallpox had occurred or might occur in the future. Concern about inadequate supply of vaccine was clear from the call for the immediate development of suitable facilities for the production of sufficient quantities to eradicate the disease throughout the country.[42] The onus, then, was on the Japanese to contain local outbreaks of the disease at the same time as they prepared to meet the challenge of a wide-ranging epidemic by means of mass vaccination. They could not expect more than very limited assistance from the US in meeting this challenge.

The need to conserve vaccine by targeting scarce resources is evident from newspaper coverage of the emerging smallpox problem in January 1946. The prefectural authorities in Yamaguchi and Tokushima prefectures vaccinated those in particular districts close to confirmed cases, and stressed the need to report suspicious symptoms to doctors immediately. Mayors of cities, towns and villages were likewise required to act quickly to inform the prefectural government of any outbreaks of disease.[43] At the end of January, the *Tokushima Shimbun* reported that officials of the hygiene section were on a mission to buy vaccine in Tokyo, Osaka and Kobe, but that supplies had been diminished by the 'sudden rise in the price of cows'. Moreover, it was difficult to acquire vaccine in cities where the incidence of smallpox was growing rapidly. In view of these difficulties, the article reiterated the need to report suspected cases of smallpox to a doctor as quickly as possible and for the doctor confirming a case to inform the police at once.[44] Around three weeks later the *Tokushima Shimbun* stated that enough vaccine for only 300 people, purchased in Osaka and Kobe, had been quickly used up, but that this was just the prelude to a large-scale, compulsory vaccination programme for the whole prefecture that would be undertaken as soon as the prefectural government acquired vaccine for 100,000 people. This was expected to arrive from Tokyo, Osaka and Kobe shortly.[45] The dilemma for all involved in the struggle against the epidemic is captured in SCAPIN 610, which called for targeted vaccination campaigns at the same time as it demanded the reinstatement of the pre-war compulsory vaccination programme. Such ambiguity reflected the problem of vaccine supply.

This much is clear from developments in Tokyo, where 'nearby residents were compulsorily vaccinated' following the first confirmed case of smallpox in central Tokyo. The unfortunate 47-year-old teacher was isolated in Toyotama hospital and the school premises where he worked were disinfected.[46] These actions complied with the advice of Dr Yahagi of the Infectious Diseases Investigation Laboratory, who highlighted the merits of vaccination but reminded everyone of the equal importance of 'early medical examination and isolation of cases'.[47] Again, on 21 February 1946 the *Asahi Shimbun* reported that smallpox patients were being isolated in Toshima and Toyotama hospitals and compulsory vaccination was confined to residents in the immediate vicinity of an outbreak.[48] The same article maintained that only 'increased production of vaccine and its effective application' could really contain the epidemic. Just five days later the same newspaper complained of doctors' inadequate stocks of vaccine and the resulting vulnerability of many babies, whose vaccination was prevented by the air raids in the closing months of the war.[49]

In contrast, the *Hokkoku Mainichi* praised the wartime efforts of prefectural health officials in Ishikawa prefecture for maintaining rigorous vaccination schedules, thus ensuring high levels of immunity. Still, there was no room for complacency, particularly as around 11,000 people, including children and those over 40 years old, had been identified as in need of vaccination. Three thousand doses of vaccine had been supplied, and a further 20,000 were expected shortly. This wait for vaccine, experienced by prefectural governments all over Japan, seems to have ended in March. From this time, invitations to factories, companies, schools and other organizations to submit their charges to vaccination gave way to commands to undertake large-scale campaigns that must include all sections of society.[50]

Thus, the provincial newspaper of Yamaguchi prefecture reported on 2 March 1946 that public health officials were demanding that everyone must be vaccinated in accordance with a prefectural ordinance enacted on 21 February. It was stated that 'Vaccination must be completed by officials of towns, cities or villages, who can determine the date and place. Those who avoid vaccination wilfully will be fined.'[51] The following day, 3 March, the *Asahi Shimbun* declared that those responsible for tackling the epidemic in Tokyo had received more than two million vials of vaccine, and that arrangements were being made to target areas where 'vagrants, war sufferers and evacuees from overseas are crowded'. This was in addition to vaccinating all residents through the neighbourhood associations at two or three places in each ward.[52] On 13 March it was announced that the metropolitan police authorities were determined to strengthen 'epidemic prevention squads' by deploying more hygiene police and rigorously enforcing compulsory vaccination. The latter necessitated the cooperation of neighbourhood associations, primary schools and businesses. It also involved teams, made up of volunteer medical students, offering vaccination at train stations, and police officials coordinating efforts to vaccinate the homeless and destitute as well as those detained in prisons.[53] All over Japan, according to the *Mainichi*, prefectural authorities were acting on the instructions of central government to enforce vaccination.[54] On 16 March 1946 the *Yomiuri Hōchi* declared that 'compulsory inoculation' was underway in Osaka, Kobe and Kyoto.[55]

While the Japanese themselves were responsible for producing vaccine and carrying out and submitting to vaccination campaigns, the Occupation apparently assisted in the rapid transport of vaccine to needy areas – more than three million doses from the Otawara laboratory in Kumamoto to Tokyo in early March 1946.[56] According to the *Tokyo Shimbun*, the manufacture of vaccine had been eased by the import of cattle from Korea. Despite a decline in its quality during 1945, it was now being effectively 'manufactured at the Infectious Diseases Research Institute of the Welfare Ministry and the Otawara Institute at Kumamoto *in cooperation with the Allied Forces*' (my italics).[57] Sams describes the efforts of Americans as being primarily directed at facilitating the resumption of vaccine production – coordinating provision of suitable buildings, refrigeration, personnel, calves, etc.[58] Despite what seems an impressive recovery of vaccine production facilities in February and March 1946, Sams was scathing about the Japanese vaccination effort. He argued that the decline in smallpox incidence was 'not as rapid as it should have been given mass vaccination carried out during January and February', attributing this to 'serious deficiencies in Japanese vaccination technique' – namely the use of alcohol on the vaccination site, which killed the vaccine virus on contact.[59] In fact, as the foregoing analysis has shown, the smallpox epidemic was brought under control only when sufficient vaccine was supplied for mass vaccination. That came about in March and so the epidemic peaked at the end of that month. In light of that fact, the arrival on 27 April 1946 of 49 medical officers from the 5th Air Force 'to help Japanese teams conquer typhus and smallpox' in Tokyo, Yokohama, Osaka and Kobe seems a little tardy.[60]

The official line on the 1946 smallpox epidemic and the measures taken to bring it under control was expressed by Sams in his address to the Allied Council for Japan on 30 April 1947. He told the assembled delegates that 'we produced vaccine here and immunized 78 million people', suggesting a much larger and more active role for the Occupation than was assumed in practice. He went on: 'I might say we actually immunized 78 million, but we vaccinated 130 million', attributing the need to re-vaccinate millions of Japanese to major flaws detected in vaccination technique. Indeed, he declared that 'They did not know how to vaccinate.' Given that the Americans only had a bit part in this particular drama, the claim that the Japanese were not competent vaccinators was untenable. Its purpose can only have been to embellish the reputation of the PH&W in this instance at the expense of those Japanese public health officials who expanded the range of their vaccination efforts as vaccine supply permitted. The lion's share of the credit for bringing the epidemic under control is indisputably theirs.

The Occupation played a more active – perhaps decisive – role in bringing the typhus epidemic under control.[61] There was real anxiety about the speed of its spread throughout Japan, and concern about its potential impact on US forces.

As was the case with the smallpox epidemic, much attention was paid to the sources of typhus, the course and distribution of the disease and the causative and enabling factors that produced a high degree of virulence, particularly in Osaka and Tokyo in the spring of 1946. These were important factors that shaped the control programme, and merit detailed analysis, as does the partnership between American and Japanese personnel struggling to contain and eradicate the disease. So serious was the typhus threat that it necessitated the active intervention of American experts, particularly those working for the USA Typhus Commission, as well as military government officials and tactical troops, all of whom worked to train, educate or supervise Japanese personnel engaged in carrying out the control measures.[62]

Although immunization was actively promoted, finding ways of keeping people free of body lice was considered the key to combating the epidemic. Louse-borne, epidemic typhus was the most serious of the typhus fever group of diseases, which also included scrub typhus and murine or endemic typhus. Historically it was associated with social dislocation, characterized above all by hunger, homelessness and overcrowding, and very poor standards of personal hygiene. A lack of opportunities and facilities for keeping clean, together with a scarcity of clothing, give rise to the proliferation of body lice, which act as the agents of transmission of the causative organism (*Rickettsia prowazekii*).[63]

Hans Zinnser, the author of a fascinating history of the typhus group of diseases, published in 1935, observed that in early modern Europe 'The disease became an almost incessant scourge of armies and was scattered far and wide among the wretched populations under conditions – ideal for typhus – of famine, abject poverty, homeless wandering, and constant warfare.'[64] Regarding the evolutionary history of the disease, he explained that epidemic, louse-borne typhus had evolved from murine (rat-borne) or endemic typhus, passed to man by fleas. In his view,

> The human louse was possibly last of the series of hosts to acquire the virus
> – for it had, long before this time, become inseparably dependent upon man.
> And this surmise is in keeping with the fact that in the louse the Rickettsiae
> are more predatory than parasitic. The infected louse always dies.[65]

However, there are sufficient opportunities amidst the press of unwashed bodies for it to transmit the infection to a new victim before it succumbs itself. In sum, as Winslow puts it, 'From the simple and direct louse–man cycle arise the great epidemics of classical typhus fever.'[66]

Clues as to the origins of the 1946 typhus epidemic in Japan are provided by the geographical distribution and seasonal incidence of typhus in 1943, 1944 and 1945. It seems that 1,008 of the 1,374 cases in 1943 occurred in Hokkaido and that the remaining cases were concentrated in Miyagi (25), Akita (50), Yamagata (53), Fukushima (38), Tokyo (59) and Hyogo (28). The statistics by prefecture for 1944 and 1945 show a similar pattern of distribution, the majority of cases still occurring in Hokkaido – 2,067 of 3,955 in 1944 and 1,669 of 2,508 in 1945

– although its predominance is no longer so marked. Most notable other foci for the disease in 1944 are Aomori (105), Miyagi (162), Tokyo (840) and, interestingly, Kagoshima (202) in southern Kyushu, and for 1945 Fukuoka (401).[67]

This concentration of cases in Fukuoka in 1945 could be explained – as it was by a number of commentators at the time – by the trickle and then torrent of Korean coal miners, accounting for 41.2 per cent of the workforce in Hokkaido, who departed these mines from the spring of 1945 to return to Korea via the ports of southwestern Japan.[68] For example, Crawford Sams declared that

> Korean slave laborers in the coal mines of Hokkaido ... revolted and ... proceeded to travel the length of the main island of Honshu to the ferry points of Shimonoseki and Moji, carrying lice and rickettsia and spreading typhus throughout Japan ... before we even arrived.[69]

Another explanation might be that the disease was already present in Kyushu at the beginning of 1945 (89 cases had been recorded in Fukuoka and 59 in Saga in 1944),[70] originating perhaps among coal miners in this region. All miners – indigenous and colonial labourers alike – experienced very harsh working and living conditions conducive to the spread of typhus, the difference in their treatment being 'a matter of degree rather than kind'.[71] The link between the deprivation experienced by coal miners and the pattern of typhus infection, reflecting the concentration of productive mines in the north and south of Japan,[72] is suggestive of a strong association of typhus with impoverished labourers (as in Tokyo in 1914) rather than a particular racial or ethnic group.

Indeed, a hint of scepticism towards the Korean-centred interpretation can be found in the official history of the Occupation, published in 1950, which observes that 'in October 1945 epidemic typhus was identified and found to be widespread in Hokkaido, *supposedly imported by Korean coal miners and other labourers*' (my italics).[73] Moreover, statistics presented earlier demonstrate that there were cases of typhus in Tokyo (840) and Kagoshima (202) in 1944 before the exodus of Koreans out of Hokkaido. These points direct attention to earlier observations on areas within Japan where typhus was endemic. Indeed, an extensive report of the USA Typhus Commission of 25 May 1946 contended that 'some small endemic foci existed in Honshu and Kyushu'.[74] Furthermore, Sams later remarked of the epidemic in 1946 that 'the peak incidence of typhus was in May, with a lower peak in January which was not as it should be' – in the sense that it usually peaked in the winter months, particularly January.[75] Sams argued that murine typhus, acquired from rat fleas, constituted the first spike, and epidemic, louse-borne typhus the second; the intervening period witnessed the proliferation of body lice and the consequent rapid spread of infection.[76] His explanation of how endemic typhus can give way to its epidemic counterpart is acknowledged as valid in *Black's Student Medical Dictionary*, published in 2004. This is significant, because it directs attention to domestic sources of disease – i.e. there were areas within Japan where typhus was endemic and these acted as potential seedbeds for future epidemics. All this suggests that too great an emphasis on Korea and Hokkaido (with its large population of Korean coal miners) as the sources of the epidemic of 1945–46 tends to underplay the degree to which pockets of murine typhus throughout Japan expanded under conditions of general lousiness into regional epidemics.

Viewed in this way, it is not surprising that during the epidemic of the winter and spring of 1945–46 cases of typhus were reported from each of the 46 prefectures of Japan. However, about 75 per cent of these cases occurred in three areas – Hokkaido, the Osaka–Kobe region and the Tokyo area – from which it was believed many of the smaller outbreaks subsequently stemmed.[77] In terms of the chief focus of efforts to contain major outbreaks of typhus, US public health officials first concentrated in the closing months of 1945 on the mining districts of Hokkaido. Indeed, it was noted in the Occupation's summation for November 1945 that 'reports of increasing prevalence of epidemic louse-borne typhus fever in Hokkaido were considered sufficiently serious to justify a special study of the situation in cooperation with the US Army Typhus Commission'.[78] The chief focus of American efforts then became Osaka, where a major outbreak of typhus fever was reported in February 1946.[79] This peaked in the week beginning 9 March, with over 1,200 new cases reported, followed closely by Tokyo, which recorded just under 1,000 at the time. The outbreak in the capital peaked in April/May when the number of new cases per week reached levels seen only in Osaka.[80] According to a later study, 'the disease ... spread from the Osaka area to Tokyo and then to such distant cities as Nagasaki in Kyushu and Aomori in northern Honshu. It is interesting that the Aomori outbreak originated in Osaka rather than in neighbouring Hokkaido.'[81]

How do we account for the virulence of the disease in Osaka and Tokyo? Why did it spread so rapidly, infect so many people and prove so difficult to bring under control? The answers to these questions relate to the suffering and hardship of countless Japanese struggling to survive in the ruins of these cities. Writing about typhus in their book *Disease and History*, Frederick Cartwright and Michael Biddiss admit that 'a certain mystery still surrounds the infection, for it seems that very special conditions are necessary before it will flourish in a virulent form even when there is gross infestation with lice'. They argue that 'typhus seems to require concomitant malnutrition and sordid living before it will produce a lethal epidemic'.[82] Likewise, an editorial in the provincial newspaper *Tokushima Shimbun* on 27 March 1946 maintained that 'malnutrition is an indirect cause of the disease'.[83] According to John Dower, malnourishment was a problem that affected the majority of Japanese by the end of the war, that it was most serious in the cities and was compounded by a disastrous rice harvest in 1945 (nutrition is examined at length in Chapter 5).[84] Indeed, Takemae Eiji states that 'some 14.5 million people, or one out of five were indigent..., and 10 million of these were on the verge of starvation'.[85] Nutrition surveys carried out by the Occupation authorities in May and August 1946 provided evidence for Crawford Sams that 'people in the major cities were near the danger point of mass starvation as their total quantitative food consumption had dropped to 1,570 calories, of which only 760 were being received from rationed foods'.[86]

This slide towards starvation coincided with the most serious typhus epidemic in Japan's history, surely demonstrating that people were particularly susceptible when their immune systems were dangerously compromised by malnutrition.

Equally important were sordid living conditions, where lice thrived due to overcrowding and shortages of clothing, fuel and soap. These deficiencies, together with the destruction of many public baths, made it impossible for people to change or wash clothing or indeed themselves as frequently as they would like. Writing in particular about Tokyo's experience, Edward Seidensticker remarks that 'the really terrible time was the first winter after the war, a time of cold, disease and hunger', adding that 'typhus was the worst plague' because it 'bespeaks lice and unwashed bodies, very distressful to the well-washed Japanese'.[87] The lice moved easily among a restless population, pressed together on trains, trams and buses in their common struggle to eke out an existence. Likewise, they moved from host to host amidst crowded dwellings, the number of which had been much depleted by the effectiveness of American incendiary bombing (and by such defensive measures as the destruction of houses to provide fire breaks).

These cramped living conditions were made worse by the large numbers of people returning to the city from the countryside, where they had fled to escape the bombs, and the repatriation of several million civilians and servicemen from Japan's former colonies. The occupiers were only too aware of the implications of this shifting population for the spread of disease and the degree to which its concentration in particular cities threatened to overwhelm them. It was presumably to alleviate the deleterious health effects of high numbers of rootless people congregating in cities that SCAP announced a plan in March 1946 that prohibited

> the influx of population into certain specified urban areas (in most cases cities of 100,000 and over) until such times as problems of unemployment, food distribution, housing, sanitary and public utility facilities are sufficiently controlled to prevent any danger of over-crowding.[88]

Likewise, with regard to the galloping typhus epidemic in Osaka that had produced 4,296 cases by 14 March 1946, the *Mainichi* reported that the gravity of the situation necessitated 'the isolation of affected areas, if not the whole of the city itself'.[89] Regarding the outbreak in Tokyo, the *Nippon Times* reported on 2 April 1946 that the number of fresh cases of infection had forced the metropolitan authorities to strictly regulate the movement of people into the city, particularly the return of evacuees.[90]

A study of the typhus epidemic in Tokyo, carried out by Major Addison B. Scoville of the USA Typhus Commission and dated May 1946, noted various predisposing factors. These provide a useful summary of what were perceived to be the complex of factors that caused the explosion of typhus in 1945–46. At the outset he bows to the most popular view that has already been discussed: that many of the people who had arrived in the capital in the previous eight months, causing its population to swell by about two million, had come from Korea and Hokkaido where typhus fever was endemic. He then acknowledges that 'there have been epidemics of typhus fever in Tokyo prior to this year' and that 'it should be concluded, therefore, that a small endemic focus of typhus fever [already] existed in Tokyo'. Scoville then discussed the problems of 'extrinsic' and 'intrinsic travel'. He maintained that 90 per cent of the mass of people leaving Tokyo each day 'for areas which were also endemic foci of typhus fever' were seeking food, attempting to find new homes, searching for relatives and recovering hoarded goods. As for travel within the city, he stated that about one million people, forced to relocate from the centre to outlying areas due to bomb damage, travel each morning on public transport 'severely taxed' by the large number of passengers. He explained:

> There is crowding on all trains and streetcars, with people sitting and stand-ing very closely together. This not only allows lice to transfer from person to person readily but also may permit the inhalation of lice faeces from other people's clothing and from the dust in the cars.

Finally, he blamed overcrowded homes, poor standards of personal/public hygiene and the 'Japanese Public Health Department'. The latter, he argued, had been reorganized so as to be free of police control, leaving insufficient trained personnel to control any epidemic effectively.[91]

This begs the question of just how dependent the Japanese were on their Ameri-can overseers when it came to tackling the scourge of typhus. How effectively did the two parties work together to bring the epidemic under control and what is the balance of credit due to each of them? Of course, the chief weapon in the Occupa-tion's arsenal was DDT,[92] described apocalyptically by C. H. Curran of the Ameri-can Museum of Natural History as 'the atomic bomb of the insect world'.[93] Although mass dusting with DDT was credited with halting a typhus epidemic in Naples in December 1943, it has recently been argued that more finely tuned measures were less visible but more effective in combating the outbreak. These included case finding, isolation of patients and 'contact delousing' – that is to say, dusting anyone who had been in contact with the patient.[94] In fact, as Edmund Russell states, 'older pyrethrum powder (and rotenone powder, another plant-derived insecticide favoured by the British) "broke the back" of the epidemic, and DDT swept in to finish the job', getting the 'lion's share of publicity'.[95]

The excitement generated by DDT's debut in Naples and the huge confidence now invested in it ensured it would be actively promoted in occupied Japan, despite the fact that 'Japan was one of the leading producers of pyrethrum flowers'.[96] This raises interesting questions, explored further in Chapter 4, about the degree to which enthusiasm for DDT derived from American self-interest as its leading supplier rather than sober, balanced assessments of its actual efficacy. Certainly, the statement made by General Stanhope Bayne-Jones of the Army Surgeon General's Office that DDT could 'change the history of the world'[97] suggests an uncritical endorsement of American science and technology.

It is not surprising, therefore, that as the epidemic worsened in Osaka – the most serious of the outbreaks – more and more DDT was literally sprayed at the problem. Official sources contend that the first typhus fatality was Sawada Shigetarō, imprisoned for illegally importing Japanese army uniforms and blankets from Korea and Manchuria that contained infected lice. Once again, former Japanese colonies were confidently identified as the source of the epidemic. Sawada was detained in Ikuno jail from 12 to 16 December 1945, when he became ill, was hospitalized and then died on 6 January 1946. Other cases of typhus then occurred in Ikuno police station and prison. Investigations revealed that all prisoners and about half of the policemen were infested with lice. Meanwhile, 16 prisoners had been transferred to a remand prison, and 26 others had been released. Up to 11 January 1946, seven cases of epidemic typhus had been identified, six of which were traced to Ikuno jail, the seventh a woman living about one mile from the police station.[98] In order to prevent the problem from escalating, the 98th Infantry Division organized teams of Japanese to dust the inmates of Ikuno jail and other jails to which detainees had been transferred. This programme of action was completed on 14 January 1946. Simultaneously, 'focal dusting' with DDT of 300–500 people was carried out in 39 districts to which contacts of typhus patients had returned following their release. In addition, an area of about 2.5 square miles around Ikuno jail – with an estimated population of 112,000 people – was dusted with DDT, a programme that came to an end on 31 January 1946.

Up until 1 February 1946, the only people vaccinated in Osaka were nurses and doctors in the hospitals where patients were isolated.[99] As was the case with DDT, the large-scale production of typhus vaccine was beyond the capability of the Japanese until the autumn of 1946.[100] Supplies came in the meantime from the US. Inoculation with two doses of typhus vaccine one week apart was deemed an effective preventive measure, increasingly employed to protect those living or working in the vicinity of confirmed cases of infection as the epidemic worsened.[101]

The sense of an escalating, increasingly desperate campaign against typhus in Osaka is provided by a lengthy report, authored by Franklin Blanton of the USA Typhus Commission on 29 April 1946. He describes how on 2 February 1946, a day on which 40 new cases were recorded, the 94th Military Government Group took over responsibility for typhus control. It set about organizing 'case-finding teams' that included a doctor, a policeman and an assistant, and 'dusting teams', each composed of five policemen. Plans stated that 500 people within the vicinity of a typhus case should be dusted and 25 contacts vaccinated. Blanton maintained that this programme, which should have worked, failed due to late reporting of cases, the general inefficiency of the Japanese and a lack of US army supervision. As a result, on 16 February, a programme of 'mass dusting' of the entire population of Osaka and neighbouring cities was initiated, which by its close three days later had dusted 1,837,511 people. In many cases, Blanton observed, supervision of the dusting process was poor and there were too few interpreters. Despite these efforts a daily total of 290 new cases was recorded on 28 February.[102]

After a conference in Tokyo in late February 1946, a new approach was adopted based on careful mapping of cases. A total of 390 areas of Osaka were identified as concentrations of cases, and 215 teams were established (composed of five Japanese dusters, one police supervisor, one interpreter and two American soldiers) to apply DDT to individuals in their homes, and to all extra clothing, blankets and mats. This programme was carried out between 19 March and 1 April 1946 and involved the dusting of 1,306,360 persons and their homes and the vaccination of 132,574 people. When it was completed, new areas were marked out, based on cases occurring since 17 March, leading to a second round of DDT dusting of 188 areas over three days. When these area-dusting operations had finished, 'focal delousing teams' continued to act as rapid response units, rushing to the address of a new patient and promptly dusting all houses within a radius of 100 yards and vaccinating 100 of those in the immediate environs. These efforts broke the epidemic that had affected 7,000 people by the end of 1946. Blanton argued (in relation to a division of opinion on the subject) that mass dusting was no more effective than its more targeted counterparts – indeed, he seems to be suggesting that it was less so.[103]

The visibility and symbolism of mass dusting was perhaps more important than its efficacy. As Yoshikuni Igarashi explains, 'DDT sprayed in the ruins of Japanese cities was material proof of Japan's humiliation.'[104] It also underlined the scientific and technological superiority of the US and the loss of Japan's self-respect, the white powder literally cleansing dirty, diseased bodies. This was a lesson learned immediately by those repatriated to Japan in the months following surrender; their bodies were subjected to rigorous 'disinfestation procedures ... in order to prevent the promiscuous dissemination of lice and typhus fever throughout Japan'. When typhus emerged as an urgent threat to public health in 1946, those applying the DDT were told to do so more thoroughly, 'to dust the top of the shoulders, around the neckline, waistline and between the many layers of clothing'.[105] This was a highly intrusive, demeaning procedure for repatriates, presumably made worse by the assembly-line dusting technique that was often used. It underlined the reality of defeat for the Japanese, expressed the scientific and technological superiority of the US and, once again, framed the problem of typhus as an external one.

Confronting an epidemic the like of which they had not experienced before, the Japanese authorities endorsed the large-scale use of DDT, the great bulk of it being applied by Japanese medical personnel. Working with the PH&W, the Welfare Ministry exhorted Japanese citizens to cooperate completely and whole-heartedly with medical officials. They were ordered to report any cases of suspected typhus immediately to a doctor or head of a neighbourhood association, to consent willingly to dusting with DDT and vaccination of all family members, to desist from crushing lice between fingers, to wash as frequently as possible, to avoid travel and crowded places and to follow medical advice given in newspapers or radio broadcasts. This particular advice was proffered by a radio programme, broadcast on Radio Tokyo on 5 November 1946, which opened with the statement:

The people of Japan, I feel, now realise that shirami [louse] typhus can strike and strike hard in Japan – over 30,000 cases of this disease between January 1st and July 1st 1946: This is certainly not a record of which to be proud.[106]

The seriousness of the epidemic and the explosion of cases in Tokyo and Osaka were often blamed by Occupation officials on slow-witted Japanese. However, the many reports and memoranda of members of the USA Typhus Commission in Japan frequently highlight inadequate quantities of DDT, unwarranted delays in releasing it to Japanese medical authorities, sloppy dusting procedures, even its overly liberal use in mass dusting when more careful, targeted application was called for.

Several interesting themes emerge from the story of the 1946 typhus epidemic. Clearly, American officials, particularly those working for the USA Typhus Commission, played a leading role in coordinating efforts to tackle the problem.

For example, Major Blanton and Sergeant Tani (interpreter, assistant, photographer) of the Typhus Commission, who were responsible for training personnel at 11 ports in 'disinfestation procedures', were 'on the road constantly from early November 1945 to 1 May 1946', making 'three round trips' of Honshu and Kyushu and two visits to Hokkaido. They spent their time training Allied and Japanese personnel in delousing techniques with hand (manual) and power dusters; for the most part, the Allied soldiers acted in a supervisory capacity. They complained that neither party fully appreciated the importance of their work, there were constant changes of personnel and Japanese were poorly paid. While US officers were criticized for 'rushing people through', frustration at the Japanese was couched in terms of their 'natural inertia' and their 'usual laxness ... when not being "punched"'. Added to these problems was the issue of supply – it wasn't until 1 February 1946 that adequate stocks existed for all repatriates to be vaccinated and their bodies and baggage dusted with DDT.[107]

Another member of the commission, Major Berge, assisted the Japanese in developing a programme of vaccine manufacture. Although it was noted that Japan had some relevant expertise in this area, producing vaccine by a modification of the preferred Cox method, it was clear that it could not produce enough typhus vaccine of the required standard to meet the demands of the developing epidemic. Due to the dearth of fertile egg supplies required for the Cox method, vaccine production was initiated in relatively small laboratories throughout Japan. These were located in Sapporo, Niigata, Chiba, Tokyo, Osaka, Hikari and Kumamoto, and a model one set up in the Institute of Infectious Diseases to train technicians and to produce and test vaccines.[108] Although there were apparently some teething problems with the programme, it was anticipated in April 1946 that typhus vaccine would be 'coming on stream' the following September.[109] Major Berge, together with other members of the USA Typhus Commission (Lieutenant Colonel Wheeler, Major Chorpenning, Major Blanton and Major Scoville), also played an important role in planning programmes for typhus control, particularly in Osaka and Tokyo, where they convened meetings and conferences with Japanese officials and US military personnel.

Sams was thus right to acknowledge the 'technical advice and assistance of the US Typhus Commission' in a *Nippon Times* article of 12 April 1946, where he expressed confidence that the epidemic was at last on the wane. Interestingly, he first lauded the work of the Occupation units whose 'concentrated drive' over the last two months had triumphed against the disease. Singled out for praise were the 94th Military Government company assisted by around 600 enlisted men of the 4th Infantry in Osaka, and the 31st Military Government company, supported by officers and men of the 1st Cavalry in Tokyo. After expressing gratitude to the Occupation's Civil Information and Education Section for publicizing details of the anti-typhus programme, he finally acknowledged 'the efforts of the Japanese people'.[110]

Of course, this tendency to highlight the work of the Occupation is understandable, given the impressive commitment shown by Allied forces in combating the typhus epidemic. Still, relatively few Occupation personnel had the necessary expertise to supervise the Japanese operation effectively, and for this reason the US Army's malaria control units were considered invaluable. Indeed, it was acknowledged that only in a few of the larger cities were qualified medical personnel 'made available in sufficient numbers to aid the program materially'. Ordinarily, the military government companies would have monitored the operations of Japanese teams. Deployment of tactical troops was necessitated by the scale of the endeavour.[111] The great majority of these soldiers were deployed in a supervisory capacity. Almost all the case finding, vaccinating and dusting was carried out by hundreds of teams of Japanese police, doctors, nurses, and ward officials, some of them under the watchful gaze of one or two soldiers. How could it have been otherwise in the context of an indirect occupation?

Ultimately, the energetic, sometimes desperate, campaign against typhus was a very unequal partnership. On one side were the Occupation and the USA Typhus Commission, responsible for direction, training and supervision of Japanese personnel charged with carrying out the programmes of disease control. In a way they were strangely divorced from the problem; only three American soldiers were ever diagnosed with typhus, and all three quickly recovered. On the other side were the Japanese government, which was primarily responsible for dealing with the epidemic, the virulence of which was unprecedented in Japan. Although some hospitals and ports had steam sterilization equipment for delousing clothes, the Japanese had no DDT, no dusters for delivering it and very little effective vaccine. In all these respects they initially depended on the Occupation, although it was not long before they were mixing DDT concentrate with talc available in Japan, manufacturing their own hand dusters and producing their own typhus vaccine.[112] As for the lessons of the epidemic, the USA Typhus Commission suggested that both the Occupation and the Japanese authorities had reacted too slowly in the early stages. It commented in relation to Osaka that 'unfortunately the typhus epidemic ... got out of hand before proper control measures could be put into effect'. In contrast, no such mistakes were made when cholera appeared off the coast of Japan in April 1946.

Cholera and diphtheria

As discussed in Chapter 1, the Meiji government suffered a wave of cholera from 1877 that necessitated a strict quarantine regime and immunization with cholera vaccine of population groups at risk of infection. By the turn of the twentieth century these measures were largely in place, and the incidence of the disease on the decline to the point where it hardly figured as a public health problem during the 1920s and 1930s. The US Army *Civil Affairs* Handbook, highlighted the rigour of Japan's quarantine system. It stated that 11 ports in Japan boasted a 'permanent quarantine organization', and that 2,877,586 crew and passengers on 24,281 Japanese vessels and 5,978 foreign vessels were subjected to inspection in 1937. These checks resulted in the discovery of just three cases of cholera, nine of smallpox and 81 of other diseases.[113] The claim made by Sams that quarantine stations at ports 'had been discontinued during the war' seems unlikely given that the incidence of the disease within Japan did not rise during this period.[114]

In any case, the end of the war brought the immense challenge of repatriating more than six million Japanese from Japan's former empire, many of them through foreign ports threatened by epidemics of communicable diseases. The Occupation authorities instructed the Japanese government to establish agencies to administer quarantine and reception centres at specified Japanese ports, to equip them with the necessary medicines and food supplies, and to staff them with Japanese doctors and nurses. Repatriates were to be immunized without charge against smallpox, typhus and cholera and the government was to further care for them and feed them until they had been safely returned to their homes. Responsibility for all of this was vested in the Welfare Ministry, which set up a temporary quarantine section and a repatriates' relief bureau. The former was charged with the all-important job of medical processing, which involved examination, quarantine, hospitalization/isolation, disinfection, disinfestation and immunization.[115]

These procedures took on tremendous importance when cholera broke out among repatriates returning home from Canton in early April 1946. Soon after passengers on the first of these vessels disembarked on 4 April at Uraga port, at the entrance of Tokyo Bay, a case of cholera was detected, necessitating examination and immunization of as many of the other passengers as could be found.[116] By this time other repatriation vessels, en route from Canton to Japan, were reporting cholera cases on board, necessitating the institution of rigorous quarantine procedures by the Japanese port authorities. On 6 April 1946 GHQ SCAP specified those procedures in SCAPIN 865. This stipulated that for passages from China of more than six days where the vessel was free of cholera, all personnel would be 'inoculated with 1.5 cc of cholera vaccine' and allowed to disembark for processing. If the voyage had taken less than six days, no one would be permitted to leave the ship until that period had elapsed, at which time everyone would be physically examined for the disease.

When ships arrived in Japan *with cholera aboard*, the SCAPIN continued, they were required to 'use only Uraga and Sasebo until directed otherwise by this Headquarters'. They were to be anchored sufficiently far from shore to preclude the possibility of anyone swimming to shore or contamination from the vessel washing ashore, to keep everyone on board for 14 days after the development of the last case, and to cooperate in the removal of cholera patients to a hospital ship provided for that purpose. Since hospital ships for isolation of patients could not be provided immediately, temporary use would have to be made of the hospital at the reception centre, where it would be necessary to sterilize all discharges from the patients (using 2 per cent cresol solution), and to provide screening to protect them from flies. Those remaining on the vessel would be immunized with cholera vaccine, their faeces and urine treated with a 2 per cent cresol solution before its discharge into the sea, stool examinations conducted of everyone to detect carriers, and their baggage and clothing sterilized.[117] As it was the beginning of the epidemic season for intestinal diseases and unsanitary conditions within Japan increased the potential for a major outbreak,[118] Japanese officials responsible for quarantine and their counterparts within the Occupation were mindful of the real possibility of a devastating cholera epidemic should these regulations be infringed. Indeed, careless treatment of Korean repatriates from Canton apparently led to 17,000 cases and 11,000 deaths from the disease in Korea during the summer of 1946.[119]

In the event, Japan escaped such a fate. The number of cases and deaths from the disease in 1946 were limited to 1,245 and 560, respectively.[120] Nevertheless, the outbreak of cholera on the repatriation vessels provoked something of a crisis. On 14 April it was reported in the *Tokyo Shimbun* that new cases of cholera had broken out among repatriates on board six ships, which had dropped anchor on 11 April 4,000 metres from Uraga harbour. The isolation hospital at Uraga was already 'nearing saturation point', and a camp was being made ready to accommodate others. Around two weeks later, on 26 April, the *Asahi Shimbun* cautioned that 'the population of the floating city' ('cholera ships') was likely to reach 130,000 in the next few days, in the face of insufficient isolation facilities and a dearth of food with which to supply them.[121] Just two days later the same newspaper captured the crisis in poignant terms, reporting that this huge number of repatriates were 'struggling against terrible disease, with their mother country, which they have longed to see for so long a time, only a short distance away'.[122] Newspaper coverage became ever more graphic and disturbing, so much so that the US censorship authorities suppressed a story in the *Yomiuri Shimbun*, which referred to 'tired bodies tortured by disease and starvation', a scene that was 'nothing short of a picture of hell'.[123]

The decision to censor the *Yomiuri* story was disclosed in a report to Sams, occasioned by the latter's concern about the repercussions of the Uraga cholera siege for the US's reputation in Japan. The censor in charge was Richard

Kunzman. He explained how a story had been submitted towards the end of April, claiming that 'there was danger of starvation because of shortage of food and water and inability to get Japanese merchant seamen to take supplies from land to the boats'. The article and others like it had been discussed with the PH&W, and approved after confirmation that there definitely was a shortage of food, but that this was the responsibility of the Japanese government to alleviate. In other words, the news stories were considered useful as a means of spurring the Japanese government to action. Kunzman than related how he had personally called Major Bourland (of the PH&W) concerning an article submitted by the Kyodo News Agency on 27 April 1946. This had been passed with just a few deletions deemed necessary to 'tone down the effect of the story'. The first two paragraphs of copy read as follows (underlined words were to be deleted):

> YOKOSUKA, April 27 – Eighty thousand Japanese home-bound from China today are leading perilous lives dangerously exposed to cholera infection aboard 14 'death ships' which are quarantined outside Uraga harbor.
> The threat of sudden death hangs heavy over these unfortunate repatriates who are jammed in the ships' holds unable to disembark until the quarantine ban is lifted.[124]

These deletions highlight the balancing act being performed by the US censorship authorities. They were keen to pressure the Japanese government to take action but also mindful of the potentially explosive nature of the story. The latter was captured by an *Asahi Shimbun* article, passed by the censor on 26 April 1946, with the headline 'Disturbance on both land and sea'. This reported that the cholera ships were causing anxiety among coastal residents, alarmed at the decision to move the vessels closer to shore (a distance of one mile rather than three) to ease the supply situation.[125] Also, there were 'signs of agitation' among healthy repatriates on board the ships, some voicing their desire to make a forcible landing or be infected by the epidemic and sent ashore to the hospital.

Sams' concern with skilfully managing the crisis, his anxiety about its potential to become a public relations problem for the US, were allayed by one of the concluding statements of Kunzman's report – that none of the stories 'casts discredit upon the SCAP agencies involved in the situation, and several involve praise for the Americans'. In any case, Sams' determination to restore some calm to the situation seems to have resulted in a clear statement on the part of the Occupation denying a crisis of supply: 'SCAP blasts reports that repatriates are not getting enough food and water' was how the *Nippon Times* reported it on 2 May 1946. Quoting an Occupation source, the article stated that 'reports that Japanese repatriates held aboard quarantined cholera ships off Uraga are not receiving food and water are "unfounded"'. Regret was expressed about quarantine or inspection immobilizing 20 per cent of the fleet of liberty ships, so impeding the progress of repatriation. At last, on 4 May 1946, the *Mainichi Shimbun* declared that the incidence of cholera at Uraga was on the decrease, and that rice, meat and canned foods would be sent out to the ships 'today or tomorrow'.[126] Nevertheless, cholera remained a serious threat during the summer of 1946, particularly following its eruption in Korea in July. Sams remained vigilant about the disease itself and how it was reported in Japan, alert as always to the politics of the issue. For example, on 4 November 1945 he summoned Dr Ōtsubo, an epidemiologist in the Tokyo Health Department, to challenge him about statements he had made to the *Nippon Times* on 25 October, suggesting that cholera was one of a number of diseases present in Japan 'in epidemic proportions'. Dr Ōtsubo was advised of pre-war and current figures that presented the Occupation's record in a favourable light. He received a rebuke for scare mongering, and was 'directed to prepare and have available for Colonel Sams a correcting statement for newspaper publication regarding cholera and present, past disease prevalence by 1400 hours on Monday, 5 November'.[127] Such was the determination of Sams to burnish the Occupation's impressive record on public health in Japan that absolutely no ground could be given to counter-narratives of failure or even partial success.

Interestingly, the head of the PH&W praised the labours and achievements of the Japanese in relation to cholera, presenting a more credible story of partnership and joint endeavour than was accorded the other epidemics. His positive view of the Japanese contribution to preventing a serious outbreak of cholera in Japan was expressed in an article in the *Nippon Times* on 11 May 1946. This reported Sams' appraisal of 'a month of intensive work to combat the spread of cholera from repatriated Japanese ... work undertaken by Japanese quarantine authorities under the supervision of the PH&W Section of SCAP'. 'This almost insurmountable job', Sams declared, 'could never have been accomplished without the outstanding cooperation of the Japanese and American army units working closely together, and by the loyalty and fortitude of the Japanese nurses.'

In his memoirs, he indirectly acknowledged Japanese endeavour and expertise by revealing, in relation to the Uraga crisis, that he quickly assembled personnel and supplies capable of handling 15,000 stool cultures and examinations per day. Moreover, he paid tribute 'to those Americans and Japanese who worked night and day to prevent a greater catastrophe which this dreaded disease might well have caused'.[128] Of course, the Americans actively involved in confronting the potential epidemic were far outnumbered by their Japanese counterparts. One indication of this was a report in the *Mainichi* on 27 April 1946, towards the end of the Uraga outbreak, that just six American medical officers were being assigned to the port of Uraga to assist Japanese teams in cholera control. Later, on 24 June 1946, the general delegation of cholera control to the Japanese authorities was highlighted by a report on repatriation at Sasebo, which was blocked by an 'explosive outbreak' of the disease, and a backlog of repatriates quarantined offshore. Apparently, there were too few American personnel available to supervise Japanese operations properly at this large reception centre.[129]

As for the measures taken to prevent isolated cases of cholera sparking off an epidemic, both the Japanese and their American supervisors stressed the importance of thoroughness and rigour. Laboratory technicians, often working in 'overtaxed facilities',[130] checked an enormous number of stool samples for the cholera vibrio; their labours ensured that active cases and carriers were quickly identified and isolated, so preventing dispersal of the disease throughout the country. Where cases did slip through the net, Japanese governmental agencies moved swiftly to contain any potential outbreak. For example, a Japanese repatriate arriving in Hakata from Shanghai on 31 May 1946 was hospitalized and died of cholera on 3 June, followed quickly by another passenger from the same vessel, who became ill in Kyoto and died of cholera the following day. The Japanese authorities, liaising with 8th Army HQ, IX Corps, then worked quickly to establish the movements by ferry and train of these unfortunate individuals to try to contain the outbreak. Indeed, it was deemed necessary to quarantine two Aomori–Hakodate ferries with 3,000 people, including 500 repatriates, on board. A subsequent telephone conversation between Major Bourland of the PH&W and Major E. Sunderville, Surgeon's Office, 8th Army, disclosed that only three of the 500 repatriates aboard the quarantined ferries had been passengers on V-068, the liberty ship transporting the original cholera victims.[131] Likewise, when one Morita Toramatsu slipped out of the camp at Uraga to have a meal at Yokosuka and fell ill on his return after vomiting in the city, the Japanese Welfare Ministry and Kanagawa prefectural hygiene section reacted with alarm. Working closely with the US Army, they warned people not only to suspend fishing and salt-making within Tokyo bay, but also to stop coming to Miura peninsula [Uraga] to receive repatriates.[132]

The issue of contaminated fish acting as a conduit for cholera infection was discussed in a memo to Sams from an American laboratory consultant, who recommended that quarantine personnel and all other official agencies be duly reminded of the dangers of inadequate control of fishermen in these areas.[133] In response, the Natural Resources Section (NRS) of GHQ SCAP cautioned that prohibition of fishing in the areas of Uraga and Sasebo, the two main cholera ports, would deplete Japanese supplies by 5,000 tons per month at a time of serious food shortages; thus, the restrictions must be lifted as soon as possible.[134] Two months later the case was made for ending the ban on fishing in Tokyo Bay. The key arguments revolved around the food supply situation and the failure of laboratory examination of marine products from the area around Uraga to detect a single instance of cholera infection. Moreover, the quarantine officer at Uraga stated that contamination of the sea was precluded by the thorough treatment of excreta on board the repatriation vessels. Nevertheless, the Preventive Medicine Division of the PH&W advised that quarantine of the area around Uraga port continue until 14 days after the departure of the last cholera ship.[135]

Although some of these prescriptions may seem overly rigorous, the precautionary approach adopted may explain why there was no major outbreak of cholera. Yet another example of playing it safe was an article in the *Tokyo Shimbun* on 18 April 1946. This advised residents of the dangers of consuming seafood caught in the vicinity of the cholera ships, the ability of flies to 'carry the germs' and the resultant need to desist from eating raw foods and to undergo preventive inoculation.[136] Regarding the supply of cholera vaccine, it seems that the Japanese government had less than adequate stocks at the beginning of the cholera siege, but was considered capable of producing sufficient quantities over the next few months. That at least was the judgement of the Deputy Chief of the PH&W, Colonel Weaver, who noted on 15 April 1946 that there were five million doses available and a 'production capacity' of 100 million by 1 July.[137] Around a fortnight later, on 28 April 1946, the *Nippon Times* stated that the metropolitan authorities were preparing an extensive cholera prevention campaign – they already had the capacity to immunize 400,000 people and would soon have enough to protect one million residents. Sure enough, an article in the *Mainichi Shimbun* on 4 May 1946 stated that about one million people living in the 23 wards would receive preventive injections for cholera through their neighbourhood associations by 10 June 1946.[138]

Determined to keep up the momentum, Major Bourland, Acting Chief of the PH&W's preventive medicine division, reported on 16 May that he had discussed acceleration of the cholera immunization programme for metropolitan Tokyo with Dr Yosano, chief of the communicable disease section of the metropolitan health department. Dr Yosano was instructed to finish the immunization drive, involving around four million people, by the middle of June rather than by 10 July as originally planned.[139]

A chronology of cholera prevention activities, produced by the Welfare Ministry at the beginning of September 1946, highlights the control measures coordinated with prefectural chiefs of public health. Apart from regular updates on the progress of immunization throughout prefectures, these included the utilization of neighbourhood associations and health centres for early discovery and confirmation of cholera cases; emergency disinfection of vehicles or buildings used by cholera patients; and sharing of information between train station staff and police authorities about the movement of repatriates, required to submit cards specifying their name, age and the details of their journey home.[140] All this testifies to a fairly sophisticated cholera control operation, founded on effective quarantine, disinfection and local immunization. The latter expanded with the availability of cholera vaccine to reach around 36 million people during June–September 1946.[141]

So great was the menace represented by cholera and so urgent the need for vaccine during the summer of 1946 that the planned immunization campaign against diphtheria had to be postponed. Attributing the delay to the 'diversion of production facilities from diphtheria toxoid to cholera vaccine', the *Summation of Non-Military Activities in Japan* for June 1946 stated that the diphtheria immunization campaign was now scheduled to take place between 1 September and 15 October 1946.[142] It had not occurred earlier despite an expected rise of incidence in November and December 1945 due to what the Occupation's official history referred to as the 'nonavailability of toxoid'.[143] Indeed, Sams claimed in his memoir that while 'the Japanese had produced diphtheria antitoxin ... for treatment and occasionally for passive immunization, they were not familiar with the comparatively modern diphtheria toxoid for active prophylactic immunization'.[144] In his address to the ACJ, he put it more starkly when he declared that 'the Japanese did not know how to make diphtheria toxoid ... so we showed them how'.[145] Contrary to these assertions, previous chapters have shown that school children had been immunized with diphtheria toxoid prior to the Occupation, but that problems of quality and availability had become pronounced during the war years. The fact that supply of diphtheria toxoid was recorded for September 1945 at a very low 70,950 cc demonstrates both that the Japanese had the necessary expertise to produce it and that output had seriously declined as a result of the war (it quickly rose to 285,960 cc in November 1945).[146]

SCAPIN 698 on diphtheria control was issued on 4 February 1946. This highlighted the unacceptably high rates of morbidity and mortality from diphtheria, particularly among children, and called for the nationwide immunization of Japanese between the ages of nine months and ten years with 'an approved immunizing agent'. The Japanese government was required to draw up a complete operational plan by 1 March and to implement it from 1 June 1946 – a deadline postponed for reasons explained above. When it did take place it seems not to have been implemented with quite the energy and commitment associated with other immunization programmes. This is indicated by a meeting between members of the PH&W and the Welfare Ministry on 11 December 1946, when Philip Bourland of the Preventive Medicine Division expressed doubt that the Ministry's directives regarding diphtheria immunization had been issued in sufficiently strong language. Other concerns expressed related to the programme being behind schedule (it had originally been scheduled for completion on 15 October 1946) and the failure to subject the toxoid to proper testing and standardization.[147] In his comments to the ACJ, Sams maintained that around 16 million children had been immunized by the end of 1946, and that the campaign's success was demonstrated by a significant fall in the disease's incidence compared to 1945 (for which incidentally there were no reliable figures). Nevertheless, he acknowledged that a more comprehensive programme was necessary to bring the disease properly under control.

This view was reiterated by Lucius Thomas of the PH&W's Preventive Medicine Division in a memorandum dated 28 July 1947, which drew attention to a large number of non-immunized or partially immunized children ten years of age and under. It was proposed that Japanese health workers immunize all children 9–21 months old, who had not been previously immunized, with three doses of toxoid 2–3 weeks apart. A single dose would suffice for all children over 21 months and less than ten years old. The inoculation drive would take place between 1 September and 31 October 1947, and the Welfare Ministry was urged to notify the prefectures of these requirements as soon as possible so they could begin planning the operation.[148] Although the incidence of diphtheria continued to fall to levels last seen in the early 1930s and rates of mortality fell even more steeply,[149] it was stated by the PH&W that this second nationwide immunization effort was 'hampered by difficulties involving production and assay [testing] of vaccine'.[150]

The problem of poor quality control came to a head in November 1948, following the promulgation of the Preventive Vaccination Law on 30 June 1948.

This required diphtheria toxoid to be administered to babies from six to twelve months after birth, and re-immunization within six months of starting and leaving elementary school. In line with these requirements, vaccine was administered to babies and infants in Kyoto and Shimane in November 1948. Unfortunately, not all the batches of vaccine produced by the Osaka Red Cross Research Institute had been properly tested, causing some defective samples to slip through. Sams commented in his memoir that 'those children ... immunized with this vaccine became seriously ill; there were a few deaths'.[151] In truth, there were a lot of fatalities – 68 in Kyoto and 15 in Shimane, with many more children hospitalized. The public health officer of Kyoto Military Government Team, John Glismann, captured the impact of the tragedy in a letter to his parents: 'The accident has been a blow – improperly detoxified and improperly sampled and assayed, we took it in the neck.' Glismann's view was that the PH&W had failed in its supervisory role and had 'rushed the vaccine production to an unreasonable degree'.[152]

Sams swiftly distanced himself and his section from the affair. In a letter to Dr Meyer of the George William Hooper Foundation, San Francisco, he was typically dismissive of Japanese laboratory science. Indeed, he stated that the great majority of laboratories, which were producing biologics at the end of the war, have been closed. This presumably left too few to manufacture the huge quantities of smallpox, typhus and cholera vaccine required during the first year of the Occupation. Moreover, while he praised the Japanese for manufacturing diphtheria toxoid 'with a considerable degree of success until the Kyoto incident marred their record', he noted that 'Japan has always been known for its cheap products of poor quality and vaccines have been no exception to the rule'. It was thus necessary, he explained to his correspondent, to suspend all immunizations with vaccines manufactured in Japan until every biologic laboratory had been properly evaluated and existing stocks of vaccine had been re-tested to confirm their suitability for use. In the meantime he had made it clear to the Welfare Ministry, the laboratory inspectors, the National Institute of Health and other interested parties that he would 'not tolerate inferior biologic products in the future'.[153] A period of around one year elapsed before diphtheria immunization resumed, during which time the incidence of the disease continued to fall. By 1949 its morbidity profile was much the same as that of the early 1920s, with a mortality rate of around 11 per cent. The PH&W's annual summary for 1949 anticipated that all legally required diphtheria immunizations would be completed by the autumn of 1950, bringing a very protracted process to its conclusion.

Conclusion

Several important themes emerge from this lengthy analysis of the Occupation's endeavours to combat 'wildfire diseases' in concert with the Japanese government. First, Sams was always alert to the politics of public health, and in relation to the epidemics of smallpox, typhus and diphtheria he tended to exaggerate US initiative and innovation and to present the contribution of his own team in the PH&W, military government medics and US soldiers acting in a supervisory role as pivotal to any success in bringing them under control. Determined to represent the mission of his section as a modernizing one, Sams missed no opportunity to highlight poor practice, outmoded thinking and relative scientific backwardness among Japanese officials, doctors and public health workers. He claimed, for example, that they did not know how to vaccinate people against smallpox, and that they had no experience of diphtheria toxoid, neither of which were valid assertions. In relation to cholera, he was much more willing to acknowledge a successful partnership between US medical personnel and their Japanese colleagues, but even here he tended to emphasize the effectiveness of American supervision of quarantine rather than its able management by prefectural authorities.

The Japanese themselves tended to view epidemic diseases as alien invaders. They blamed outbreaks of smallpox and typhus on their former colonial subjects, principally Koreans, rather than recognizing endemic foci of such diseases within Japan and the social conditions attending defeat that caused pockets of disease to spark regional epidemics. Just as there was arrogance among the Occupiers, so there was pride among Japanese officials. This apparently inhibited a full acknowledgement of the limitations of their public health organization, defined according to modern concepts of hygiene, and the damage done to it by war and defeat. In a sense, their colonial attitudes towards the continent of Asia were a natural correlate of American perceptions of their superiority vis-à-vis the Orient. The ready submission of Japanese to DDT dusting, actively promoted and represented in dramatic terms by US officials, underlined the unequal relationship between the two parties – the depths to which the dirty, diseased Japanese had fallen in defeat and the scientific prowess of the victorious Americans. Images from this period often show Japanese citizens being dusted by US soldiers, when in fact the huge majority of dusters were Japanese, as were almost all those engaged in case finding and inoculation.

Perhaps the most striking aspect of this story of epidemic control is the speed with which the strengths of Japanese public health reasserted themselves. Rigorous quarantine procedures for foreign vessels and medical processing of travellers seem to have been second nature to the Japanese. Rapid disinfection of local environments and swift isolation of suspect cases were carried out by officials working closely with the police and neighbourhood associations. Despite some understandable delays in resuming large-scale production of vaccines for smallpox and cholera, the successful immunization drives against these diseases testify to Japanese expertise and ingenuity in producing millions of doses of effective vaccine in what seem to have been less than perfect surroundings. Also impressive was the speed with which they were manufacturing their own typhus vaccine and increasing production levels of diphtheria toxoid. Of course, the latter produced a scandal in late November 1948, but Sams was surely disingenuous in his condemnation of Japanese quality control of vaccines. He could not have it both ways – taking the credit for very successful immunization campaigns against smallpox and cholera and then blaming the Japanese laboratories for incompetence in vaccine production. There is undoubtedly some truth in Wildes' claim that Sams' team 'sparkplugged' these achievements in public health, 'cudgelled and cajoled the health and welfare authorities intro remedial action and ... provided essential technical advice',[154] but lost from this narrative is Japanese experience, energy and initiative. The next chapter will again explore this dichotomy, this time in relation to environmental sanitation and Sams' drive to 'clean up Japan'.

4 'We're cleaning up Japan'

'We're cleaning up Japan' was the title of an article by Kate Holliday in an American magazine in 1951, and captured a common sentiment in Occupation circles that all around them was filth and disease, insalubrious conditions that threatened Occupation forces and Japanese society more generally. The article's subtitle, 'The Orient's plague spot is now the healthiest nation in Asia thanks to our Army doctors',[1] expressed the prevailing view that the Public Health and Welfare Section (PH&W) had transformed Japan's disease environment. It had done so by spearheading campaigns against contaminated water, the use of night soil as fertilizer, poor food hygiene and the proliferation of rats, flies and mosquitoes. These menaces to public health concerned Sams and his team in the PH&W as, first and foremost, a threat to the health of American troops, but beyond that as representative of attitudes, customs and conditions in Japan that obstructed the improvement of standards of public health.

While immunization programmes and effective quarantine regimes could be celebrated as effective means of preventing or checking disease, the Occupation found it more difficult to demonstrate success against diseases rooted in particular environmental conditions for which there was no vaccine. Hence the unease caused by rising incidence of dysentery from 1949, which suggested that the clean-up effort was by no means complete. When this was pointed out to Sams – as it was by an American correspondent in 1951 – he was at pains to deny any suggestion of failure, stating that 'although dysentery this year in Japan has been about three times as prevalent as last year, it is still less than 50% of the seven year pre-occupation average'.[2]

When it came to sanitary conditions and insect and rodent control programmes, such sensitivity could give way to outright frustration and anger at times. In response to scepticism about the positive impact of Occupation-sponsored 'sanitary teams', he insisted that 'this country hasn't been cleaned up by magic. The streets are clean, the drains are clean, compared to what they were when we came in.' Such hyperbole about the perceived contrast between Japan's predisposition to filth and the US as a champion of hygiene and cleanliness betrayed Sams' political priorities. It revealed his determination to attribute any advances in environmental hygiene to guidance and initiative on the part of the PH&W rather than acknowledging Japanese endeavours in this regard, both before and during the Occupation. This chapter will begin with a brief analysis of disease trends during the Occupation period, focusing on such environmental disorders as typhoid, paratyphoid, dysentery, typhus, plague, malaria and Japanese B encephalitis. It will then explore such important contributory factors as insect and rodent control, water supply and sewage disposal. As in Chapter 3, the success of American prescriptions and the degree to which they represented a break with Japan's past will be discussed, as will the nature of the partnership between officials of the PH&W and Japanese involved in improving sanitary conditions.

Disease trends: immunization versus environmental controls

As has already been intimated in relation to dysentery, Sams was always keen to demonstrate declining incidence of disease during and as a result of the Occupation. In the lengthy briefing note that accompanied his address to the Allied Council for Japan (ACJ) in April 1947, progress against each disease was gauged according to three criteria: conditions in Japan prior to the Occupation; actions taken by the PH&W; and the present situation as a result of those actions. This format was obviously designed to highlight American-inspired measures and achievements. As regards typhoid and paratyphoid, Sams stated that disease rates are 'presently at their lowest point in seven years',[3] that is to say since 1940, when Japan had been at war with China for more than two years. The yardstick for comparison is of course crucial, and Harry Wildes makes the highly suggestive point that Sams 'fell back perforce upon the late war years, particularly 1943, 1944 and 1945; but these chaotic years were far from satisfactory as an index base'.[4] In contrast, a long-term survey of the incidence of enteric diseases properly contextualizes their rise or fall during the Occupation. It shows not only that wartime problems caused the incidence of typhoid and paratyphoid to climb, but also that they were checked at a fairly constant level from the beginning of the Shōwa period in 1926 until 1942.

Figure 4.1 illustrates the increasing incidence of typhoid at the beginning of the Taishō period (1912–26) that peaks in the mid-1920s at around 60,000 cases and then oscillates slightly around the 40,000 cases mark until around 1942. Thereafter, the number of cases climbs steeply to around the level experienced in 1924, only to fall precipitously from 1945 onwards. The year 1947 witnessed the lowest number of cases (17,810) since 1900. Similarly, the number of paratyphoid cases seems to have declined steeply from the beginning of the Occupation, so much so that one British observer declared that after four years of Occupation, Japan was experiencing 'the lowest typhoid and paratyphoid case rate in Japanese history'.[5]

However, there are grounds for doubting the accuracy of the figures for 1946 and 1947. The data sets produced by the PH&W single out the figures for these years as 'provisional, based on periods of 4 or 5 weeks as taken from the regular weekly reports of the Welfare Ministry'.[6] Also, the depth of the gorge for dysentery between 1945 and 1952 must cast doubt on the accuracy of the statistics, as

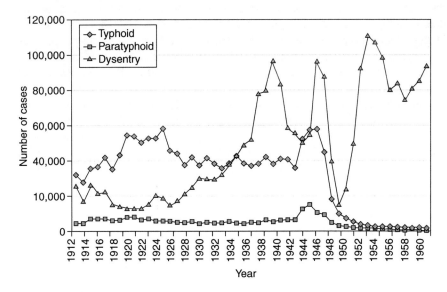

Figure 4.1 Cases of enteric diseases, 1912–45 (source: cases of enteric diseases PHW 92491 (for the period 1912–45), F. Ohtani, *One Hundred Years of Health Progress in Japan*, Tokyo: International Medical Foundation of Japan, 1971, pp. 82–83 (for the period 1945–60)).

does the less noticeable trough between 1939 and 1945. According to Eiji Marui, 'What the GHQ/SCAP staff confronted in its initial survey in early 1946 was a vital statistics system that had in fact broken down.' Marui contends that the collapse of the system was particularly evident from 1944, due to the adverse impact of the war on transport and communications.[7] Still, even if the accuracy of the official statistics is questionable for the period 1944–48, the downward trend of typhoid and paratyphoid incidence is surely indisputable. How can this be explained?

During his confident performance before the ACJ on 30 April 1947, Sams attributed this success to Occupation-inspired initiatives on environmental sanitation, insect and rodent control, the improvement of water supplies and the immunization of 23 million Japanese. At the same time he admitted that in the case of dysentery there had been 'no material change in incidence or mortality rates during the past seven years'. However, it was his firm belief that 'improvement will be forthcoming as environmental sanitation, water supplies and education programmes progress'.[8] This turned out not to be the case, and later on in his memoir Sams tried to explain the divergent trends of dysentery and typhoid/paratyphoid by singling out the efficacy of programmes of inoculation in relation to the latter. Indeed, he believed that this discrepancy 'settled a scientific controversy which had been going on in the medical profession throughout the world since 1910' – the question of whether it was the typhoid vaccine itself or improvements in environmental sanitation that caused the incidence of these diseases to fall. Arguing that the drop in typhoid/paratyphoid occurred despite deteriorating sanitary standards in Japan, evidenced from 1949 by steep increases in dysentery (for which there was no effective vaccine), Sams stated that this must mean that 'typhoid vaccine will protect in spite of poor sanitary standards'.

Keen to underline Japan's debt to the US, Sams extolled the virtues of 'our vaccine', developed in 1910, and claimed that its success 'caused the Japanese scientists to lose face in the eyes of their own people and the Americans who were responsible for the introduction … of the program to gain the confidence of the people as a whole'.[9] No evidence is provided to substantiate these claims, nor is due attention paid to historical antecedents for typhoid immunization in Japan (see Chapter 1). Indeed, the head of the PH&W need have looked no further than the US Army's *Civil Affairs Handbook on Public Health and Sanitation*, issued in February 1945, in which it is made clear that not only does a mixed typhoid–paratyphoid vaccine exist in Japan, but also that 'both the Japanese navy and army submit their entire strength to vaccination once each year'.[10] Likewise, a contemporaneous study of global epidemiology, co-authored by General James S. Simmons, stated that the Japanese military had been vaccinated against typhoid and paratyphoid fevers for many years, adding that in recent times the vaccine had been made available to the general population.[11] This is evidenced by Manabe Ichirō's diary, discussed in Chapter 2, where he records being inoculated against typhoid on the ninth and sixteenth of August 1944.

The fact that the Occupation authorities record a figure of 1,163,044 cc of triple typhoid (TAB) vaccine[12] for September 1945, deemed 'far below requirements',[13] suggests that its production continued throughout the war. Also, we know from the briefing document that formed the basis for Sams' address to the ACJ in April 1947 that around 20 million Japanese had been immunized against typhoid and paratyphoid in 1946. This was presumably with Japanese vaccine, as it is stated in the relevant volume of the *History of Non-Military Activities* that this predated a nation-wide immunization programme, 'using TAB vaccine and cultures equal in standard to those of the US'.[14] The latter did not get under way properly until 1948, by which time the incidence of typhoid and paratyphoid had apparently been falling for some time. In March 1948, Lucius Thomas, the chief of the Preventive Medicine Division of the PH&W, disclosed that only 35 million people out of 65 million had received their typhoid immunizations. Dr Kinugawa of the Welfare Ministry was told that the PH&W required that this programme be completed by fully immunizing (three inoculations) the remaining 30 million individuals.[15] According to the official history of the Occupation, the Japanese responded effectively to Thomas' urging, administering a full course of inoculations to approximately 50 million of the 60 million designated persons by the end of 1948. The same source seems ambivalent about the Sams line on TAB vaccine as the key to disease control in this case. On the one hand, it contends that 'These immunizations *combined with the other control measures* resulted in the lowest typhoid–paratyphoid case rate in Japanese history' (my italics). On the other hand, it states that the constant decline indicated that the immunizations were 'the primary and effective factor in reducing the incidence of these diseases'.[16]

It seems likely that the decline of cases resulted as much from the effects of peacetime and the associated resumption of local campaigns to improve sanitary conditions as it did from inoculation. After all, it is conceivable that typhoid/ paratyphoid was more susceptible to these sanitary programmes than dysentery. Such a trend was noted by one authority in relation to the US in the 1930s and early 1940s: 'Sanitary and hygienic measures among the civilian population in times of peace have reduced typhoid fever measurably, while bacillary dysentery remains widely prevalent.'[17] In any case, if there really was a 'retrogression in environmental sanitary standards',[18] as Sams claimed in relation to dysentery, then other diseases associated with insalubrious neighbourhoods – typhus, plague, malaria and Japanese B encephalitis – might have likewise registered rising incidence.

After its extraordinary eruption in 1946, typhus incidence fell considerably. It registered just 1,106 and 475 cases in 1947 and 1948, respectively, dropping to just 111 in 1949, but then jumped suddenly to 938 cases in 1950.[19] Determined not to repeat the mistakes that contributed to the 1946 epidemic, the Occupation authorities worked to inculcate a high level of preparedness on the part of the Japanese authorities. They encouraged inoculation of populations at risk and established 'routine dusting' of such potential sources of disease as prisons, railway stations, orphanages, public baths and public transport facilities. The spike in cases in 1950 was blamed on complacency among Japanese officials, whose belated but 'intensive' efforts nevertheless successfully checked the disease. Just four cases were recorded for the following year, demonstrating both the importance of improving living standards and effective proactive measures against the vectors of epidemic and endemic typhus – body lice, rats and rat fleas. The apparent absence of perhaps the most notorious rat-borne disease – plague – during the Occupation indicates the effectiveness of such preventive measures as the inspection and fumigation of vessels and cargoes at Japanese ports, together with the control of rat populations in the harbour areas.[20]

Similarly, effective quarantine and environmental controls brought the incidence of malaria down from 28,825 cases (and an undisclosed number of deaths) in 1946 to just 1,016 (73 deaths) in 1950.[21] While the disease's profile had been a relatively slight one in pre-war Japan, rarely causing more than 200 deaths from 1920 to 1943, it was endemic in Ehime, Fukuoka, Hiroshima, Kagoshima and particularly Saga prefecture. Its explosive growth at the war's end was due principally to recurrences among the demobilized military personnel repatriated from the southwest Pacific and Asian mainland. With the end of repatriation from those regions, areas of 'indigenous malaria' could be subjected to more rigorous control measures, most notably the use of larvicides and insecticides to eliminate mosquitoes' breeding places. Consequently, in Shiga prefecture, where the problem was most severe, the number of cases dropped from 2,200 in 1949 to 292 in 1950.[22]

In contrast, another mosquito-borne disease, Japanese B encephalitis, proved more difficult to control. Here, again, the tension between immunization and environmental measures, in this case the eradication of mosquitoes, was evident from the start. Designated type B to distinguish it from lethargic encephalitis (type A), which emerged in the early 1920s, the Japanese variant produced serious summer epidemics in Japan in 1924 and 1935. The 1924 outbreak was described in *Public Health Reports*, the official journal of the US Public Health Service, as 'explosive', comparable to 'more severe epidemics of acute poliomyelitis' (in the US). It was concentrated in the prefectures bordering the Inland Sea, most notably around the city of Okayama.[23] More than 6,000 cases of the disease were recorded in 1924, resulting in 3,797 fatalities (62 per cent). From 1924 to 1937 there were 21,355 cases of Japanese B encephalitis and 12,159 deaths from the disease (a fatality rate of 57 per cent).[24] In 1935 Japanese scientists had successfully demonstrated that the disease was a virus, and two Japanese virologists (Mitamura and Kitaoka) correctly surmised that it was spread by special varieties of *Culex* mosquitoes. All of this was of great interest to the US Army in the closing months of the Pacific War as there was much anxiety that previously unexposed American troops would prove particularly susceptible to this nasty disease of the central nervous system.[25]

With the end of the war in August 1945, the Neurotropic Virus Disease Commission of the US Army Epidemiological Board set about analysing the available Japanese research findings and preparing strategies to combat the disease, including the manufacture of a vaccine. American encephalitis specialists, including John Paul and William Hammon, investigated the problem *in situ*. They contacted Mitamura and Kitaoka 'to congratulate them for having been the first to have seen the light and to have maintained that a particular epidemic form of human viral encephalitis was mosquito-borne'. SCAP was advised to adopt a dual strategy of immunization and mosquito eradication. With some relief, John Paul remarked that 'the disease, with all its ugly implications, did not prove to be the serious menace to American soldiers that was expected'. Nevertheless, his research in Japan represented a rare opportunity 'to study this important infection in its native environment, and to prepare and use for a time a formalinized (inactivated) vaccine on civilian and military personnel alike'. When the latter turned out to be of limited effectiveness, provoking a feeble antibody response among US troops, it was abandoned; reliance was placed instead on environmental measures such as screening and other types of mosquito control.[26]

In contrast to its limited impact on Allied forces during the Occupation, Japanese B encephalitis proved much more problematic for the native population. We learn from official Occupation sources, namely the *Summations* and the *History of Non-Military Activities*, that the disease was made a reportable one in June 1946, and that 20,000 Japanese in Okayama prefecture were given the newly developed vaccine around that time. In addition, a special research programme was initiated in March 1948 at the National Institute of Health in Tokyo in concert with the PH&W and Okayama's prefectural health department and medical school. This was just before a serious outbreak of the disease in August 1948, disturbing a trend of low incidence until that time.[27] There were 2,620 deaths recorded among a total of 7,208 cases. The concentration of cases occurred in central and northern Honshu rather than in the endemic area border-ing the Inland Sea. Reflecting doubts about the quality of the vaccine, together with problems of supply, the official record states that control measures were necessarily of an environmental nature, targeting the mosquitoes responsible for transmitting the disease. When another epidemic occurred in 1950, causing 2,430 deaths among 5,196 cases, blame was laid at the door of the sanitary teams as 'field observations had revealed serious deficiencies in applying mosquito control techniques and in materials used'.[28] Whether these factors satisfactorily account for the recurrence of Japanese B encephalitis in 1950 is very difficult to establish due to the complex epidemiology of the disease in question. The same can be said of Sams' claim about the rising incidence of dysentery being due to the decline in standards of sanitation. This he apparently attributed to a loss of effectiveness on the part of sanitary teams, in which he set great store. These teams were the key to the insect- and rodent-control campaigns that were pivotal in Sams' view to the control of enteric and insect-borne diseases. It is to this subject that we now turn.

Vector control

Several questions come to the fore in relation to insect and rodent control. Why did the Occupation authorities so vigorously promote these campaigns and how justified was their representation of them as exciting new developments? To what extent was Japan able to supply itself with the requisite equipment and materials? How does DDT, most often associated with delousing powder, fit into this broader narrative of insect control, and to what extent and why did it eclipse pyrethrum? Is there sufficient evidence to support Takemae's claim of a 'DDT revolution' and what concerns were revealed by the debate over the legitimacy of aerial spraying with DDT of areas of troop concentration? How did the sani-tary teams, so keenly promoted by Sams as the shock troops of insect and rodent control, differ from their precursors, the sanitary associations or *eisei kumiai*? Why did these established local agencies soon became a major bone of conten-tion between the Welfare Ministry and PH&W?

The Occupation's commitment to preventing or at least checking communica-ble diseases in order to safeguard Allied personnel and to prevent unrest conse-quent on the outbreak of serious epidemics necessitated active control of those insects and rodents responsible for transmitting infections. Much was made of Japan's apparent disregard for such environmental controls in the past. For example, Sams declared that 'The Japanese had never attempted large-scale fly, mosquito, or rodent control programs', citing 'an old Japanese saying that the better the cook the more flies she attracted to her kitchen'. Moreover, the public health volume of the official history referred to 'the superstition that the pres-ence of rats marks a happy and prosperous house'.[29] Takemae supports these assertions, contending that the Occupation-sponsored campaign to systematically eliminate flies, mosquitoes, fleas, mites, lice or rodents was unprecedented in Japan, reiterating the traditional view of rats around a house as signifying affluence.[30] However, there are grounds for doubting the validity of these statements. First, it is surely inconceivable that the Japanese authorities, whose pre-war/wartime commitment to modern forms of disease control has been documented in previous chapters, would disregard the potential threat posed by large populations of insects and rats as reservoirs of epidemic disease. Indeed, paragraph 2 of article 16 of the Law for the Prevention of Infectious Diseases of 1897 stated that cities, towns and villages were responsible for the elimination of rats and insects and article 21 charged them with funding these activities. Referring also to legislation concerned with water works (1890), sewerage (1900) and 'filth cleaning' (1900), the Welfare Ministry was at pains to contrast pre-war standards, when families and communities took insect and rodent control seriously, with the deterioration of conditions towards the end of the war, which caused a plague of pests.[31] The official history of the Occupation was generous enough to acknowledge that 'war conditions weakened or destroyed such measures as had previously existed'.[32]

Statements made about the subject in the *US Army Civil Affairs Handbook* similarly conflict with Sams' view that Japan's record on insect-borne diseases was one of neglect. Indeed, it maintained that 'considerable results' were obtained through the rigid operation of relevant legislation. It detailed the efforts made by prefectural authorities working with local hygiene associations (*eisei kumiai*) to eliminate flies and to destroy their breeding places. A number of measures were listed, including reconstruction of storehouses for manure and night soil to make them fly-proof, promotion of fly traps, distribution of larvicides and 'anti-fly propaganda'.[33] As for the comment made by ministry officials to members of the PH&W on 19 April 1946 that 'mosquito and fly control had never been accomplished on a national level', this merely reflected the historical devolution of these functions to the prefectures rather than suggesting general disregard for their importance (as was implied). Indeed, further evidence of a long-term commitment to these kind of environmental controls was the existence of substantial industrial capacity for the production of insecticides and rat poison (Antu), which was revealed in a conference between interested American and Japanese parties on 10 April 1946. Much effort was being made by Occupation officials at this time to marshal what were quite extensive Japanese resources for the prevention of epidemics of enteric diseases during the coming summer months.[34]

There were, for example, substantial stocks of pyrethrum, a natural insecticide extracted from dried chrysanthemum flowers. A PH&W memo of 12 April 1946 stated that its supply amounted to 3,006 tons, 1,600 of which had been allocated for home use, 1,031 for agricultural insecticides and 375 provisionally for export. Also available were 60 tons of aqueous emulsions, 260 tons of insect powder and 245 tons of mosquito sticks.[35] As mentioned in Chapter 3, Japan had led the world in pyrethrum production during the 1930s, exporting more than two-thirds of its annual production of dry flowers and manufactured products. The US was the main recipient of the raw material. Its imports accounted for 89.9 per cent of total Japanese exports in 1936.[36] Although Japan was beginning to lose ground to competition from Kenya in the late 1930s, it still remained the dominant supplier. As regards Japanese consumption, 3,863 metric tons of dry flowers were used in the production of pyrethrum insecticide spray solutions in 1939. This was indispensable for community insect control programmes. Moreover, an average of 3,000 metric tons was processed into agricultural insecticides annually from 1941 to 1945. In 1938, 1,913 metric tons of dry flowers were used for the manufacture of insect powders, and 2,250 for the production of mosquito sticks or coils, both associated with household use. The NRS concluded its 1947 report on pyrethrum in Japan with a ringing endorsement of the industry. Ample manufacturing facilities existed for the processing of the raw material into agricultural and household insecticides, domestic demand exceeded supply and Japanese researchers continued to advance scientific understanding of the field.[37]

Despite all the evidence to the contrary, Sams opened a conference on insect and rodent control in April 1946 with the statement: 'In the past little effort has been made in Japan to control insect-borne diseases.' The chief of the PH&W then advised his audience of military government public health officers of their pivotal importance to the Occupation. He noted the high case rate of dysentery that occurred among the first troops who came to Japan, largely due to the abundance of flies, and highlighted the dangers of Japanese B encephalitis. Another conference would soon be convened for Japanese public health officials, and Sams urged his audience to foster close cooperative relations with their Japanese counterparts. He further underlined the politics of their mission by reminding them that 'the Japanese are watching us closely. Falling down on our important jobs affects the prestige of all Americans.'[38] Here was a declaration of the need to impress the Japanese with the superiority of US know-how, commitment, equipment and materials.

While DDT had already made a rather dramatic entrance in recent months as a delousing powder, this was by no means the limit of its usefulness. As well as being deployed as a powder dust, it could also be delivered in the form of aqueous emulsions, targeting larvae as well as adult flies and mosquitoes.[39] Sams fully appreciated that DDT's importance transcended its perceived public health and later agricultural benefits; ultimately, it recommended the US as a global leader in science and technology. While this 'scientific supremacy' had been most powerfully demonstrated by the atomic bomb, Igarashi draws a parallel between the bomb and DDT as expressions of the promise of science. He cites a Japanese newspaper article that reported the avowed commitment of the Minister of Education, Maeda Tamon, to build a nation founded on scientific knowledge.[40] This ambition complemented Japan's constant 'pursuit of modernity', identified by Barak Kushner as the dominant theme of its wartime propaganda, and the chief justification for its turn to the US after 1945.[41] For the Occupation, DDT was a means of convincing the Japanese people of the merits of close ties with the US – Kate Holliday described the process in February 1951 as 'helping the Japanese people to understand that the people of America are their friends'.[42]

Like penicillin and streptomycin, which would also impress the Japanese as examples of American scientific prowess, DDT epitomized the power of the US to control infectious diseases.[43] Sams was only too aware of DDT's potential to cement the US's reputation in Japan as a modernizing, progressive force in public health, and so to foster closer ties between the two countries. His urgent endorsement of insect control can be seen as motivated as much by these considerations as it was by fears of enteric and insect-borne epidemics. Interestingly, large amounts of pyrethrum continued to be deployed as an insecticide, and a memo of August 1946 called for it to be used 'to the maximum extent'.[44] Still, it was invariably eclipsed by DDT, which generated much excitement and most of the credit for averting epidemics. The Occupation enabled the US to influence and guide the Japanese approach to insect control, aggressively promoting DDT at the expense of pyrethrum, which had been losing ground to its rival since the US army adopted it in May 1943 as its preferred insecticide.

The background to this decision in 1943 highlights the politics of the issue, the urgent need for the US to secure its supply of vital wartime insecticides by producing its own. Only too aware of the potentially disastrous impact of insect-borne diseases, chiefly typhus and malaria, on their troops, the US military authorities vigorously sought solutions to these problems. They demanded a louse-killing powder that soldiers could use on themselves and that worked quickly and effectively to eradicate adult mosquitoes. Such established measures as draining, oiling or poisoning mosquito breeding sites were not deemed suitable for highly mobile warfare. American researchers confronted these challenges with great ingenuity, but 'unfortunately for the army, the two most effective advances in insecticide technology, louse powder and aerosol bombs, relied on dwindling supplies of pyrethrum'. By July 1943, James S. Simmons, the chief of preventive medicine for the US Army, was extremely concerned by the need to find a viable alternative to pyrethrum. He thus welcomed the discovery of DDT, which seemed to more than fit the bill. It was highly toxic to insects, more persistent than pyrethrum powders (i.e. its deadly effect continued for weeks or even months) and, most importantly, it could be manufactured in the US. Reassured in September 1943 that DDT as an aerosol, dust or mist was not hazardous to humans, the army authorities embraced the new chemical insecticide. So rapid was the growth in its production that it played a role in the final phase of the typhus epidemic in Naples in early 1944.[45]

Described by the *Chicago Tribune* as being 'as miraculous a substance as the sulfa drugs or penicillin',[46] DDT continued to win many plaudits after 1945. Most notable among these was the 1948 Nobel Prize in Physiology and Medicine for Paul Mueller of the Swiss firm J. R. Geigy, who had developed it in 1939. Mueller's work had been informed by a number of exacting criteria: the product's high toxicity to insects, its swift effects against a broad spectrum of pests, its harmlessness to mammals, fish and plants, its 'long duration of action' and its commercial viability.[47] While DDT's only apparent drawback was the delay of several hours before insects began to die, some of the judgements made about its low toxicity to animals and fish turned out to be premature. As one entomologist succinctly explained in May 1944, the very qualities that made DDT so attractive to the army – its persistence in the environment and its usefulness against a host of insects – caused great anxiety among civilians. Concern was expressed about chemical residues on food, and the disruption to natural checks and balances that followed indiscriminate killing of insects.[48]

These misgivings would culminate in Rachel Carson's compelling indictment of DDT and other chlorinated hydrocarbons in her book *Silent Spring*, published in 1962. Her book equated the long-term effects of chemical insecticides with nuclear fallout, describing them as the 'little-recognised partners of radiation in changing the very nature of the world – the very nature of its life'. As for DDT's perceived usefulness, Carson condemned such

> non-selective chemicals that have the power to kill every insect, the 'good' and the 'bad', to still the song of birds and the leaping of fish in the streams, to coat the leaves with a deadly film, and to linger on in soil.

Rather than being described as 'insecticides', she claimed, chemicals like DDT should be called 'biocides'.[49] Interestingly, her rejection of aerial spraying of DDT – 'indiscriminately from the skies'[50] – echoed concerns expressed by the NRS of GHQ SCAP in 1946.

These anxieties were expressed following a memorandum from Sams to the Chief of Staff, dated 16 April 1946, in which he recommended that 'airplane spraying with DDT be approved for areas of heavy troop concentration'. The chief of the PH&W praised this approach as an effective and economical method of control, necessitated by prevailing sanitary conditions in Japan and the consequent potential for outbreaks of intestinal diseases, malaria and Japanese B encephalitis during the summer months. This was despite his awareness of its indiscriminate effects, killing those insects essential for agriculture and sericulture as well as the targeted ones, and adversely affecting fish stocks. Nevertheless, he contended that these were problems unlikely to arise in areas with large concentrations of troops. If substantial Allied forces were stationed in or near centres of agriculture or sericulture, he added, then 'hand control methods' were obviously preferable.[51]

In response, the NRS stated that it could not concur with widespread aeroplane spraying of DDT in Japan without 'proper consideration of its effect upon the biological resources of the area to be treated'. Here it had in mind its deleterious impact on fish grown for food purposes, the important economic resource of silkworms, the biological balance between insect pests and their natural parasites or predators, and bees and other insects essential for pollination of crops. Also expressed was an anxiety about the accuracy of spraying and the care needed to confine the spraying to areas carefully evaluated and approved by the interested agencies of SCAP. Acknowledging that there were predominantly urban areas where the benefits of aerial spraying would outweigh the risks, the NRS authorized the practice over just 11 designated areas. These included the First Cavalry Area in Tokyo, Tokyo–Yokohama area, Kobe proper, Okayama area and Kyoto area except the Imperial University Agriculture Department. Finally, advance notice of any spraying was requested so carp farm and fish hatcheries were ready 'to flush their ponds immediately after the application of DDT in order to reduce its concentration'.[52]

These exchanges highlight the different perspectives and priorities of the PH&W and NRS. Whereas the former was charged with protecting the health of US troops and preventing epidemics, the latter focused on safeguarding and maximizing the use of Japan's natural resources, particularly potential sources of food. While DDT's potency was the cause of enthusiasm for Sams and others anxious about the disruptive effects of insect-borne epidemics, the potential for its overuse concerned those more wary of its possible long-term effects, particularly in relation to what we now call 'the environment'. Their concerns reflected more critical opinion in the US, where DDT was considered to be still in the trial phase of its development, so much so that aerial spraying was only permitted in exceptional cases. Only seven applications to spray military bases were approved by a special Army committee in August 1945.[53]

Nevertheless, such controls over the new product's use soon yielded to market pressures. The American public's embrace of DDT was largely a response to its perceived importance in protecting the health of US troops during the war. Japan was caught up in this 'general rhetoric of scientific and technological miracles flowing from World War II'.[54] What Takemae calls the 'DDT revolution' was made possible not just by the realities of military occupation, the US's control and aggressive promotion of this product, but also by the apparent readiness of many Japanese to acknowledge the need for effective insect control amid the social privations they were experiencing. Still, the story of DDT in Japan begins with that decision by the US Army to endorse it in May 1943, largely as a result of the need to free itself from dependence on Japanese pyrethrum. As the Occupation was largely a military exercise, it was perhaps inevitable that the importance attached to DDT in safeguarding the health of US troops would expand to include the Japanese public more generally. Add to this the political benefits of bestowing this exciting new insecticide on the Japanese people, the prestige it conferred on the US, then it is not surprising that DDT figures prominently in Sams' memoir and pyrethrum merits hardly a mention.

Yet large quantities of pyrethrum emulsion continued to be used in insect control during the Occupation. Indeed, this was in line with the US policy of utilizing Japanese resources rather than substituting US products wherever possible.[55] Still, the strong urge to recommend DDT to the Japanese justified imports of US-produced concentrate until Japan could produce sufficient quantities of its own (achieved by the end of 1948).[56] Meanwhile, the insect control programme depended on a mix of pyrethrum emulsion and 5 per cent DDT residual effect spray. On 22 May 1946, a request was made for imports of fuel oil (diesel) and gasoline to be used in the production of pyrethrum emulsion. These were to be included under the category 'for prevention of disease and unrest', and stress was placed on the need for rapid delivery so that manufacturers could produce sufficient pyrethrum emulsion for the imminent summer programme of insect control.[57] The previous month it was disclosed that there were 3,006 metric tons of pyrethrum powder on hand, and that 1,600 tons were allocated to the production of insecticides for home use.[58] On 23 August 1946 it was reported that the Welfare Ministry's schedule for production of pyrethrum emulsion for mosquito and fly control had been achieved. This amounted to 1,819,000 gallons, produced in two months almost exclusively from Japanese materials, requiring only US provision of gasoline and fuel oil. It was the view of Harold Cummings of the PH&W's supply division that 'accomplishment of this program as desired by this headquarters deserves commendation to responsible officials in the Welfare Ministry'.[59] Likewise, it was stated in the Occupation's monthly summation of August 1946 that production of sufficient pyrethrum emulsion, phenothiazine (another established larvicide in Japan) and other insecticides had resulted in a successful mosquito and fly control programme. The insecticides had been dispensed by means of more than 4,000 knapsack and semi-automatic pump sprayers manufactured within Japan.[60] Although the monthly summation for April 1946 made the bizarre claim that 'there have always been adequate quantities of pyrethrum in Japan [but] there is no indication that any significant amount was ever used for insecticides', the official history of the Occupation attributed the domestic supply of effective insecticides in 1946 to Japan's history as a major producer and user of pyrethrum flowers.[61]

Interestingly, pyrethrum emulsion dominates the narratives of insect control during the summer of 1946, DDT attracting relatively little attention at this time (in contrast to its very high profile as a delousing powder during the typhus epidemic). Indeed, it was stated in a memo of 19 April 1946 concerning supplies for the mosquito and fly control programme that Dr Paul's 'preferred agents' were pyrethrum extract and phenothiazine (no mention was made of DDT).[62] It seems that the Japanese government itself continued to rely on pyrethrum emulsion, as demonstrated by correspondence between the PH&W and the Welfare Ministry in June 1947. In a PH&W memo, dated 27 June, it was noted that the ministry had 'omitted use of five per cent DDT residual insecticide in their insect and rodent control directive to prefectures'. This was in spite of available supply of 500,000 gallons of DDT 5 per cent solution, which nevertheless was dwarfed by 600,000 gallons of pyrethrum 30× concentrate, amounting to 18 million gallons of diluted solution. The memo called on the Ministry to advise prefectures of the need to use DDT 5 per cent solution for residual spray programmes. They were to target theatres, bath houses, public toilets, rubbish dumps and private houses in areas where the incidence of insect-borne diseases was high. Furthermore, it was recommended that the supply of DDT liquid insecticides be increased to eight million gallons, including water emulsions, wettable dusts and solutions. This was a substantial increase on the current year's supply of just one million gallons (of 5 per cent solution only). In contrast, the memo declared, the 1948 production level of pyrethrum emulsion was to remain the same as 1947.[63]

This suggests a deliberate effort to shift the emphasis in insect control from pyrethrum to DDT. Only the following month – July 1947 – production of DDT residual effect spray (made with US-produced DDT concentrate) exceeded production of pyrethrum emulsion for the first time, jumping from 68,858 gallons in June to 204,712 the following month.[64] This was in spite of continued high levels of domestic demand for pyrethrum, as noted in a meeting between interested Japanese and American parties on 17 September 1946. Output for 1946 was recorded as 2,100 tons, when the NRS indicated that about 3,000 tons were needed for the production of agricultural insecticides annually, 1,000 tons for pyrethrum emulsion and a substantial quantity for mosquito sticks and other products used in the home.[65] Regardless of DDT's role as a highly effective delousing powder, pyrethrum remained the insecticide of Japanese choice, principally due to familiarity and confidence in its efficacy. Indeed, the NRS report on pyrethrum in Japan noted that domestic demand for it had greatly increased since the end of the war.[66]

Despite Japanese preferences, the gradual eclipse of pyrethrum by DDT was increasingly evident from the closing months of 1947. In October 1947 it was reported that the harvest of pyrethrum flowers was half that of the 1946 crop, which had nevertheless failed to meet domestic demand.[67] The monthly summation for December 1947 recorded a 74 per cent increase in output of 5 per cent DDT residual-effect spray. Moreover, figures specified in the monthly accounts of the following year make no mention of pyrethrum at all, distinguishing only between DDT spray solution manufactured from Japanese-produced concentrate and that made from imported US supplies.[68]

In May 1949 it was reported that the increased production of DDT and benzene hexachloride (BHC), another chlorinated hydrocarbon, had caused demand for pyrethrum to drop, and that this trend, exacerbated by the increased import of agricultural chemicals, was likely to continue.[69] In July of the same year a PH&W official explained that production of pyrethrum emulsion had been suspended, because prefectural officials were cancelling sales contracts and producers had stockpiles of 99,300 gallons in their warehouses (equivalent to 2,979,000 gallons of finished insecticide). Also quoted was the view of Mr Turner, the PH&W's chief sanitary engineer, that the current pyrethrum production was of inferior quality (subsequent checks failed to verify this claim) and, perhaps more significantly, far too costly to the consumer.[70] Due to rising prices and a consequent drop in demand, 216,000 gallons of pyrethrum concentrate was produced in 1950, far short of an original production goal of 413,750 gallons (12,412,500 gallons of diluted emulsion).[71] This compared with a total production of 2,642,603 gallons of 5 per cent DDT residual-effect spray.

Given that the amount of pyrethrum emulsion being produced in 1950 still amounted to a considerable quantity, apparently more than twice the figure of its chief rival, the claim of a 'DDT revolution' needs to be treated with some caution. There is no doubt that DDT was of pivotal importance as a delousing powder and helped to arrest a serious typhus epidemic in 1946 and to prevent any recurrences thereafter. However, the publicity surrounding its use against typhus has tended to produce assumptions about its similar importance in fly and mosquito control. The foregoing analysis of pyrethrum's continued dominance in vector control suggests that DDT failed to displace its chief rival despite claims to the contrary. Indeed, there is evidence to suggest that the Japanese public knew little about the new insecticide. They dismissed household DDT preparations as 'not any good' against flies and mosquitoes, because they were ignorant of DDT's delayed action – disappointed that insect pests did not die on contact with the powder or spray. The PH&W official who revealed these misconceptions in August 1949 stated that he used a mixture of 5 per cent DDT spray and the familiar pyrethrum product in the homes of some Japanese acquaintances (who were complaining). 'The immediate effect of this mixture', he reported, 'was very gratifying to these people'.[72]

This suggests that the strong endorsement of DDT products by Occupation officials largely failed to detach Japanese from indigenous products and practices. Moreover, by the end of the Occupation, there was increasing awareness of the limitations of DDT, most notably the development of insect resistance to it. As one later study of pyrethrum puts it, DDT became a major rival to pyrethrum due to 'great cost advantages', but 'the bloom eventually came off the rose'. As a result, pyrethrum 'became even more in demand for quick killing effect and the inability of insects to develop significant resistance under normal use conditions'.[73] Ultimately, DDT was something of a false dawn in Japan, vying with an indigenous product that turned out to have much greater longevity.

Sanitary teams or *eisei kumiai*?

As well as making a great deal of the public health significance of DDT, Sams and his colleagues in the PH&W put great store in the so-called 'sanitary teams', ostensibly new organizations for undertaking and spreading awareness of environmental hygiene. These were agencies consistently represented as a major break with the past. Indeed, formally acting under the supervision of American officials or military personnel, they were publicized as pivotal to the effort to clean up Japan. Sams drew a clear distinction between the new teams and existing *eisei kumiai* or hygiene associations, dismissed as having failed over several decades to 'materially reduce the incidence of diseases attributable to poor environmental sanitation'.[74] In practice, however, it seems that the distinction was more blurred than he suggested. Indeed, Takemae explains that the sanitary teams were 'formed around' the pre-war organizations,[75] so explaining their rapid emergence during 1946. The official history of the Occupation maintains that by the end of 1946 9,000 sanitary teams, involving 54,000 Japanese, were actively involved in insect and rodent control. At the same time there were 57,620 sanitary associations with a membership of 9,848,545, presumably providing sufficient skilled personnel to staff the sanitary teams.[76]

Furthermore, the admission that the shortage of American military government personnel with the requisite expertise caused supervision of sanitary teams to be inadequate suggests that any credit due these organizations lies with the Japanese involved. Conversely, any problems were blamed on lack of US scrutiny. This apparently caused haphazard insect control: breeding places were frequently missed, toilets were often inadequately sprayed and there was a general lack of thoroughness.[77] The limited opportunities available for US personnel to train and supervise Japanese charged with cleaning up local environments suggests that members of *eisei kumiai* resumed practices of local environmental hygiene disrupted by wartime dislocation.

While Sams presented the sanitary associations as hopelessly inadequate so as to highlight the importance of the 'new' teams as agencies of modernization, it seems that their pre-war record (as suggested in Chapter 2) was at least satisfactory. Although the performance and leadership of the associations during the decades that followed their establishment in 1897 were variable, Masami Hashimoto judges their overall contribution to have been a very significant one. He contends that few communities were without them; their scope of activities expanded to encompass all aspects of public hygiene; they served as effective agencies for the dissemination of preventive health strategies; and their impact on public health, particularly when epidemics threatened, was decisive. On the other hand, these semi-official groups inevitably displaced more formal structures at the local level, a deficit that the Occupation was keen to correct.[78]

In his fascinating study of state and society in modern Japan, *Molding Japanese Minds*, Sheldon Garon alludes to the Occupation's dislike of the many intermediary organizations, 'preferring a more direct relationship between the state and individual'.[79] Still, the sanitary associations proved impervious to reform, perhaps because the Americans themselves were ambivalent about them, wary of what they perceived to be 'fascistic' overtones but grateful for the community cohesion they fostered. For example, E. A. Turner, the PH&W's chief sanitary engineer, accorded them an important wartime role that included mass immunizations, dissemination of hygiene information and education, insect and rodent control activities and national clean-up campaigns twice per year. He praised the latter, stating that it should continue under the aegis of the health centres, which were to be the new guardians of community health. Promoting these new agencies might be difficult, however, when 'The sanitary associations have and still do carry most of the responsibility for municipal sanitation' despite being 'outlawed by order from SCAP'.[80]

More important than American ambivalence, however, was the strong sense of attachment the Japanese authorities had towards these semi-official organizations.

Evasion was thus preferred to compliance. Turner argued that many of the associations had not been dissolved as required but had been 'simply changed around to comply with the new regulations, which finds them functioning as in previous times'.[81] The Occupation authorities were prepared to tolerate hygiene associations only if they were purely voluntary, organized along democratic lines and restricted to the dissemination of health education and information, refraining from 'assuming functions which properly belong to government'.[82] The lack of progress on this issue reflected the Japanese government's reluctance to pay for official governmental organizations, when it could instead make substantial savings by devolving responsibility to community groups that largely financed themselves through membership fees. More to the point, the Japanese authorities were loath to dissolve organizations that were rooted in communities and served in the front line of disease prevention. The Welfare Ministry under-lined their importance by specifying the following functions: acute infectious diseases control (including prophylactic inoculation, disinfection, case finding) and 'cleansing works' (disposal of refuse and night soil, control of insects and rodents and the purchase of associated chemicals, cleaning drains and ditches, plans for general cleaning of homes of members).[83]

So determined, however, was Sams to project the work of the Occupation as novel and innovative, that he claimed that the new sanitary teams brought about the education of Japanese families 'in the importance of good environmental sanitation'. He was convinced that this function was

> one of the most important jobs of the team, since the idea of sanitation ... is entirely new to the Japanese who have previously been content to live in areas in which flies and mosquitoes were accepted as normal and in which rats were looked upon as friendly inhabitants of the house.[84]

These statements were closer to propaganda than an accurate rendering of past practices or indeed current developments.

The story of the sanitary teams is a confusing one. After all, apart from over-lapping with *eisei kumiai* or supplementing them at times of crisis (such as when typhus erupted in 1946), the sanitary teams also seem to have been short-lived. They experienced only a brief burst of activity from 1946 to 1948, by which time they had apparently fallen victim to budgetary cuts. According to Sams, this was the main reason the incidence of dysentery 'began a steady return to its prewar rate, which was reached by 1951 and exceeded in 1952'.[85] And yet Turn-er's report of early 1950 casts doubt on this version of events. It continues to present the teams as central to a new system of environmental sanitation coordinated by health centres.[86] Regardless of how sanitary teams and *eisei kumiai* interacted, it is clear that Sams exaggerated the former's significance as agitators for a new public health consciousness. Just as DDT was promoted at the expense of pyrethrum to highlight the Occupation's contribution to higher standards of environmental hygiene, so too were 'sanitary teams' deliberately designed to eclipse *eisei kumiai* as exciting, US-inspired innovations.

While insect control lay at the heart of the Occupation's drive to reduce the incidence of enteric diseases, and to prevent epidemics of typhus and malaria, attention was also directed to the eradication of rats by means of traps and poison. Here there was no great fanfare over the introduction of superior Ameri-can products or methods, rather a commitment to ensuring that established Japa-nese practices were carried out satisfactorily. In April 1946 H. Cumings of the PH&W's supply division stated that at least one company – Hodagaya Chemical Company – was capable of producing two tons of Antu rat poison per month.[87] Just ten days later Sams reported that production of effective rodenticides was being re-established at all plants where this was possible, but there was little likelihood of sufficient supplies for an effective control programme in the coming months.[88] In the meantime, he declared, the shortfall would have to be met by 8th Army and the Japanese government charged accordingly. Just a few months later, in August 1946, Warren Bradlee of the PH&W's Preventive Medicine Division assessed the rat control measures undertaken by many cities, using rat poison and traps, as 'fairly effective', although he regretted the lack of 'trained supervision'.[89] The 4,100,000 packages of Antu reportedly produced by Japanese factories between June and August 1946 obviously contributed to the campaign's modest success.[90] From May to July the following year, Japanese factories manufactured 25,763 kg of Antu, 8,915 kg of Nekoirazu rat poison and 14,000 rat traps.[91] These supplies enabled prefectural governors to oversee more rigorous control measures. Given that the official history of the Occupation maintains that rodenticides such as Antu and phosphorous compounds were manufactured 'to satisfy all needs', it can be assumed that production levels soon returned to pre-war norms.[92]

According to a report on the development of sanitary conditions in Japan from 1946 to 1949, compiled by the environmental sanitation section of the Welfare Ministry, there was a history of community observance of laws and regulations regarding the extermination of insects and rats since the early twentieth century. It was only the pressures of war that had caused controls to lapse and the consequent deterioration of environmental conditions.[93] Removing and disposing of rubble and garbage that provided food and habitats for rodents contributed as much to the success of post-war rodent control as did widespread baiting and trapping programmes.[94] Indeed, the Occupation presented the issue of rodent control not only as a public health problem but also as an 'economic' one. This was evidenced by an 8th Army memo of May 1948 on civil information activities that stated that there was one rat for every person in Japan, and 'besides the food these 78 million rats eat – the equivalent of 35,100,000 ton shipments each year – the fleas they carry transmit typhus'. Households were urged to continue to poison and trap rats throughout the year.[95] In 1950 a detailed schedule for 'fall cleaning week' specified the fifth and sixth day for rodent control. Recommended approaches to eradicating rats included: 'starvation' (i.e. depriving them of access to food waste and garbage); 'rat proofing' premises; trapping them; and poisoning them. Further, it was recommended that rat runways, burrows, holes and harbourages be dusted with DDT,[96] perhaps the only proposed measure that was unfamiliar to the Japanese.

Night soil and water supply

There were no major changes to established Japanese practices when it came to sewage disposal and water quality. That is to say, the US had no quick fixes for what were generally perceived to be highly deficient systems. Nowhere was the American tendency towards derision more apparent than in the case of night soil. This drew scathing criticism as alien and primitive and captured for many Americans the limitations of Japanese hygiene. The relevant volume of the *History of Non-Military Activities of the Occupation of Japan*, for example, described the utilization of night soil as fertilizer as the 'greatest single sanitation problem' the

US faced. Despite this, they could do very little about it other than return to the best practice of the pre-war years. As the official history puts it rather succinctly, since 'there was no prospect of Japan being able to discontinue the use of night soil for fertiliser in the near future', the emphasis should be on enforcing regulations for proper storage and composting so as to destroy pathogenic organisms and helminth ova. These regulations, it was noted, had been 'relaxed during the war'.[97]

Interestingly, the problem was unavoidably tied up with that of food shortages during the Occupation. An important report on the food and fertilizer situation in Japan, dated 4 April 1947, stated that the country had historically depended on commercial fertilizer for maximum crop production, that the consumption of plant food had dropped steeply during the war years, and that only repair of existing plants and imports of vital raw materials would enable Japan to resume its pre-war practices. 'Before the war', William Tsutsui points out, 'Japanese agriculture was one of the world's most intensive users of chemical fertilisers.'[98] At this time, night soil accounted for only a small proportion of fertilizing materials, contributing a combined total (nitrogen, potash and phosphorous) of only 6.8 per cent in 1937, the 'maximum consumption year for commercial fertilisers'.[99] By 1945, however, these had lost some ground to night soil – about 12 per cent of all plant foods applied to growing crops now came from this source.[100] The increase reflected the disruptive effects of the war on external supply of chemical fertilizers and diversion of ammonia, for example, from nitrogenous fertilizers to the munitions industry.[101] It is clear, therefore, that when Sams' staff, in tandem with the NRS, 'encouraged the domestic production and use of chemical fertilizers to replace night soil',[102] they were preaching to the converted.

With typical directness, Sams singled out the practice of using night soil as chiefly responsible for the pronounced profile of dysentery and other enteric infections in Japan:

> In a land where untreated human excrement … is habitually used on the land for fertilizer, the causative organisms are spread on the fields and then spread to uninfected persons through vegetables or other foods that are grown on the ground and normally eaten uncooked. They are also spread to all of the surface streams and shallow wells when rains wash the fertilizer into these streams or wells.[103]

Clearly, the use of 'untreated human excrement' was a reference to wartime malpractice rather than a fair appraisal of pre-war standards. Moreover, his failure to mention Japan's intensive use of commercial fertilizer detracts from the reality of the situation. Still, his characterization of streams and wells as conduits for infection from run-off is a fair one, given that around three-quarters of Japanese obtained their water from such sources.[104] Certainly, the high incidence of intestinal parasites in Japan at this time may be attributed to these circumstances, as was explained in the *Civil Affairs Handbook on Public Health and Sanitation.*

This astutely observed that 'the need of fertilizer, and the availability of human night soil, have created a strong block against the installation of widespread sewerage systems, and as long as this condition persists, intestinal parasites will remain a serious problem'. It also stated that pre-war concerns about the problem had engendered subsidies for adequate sewerage systems and promotion of the 'sanitary privy'. There was recognition of the Japanese government's efforts to reduce parasitical diseases, found to be more entrenched than it anticipated, as early as 1920, when it informed local governments that it would provide one-third of the funds necessary to tackle them. Moreover, specialists were charged with assisting districts particularly affected by parasitism. In one such prefecture, Saitama, where hookworm (a roundworm) was most prevalent, the local authorities treated 400,000 people with antihelminthic drugs like santonin that expel parasitic worms (helminths) from the body. In 1937, 581,809 Japanese were examined according to the provisions of the Law for the Prevention of Parasitic Diseases; of this number, 282,004 – or 48 per cent – were recorded as carrying eggs (roundworm eggs were found in 83 per cent of the infected group).[105]

The Occupation acknowledged past Japanese efforts to confront the problem, and acquiesced in Japanese strategies for bringing it under control. This much was clear from a conference on the subject on 28 August 1947, attended by members of the PH&W and Welfare Ministry. The single agenda item was a plan for a programme of parasite control, prepared by Dr Kanai of the Ministry's Chronic Infectious Diseases Section. This examined the subject under six headings: treatment of those affected; control of night soil; public health education; research on vermifuges (drugs used to expel parasites from the intestinal tract); increased production of vermifuges; and establishment of demonstration districts for parasite control.

For Kanai, the problem was essentially one of resources. The dearth of chemical fertilizers was causing over-reliance on night soil and the shortage of vermifuges constraining the effectiveness of treatment programmes at a time when 'in many places more than 80% of the population have ascaris (roundworm) eggs in their faeces'. Apparently, all those at the conference agreed that Kanai's plan represented 'a very weak attempt at a solution of the parasite problem but that it was probably worth dispatching to the prefectures' in any case, suggesting low expectations among the participants. The best that could be achieved in the short term was to improve supplies of vermifuges, relegating more fundamental improvements in sanitation to the long term.[106] In the meantime, Sams and his colleagues tended towards ambivalence about night soil; on the one hand, it was seen as a source of enteric diseases, on the other, it was a key part of the fertilizer mix required to maximize crop yields as desired by the NRS.[107] As a result, the Occupation authorities encouraged the Japanese to act on the findings of Dr Tokurō Takano, whose research, conducted over many years, examined the destruction of pathogenic bacteria and parasites by the simple method of storage of excreta. The PH&W's Preventive Medicine Division urged Japanese officials to reinstate the educational and publicity programmes in use before the war for the construction of sanitary privies and storage vaults.[108] It seems that the Occupation made few inroads into the problem. The British social scientist, Ronald Dore, later remarked that a survey of Tokyo school children in mid-1951 revealed that 51 per cent were hosting parasites, with one district recording a figure of 72 per cent. Reiterating that the chief causal factor was the use of night soil as fertilizer, he attributed 'gradual improvement' in the situation to 'the increased use of preventive and curative medicines'.[109]

Dore also referred to publicity in 1951 encouraging households to install modern plumbing – 'A flush toilet is the first condition of Civilized Living' was the favoured slogan. As the main impediment to the 'popularisation of the water closet' was the cost of its installation, cheaper models using kitchen waste water were promoted, and short-term loans provided by the authorities. In 1951, 90 per cent of the households in Shitayamacho, the object of Dore's study, were connected to the sewer, the remaining 10 per cent relying on others to empty their pit-toilets.[110] Here there were gradual improvements from an aesthetic as well as a hygienic point of view. One group of Japanese reformers called for the substitution of vacuum pump trucks for the traditional manual means of removing night soil in wooden buckets slung from carrier poles and onward transport by hand cart or barge. To accommodate Tokyo's narrow back streets, 'an auto-tricycle', equipped with a vacuum pump and trailer, was developed. This method, its advocates enthusiastically declared, made for a much more hygienic, less smelly removal process.[111]

The trend towards installation of modern sewerage systems and the gradual replacement of night soil with commercial fertilizers were developments that had been interrupted by the war and were resumed during the Occupation. Future prosperity would bring real advances in these areas, but in the meantime – as one Japanese official put it in relation to night soil – Japan had no choice but to make full use of it 'since she is a poor country'.[112] Similar inertia characterized efforts to improve the quality of Japan's water supply. Clearly, there was little likelihood at this time of piped, treated water being extended to the large number of rural communities dependent on wells or polluted streams.[113] Indeed, the civil affairs guide on water supply and sewage disposal, issued in September 1945, advised that the ambitions of military government largely be limited to returning to the status quo ante, to pre-war standards of water purification that were deemed to 'compare favourably with those in the United States'. It recommended that restoration be done speedily to the sacrifice of quality; that facilities be restored along existing lines, using Japanese equipment wherever possible; that expansion of facilities be undertaken only in cases of extreme necessity; and that the Japanese be encouraged to adopt more modern techniques.[114]

Acting on these recommendations, the PH&W advised the Welfare Ministry in December 1945 to expedite the restoration of all public water supplies to ensure the provision of water of quantity and quality at least equal to that produced before the war. The only change to established practice that was recommended was more rigorous water analysis and more attention to 'residual chlorine found in active parts of the distribution system, rather than at the treatment plant'.[115]

The issue of chlorine and associated problems of supply and equipment, together with the consequences of bomb damage to water supply infrastructure in the cities, were the principal concerns of Occupation officials at least until 1948.[116] In February 1946 the *Asahi Shimbun* reported plans to restore the metropolitan water supply to pre-war standards by mobilizing 1,000 specialist workers. Extensive leakage of underground water was considered the principal reason for erratic fluctuation of water pressure and consequent suspension of supply. In an effort to tackle these problems, the metropolitan water supply bureau divided the city into seven blocks, assigning teams to liaise with neighbourhood associations to detect leaks and repair or replace damaged pipes.[117] In June 1946 there was evidence of progress made but much still to do. According to the Occupation's monthly summation, several cities had reported a 50 per cent reduction in leakage since December 1945, but the problem was still believed to exceed 30 per cent in most cities.[118] Apart from the dangers of 'back siphonage' and pollution from low water pressure,[119] there was also the problem of a complete cessation of supply to homes on higher ground, particularly during the hot summer months. Indeed, the *Asahi Shimbun* reported that 'public disturbances' had broken out in July 1946 as a result of a 'water famine' during 'the heat of July'. In response, an official of Tokyo's water supply section reassured readers that, despite damage to 600,000 of 900,000 hydrants during the war, an ambitious repair and reconstruction programme involving 700 workers was now 70 per cent complete.[120] Repair and maintenance of existing infrastructure was the priority until 1950, when ¥14 billion of expenditure was earmarked for extension and improvement of 310 water supply systems and 70 sewerage installations. This was regarded as largely a continuation of construction begun during the past ten years. Until then the emphasis was on meeting the basic needs of the Japanese public and protecting them, together with Occupation personnel, from enteric diseases.

Safeguarding public health was strongly linked in American minds with higher concentrations of chlorine in the water supply. Much was made of the gap between American and Japanese requirements in terms of water quality, one source stating that it was 'generally satisfactory according to Japanese standards but ... non-potable according to those of the US army'. According to the official history of the Occupation, the Japanese had tended to rely on water purification by infiltration alone, reserving use of chlorine for water definitely known to be non-potable and even then the acceptable dosage was only about one-quarter of the proper quantity.[121] Some impatience on the part of the Occupation authorities with this problem reflected the logistical difficulties of supplying their troops with safe drinking water. On 21 November 1945 the *Stars and Stripes* reported the view of Brigadier General G. W. Rice of 8th Army Headquarters, Yokohama, that military personnel in the Tokyo–Yokohama area would have to use 'lister bags' until chlorination units arrived. Insufficient supplies of salt, which could not be imported from Korea, made wholesale chlorination of the Japanese water supply impossible under present circumstances, and no action would be taken as long as there was no outbreak of water-borne disease among the civilian population.[122] No such epidemic developed, suggesting that Japanese efforts to 'provide chlorine for all cities in sufficient quantities to treat to prewar standards' met with some degree of success.[123]

During the summer of 1946 the Occupation received imports of liquid chlorine from the US, but this was justified as necessary to safeguard the quality of drinking water in cities with large concentrations of Occupation personnel.[124] This may have continued up to 1948, by which time Japanese manufacturers were apparently producing sufficient quantities of chlorine to meet American requirements.[125]

Despite such improvements in chlorination, there seems to have been persistent anxiety among American officials about the quantity and quality of water in Japanese cities. On 25 February 1948, the *Nippon Times* reported the concerns of Mr Kaufman, one of the PH&W's sanitary engineers, about water shortages in Tokyo and the Kanto plain, the rigid water conservation measures that these justified and the consequent risk of people resorting to other, less safe sources, namely shallow wells. Local health centres and ward sanitary offices were thus advised of the need to instruct people in the use of chlorinated lime so as to avoid a rise in the incidence of enteric diseases.

Eighteen months later, on 1 September 1949, Occupation personnel were warned that the water supply in the Yokohama area was not safe due to breaks in the water mains and low pressure causing possible pollution. They were advised to boil water for not less than five minutes or to treat it with purification tablets. Similar warnings were issued to those living in Tokyo.[126] In short, the limitations of Japanese water supply infrastructure, the inadequacy of storage and treatment facilities, were problems that the Occupation authorities had to accommodate rather than try to solve. It was understood that improvements in this area would be gradual and incremental, and would depend on economic recovery and rehabilitation. Although rather absurd claims were made about a lack of Japanese expertise – Sams complained, for example, that there were only two sanitary engineers in all of Japan at the beginning of the Occupation[127] – the reality of the situation was that responsibility for water quality and supply lay with the relevant Japanese authorities. They were constrained above all by a lack of resources and the scale of the task of reconstruction.

Conclusion

Shattered cities and damaged sanitary infrastructure, piles of debris and refuse, the accumulation of untreated night soil and the rise of insect and rodent populations produced conditions ripe for epidemics. Viewing the devastating consequences of Japan's defeat, Sams and his colleagues in the PH&W can have been in no doubt about the urgent need to clean up Japan, to establish sanitary standards that would safeguard public health. Usually this meant re-establishing or reinstituting procedures and practices associated with Japan's pre-war and wartime hygiene regime rather than introducing novel, innovative approaches. The key exception to this, of course, was the deployment of DDT, which attracted much publicity as a public health panacea.

Indeed, the dusting of Japanese with delousing powder is the image that dominates accounts of public health during the Occupation, perhaps unsurprising given the Occupation's sophisticated censorship apparatus. As William Tsutsui succinctly puts it, 'Allied Occupation advisers aggressively promoted the use and production of DDT in Japan, all but assuring that the Japanese pyrethrum industry would not rebound from the wartime rupture in global markets.'[128] Nevertheless, pyrethrum remained the more familiar and arguably the more vital means of insect control in the home and local community. Early on, the PH&W disclosed that they had discovered that at least three commercial preparations containing pyrethrum were made in Japan, and that the only one that they knew how to use was the 3 per cent emulsion.[129] The insect and rodent control programmes, in which Sams set great store, were not the novel developments that he claimed. His declarations to that effect may have been influenced as much by the politics of DDT promotion as the threat posed by insect-borne and enteric diseases. The political importance of DDT is hinted at in a much broader analysis of its deployment against malaria elsewhere, which alludes to an 'over-reliance on DDT', and the stress placed on vector control 'to encourage capitalist development and to fight communism'.[130]

As to who was engaged in 'cleaning up Japan', there is no doubt that Kate Holliday, and her principal source, Crawford Sams, exaggerated the role and significance of Occupation personnel. Of course, members of military government teams and US Army sanitary engineers may have supervised and assisted their Japanese counterparts in the cities where they resided, but they were too few to be accorded a dominant role.

In the context of an indirect Occupation, responsibility lay with the Japanese authorities, working with neighbourhood associations and *eisei kumiai* or sanitary teams to carry out the policies of the Japanese government, prompted of course by GHQ SCAP, but seldom controversial. There was general agreement on methods of disease control, but some conflict over associated local agencies, principally the semi-official nature of the *eisei kumiai*.

Just as the rhetoric about sanitary teams eclipsing *eisei kumiai* and DDT revolutionizing public health was overblown, so too were Sams' claims about the lack of Japanese expertise in modern forms of sanitary engineering. Such a deficit is difficult to reconcile with the Occupation's limited ambitions regarding the supply of treated water and the disposal of sewage, focused largely on the resumption of pre-war practices and standards. These would not have been considered acceptable if the Japanese authorities were as ignorant of sanitary science as Sams suggested.

This is not to discount the fundamental, structural problems besetting Japan's sanitary infrastructure, most notably its very limited reach. However, the scarcity of resources and the scale of the challenge were such that they transcended any ambitions of the Occupation to do more than exercise limited supervision over Japanese efforts to repair existing infrastructure and to encourage aspirations for improvement. Much to Sams' frustration, the intractable problem of dysentery reflected these realities.

5 Nutrition and disease

Previous chapters have illuminated American assumptions and prejudices about the shortcomings of disease control in Japan and the primitive nature of its sanitary infrastructure. Although some of these judgements may have been at least partly justified, more often than not they drew on rather crude comparisons with practices in the US rather than reflecting a proper understanding of the particular historical and cultural influences that had shaped the Japanese experience. A similar Occupation mindset was evident in the case of Japanese nutrition. Its perceived shortcomings were largely a reflection of how it differed from dietary practice in the United States. Sams, for example, observed that long ago 'the Japanese had made a fundamental decision ... to rely on grain crops as the principle source of food, rather than a combination of grain and domestic livestock', as was the norm in the US. Further, he argued, this adoption of 'faulty nutritional patterns' had 'contributed to the exceptionally high beriberi and tuberculosis incidence in pre-war Japan' and (rather implausibly) 'the steady decrease in the height and stamina of the people'.[1]

A number of questions arise from these representations of the 'problem' of Japanese nutrition. Was it as fundamental as Sams claimed or more a case of war-induced malnutrition, best corrected by a return to pre-war dietary norms? How direct a relationship was there between (mal)nutrition and the very high incidence of tuberculosis in Japan? What is the relationship between diet and disease more generally? How justified was the vigorous promotion of animal protein, what measures were adopted to increase its consumption and to what extent did they meet with success?

Before these more ambitious endeavours to rebalance diets could be undertaken, however, the Occupation had to contend with a grave shortfall of food, caused chiefly by a very poor rice harvest in the autumn of 1945 and the cessation of food imports. The latter had accounted for 15–20 per cent of Japan's pre-war supply by caloric value.[2] SCAP had little choice but to appeal to Washington for food aid at a time when the US administration was confronting a global food shortage. The early obsession with counting calories, with ensuring sufficient food supplies were on hand to avert a famine, reveals much about the Occupation's anxiety that consequent 'disease and unrest' would seriously undermine its ability to carry out its programme. Initially, then, food aid was justified in terms of protecting Allied personnel from the social and medical consequences of pervasive starvation. Only with the end of 1947, when the threat of famine had diminished, did nutrition become more explicitly linked to correcting dietary deficiencies and concomitantly improving standards of public health. For Sams, this was the key to a healthy, robust democracy. He believed that countries like Japan were 'underdeveloped because most of their populations are chronically ill and malnourished'.[3] Perhaps that was why he set such great store in the school lunch programme, which aimed to reverse the apparent decline of children's physical stature and resilience during the war years. Together with assessing the success of this programme, this chapter considers the relationship between diet and disease and explores how the Occupation represented that relationship to secure food aid. Also discussed are the nature and legacy of its nutritional reforms. Ultimately, prosperity changes diets, and so the kind of dietary change favoured by Sams could not occur until Japan had moved beyond the rehabilitation phase of the 1950s to high rates of economic growth and rising affluence thereafter.

Diet and disease

The quantity of food consumed by an individual measured in calories, the dietary balance of his/her diet in terms of macronutrients (carbohydrates, protein, fats), and the presence of micronutrients (vitamins and minerals) all have a bearing on that person's health – his or her susceptibility to infection. With the exception of those diseases directly caused by micronutrient deficiencies (e.g. beriberi, rickets, pellagra and scurvy), the relationship between diet and disease is invariably a complex one. It is difficult to separate nutrition from other environmental influences such as congested or unsanitary living conditions. Jannetta makes the point that changes in the morbidity and mortality rates of acute infectious diseases 'are often a response to environmental changes that affect one or more links in the chain of infection', involving the pathogen itself, its routes of transmission and the human host. The relationship between malnutrition and epidemics, she argues, is an 'indirect' one. More direct influences, she suggests, are the consequent relaxation of public health controls and the ease with which hungry people travelling to find food can spread infection.[4]

However, Occupation officials and their Japanese counterparts more explicitly linked nutrition to the high incidence of chronic infectious diseases, most notably tuberculosis. Indeed, a direct relationship between what William Johnston has referred to as Japan's 'modern epidemic' and malnutrition was postulated in a memorandum of October 1947 from the War Department in Washington. This stated that in order to demonstrate the urgent need for food relief the latest data on incidence of tuberculosis was required, among other factors – most notably pictures showing famine conditions and evidence of people's loss of weight.[5] A more recent study of tuberculosis suggests that the War Department's approach was justified: 'Of all the factors involved – housing, fatigue, anxiety, uncleanliness – poor nutrition with the impaired resistance that accompanied it, seems to have been the crucial divider between exposure and active manifestation of the disease.'[6]

In the early years of the Occupation 'poor nutrition' principally referred to insufficient calories, regardless of the division of nutrients. Later, dietary balance increasingly came to the fore, particularly with regard to the very low intake of animal protein. In a paper on the efficacy of BCG immunization written for an American audience in the mid-1950s, Crawford Sams asserted that epidemiological studies of the link between nutrition and tuberculosis demonstrated that food shortages caused by war compromised resistance to the disease, producing marked rises in rates of morbidity and mortality. He contended that nutrition surveys carried out in Japan as late as 1949 revealed that rural Japanese were still consuming insufficient amounts of animal protein for normal growth and resistance to disease, particularly diseases of chronic nature such as tuberculosis.[7] The latter was the leading cause of death in Japan until around 1950, with a mortality rate of 187.5 and 168.8/100,000 in 1947 and 1949, respectively.[8] It was thus not surprising that diet and nutrition were major preoccupations of the chief of the PH&W for the duration of the Occupation.

Some of Sams' colleagues, however, were less willing to accord nutrition such prominence in explaining rising mortality from tuberculosis during the war years and their aftermath. In his detailed and sophisticated study of Japanese food management, Bruce Johnston acknowledged that tuberculosis' high incidence might by explained 'in part' by dietary deficiencies, but wished to give equal salience to non-nutritional factors, namely poor sanitation and crowded living conditions. Regarding the steep increase of incidence towards the end of the war, he insisted that 'deterioration of the diet was unimportant'. Rather, it was explained by the 'congestion of population in industrial centres and lowered standards of sanitation and public health services'. In contrast to Sams, who typically adopted a strongly negative position on Japanese nutrition, Johnston was more willing to judge it on its merits. He acknowledged that compared with Western countries, the Japanese pre-war diet was principally vegetarian and incorporated little animal protein, but maintained that consumption of other forms of protein was adequate. Soybeans, which represented an important part of the Japanese diet, were a source of 'complete protein', containing all nine of the essential amino acids in adequate measure.

As far as micronutrients were concerned, Johnston took issue with Sams' assertion that comparatively low consumption of calcium in Japan represented a major nutritional deficiency. However, he acknowledged that the figure of 10,600 deaths and the high incidence of incapacitating illness attributable to beriberi in 1937 highlighted the problem of an insufficient intake of vitamin B1 (thiamine). This was associated with a dietary over-reliance on polished rice, the milling and washing of which caused the loss of most of the antineuritic vitamins. Still, beriberi was responsible for the huge majority of the 11,000 deaths from 'vitamin diseases' recorded in 1937. The incidence of pellagra (deficient niacin or vitamin B3), scurvy (ascorbic acid or Vitamin C), xeropthalmia (Vitamin A) and rickets (Vitamin D) was very low. Interestingly, the pressure on rice supplies during the war years caused the incidence of beriberi to fall as it forced the Japanese government to take steps to reduce the polishing of brown rice, so retaining thiamine content.[9]

Moreover, the increasing need to adulterate the rice ration with other grains and potatoes had a largely beneficial effect in nutritional terms. When wheat was substituted, the ration contained less calcium and niacin (vitamin B3) but more protein, thiamine (B1) and riboflavin (vitamin B2); barley was beneficial in all respects, particularly with regard to vitamins B1, B2 and B3; white potatoes provided more calories, protein, calcium and all vitamins, but less fat; sweet potatoes were even richer in terms of vitamin A, but less so in terms of protein.[10] These benefits, however, have to be considered alongside grave food shortages and under-nutrition from 1944. While the pre-war diet of the Japanese may be considered nutritionally adequate, it was barely so and thus could not easily accommodate the pressures of war, naval blockade and defeat. As Johnston puts it, 'the caloric intake and the supplies of essential nutrients were too close to the margin to permit marked reduction in food supply without adverse effects on the health and working efficiency of the population'.[11] Those adverse effects, of course, could manifest themselves as less dramatic markers of ill-health, namely fatigue and lassitude. Members of the PH&W, NRS and Economic and Scientific Section constantly wrestled with these issues, endeavouring to ease the food supply problem not only to prevent the outbreak of 'disease and unrest', but also to facilitate the economic rehabilitation of Japan. Justifying US food relief for Japan necessitated detailed studies that dramatized the spectre of famine and latterly represented the Japanese as chronically malnourished. For Sams, tackling the problem of Japanese nutrition was as intrinsic to the success of democratization as was the 1947 constitution.

Measuring nutrition

As discussed in Chapter 2, the Japanese authorities had long taken an interest in prevailing standards of nutrition, fully aware of the economic and military implications of deficiencies in this regard. From 1932 the Japanese Education Ministry provided subsidies for school meals, and by 1940 more than 12,000 schools were making use of them. The establishment of the Welfare Ministry in 1938 served to heighten nutritional awareness, as shown by growing numbers of trained dieticians during the war years. According to Cwiertka, 'total war' brought nutritional principles to the fore; the state viewed 'diet as an important home-front weapon essential for preserving order and productivity'.[12] The lengthy discussion on wartime nutrition in the report of the US Strategic Bombing Survey draws on several Japanese nutritional studies to inform its judgements.[13] Interestingly, the nutrition survey set up by the Dieticians' Association of Japan in June 1945, but not concluded due to Japan's surrender, anticipated the national nutrition surveys ordered by the PH&W from the end of 1945.[14] Indeed, a memo on the caloric and protein intake of the Japanese, dated 27 October 1945, referred to discussions with Dr Sugimoto of the Japanese

National Nutrition Laboratory and Dr Oiso of the Welfare Ministry concerning the June 1945 surveys. It was noted that the sample had been perhaps narrowly conceived – limited to the diets of middle-class families – but was nevertheless useful.[15]

It seems that there was sufficient confidence in Japanese nutritional expertise to entrust the task of nutritional surveys to the relevant authorities with minimal oversight by their American counterparts.[16] In a memo of October 1946 it was stated that military government officers, preferably the medical officer, in the cities and prefectures should review the conduct of nutrition surveys in November 1946 and subsequent surveys in their areas, monitoring 'the uniformity of observation in the physical examinations'. Their presence served chiefly to demonstrate to the people concerned the official importance of the surveys.[17] Presiding over this nutritional research was Aritomo Kunitarō (1898–1984), an impressive dietician who headed the nutrition division in the Ministry's Public Health Bureau. For Cwiertka, he represents 'the trans-war continuity in the popularization of nutritional knowledge in Japan'.[18]

Survey results were carefully scrutinized by members of the PH&W for signs of famine and serious malnutrition. They were reproduced in the monthly summations and later the official history to highlight the grave shortage of food in the cities and the Japanese diet's perceived physiological inadequacy more generally. The latter concern, however, did not dominate until around the end of 1947. Until that time the nutrition surveys served as the chief instrument for convincing the US administration in Washington of the dire food supply situation in the cities and the consequent urgency of food aid. Indeed, according to SCAPIN 422 of 11 December 1945, the express purpose of the surveys was to provide factual information on the nutritional health and actual food consumption of the Japanese people.[19]

In terms of the survey's development, attention was first focused in December 1945 on Tokyo, where rumours were circulating about deaths from starvation.[20] Its range was then expanded in February 1946 to include four other large cities (Nagoya, Osaka, Kure and Fukuoka) and rural areas in 19 prefectures (Aichi, Chiba, Fukuoka, Gunma, Hiroshima, Hyogo, Ibaraki, Kanagawa, Kumamoto, Kyoto, Okayama, Osaka, Saga, Saitama, Shiga, Shizuoka, Tochigi, Tokyo and Wakayama). That is to say, the survey spread out from Tokyo to include neighbouring prefectures in central Honshu, extending to the Kansai region, southern Honshu and northern Kyushu. From May 1946 its range was expanded to include northern Honshu and Hokkaido, several prefectures on the Japan Sea coast and Shikoku. It now encompassed nine cities (Kanazawa, Matsuyama, Sapporo and Sendai in addition to the five already specified) and rural designations in a total of 27 prefectures. That prefectural total was made up of the 19 already specified plus Ehime, Fukui, Hokkaido, Ishikawa, Iwate, Kochi, Miyagi and Toyama. The pattern of four surveys per year, undertaken during the months of February, May, August and November was established in 1946 and 1947. However, the nutritional survey did not become a truly national one until February 1948, when it expanded to include any remaining cities with populations greater than 30,000, namely Yokohama, Kyoto and Kobe, and the rural areas of all 46 prefectures.[21]

Coordinated by the Welfare Ministry, the surveys incorporated two investigative processes. One was conducted by Japanese nutritionists, who recorded three-day dietary histories of subjects. The other was undertaken by doctors and nurses, checking for symptoms associated with nutritional deficiencies, including body weight and height. The number of people who submitted forms detailing their food intake over a three-day period was about half the number subjected to physical examination for malnutrition. Those undergoing physical checks amounted to around 150,000 per survey (about 1 per cent of the population in the designated areas, representing all ages and socio-economic groups).

This changed in February 1948 when not only was the scope of the surveys widened, but also their methodology was changed with a view to improving their usefulness. Although the population sample became smaller (around 42,000), it was regarded as more representative, distinguished between 'farmer' and 'non-farmer' categories, and examined all those providing dietary records for symptoms of malnutrition. The latter were listed as follows: anaemia, hyperkeratosis (thickening of the skin), xeropthalmia (dryness of the conjuctiva and cornea), glossitis (inflammation of the tongue), cheilosis (inflamed lips and cracking at the corners of the mouth), loss of knee jerk, oedema (swelling of the feet and legs due to excess fluid), chronic diarrhoea, bradycardia (slowing of the heart rate), 'bone malgrowth' in children aged six and under, delayed menstruation and impaired lactation (percentage of lactating women who had to supplement breast with bottle feeding or completely rely on the latter).[22]

Anaemia signalled iron deficiency, as did cheilosis and glossitis. More important in the case of cheilosis and glossitis was a lack of vitamin B2 (riboflavin).[23] Loss of knee jerk was often attributed to a deficit of vitamin B1 (thiamine), as were bradycardia, oedema and anaemia.[24] In the case of xeropthalmia and hyperkeratosis, vitamin A was deficient. Symptoms of delayed menstruation indicated under-nutrition or diets lacking in essential nutrients, as did problems with lactation among new mothers, who obviously needed to consume more calories and such essential nutrients as calcium and iron. Whereas before the war, most Japanese people could expect to consume reasonably balanced diets with adequate quantities of protein from fish or soya, this was not the case during the early years of Occupation.

From the beginning, the surveys made a clear distinction between urban and rural nutrition levels. By 1948 the data displayed in the Occupation's monthly summations and the PH&W's annual summaries distinguishes between three or four categories, namely Tokyo, the next 11 largest cities, sometimes 'other cities' as well, and 'rural areas' (defined as existing outside legally recognized cities with populations equal to or greater than 30,000). This approach served to highlight the food supply crisis in the cities, driving home the case for urgent food aid from the US.

The case was strengthened from January 1947, when the series of monthly summations started detailing diets of industrial workers – employees of Kosaka copper mine in Akita, railway workers in Tokyo and miners from a number of coal fields – with a view to illuminating the economic implications of the food crisis.[25] It is clear that right from the start of the nutrition studies the Occupation authorities adjusted their message according to the audience they were addressing. Domestically, the data was used for the most part to demonstrate satisfactory management of the food crisis. Internationally, it was presented in much more alarmist terms to those making decisions about food relief in Washington and those allies in the Far Eastern Commission complaining about the US's perceived generosity to Japan.

The contentious nature of the problem, the degree to which famine and associated disease threatened the Occupation's reform programme, caused the key governmental departments in Washington to send food missions to Japan to investigate claims of imminent crises in 1946 and 1947. Much of the discussion that took place between members of these missions and Occupation officials in Tokyo was coloured by the results of the nutrition surveys. It was clear from close scrutiny of the data that the spring and summer months were the time of most serious shortage, when stocks of indigenous staple crops harvested in the autumn became seriously depleted. Such was the urgency of the situation in March 1946 that Colonel Raymond Harrison, chairman of the special Japan food mission, decided to radio his final report to the Secretaries of Agriculture and State in Washington.[26] Harrison declared that a minimum of 200,000 tons of grain per month was required for April, May and June 1946 to avert 'serious food shortages in deficit areas'. Informing this judgement was the data produced by the nutrition surveys of December 1945 and February 1946, together with assumptions based on current stocks of indigenous food, the failure of the Japanese government to prevent hoarding and extensive black market activity, and Japan's pre-war food import requirements. Due to a dearth of fertilizer, serious typhoons and floods in the autumn of 1945, and negligible imports for the past year, there had been a 41.5 per cent reduction in the total amount of food available on a per capita basis compared with pre-war years. It was explained that the impact of this reduction would fall almost entirely on the urban population, resulting in 'a reduction in their caloric intake to starvation levels'. The radio ended with a statement that the final decision on allocation should be made immediately so as to relieve the Occupation of its present anxieties.[27]

Little more than a month later Japan was one of 25 countries visited by the Famine Emergency Committee, chaired by ex-president Herbert Hoover.[28] A briefing paper prepared by the NRS reiterated the imminence of a food crisis, contending that it would 'threaten to an alarming degree the success of the occupation by the Allied Powers'. Running to 73 pages, including 22 pages of graphs and charts, this document was primarily designed to highlight the danger of widespread starvation and associated disease and unrest should the required imports of food not be authorized.[29] Nutrition was analysed at length (Section III), together with related issues of indigenous food production (Section IV), food distribution and supply (Section V), food import needs (Section VI) and US Army stocks suitable for food relief purposes (Section VII). Noting the confusion that had arisen from poorly differentiated measures of caloric intake in countries threatened by famine, the discussion of Japanese dietary requirements began by distinguishing clearly between the consumption requirement, the food ration and the staple food ration.

The starting point for all of these, it was explained, was the 'basal metabolic rate', a scientific measure of the energy requirement of the human body at complete rest; that is to say, the minimum number of calories needed to sustain life. Saiki Tadasu had established this as 1,373 calories for Japanese men and 1,073 for women (average 1,223 calories), approximately five-sevenths of the rate for Westerners.[30] Allowing for the energy needed for work and daily life increased the average consumer's requirements to 1,800 calories. This was a figure much less than that required for workers in heavy industries like mining, but more than the minimum intake for non-workers, women and children. It was stated that this figure was a very conservative one, around 10 per cent less than that required for light work, and nowhere near the caloric equivalent of the ration. The latter, including staple and supplementary foods, was only 55 per cent of the food actually consumed in Tokyo in December 1945, the balance made up by black market produce, home gardens and gifts from relatives and friends. However, the nutrition survey of February 1946 registered a slight improvement, the proportion of food intake attributed to rations rising to 64 per cent. Given the preponderance of rice, other grains and potatoes in the Japanese diet, accounting for more than 80 per cent of the calories consumed, the 'staple food ration' was considered the most important yardstick for relief programmes.

As mentioned in Chapter 2, it was not until the final months of the war that the staple food ration was reduced by 10 per cent to 2.1 *go*, just 1,046 calories. It was clear to interested parties in GHQ SCAP, as well as such investigators as Harrison, that any further erosion of the staple food ration, which they considered inevitable in the absence of food imports, would have serious consequences. Noting the shipment of only 32,000 tons of food relief in April, despite Harrison's dire warnings, the briefing paper for Hoover cautioned that the 600,000 ton emergency programme would deliver only approximately 900 calories per day for non-self-suppliers for the critical five-month period, May through September 1946. Such a diet, it was argued, would cause 'acute mass starvation and civil disturbance' and would 'constitute a continuing threat to the safety of our occupation forces'.

The question then arises as to how this slide into famine and disorder was averted. Agitation for more fair distribution of scarce food supplies grew in the wake of the campaign for the general election of 10 April 1946, culminating in huge rallies on May Day, when 500,000 demonstrators congregated in front of the Imperial Palace. The scale of protest in Tokyo reflected the irregular distribution of rations and a consequent serious drop in caloric intake.[31] Indeed, it was in May 1946 that the food supply crisis in the capital reached its nadir. 'Food May Day' on 19 May served to dramatize the plight of those struggling to eke out an existence in the face of a dysfunctional rationing system.[32] The following day General MacArthur intervened decisively against this explosion of protest, publicly declaring that 'the physical violence which undisciplined elements are now beginning to practice will not be permitted to continue' as it represented 'a menace not only to orderly government but to the basic purpose and security of the Occupation itself'.[33] Although the Supreme Commander conjured up images of mob rule, the demonstrations were legitimate, largely peaceful acts of protest by hungry, disaffected Japanese. At the same time MacArthur assured Yoshida that the US would provide the necessary food aid to avert famine.[34] Still, it was not until July and August 1946 that imports began arriving in large quantities (330,000 tons),[35] enabling the release of 388,022 tons for staple food rations in the cities.[36] During September, the final month of the 1946 rice year, 114,360 tons of imported cereals/beans and 67,300 tons of canned foods were released for Japanese consumption. Nevertheless, the total amount of imported food released from April to October 1946 was only 687,266 tons.[37] This was a figure not much more than Harrison had defined as the bare minimum for just three months (600,000 tons) at the end of March 1946.

In order to gauge the impact of this shortfall on standards of public health we need to look closely at the results of the May, August and November 1946 nutrition surveys. According to the July issue of the monthly summations, food consumption in Tokyo dropped dangerously low in May – with around 700 calories provided by the ration and another 600 acquired principally from the black market (euphemistically described as the 'free market').[38] The public health volume of the official history states that total caloric intake in the capital dropped to 1,352 calories at this time.[39] This was effectively a starvation diet, hardly even reaching the basal metabolic rate. In such circumstances, the human body must start using its reserve of calories stored in tissue, an alarming prospect for those already lean from prolonged food deprivation. The food supply situation seems to have been less serious in the other 'large cities' surveyed (Nagoya, Osaka, Kure, Fukuoka, Sendai, Sapporo, Kanazawa, Matsuyama), where official rations generated around 1,100 calories; the average total intake increased to about 1,600 when other food sources, namely the black market, were included. In contrast to these cities, the rural areas of 18 prefectures managed to consume nearly 2,000 calories, including around 400 provided by official rations.

According to the nutrition survey of August 1946, the rural advantage remained, but the relative positions of Tokyo and the 'other cities' were reversed. The capital seems to have been the chief beneficiary of food imports, pushing the total intake to around 1,800 calories. Although food consumption in the eight cities averaged out at 1,567 calories, in four of them it fell to about 1,300 calories due to fitful distribution of rations. Again, this was dangerously low and in the absence of available indigenous crops could only be relieved by food aid from the US. Imports presumably provided vital relief until the autumn harvests of rice and sweet potatoes. These produced much more favourable data in the November 1946 nutrition survey, when Tokyo's residents were apparently consuming just over 2,000 calories, their counterparts in the other large cities just a little less, and those in the rural areas in excess of 2,250 calories.[40]

Not surprisingly, the data from the quarterly surveys relating to symptoms associated with nutritional deficiencies reflected these seasonal variations of food supply and caloric intakes per capita. In May 1946 nearly 10 per cent of the Tokyo sample suffered from anaemia, just under 8 per cent from cheilosis, 12 per cent exhibited loss of knee jerk, 4 per cent oedema, 3 per cent hyperkeratosis, just over 2 per cent chronic diarrhoea, 7 per cent bradycardia, and 19 per cent of women aged 17–45 experienced delayed menstruation. On the whole the figures for Nagoya, Osaka, Kure and Fukuoka roughly corresponded with those for Tokyo, although anaemia was much lower at 3 per cent and loss of knee jerk slightly so at just under 9 per cent. As might be expected given the greater availability of food in the countryside, fewer people from rural areas presented with symptoms associated with malnutrition in May 1946 than in Tokyo or the other cities. The only exception to this was cheilosis, which at just over 12 per cent was clearly more of a rural than an urban problem. The caloric advantage generally enjoyed by those in the countryside did not necessarily mean that they were receiving sufficient amounts of all nutrients.

Perhaps as a result of the seriousness of the nutritional crisis in the cities, the definition of 'underweight' was changed from 5 per cent below the 'standard weight' in February 1946 to 10 per cent below the norm in May.[41] Figures 5.1, 5.2 and 5.3 highlight a number of trends across age group and time period: the degree to which the situation deteriorated between May and August 1946, only to improve after the harvest of the rice crop in the autumn; the disproportionate

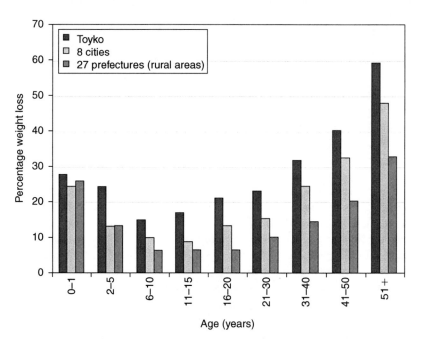

Figure 5.1 Weight loss by age group (%) May 1946.

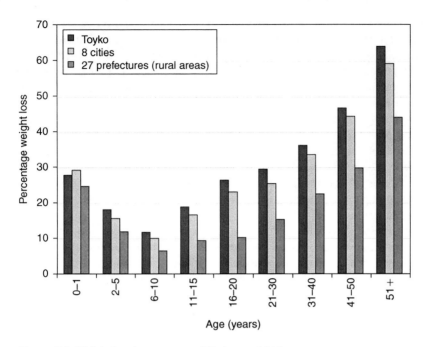

Figure 5.2 Weight loss by age group (%) August 1946.

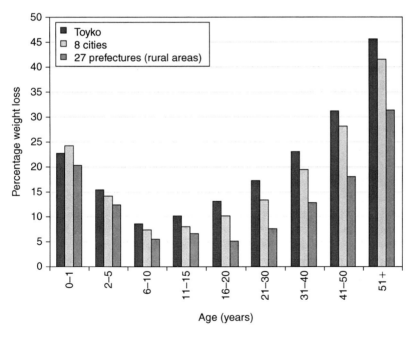

Figure 5.3 Weight loss by age group (%) November 1946 (source: data from nutrition surveys of May, August and November 1946 [PHW 02158]).

impact of food shortages on the very young and elderly; and the advantageous position enjoyed by rural communities compared with urban ones, particularly Tokyo. Only once – in May 1946 – did a rural category – babies (aged 0–1) – exceed an urban one, presumably due to inadequate supplies of milk. Otherwise percentages for those living in the countryside tended to be significantly lower than for urban residents.

More surprising evidence of inequitable distribution of available food supplies was provided by figures for those recorded as overweight (i.e. exceeding normal weights by more than 10 per cent): 15–20 per cent of these fell in the first age categories (0–20). The figure fell to around 10 per cent for the 31–40 and 41–50 age groups, and just 5 per cent for the rest.[42] Obviously, the wealthier the social group the greater their access to black market produce and presumably the more robust their health.

By the end of 1946 both the Japanese government and Occupation authorities were expressing anxiety again about the exhaustion of food supplies by the following spring and the consequent urgency of food relief from the US. The first nutrition survey of 1947 took place in February, by which time the number of calories being consumed was declining due to the steady depletion of food stocks from the previous autumn.[43] Medical checks of the survey population in Tokyo and the eight selected cities revealed that 22.3 per cent were suffering from one or more symptoms associated with nutritional deficiencies. This included a figure of 29.9 per cent for deficient lactation (among women with children up to six months old) in the capital and an even higher one of 31.4 per cent in the other cities. Interestingly, this problem was only slightly less marked in the rural areas (27.5 per cent), and the overall figure for those presenting with symptoms of malnutrition was actually higher than the cities (25.6 per cent). Again, this demonstrates that more calories did not necessarily equate with a proper balance of nutrients. For example, twice as many of those seen by doctors in the countryside suffered from cheilosis (13.3 per cent) than did their counterparts in the cities (5.75 per cent).[44]

These distinctions were acknowledged by the food and fertilizer mission sent from Washington in February 1947 to ascertain Japan's food requirements for the months ahead.[45] Again led by Colonel Raymond Harrison, the mission's report stated that the diet of farmers or 'self-suppliers' was quantitatively sufficient but qualitatively deficient and that of urban residents was inadequate in both senses.[46] While the report's authors 'found no evidence of acute malnutrition on a mass basis' in Japan, they nevertheless warned that 'overall health conditions are not good'. Acknowledging that timely imports of food from the US had prevented 'acute malnutrition' and mass starvation during July and August 1946, they interpreted the data of the nutrition surveys as indicating a state of 'chronic malnutrition' among various sections of the population. This was apparently caused by a shortage of protein, milk and fat products. Harrison and his colleagues (Captain Kittredge, Mr Tuck, Mr Koenig and Mr Whitman)[47] concurred with the view of Sams and others in the PH&W that even before the war, when sufficient calories were consumed, the 'nutritional content' of the average diet was 'not physiologically adequate'. The exigencies of war and defeat had only made matters worse. This was evidenced, the report maintained, by the results of health checks carried out as part of the nutrition surveys in 1946, which revealed that 30 per cent of the urban population and 27.5 per cent of those in the countryside showed clinical symptoms associated with malnutrition (these were slightly higher figures than those presented by the PH&W). Also discussed was the high death rate from tuberculosis – seven times that of the US and four times that of Germany – and statistics showing diminished stature. An average reduction in height of one inch and weight of 8.6 pounds since 1938–40 had affected 66 per cent of children under six years of age and 83 per cent of school children and adolescents 'suffering from chronic malnutrition'.

Although the autumn harvests of rice and sweet potatoes had generated large stocks of these staples, new pressures were created by the increase of the staple food ration from 2.1 *go* (1,042 calories) to 2.5 *go* (1,246 calories) in November 1946 and the rise in population of around four million due to repatriation. Harrison and Koenig called on the Japanese government to tighten its systems of collection and distribution so as to maximize the amount of food in official, rather than black market, channels. While they encouraged SCAP to take a stronger stance on this, they did not doubt the existence of a shortfall and the urgent need to bridge it by importing 1,100,000 tons of cereals and other foodstuffs by 30 June 1947. This was Japan's share of a proposed allocation for the Far East, which also included South Korea and the Ryukyu Islands, of 1,473,000 tons of cereals and 331,000 tons of other foodstuffs such as dry skim milk, pulses and fats and oils.[48]

The designation of these particular kinds of food represented an effort to move the debate on from emergency relief diets, defined by the staple food ration and imports of cereals, to a more sophisticated, targeted approach. This aimed to improve the dietary balance and health of the Japanese people. Particularly important were extra rations for industrial workers, on whose shoulders the main responsibility for economic rehabilitation rested, and supplementary feeding programmes for such vulnerable groups as infants and school children. An interest in the phenomenon of 'chronic malnutrition' now dominated discussions of diet rather than its 'acute' counterpart. Such language reflected a longer-term prospect. There was now a commitment to bringing about a more equal distribution of indigenous food supplies and to move towards a more stable inflow of food relief so as to avoid caloric intake levels dropping to levels of bare subsistence (as had occurred in May and August 1946). As caloric intakes stabilized, so the Occupation could pay more attention to the balance of nutrients in the Japanese diet.

Such an approach would have been recommended also by the divergent trends of weight loss on the one hand and conditions associated with nutritional deficiency on the other, evident by the summer of 1948. While the former generally exhibited a downward trend, presumably reflecting higher average caloric intakes, the number recorded as presenting with symptoms of malnutrition seemed more stubbornly entrenched. It is stated, for example, in the July 1948 issue of the monthly summations that although the May 1948 nutrition survey had revealed a decline in the proportions of those classified as underweight, the percentage of people exhibiting symptoms of nutritional disorders in Tokyo had increased for all conditions except glossitis, cheilosis and impaired lactation. As regards the latter, this was a major problem in the other 11 cities surveyed and throughout the rural areas of the 46 prefectures where it affected 27.8 per cent and 26.4 per cent of nursing mothers, respectively.[49]

Against a backcloth of general scarcity, seasonal availability and balance between the various food groups largely explain the fluctuations in the incidence of nutritional deficiency from one survey to another. Hence the PH&W warned against too strong an emphasis on supplies of staple food as the key factor in nutritional disorders, when an increase of symptoms might be equally due to a lack of 'supplemental foods, including vegetables, during the winter months'.[50] The monthly summation for October 1947 observed, for example, that an important factor influencing the nutritional status of the Japanese people from June to August was 'seasonal availability of leafy vegetables which tended to improve the vitamin and mineral content of the diet'.[51] This recognition of the importance of micronutrients alongside the major measures and elements of dietary intake (calories, carbohydrates, protein, fats and oils) is evident from the changing data sets in the monthly summations. For example, indicators of average daily per capita consumption of minerals (calcium, iron and phosphorus) and vitamins (A, B1, B2, B3, C) first appear in graph form in the monthly summary for October 1947. This data is presented in a detailed table from February 1948, accompanied by graphs depicting average daily consumption of vegetable proteins, animal proteins, fats and carbohydrates in Tokyo, other cities and rural areas.[52] Also depicted is average daily food consumption, detailing grams per capita per day of the various foods (rice; other grains; sweet potatoes; other potatoes; leafy, green and yellow vegetables; other vegetables and fruits; fish products; meat and dairy products; legumes; other foods). These graphs provide a visual representation of both patterns of seasonal availability of various foods from May 1946 to May 1948 and the huge dependence of Japanese on carbohydrates and vegetable proteins at the expense of animal proteins and fats. Such dietary imbalance is clearly demonstrated in Figure 5.4. Also evident from the graph is the advantage enjoyed by rural residents in terms of consumption of grains, although their intake of animal protein was only about half that of urban residents.

It was the dearth of animal protein that, for Sams, came to epitomize Japan's 'faulty nutritional patterns' and their adverse effects on standards of public health. While the chief of the PH&W seems to have advocated a fundamental reconfiguration of the Japanese diet, others merely sought a resumption of dietary trends interrupted by the demands of war and defeat. What seems to have united all parties, Japanese and American alike, was a determination to boost animal protein intake among Japanese so as to strengthen resistance to chronic infectious diseases. The challenge for them all, however, was bringing this about at a time when grain was too scarce to feed to livestock and Japan's fishing grounds were much diminished compared to her pre-war range.

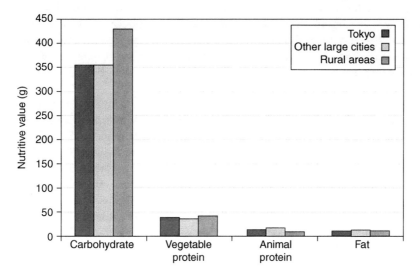

Figure 5.4 Nutritive value of food (grams) consumed per capita daily, 1947.

Promoting animal protein

As evidenced by nutrition surveys between May 1946 and May 1948, the average daily consumption of meat and dairy products was negligible and fairly flat. Recovery from a drop in the average intake of fish products, albeit from a much higher base level, likewise seems to have been at best gradual. This final section explores the efforts made to increase availability of key sources of animal protein. It evaluates the extent to which they met with success by the end of the Occupation, and their impact on patterns of nutrition and, so far as can be estimated, the incidence of chronic diseases and conditions associated with malnutrition. Particularly significant in this regard was the emphasis placed on improving the diets of primary-school children through the school lunch programme. Finally, this section briefly considers the legacy of the Occupation's nutritional reforms for post-war dietary patterns in Japan.

There was a consensus in US and Japanese circles that increasing supplies of fish, meat, eggs and dairy products would improve nutritional standards by rebalancing the Japanese diet away from its overdependence on carbohydrates and vegetable protein and towards greater consumption of animal protein, fats and oils. Fat consumption in particular was considered 'remarkable by its lowness' – even before the war it was 'far below amounts considered essential in Western countries'.[53] More critical, however, against a backcloth of low caloric intake was the deficiency in protein-rich foods. Indeed, the report of the food and fertilizer mission of 1947 highlighted the lack of 'body-building proteins', noting that Japanese consumed 'only one third of the animal protein necessary for maintenance of good health'. In the view of the PH&W, the report added, this was a major factor in their under-nourishment and low resistance to all diseases, particularly such chronic diseases as tuberculosis.[54] Moreover, the vitamins (A, B1, B2 and B3) and minerals (calcium, phosphorus and iron) found in meat, fish, eggs and dairy products would enhance Japanese diets and reduce the incidence of conditions associated with nutritional deficiency specified by the quarterly surveys.

Fish was the obvious starting point for boosting intake of animal protein. It was the nearest equivalent to meat and dairy products in Western countries, and Japan had only recently been 'the foremost fishing country in the world', catching five million and consuming three million metric tons of fish in 1939. While the Harrison report of 1947 commended the NRS for the progress made in re-establishing the industry and in bringing the annual fish catch up to around three million tons, it argued that in the absence of imports of soybeans (historically an important source of complete protein) 'the urgency of increasing still further the production of fish and whale meats cannot be overemphasized'. Unfortunately, however, it was difficult to make full use of fish catches when there was a shortage of preservatives, ice, storage and canning facilities and little likelihood of rapid transport to consumption centres far from the coast. As a result, distribution of fish was almost entirely localized, with around 50 per cent of supply diverted into black market channels.

At a meeting of the members of the food and fertilizer mission with representatives of the Japanese government on 11 February 1947, Colonel Harrison called for 'the stamping out' of the black market in fish, and an increase in catches. The latter apparently was facilitated by MacArthur's 'courageous' efforts to extend the fishing areas.[55] The Supreme Commander had to face down opposition from members of the Far Eastern Commission, particularly Australia, New Zealand, Britain and the Soviet Union, to both the expansion of Japan's fishing range to include rich trawling grounds to the east and south,[56] and the dispatch of 'emergency' factory whaling expeditions to the Antarctic. These were justified with reference to 'humanitarian principles of augmenting supply of protein foods in Japan (as well as world supply of fats and oils)'.[57] In defence of its support for Japanese whaling against objections from Norway, the US Department of State contended that the 1946–47 expedition generated the equivalent of one-third of the total Japanese meat consumption from indigenous farm sources in 1946. This was all the more important, it insisted, in the absence of Japan's principal source of protein in the past – Manchurian soybeans.[58] The official history of the Occupation viewed these initiatives as chiefly responsible for the slight but steady rise in the daily consumption of animal protein between 1947 and 1952. This increased from an average per capita figure of 11 grams (7 in rural areas and 14 in the cities) to 14.3 in 1949, 17.1 in 1950, 19 in 1951 and 22 in 1952.[59]

Some contribution to these increases from meat, dairy products and eggs might be expected, given the Occupation's avowed commitment to developing livestock farming in Japan. However, the data presented in Figure 5.4 suggests that these were of negligible value. While fish and shellfish accounted for 61 grams of daily per capita intake of nutrients in 1950, meat, eggs and milk provided just 8.4, 5.6 and 6.8 grams, respectively (up from 5.4, 3.2 and 4.1 grams in 1949).[60] As was noted in Chapter 2, Saiki Tadasu, the father of Japanese nutrition, was no less determined than the members of the PH&W to promote a well-balanced diet with greater proportions of animal protein and fat. However, he found this difficult to achieve in a country where arable land was so scarce (just 15 per cent of the total area) and where rice cultivation demanded much of farmers. Despite these impediments, there was a fairly steady increase in the number of cattle, pigs, sheep and goats through the 1920s and 1930s. There were 195,642 sheep in 1940, compared with 9,353 in 1921, and the respective figures for goats were 182,465 and 40,062. The number of pigs rose less sharply from 420,132 in 1921 to 669,037 in 1940, and the cattle population went from 1,397,801 to 2,034,257 in the same period. The production of milk more than quadrupled between 1921 and 1940 (from 81,710 to 369,000 kilolitres).[61] Likewise, the number of eggs produced more than trebled between 1916 and 1932, after which it remained fairly constant until 1940, falling swiftly thereafter.[62] Interestingly, many of the animal populations cited above continued to grow during the war years, particularly goats, but most fell away sharply in 1945 or 1946 due to critical shortages of livestock feed. In response, the Occupation turned to animals existing largely on forage.

In his study of the lifestyle improvement movement in rural Japan from the mid-1920s to the mid-1960s, Simon Partner highlights the Occupation's promotion of the goat as the ideal solution to Japan's problems. Goats were undemanding in terms of food, their milk and cheese represented invaluable sources of protein, and their care could be entrusted largely to women and children. The NRS brought in a goat enthusiast, Corl A. Leach, to find ways of convincing Japanese farmers of the merits of rearing goats. These efforts at least partially explain the steep rise in the goat population from 221,725 in 1946 (representing a drop of some 30,000 from the previous year) to 418,351 in 1950. Just as important, however, was the established trend of goat ownership from the 1920s until the end of the war, which naturally resumed as soon as conditions permitted.[63] While this was an impressive advance, the number of goats (and other livestock) was still very low relative to a population of more than 80 million. Although greater consumption of goat meat and dairy products can only have been beneficial for nutritional balance, it cannot have had more than a very marginal effect on average intake of animal protein, particularly in view of apparent reluctance on the part of many Japanese to drink goat's milk.[64]

In any case, the report of the food and fertilizer mission of 1947 found no room for optimism. It declared that 'many segments of the population are not receiving even the inadequate ration schedule and living at definitely deficient nutritional level'. Some indication of the groups it had it mind was provided by the statement that there was an immediate need to increase rations of animal and vegetable proteins, fats and oils for growing children, industrial workers and the sick.[65] Arguably this was an acknowledgement of the immense scale of the task the Occupation had set itself in trying to tackle the problem of 'chronic malnutrition'. The best approach, therefore, was to identify priorities, to target specific groups so as to improve the likelihood of making measurable advances on the nutritional front.

With these considerations in mind, there is no doubt that the flagship of the protein promotion campaign was the school lunch programme, an initiative that resonated with tremendous symbolic importance. Here was the Occupation investing in Japan's future, in improving the nutrition and health of Japanese school children through supplementary feeding programmes. Its endeavours to rebalance the diets of the young and vulnerable so as to safeguard them against disease undoubtedly burnished the Occupation's humanitarian, compassionate credentials. Sams understood this, and so viewed the import of powdered skim milk that lay at the heart of the programme as not only essential to achieving its nutritional purpose, but also as a powerful weapon in the Cold War, recommending the US as a natural ally of Japan.

So strong were these convictions that there was arguably a tendency to overstate the significance of the whole project. Even its preferred designation – 'school lunch programme' – was something of a misnomer, given that its chief purpose was to provide supplementary food and not a main meal.[66] Moreover, it seems to have firmly established itself in Japan, largely because it represented a reinstatement of earlier practice. The key pre-war development occurred in 1932 when privately supported school lunches for the needy, dating back to the 1880s, gave way to state involvement in subsidizing them. By the mid-1930s there was a shift from the original emphasis on feeding the children of poor families to a more broadly conceived, explicitly nutritional approach. This arose from the authorities' awareness of poor dietary standards among the young.[67]

Given that the Japanese government had long been 'nutrition conscious', boasting highly trained nutritionists and volumes of technical data, it was not surprising that there was much enthusiasm among all concerned for 'reinstating the school lunch program'.[68] Interestingly, those in the PH&W, commonly viewed as the architects of its success, had very little experience of school feeding programmes. Indeed, this lack of knowledge caused them to send one of their number, Miss O'Donnell, on a tour of the US during the spring of 1950 to study school lunch operation as it occurs there.[69] Some years earlier, Nathan Koenig, a member of the food and fertilizer mission, had encouraged Sams to follow the example of the US Department of Agriculture, which was 'using dry skim milk in its school lunch program in some of the southern states with good results'.[70] However, the PH&W viewed the scheme as originating chiefly from Maurice Pate of the Famine Emergency Committee, who praised the success of England's school lunch programme.[71] Thus, it was to this committee, presided over by Hoover, that one Japanese official attributed the 'reopening of the school lunch program'.[72]

Regardless of the genesis of the idea, Sams drove it forward with typical determination and resolve. He convened a conference on the subject in October 1946, at which he brought together all the interested parties in the Japanese government, together with their American counterparts. While he acknowledged that 'the general framework was already established', Sams insisted that swift planning and execution of a universal programme was necessary to avoid 'an increase in incidence of chronic diseases including tuberculosis, rickets and other diseases that show up in growing children after a protracted period of inadequate feeding'. Not surprisingly, the conference concluded with unanimous agreement that 'the school lunch program was important and must be initiated'.[73] Such enthusiasm, however, could not compensate for inadequate resources. In November 1946 Sams cautioned that only 10 per cent of the 14,000 tons of protein needed was available.[74]

It seems that somehow the project got off the ground the following month, utilizing 5,000 tons of canned meat from wartime military stockpiles, powdered milk and other foods donated by the US organization LARA (Licensed Agencies for Relief in Asia), together with US Army foodstuffs surplus to requirements.[75] On the first anniversary of the programme's inauguration, Sams praised the achievements of all those involved, and claimed that 'children are much better today in physique than a year ago'. This, he claimed, was evidenced by 'our nutritional surveys', but the scope of these and their precise findings were not disclosed. As there are no records of any surveys of child nutrition conducted by the PH&W, presumably Sams was alluding to data from the quarterly nutritional surveys conducted by the Welfare Ministry. Although the school lunch programme had quickly expanded to cover four million school children and had benefited from a LARA contribution of 300 tons of powdered skim milk, Sams was impatient for more progress. He urged that it be enhanced (600-calorie meals every day of the school week rather than 180-calorie ones every other day) and expanded to include 18 million children. In response to these grand ambitions, Bruce Johnston of ESS (Economic and Scientific Section) adopted a rather pessimistic line, warning that 'continued shortages' constrained what could be achieved.[76]

Johnston was right to be more cautious about the programme's growth potential. At a meeting with colleagues in the PH&W and ESS on 10 June 1948 Sams suggested that the present number of school children involved was insufficient at 4,775,000 and would need to increase to 12 million by 1 July 1949. Moreover, he drew attention to a report on child nutrition issued by the United Nations International Children's Emergency Fund (UNICEF), noting that the Occupation was providing only half of the recommended dose of reconstructive skim milk.[77] By July 1949 the chief of the PH&W was expressing frustration at the 'constant struggle' necessary to secure supplies of powdered skim milk. At the same time he called on Japanese officials involved to 'get the school lunch program out of the present unsatisfactory state in which it is found'.[78] His criticisms were directed at poor management and coordination, deliveries to schools without adequate facilities and overpricing of the meals (they were to be set at 'the lowest possible price' for school children).[79] Clearly, some of the anger directed at Japanese officials reflected Sams' disappointment at the failure of the scheme to meet his expectations. For example, he cannot have enjoyed reading a review of the programme by Kinki Military Government region, which admitted in early 1949 that 'the majority of the children receive 105 to 180 calories only' when 'the goal is 600 calories a day for each child'.[80] Moreover, the programme's expansion was much slower than he had hoped, benefiting just over six million school children in May 1950. In view of 'the limited quantity of imports', the PH&W and ESS advised a gradual increase in uptake to eight million or about 50 per cent of those in the first nine compulsory school years by 1 July 1951.[81]

By this time UNICEF was assisting the Occupation with the provision of dried skim milk for Japanese children. Its involvement dated from July 1949, when the school lunch programme was seriously threatened by a suspension of imports.[82] Due to Europe receiving all available supplies of dry skim milk for much of 1949, a bean paste soup (presumably miso soup) of some 90 calories was substituted three times per week. The supply crisis only lifted in September 1949 when the programme received, in addition to skim milk, regular allocations of edible oils, *miso*, *shōyu*, sugar and salt, canned foods released by the 8th Army Quartermaster, and indigenous fish and vegetables.[83] Notwithstanding the prominence accorded powdered milk as a key source of complete protein and calcium, it is important to realize that the lunch programme also depended on indigenous supplies of soy sauce, *miso*, salt and sugar, as well as locally procured fresh vegetables, fresh and dried fish, meats, grains, etc. In May 1950 it was disclosed that other imports and indigenous foods under consideration for the supplementary feeding of school children were brown rice equivalents and soya beans.[84] When Mr Nakamura of the Education Ministry had informed Nelson Neff of the PH&W on 12 October 1948 that supplies of skim milk and canned meats for the school lunch programme would be exhausted by 1 November, he had nevertheless assured him that it could still be sustained, albeit on a limited basis, with indigenous stocks of 'miso, shoyu, green vegetables, oil, sugar, some fish, fresh and dried'.[85] In March of the previous year (1947), Nakamura had allocated '30 grams of whale meat and fats per day for a 7 to 10 day period' to 'all children in all schools now participating in the school lunch program'.[86]

Another consideration recommending more familiar foods may have been apparent reluctance among some Japanese school children to consume dried skim milk and other imported products. The review of the lunch programme by Kinki Military Government region, for example, remarked that tomato juice, powdered milk and soup mix had been rejected as distasteful by the children. Reminiscing about his childhood experiences during the Occupation, Nishi Toshio recalls receiving extra rations of skim milk, because most of his friends recoiled at the thought of drinking it.[87] Likewise, in a short article on the history of school meals in Japan, Ehara Ayako maintains that the 'smell and taste of powdered milk ... were disliked – so much so that the gutters were said to turn white each day after lunch hour as left-over milk was poured down the drains'. Nevertheless, as she points out, school children continued to receive it until the late 1960s, when real milk was provided in its stead.[88] So, it can be assumed that despite evidence of resistance, plenty of children during the Occupation benefited from the calcium and protein in powdered milk. This is confirmed by an editorial in the *Mainichi Shimbun* on 19 September 1951 that reported the results of a poll of 2,000 parents in 25 cities during the period May to June 1951. This revealed that only 19 per cent of parents sampled stated that their children did not appreciate school lunches, although precisely what they disliked about them was not disclosed. Indeed, the same editorial sought to safeguard the future of the school lunch programme. It stated that eight million (70 per cent) of Japanese school children were now eating healthier lunches. Four million children of 3,707 schools in 248 cities throughout the country received full meals of at least 600 calories and 25 grams of protein. About the same number received supplementary food (180 calories, 15 grams of protein). Commenting on the popularity of these arrangements, the editorial stated that its poll of parents showed that 78 per cent were in favour of the school lunch programme continuing at an average cost of ¥135 per month.

Clearly, there was much appreciation on the part of Japanese parents for the kindness and compassion shown towards their children by the Occupation and American citizens more generally (through organizations like LARA). It would be churlish not to recognize the genuine concern and generosity signalled by the US commitment to supply powdered skim milk and other products rich in animal protein. However, the degree to which the programme rested on sturdy Japanese foundations, the problems with supply of its key commodities, its consequent dependence at times on indigenous supplies, and the rather slow expansion of the programme all suggest that its significance may have been overstated. Somehow, its symbolism mattered more than its actual reach and impact.

Evaluating the nutritional effects of the school lunch programme, particularly its mainstay, the dried skim milk, is difficult. Statistics on children's average heights and weights show an improvement towards the end of the Occupation, but this may reflect higher caloric intake as well as better dietary balance. For the most part, these statistics did not distinguish between those receiving supplementary lunches and skim milk and those existing on traditional fare. Some excitement, therefore, greeted a study conducted in Sendai, which 'proves again the value and importance of milk in the diet of the growing child', although it was acknowledged that 'a complete study has not [yet] been made of all prefectures and schools' to determine the value of the school lunches.[89] The Sendai study conducted by Kondō Masaji of Tohoku University was based on measurements of height and weight of school children stretching back to 1934, and noted impressive, record gains in 1948. These were confidently attributed 'not to the improved food condition as a whole, but chiefly to the effect of the school lunch program'. Placing particular emphasis on skim milk as the key to its success, he contended that it would not be long before children's physiques returned to pre-war norms.[90] More guardedly, a pamphlet entitled 'Thanks to UNICEF', produced in 1950 by the Education Ministry, declared that children's physiques had 'improved a little' and for this progress gratitude was owed the Allied powers, but the situation was 'far from reaching the favourable situation of 1935–38'.[91]

The original purpose of the school lunch programme was to improve standards of physical health among children, increasing their resistance to disease. Again, it is very difficult to measure any improvement in health consequent on higher intake of calcium, animal protein and vitamins due to the complex relationship between diet and disease and the variety of variables influencing disease morbidity. The limited evidence for height and weight gains, however, is suggestive of more robust constitutions. A brief review of tuberculosis incidence, which does not distinguish between particular age groups, shows a rising rate of morbidity during the final years of the Occupation.[92] However, rather than reflecting nutritional problems, this was more likely due to better surveillance/ reporting and greater willingness of suspect cases to come forward for diagnosis due to therapeutic breakthroughs. In terms of diseases directly relating to nutrition, no conditions associated with particular dietary deficiencies among children stand out from the statistics.

As regards the more fundamental rationale for the school lunch programme, there is little evidence to suggest that it succeeded in 'instilling into the coming generation the habit of eating and liking the kinds of food previously neglected which would correct the unbalanced character of the traditional Japanese diet'.[93] This, of course, was one of Sams' key motivations for imports of powdered milk. While Ehara contends that the school lunch programme had 'a profound impact on the eating habits of Japanese children and led to a revolutionary westernization of household meals', her argument pays too little attention to dietary changes during the interwar period. These reflected support among Japanese nutritionists and government officials for a rebalancing of the diet away from grains towards more meat and dairy products. Imports of American flour have likewise been associated with the 'popularization of bread in Japan', but, as Cwiertka points out, 'American initiatives sustained a tendency that had become increasingly pronounced since the late 1930s'.[94] In any case, this interested Sams much less than the negligible consumption of such key staples of the American diet as eggs, meat and dairy products. Indeed, he declared himself 'much perturbed' when a 'so-called wheat mission' to Japan reported to the Department of Army that 'medical and nutritional experts found the Japanese diet to be lacking in essential vitamins and minerals, some of which are present in whole grains'. Sams retorted that this was 'a deliberate distortion of the information given to the mission ... that the basic deficiency found in the Japanese diet was animal protein and calcium, neither of which can be normally or sufficiently supplied by wheat'.[95]

The entrenched nature of Japan's nutritional patterns is demonstrated by an article on the subject published by a group of Japanese and American nutritionists some 16 years after the end of the Occupation. Their research was justified by the unique opportunity presented by Japan 'to study the relationships of growth and chronic degenerative diseases to a diet poor in fat and rich in vegetable protein and ... carbohydrate'. The article informed readers that 'nutritional science has long been active in Japan', referring to the joint discovery of vitamin B1 by Suzuki Umetarō and Casimir Funk in 1911. Its chief focus, however, was the 1963 nutrition survey, which followed the same quarterly pattern as those during the Occupation. Although the authors described the Japanese diet in familiar terms as disproportionately dependent on carbohydrates, low in fat and taking its protein largely from vegetable sources, they acknowledged gradual changes in line with the Occupation's aims. Most notable was a slight (3.7 per cent) increase in protein during the period 1950–63 to 70.6 g/person/day, with animal sources rising at the expense of vegetable ones. They reported that while consumption of fish remained fairly constant at about 75 g/day (5–6 g of protein), that of meat, eggs and milk had increased significantly. As for fat, while this had supplied just 7.7 per cent of total calories in 1950, it now accounted for 12.6 per cent. Reflecting these changes in dietary balance, the percentage of calories acquired from carbohydrate had fallen from 80 per cent in 1950 to 73 per cent in 1963.[96]

As regards their appraisal of diet and disease, the article's authors cautioned that 'the present role of nutritional disease in the public health of Japan is complex'. They highlighted the low profile of many nutritional diseases, and the difficulty of detecting subtle nutritional deficits, particularly when confined to 'limited segments of the population'. Similar difficulties marred the Occupation's effort to detect and tackle nutritional disorders in Japan. The figures from the nutrition surveys on the percentage of those presenting with symptoms associated with dietary deficiency registered very slight fluctuations over time, invariably in line with seasonal availability of foods or access to imports. Also, interesting and revealing trends relating to region and social group were presumably lost in the process of averaging out the survey results. There was more food to eat by the end of the Occupation, as is shown by higher average caloric intakes, but as regards dietary balance, there was only marginal change during the period. Just as the authors of the 1968 article argue that the three leading causes of death in Japan were influenced by diet but admit that little was known about the 'exact manner' of that influence,[97] so too can only suggestive comments be made about any connection during the Occupation between slight increases in animal protein intake and less susceptibility to chronic diseases like tuberculosis (for which there are no national statistics on morbidity until 1947).

Conclusion

Although the precise interactions between diet and disease were obscure, enough was known about nutrition and health for the PH&W to accord dietary reform a high priority. As Richard Leiby puts it in relation to the American zone of control in Occupied Germany, 'nutrition is actually the quintessential concern of preventive medicine. Good nutrition is a prerequisite of good health.'[98] This was clearly understood not only by Sams and his colleagues, but also by their counterparts in the Japanese government, who variously associated improvements in nutrition with higher standards of public health, more effective education and greater economic vigour and national strength. Sams viewed the Japanese as chronically disadvantaged by their predominantly vegetarian diet, and strongly associated the Occupation's commitment to democratization with improved diets and physiques, with introducing the Japanese to a diet richer in animal protein, like that of the US.

Nevertheless, confronted with the insurmountable obstacle of a livestock industry that was of minor importance in relation to crop production, Sams switched his attention to the next generation, to correcting 'faulty nutritional patterns' by changing the tastes and diets of Japanese school children. For all the reasons explained above, this was a mixed success, undoubtedly improving the health of those children who consumed the powdered milk on offer, but doing little to shift diets away from established patterns as was desired. While at times susceptible to Sams' high-blown rhetoric about transforming nutrition, the report of the food and fertilizer mission also characterized the Occupation's mission more realistically as re-establishing the pre-war dietary pattern that had been distorted by war and defeat.[99] Bruce Johnston of the ESS, who regarded the inter-war diet as adequate and moving in the right direction in terms of dietary balance, would perhaps have agreed with this approach.

These considerations of nutritional balance, particularly the lack of animal protein in the Japanese diet, pale into insignificance when compared with the food emergency that confronted the Occupation during the periods of serious depletion of stocks in the spring and summer of 1946 and 1947. Despite evidence of large-scale black marketing, particularly in fresh fish, and striking inequalities in access to food, there is no doubt that the timely import of cereals prevented hunger from escalating into starvation in the cities. The PH&W was keenly aware of the need to make a persuasive case for food aid to their superiors in Washington, and were also sensitive to the political implications of any steep rise in nutritional or chronic diseases. It scrutinized the data from the quarterly nutritional surveys, mining it for useful figures to support its arguments for urgent food imports on the one hand and increasingly for particular foodstuffs to help disadvantaged groups on the other. The meticulous presentation of survey results in the monthly summations and annual reports of the PH&W are a testament to the Occupation's determination to gauge nutrition in both quantitative and qualitative terms. While average caloric intakes increased as the Occupation progressed, qualitative imbalances proved more impervious to change. Rather like such chronic infectious diseases as dysentery and tuberculosis, 'chronic malnutrition' reflected a complex of circumstances that could not be significantly altered by a six-year military occupation.

6   Chronic infectious diseases

This chapter explores the PH&W's endeavours to reduce the incidence of tuberculosis and venereal disease, both of which exercised Sams and his colleagues as serious impediments to the improvement of standards of public health in Japan. Of course tuberculosis, as the leading cause of mortality among Japanese until 1950, was a higher priority than venereal disease. However, the latter's potential for undermining Allied military efficiency caused it to be at the forefront of American concerns from the beginning of the Occupation. There were effectively two policies for venereal disease control running in parallel – one reflecting a determination to protect the health of US servicemen who consorted with Japanese prostitutes; another seeking to ensure that venereal disease clinics did not just focus their energies on prostitutes, but adopted a much wider social perspective of the problem. While there was recognition on the part of Sams and his colleagues of an established, appropriate set of policies for combating tuberculosis, they did not hesitate to highlight the shortcomings they perceived in past policies towards venereal disease. Most notable among these were failure properly to diagnose the diseases and an apparent reluctance to control them by contact tracing and efficient treatment.

Policies towards both tuberculosis and venereal disease did not emerge clearly until some years into the Occupation, chiefly because such acute infectious diseases as smallpox, typhus and cholera represented more urgent threats to public health and the Occupation's viability than these more entrenched problems. Moreover, Sams and his colleagues were fully aware of the degree to which the high incidence of these diseases reflected prevailing social conditions, and so understood that progress against them would be slow and fitful. A degree of humility in relation to tuberculosis, for example, is evident from Sams' statement to the ACJ in 1947 that 'We have made a beginning and I think our program is satisfactory.... We hope within the next five years to make an impression by this program'. These were sober claims and low expectations indeed for a man who never hesitated to propagandize on behalf of the Occupation, particularly before an international forum such as the ACJ. It was not until some months after this meeting that the Health Centre Law was promulgated on 5 September 1947. This was followed by the Preventive Vaccination Law of 30 June 1948 and the Venereal Disease Prevention Law of 15 July 1948. All three signalled the joint commitment of the PH&W and the Welfare Ministry to commit more energy and resources to the control of tuberculosis and venereal disease. They expressed the need for wider and fuller public engagement with chronic infectious diseases, and the health centres were represented as key agents of education, diagnosis, treatment and control.

This chapter analyses the challenges posed by tuberculosis and venereal disease during the Occupation. It devotes a section to each one, highlighting the obstacles that frustrated effective measures in the field. Particularly significant in the case of tuberculosis was what Sams referred to as the Japanese public's tendency to view it as 'a shameful disease to be concealed'.[1] The degree to which members of the PH&W relied on existing Japanese agencies, expertise and commitment vis-à-vis these chronic diseases is examined, as are Sams' habitual claims of American-inspired progress against them. Central to this debate are the *hokenjo* or health centres, the extent to which their original purpose, functions and effectiveness were altered by PH&W's initiatives. By such measures as 'mass testing' (with tuberculin, X-rays, blood tests), immunization with BCG, diagnostic work in laboratories, 'case holding', contact tracing and treatment of those with active disease, the staff of the health centres worked to gauge the scale of the problems they faced and to bring them under control. Although the *hokenjo* were redefined as public health agencies that served local communities, their development and reach were undoubtedly limited by prevailing conditions, causing H. E. Wildes in 1953 to posit their failure to render 'full service'. This, Wildes contended, was chiefly due to a lack of resources – an inadequate supply of trained technical and professional personnel prevented 'complete examination of all suspected tubercular or venereal cases'.[2] Rather than attributing the progress made against tuberculosis and venereal disease to the efforts of the PH&W or the personnel of *hokenjo*, it is argued here that it was advances in chemoprophylaxis in the form of penicillin and streptomycin that were crucial. These slowed the spread of venereal disease and encouraged tuberculosis patients to seek treatment by fundamentally changing attitudes towards the disease.

The challenge of tuberculosis

As discussed at length in Chapter 2, tuberculosis was a disease that lurked in the background of Japanese social life, despite very high rates of recorded mortality and suspected levels of morbidity many times greater. In the absence of tuberculin testing across all age groups, it was very difficult to estimate the extent of infection across the population. Moreover, infection or latent disease was not the same as active or clinical cases, which could be detected by means of X-rays, sputum tests and blood sedimentation checks. Finding and isolating those with active tuberculosis, who exhibited symptoms and could spread the infection, was the key to controlling the disease. Those shown by the tuberculin test to harbour the bacilli but found not to have active disease might have some immunity but could also develop clinical symptoms, so putting others at risk. It would be prudent, therefore, to monitor these cases. Tuberculosis represented a tremendous challenge not just medically, but also socially. Its symptoms were slow to develop, its aetiology was complex and contested, and such was the stigma attached to it that families sought to hide cases from others. It seems too that doctors connived in this process of concealment, so hindering the efforts of central government to establish the extent of the problem and to limit its spread. Control was best achieved by removing those who were infected to sanatoria, where they could be isolated from their families and neighbourhoods and subjected to more healthy regimens and courses of treatment.

Interestingly, there was little disagreement between the PH&W and their counterparts in the Welfare Ministry about how to confront the tuberculosis menace. Indeed, the policy promoted by Sams and his colleagues was one of resuming the anti-tuberculosis campaign established during the war years. This had been a combination of prevention and containment – tuberculin testing and BCG immunization on the one hand and hospitalization of infectious cases on the other. Both of these endeavours had been severely disrupted by war and defeat. Perhaps most interestingly, Sams' decision to endorse the use of BCG did not reflect the medical consensus in the US. In his memoir, the chief of the PH&W criticizes the resistance of the American medical establishment to the BCG vaccine, explaining it with reference to trials in Europe that caused some children to contract tuberculosis. Indeed, he recalls 'the tremendous reaction among the medical profession in the US during my medical student days against the use of BCG'.[3] In contrast, the Danes and the Japanese persevered with their research endeavours, viewing the vaccine as worth expending time and effort on developing. Some years after the end of the Occupation, Sams discussed the research conducted by the Japanese in a lengthy paper on 'mass vaccination under postwar conditions in Japan', presumably aimed at convincing a sceptical US medical establishment of the merits of BCG.[4] He referred to animal experiments undertaken to study the virulence of the vaccine and to confirm its generation of antibodies. These were followed by a series of controlled inoculation experiments carried out throughout Japan for a ten-year period up to 1943, involving a variety of subjects from school pupils to factory workers and nurses. Following extensive analysis of the results of these trials, a committee of the Japanese National Research Council decided in 1943 that BCG was safe and effective, thus clearing the way for mass immunizations in 1944.

Confronted with social conditions that might lead to the tuberculosis epidemic becoming 'explosive in character', Sams examined the published work of Danish and American scientists on BCG and 'reviewed very carefully' the research conducted by the Japanese that had led to full endorsement of the vaccine. He concluded that where similar doses of vaccine had been used and comparable criteria for the tuberculin test applied, there was 'remarkable consistency in the reduction of morbidity and mortality'.[5] For these reasons, Sams decided that maximum effort should be invested in a mass campaign of immunization with BCG in Japan, so endorsing and deferring to an established Japanese position. Typically, he rather overstates his role in what he called 'the decision', given that there was presumably official and popular support among Japanese for immunization against tuberculosis. In any case, there was no real alternative to resumption of the programme as soon as it was possible to do so. Indeed, the Japanese government was advocating mass BCG vaccination as a powerful means of fighting the post-war prevalence of tuberculosis. It fully supported efforts to replace a liquid vaccine of very limited viability (around one week) with a stable freeze-dried one that could be mass-produced and retain its potency for lengthy periods of time.[6] It is surely very unlikely that Sams would have backed a programme of mass immunization with BCG if there had not been this strong record of achievement by Japanese scientists and doctors. Indeed, in later years Sams was only too willing to acknowledge their 'outstanding contributions to the control of TB, not only in Japan, but throughout the world'. He singled out his friend, Dr Minoru Katsumata, describing him as a 'great Japanese physician', who was 'responsible for mobilizing the entire resources of the Japan Anti-Tuberculosis Association and cooperating with the government agencies in carrying out this TB control program'.[7]

Sams became a committed advocate of BCG in the decades that followed the Occupation, often allying himself with those impatient with the refusal of public health authorities in the US to act on 'unequivocal evidence' that it was 'a highly effective vaccine for the prevention of TB'.[8] This was all the more frustrating when the tuberculosis problem in the US was described as 'a serious and pressing one'.[9] As late as 1969 he was still identified as a key ally by Philip Rettig of the Research Foundation in Chicago, who continued to push the US Public Health Service to change its attitude towards the vaccine.[10] There is no doubt that Sams' enthusiasm for BCG arose from his conviction that it had substantially reduced morbidity and mortality from tuberculosis during the Occupation of Japan. However, the evidence is suggestive rather than demonstrative of this. William Johnston, for example, declares that 'the actual effect of BCG remains unclear', and opponents of the vaccine emerged in the Japan Science Council in 1951.[11] Further scepticism comes from the chaotic situation on the ground in Japan during much of the Occupation, particularly the lack of personnel and resources to carry out the programme that Sams was so keen to promote. The gap between the scale of the enterprise and the very limited infrastructure in place to support it casts doubt on some of Sams' claims.

As was the case in 1943 and 1944, the tuberculosis prevention programme targeted the young on the assumption, prompted by the number of positive tuberculin results, that Japanese acquired the bacilli early in life. Under the terms of the National Physical Fitness Law of 1940, the wartime programme of immunization had focused on males between 15 and 25, together with factory workers and those with family members suffering from tuberculosis.[12] Only those testing negative could benefit from BCG vaccination, and, according to Sams, 25,500,000 or 46.6 per cent of the 54,800,000 people in Japan under 30 had acquired a natural infection (30 was the upper age limit set by the Preventive Vaccination Law of 30 June 1948). This left around 30 million who could be protected from the disease by BCG immunization.[13] Although the Japanese authorities had managed to vaccinate as many as ten million people in 1944, such was the dislocation accompanying defeat that little could be achieved in the early years of Occupation.

In his later paper recommending mass vaccination with BCG, Sams maintained that the priority cohorts in terms of elevated mortality levels were the 15–19 and 20–24 age groups. Those giving negative reactions to tuberculin in these groups must have received the bulk of the immunizations, which were recorded as numbering just over six million in 1946, nearly 7.5 million in 1947 and around seven million in 1948. However, many of these may have been re-immunizations, since an undisclosed number of those tuberculin tested again within a year revealed 'reconversions' (i.e. immunization had caused them to change from tuberculin negative to tuberculin positive, only to return or reconvert to tuberculin negative, suggesting a loss of immunity). The geographical pattern of reconversions, some as high as 30 per cent, suggested wide variation in the potency and efficacy of the liquid vaccine. Its production was undertaken by 11 widely dispersed laboratories. Given the uneven quality of the liquid vaccine, and the difficulties of producing, testing and distributing large quantities of it in the face of inadequate transport and refrigeration facilities, it was not surprising that Sams saw fit to suspend all production of BCG from December 1948 until October 1949. This decision implicitly acknowledged the undue haste with which the immunization programme had been implemented. It revealed a common tendency to command the Japanese authorities to undertake programmes for which they had neither sufficient infrastructure nor resources.[14]

The chaotic nature of much of the public health work being done during these years is illuminated by reports from the field. In the case of tuberculosis, the PH&W relied on the reports of Albert Knight, their 'tuberculosis consultant', for some insight into the actual practice of tuberculosis prevention activities throughout Japan. Knight travelled extensively in 1947, visiting the four prefectures of Shikoku during the summer and a variety of prefectures on Honshu in the autumn and winter (Iwate, Ibaraki, Miyagi Tochigi, Fukushima, Toyama, Ishikawa, Shiga, Hyogo, Kyoto and Shizuoka). During the months of February, March and May 1948 he was on the road again, surveying sanatoria, hospitals and health centres in the prefectures of Hiroshima, Wakayama, Okayama, Nara, Osaka, Saga, Kumamoto, Yamaguchi, Tottori and Shimane. His detailed reports paint a picture of a largely dysfunctional public health infrastructure, of health centres and hospitals lacking in personnel and vital equipment and often falling short in terms of their hygiene standards. Knight interviewed US military government medical officers, prefectural health officials and those responsible for tuberculin testing, BCG immunization, diagnosis of active cases of tuberculosis and care of patients in the home and the sanatorium.

It is therefore very revealing that during the course of his travels in 1947 and 1948, he drew attention to tuberculin testing and inoculation with BCG in comparatively few of the prefectures he visited – in Miyagi, Fukushima, Kyoto, Hyogo, Shiga, Shizuoka, Wakayama, Nara, Osaka and Saga.[15] It was reported that 'mass examinations' of school children and factory employees, which were supposed to be carried out throughout Japan, had been undertaken in these prefectures, and that they were complying with official policy on tuberculin testing and BCG immunization. However, some were doing better than others. Only in a couple of cases did Knight seem confident of satisfactory results. He maintained that 60,000 people had been examined in Hyogo prefecture and observed in relation to Saga prefecture that mass examination with tuberculin tests and inoculation with BCG had been 'fairly well done'. Otherwise, he was rather vague, asserting that 'tuberculin testing is being done and BCG is being given' in Miyagi prefecture, and resorting to random figures for other prefectures rather than measuring performance against targets. For example, we discover that 2,300 school children and 70 employees from three small factories had been tested in Shiga prefecture, that 7,300 had been immunized with BCG in Shizuoka prefecture and that the figure for Nara prefecture was more than 9,228 over the past year. These numbers suggest rather limited progress, as does the evidence from Kyoto. Here, one Japanese informant was calling for BCG inoculation to be completed throughout the prefecture and Knight felt compelled to remind public officials that 'All those individuals with negative tuberculin reaction should be given BCG and accurate records made.' According to the military government health officer for Kyoto, John Glismann, only around 30 per cent of those tested were negative (61,250 of 203,500).[16]

In any case, it seems that the delivery of large-scale tuberculin testing and BCG inoculation prior to the suspension of the vaccine at the end of 1948 was very patchy. The reports from his tuberculosis consultant cast doubt on Sams' figures for immunizations of 6–7 million per year from 1946 to 1948. Assuming them to be accurate, it is likely that programmes were concentrated in particular areas and that the number of re-conversions due to defective vaccine caused many school children to be re-immunized at frequent intervals. Sams himself acknowledged that 'only a fraction' of those under 30 producing negative reactions to tuberculin had been immunized for the entire five-year period, 1945–50. Moreover, regarding the vaccine's variable quality, he admitted that there were too few qualified Americans on his staff to exercise effective control of BCG in 11 different laboratories.[17]

For these reasons, Sams claims that he decided to convert to a dry vaccine which could be produced in one laboratory, over which his staff could exercise proper control. The switch, of course, was only made possible by the successful development by Japanese scientists of a mass-produced, freeze-dried vaccine, the first of its kind in the world.[18] This facilitated a more effective BCG immunization drive from October 1949, when the programmes of tuberculin testing and inoculation were resumed. During the remainder of 1949 around two million people were immunized, and in 1950 and 1951 the number of (re)immunizations was around 28 million.[19]

This represented a major escalation of the BCG programme. As part of a much stronger commitment to its universal application, we find Albert Knight touring the prefectures again in May, June and December 1950 and in February and June 1951.

His reports suggest some progress, but continue to identify shortcomings. In Osaka, there were 'fairly good mass examinations' and 'middle schools were supposedly finished'.[20] Schools were recording tuberculin tests and immunizations in Yokohama, but this information was not always properly transferred to a central database due to a lack of funds to employ the necessary clerical help. Also, there was a suggestion of 'some laxity in pushing this program' despite plentiful supplies of the vaccine.[21] A trip to the prefectures of Shikoku in February 1951 highlighted low rates of immunization, principally due to a lack of money with which to purchase it or too few personnel to administer it.[22] Likewise, a visit to northern Honshu and Hokkaido in June 1951 revealed that 'only 43% of the program was completed' in Iwate prefecture, 'because the authorities could not obtain enough vaccine when they needed it'. A contrast between urban engagement with the programme and rural inaction worried Knight, particularly in relation to Hokkaido. Here he complained of poorly trained doctors outside the cities, public apathy towards the disease and insufficient infrastructure (health centres) and personnel to tackle it.[23]

To focus energies on effective tuberculosis prevention and control, Knight identified four key priorities, namely early case finding, early diagnosis, early isolation (either at home or through hospitalization), and early prevention with BCG vaccination.[24] The latter has been discussed at length above, but what of the other three, all seen as pivotal to controlling the epidemic? Once again, these activities were compromised by a dilapidated public health infrastructure, too poorly resourced to implement the kinds of measures that all agreed were necessary. First, it was essential to establish quickly how many of those producing positive reactions to tuberculin were active cases and therefore capable of spreading the disease. As mentioned earlier, this was done by means of X-ray analysis, followed by physical examinations, sputum tests and blood sedimentation results. According to Sams, approximately 1.3 million active cases were detected among the 25.5 million Japanese under 30 who tested tuberculin positive.[25] The difficulties of carrying out the requisite tests on those shown to be infected were repeatedly described by Knight in his reports from the field in 1947 and 1948.

Time and again he referred to X-ray machines, which could not be effectively utilized due to missing parts, insufficient film or the wrong kind of film, and frequent interruptions in the supply of electricity. For example, a summary of a survey trip through Toyama, Ishikawa, Shiga, Hyogo and Kyoto prefectures observed that 'The shortage of electrical power makes impossible the use of the X-ray laboratory facilities as is absolutely necessary'.[26] In Shizuoka prefecture, Knight reported that one sanatorium had no power three days per week and on other days could not predict when the supply would be interrupted. At the same time, the staff wanted to use larger X-ray films (11×14), essential for confirming suspect cases of tuberculosis, but could not afford them.[27] Dependence on smaller film (10×12) or even paper due to budgetary limitations was a common complaint. One health centre in Tochigi prefecture had placed orders for film each month but was unable to obtain it, and a health centre in Sendai (Miyagi prefecture) was advised to make X-ray films of the proper size. In Tokushima prefecture, Knight was informed that X-ray studies were to increase in number 'as soon as film is available', and in Iwate prefecture there was the 'usual complaint of a shortage of film and the use of 10×12 size because 11×14 is not available'.[28] Also reported in relation to Iwate was a lack of alcohol for 'lab work and [sputum] staining', apparently a habitual complaint. Certainly, it was identified as a problem for laboratory technicians in Ibaraki, Tochigi, Kyoto, Toyama and Shiga prefectures. In Kyoto, laboratory studies were hobbled by a lack of electrical power to run the centrifuges and insufficient alcohol and dyes for staining. Only in Hyogo was Knight able to report 'adequate stain and alcohol'.[29]

The lower frequency of such comments in the tuberculosis consultant's reports of 1948 and their absence from his commentaries of 1950 and 1951 suggest that these problems eased over time. This supposition seems to be confirmed by the rising trend of diagnosis of new cases from 1947. These reportedly increased from more than 300,000 cases that year to 380,000 in 1948, around 400,000 in 1949, 528,000 in 1950, and nearly 600,000 in 1951.[30] The trend may be explained not just by early diagnosis, arising from mass tuberculin testing, but also by a stronger commitment among doctors to disclose cases of active tuberculosis. This was perhaps encouraged by an Occupation order of March 1947 for all infectious diseases to be reported within 24 hours of diagnosis.

Another means by which new cases could be identified was by active contact tracing and home visiting by public health nurses. During his visit to Kyoto in November 1947, for example, Albert Knight urged prefectural health officials to ensure that public health nurses contact members of patients' families with a view to their being checked for the disease.[31] Interestingly, however, the primary role of the public health nurse seems to have been less one of surveillance than of education and guidance. There are constant references in Knight's reports to the fundamental importance of teaching control of tuberculosis in the home. In 1950 'twelve rules of tuberculosis control' were publicized to limit the spread of the disease among family members. These stressed the need for the patient to have his/her own bed, preferably in a separate room, for the room to have good ventilation and sunlight, for precautions to be taken with the patient's personal effects, clothes and bedding, for sputum to be wrapped in paper and burned and excreta to be disinfected. There was to be no careless spitting, and the patient was to be isolated from babies or young adults.[32]

The emphasis on the patient's isolation at home reflected the principal problems surrounding tuberculosis control in Occupied Japan, at least until 1950 or 1951. First, there was insufficient capacity for the care and treatment of tuberculosis patients in hospitals and sanatoria. According to Sams, there were 25,000 beds for active cases of tuberculosis at the end of the war, at a time when he estimated there were 1–2 million clinical cases of the disease.[33] Apparently the situation had slightly improved by 1948, when there were just over 60,000 beds available.[34] Nonetheless, in June 1950, Knight, as the PH&W's tuberculosis consultant, stated that only 5 per cent of the known cases of tuberculosis were in sanatoria or hospitals.[35] This discrepancy, however, was not just due to a shortage of beds. More disturbingly, it reflected a strong reluctance among new cases as well as established ones to break the chain of infection by withdrawing into these institutions. Once again, this complex of problems was catalogued in some detail by Knight on his trips round Japan in 1947 and 1948. As he visited sanatoria and hospitals with tuberculosis patients in prefecture after prefecture, he constantly remarked on empty beds. Of the 25 prefectures he visited during 1947 and 1948 (listed above), he referred to unoccupied beds in 18 of them, simply neglecting to mention the issue in the other seven cases. Only once – in Ibaraki prefecture in November 1947 – did he refer to a 'high proportion of TB beds filled'. More often, he reported occupancy rates of little more than 50 per cent – for example, in Tokushima prefecture, 325 of 630 beds were occupied in August 1947, and in Kyoto and Fukushima prefectures in November 1947 the figures were 986 of 1,859 beds and 400 of 700, respectively.[36]

This peculiar phenomenon of empty beds in a country where capacity was deemed to be hopelessly inadequate was attributed chiefly to the dearth of food. Other factors were transport difficulties, financial hardship, a general resistance to hospitalization and poor staffing levels in the institutions concerned. Efforts were made to coax patients into hospitals and sanatoria by offering extra rations. This reportedly included daily allowances of 51 grams of protein (15 grams of animal protein) and 33 grams of fat in Matsuyama prefecture in August 1947. In Fukushima prefecture in November 1947, the extra ration amounted to just half of the 140 grams recommended, and even though patients in Toyama had received extra rations of 140 grams since October 1946, this was still deemed to be 'inadequate'.[37] Anxiety about food, however, was just a symptom of a much deeper problem of fear of institutionalization. This was succinctly captured by Knight in his report on tuberculosis control in Ishikawa prefecture (29 November 1947). Here he stated that the prevailing view among Japanese was that 'once a patient enters a hospital he never returns alive and only the serious cases go to the sanatorium'. Moreover, people were 'ashamed to disclose they have tuberculosis in the family and if they send a patient to a hospital their relatives and friends know of it'.[38] Bizarrely, a glut of fresh milk in Fukuoka prefecture in July 1950 was similarly blamed on the 'linkage between milk purchase and a TB patient in the household'.[39]

There was therefore little alternative to the strong emphasis on the care of tuberculosis patients in the home. In August 1947 Knight was advising health centre personnel of the need to emphasize the isolation of the patient and the control of the spread of infection in the home until bed space could be found and the people trained to accept hospitalization.[40] Given the difficulty of meeting those conditions (arguably only partially met by the end of the Occupation), it was not surprising that Knight encouraged civic engagement with the problem. He placed great trust in women's organizations, which responded well to his talks and seemed committed to effective disease control. For example, during a tour of Shimane prefecture in May 1948, he gave the 'usual address on control of TB to about 1,000 people, among whom again were many young women of high school and college age who showed marked interest'.[41] More than two years later, in July 1950, Knight was urging an audience of 800 people to view the home as the key battleground against such chronic diseases as tuberculosis and dysentery.[42]

How, then, should the Occupation's record on tuberculosis prevention and control be judged? What was achieved against this most entrenched epidemic? The statistics show a striking decline in tuberculosis mortality between 1943 and 1951 – from 171,473 in 1943 to 146,241 in 1947, 121,769 in 1950 and just 93,307 in 1951.[43] Sams attributed this to the Occupation's active promotion of tuberculin testing and BCG immunization, noting that the steepest drops occurred in the 15–25 age cohort. An alternative explanation is provided by Shimao, who observes that the steep decline was due to excess deaths of tuberculosis cases during the war. While William Johnston attributes the steep decline in mortality during these years to broader economic factors, he concedes that mass inoculations with BCG from 1943 'possibly had a cumulative effect of lowering tuberculosis mortality rates from the late 1940s'.[44]

It was typical of Sams that once he endorsed the BCG vaccine as Occupation policy, he would strive constantly as head of the PH&W to attribute its apparent success to American drive and ingenuity. He presents Japan's wartime inoculation programme as still-born, emphasizing *his* 'decision to reinstitute and expand the program for mass use of BCG in Japan as the most effective tool available in stopping this epidemic'.[45] It was the Preventive Vaccination Law of 1948 that broadened the wartime programme to include all Japanese between the ages of 6 months and 30 years who gave negative reactions to tuberculin. It appears, however, that there was a gap between Sams' rhetoric and the reality on the ground for much of the Occupation. Mass testing and immunization programmes were very patchy and the quality and potency of the vaccine uneven. Only with the launch of a dried vaccine, pioneered by the Japanese themselves, and the imposition of a proper system of quality control towards the end of 1949 could those responsible for the immunization drive have much confidence in its efficacy as a preventive measure.

Early case finding and diagnosis of active cases of tuberculosis were difficult to pursue effectively when there was defective equipment, insufficient X-ray film of the required quality, breaks in the electricity supply and poorly resourced laboratories. The urgent need to isolate tuberculosis patients was frustrated by not only a dire shortage of beds, but also – more worryingly perhaps – a deep-seated popular resistance to hospitalization due to anxieties about food supply and a cultural aversion among Japanese to revealing cases of tuberculosis in the family. Although Albert Knight was able to inform Sams in January 1954 that the number of beds for the care of tuberculosis had increased dramatically to 150,000,[46] much more important was the new willingness of Japanese to confront the disease and come forward for treatment. The key to this behavioural shift was the belated arrival of a medical cure for tuberculosis, a new drug that in Johnston's memorable phrase 'washed the disease of its stigma'.[47] Its insidious, morbid character gave way to one that was altogether less threatening, and patients now exuded hope and optimism rather than the shame and fatalism of past years.

The medical cure, of course, was streptomycin. This was first introduced into Japan in 1949, when 200 and 400 kg were imported from the US in March and October, respectively. Only those hospitals and sanatoria with excellent facilities and proficient staff were given access to the antibiotic in order to minimize wastage. It was absolutely essential that it was used to its full effect, given that the imported quantity amounted to just 1 per cent of the estimated Japanese requirements for the new drug (around 60,000 kg per year). As the official history of the Occupation explains, these imports were designed to introduce the drug to Japanese doctors and to foster sufficient demand for the product to enable potential Japanese manufacturers to secure necessary financial backing. In July 1950 Japanese companies began producing streptomycin in modest quantities on a commercial basis (118 kg by the end of the year). By 1952 the successful operation of large-scale plants brought self-sufficiency and even the opportunity for export. Also manufactured commercially for treatment of tuberculosis patients was para-aminosalicylic acid (PAS), which was successfully used to supplement streptomycin in the chemotherapy of active tubercular patients.[48] The increasing availability of these drugs and the confidence invested in them by Japanese suffering from tuberculosis account for a steep drop in mortality from the disease, from 93,307 in 1951 to 57,849 in 1953 and 46,735 in 1955.[49] Interestingly, morbidity levels remained comparatively high in Japan throughout the 1950s. They were recorded as 445.9/100,000 population in 1961, compared with 365.7 for Peru and just 29.3 for the US.[50] This highlights the entrenched nature of chronic infectious diseases – their rootedness in social environments permissive of only gradual, incremental improvement. Similar considerations apply to the US effort to reduce venereal disease, where once again a major pharmaceutical development, in this case mass-production of penicillin, masked comparatively high rates of morbidity.

Conflicts of purpose over venereal disease

For the purposes of this analysis of policy and practice in this difficult medical field, the term 'venereal disease' applies to its three chief manifestations: gonorrhoea, syphilis and chancroid. More than any other group of diseases, the problem of venereal disease was inextricably bound up with the realities of military Occupation. Prostitution rapidly expanded to meet the demand of large numbers of foreign troops, whose ready access to sexual services reflected the social deprivation that accompanied defeat. Here was a rare case where the latent tensions between the two main elements of the Occupation came to the fore. The commanders of tactical troops, answerable to GHQ FEC for high venereal disease rates among their charges, tended to view the problem through a powerful colonial lens. They attributed it to diseased Japanese prostitutes rather than promiscuous soldiers. This attitude generally conflicted with the views of public health officials in the PH&W (GHQ SCAP), who advocated an approach that necessarily transcended the health of the troops – a venereal disease control programme that involved the Japanese people as a whole rather than focusing almost exclusively on prostitutes. Between them, in a sense facing both ways, were the military government teams, sensitive to the demands of local military units but nevertheless responsible for monitoring the implementation of public health reforms sponsored by the PH&W. This issue of conflicting purposes was replicated in the Japanese medical establishment, divided over whether to trust in established policies or to embrace broader social initiatives against venereal disease. Such divisions bedevilled the efforts of Sams and his team to properly confront the problem of sexually transmitted diseases.

A report by Isamu Nieda, the head of PH&W's venereal disease control branch, on the period 1945–49, identified 'the problem of prostitution as related to venereal disease control' as 'a source of constant conflict between the Occupation force commanders and PHW'. Regrettably, he added, these tensions compromised the success of venereal disease control. Moreover, this lack of unity served to confuse the Japanese and to hamper the proper implementation of the modern, progressive venereal disease control programme favoured by Sams and his colleagues.[51] Their aim essentially was to break with the past, to end licensed prostitution and police enforcement of such measures as the regular examination of prostitutes. These checks were seldom rigorous enough to be effective and were thought to represent venereal disease as a disease affecting only licensed prostitutes. Furthermore, medical examinations and venereal disease-free certificates engendered a false sense of security among those visiting brothels, so encouraging the spread of gonorrhoea and syphilis. Ultimately, the PH&W sought to utilize the revamped *hokenjo* as centres for the diagnosis and treatment of venereal disease, which all Japanese could voluntarily make use of at reasonable cost or free of charge. As will be discussed in the next chapter on the health centres, some progress towards this goal had been made by the end of the Occupation.

For the most part, however, the PH&W had to surmount major obstacles before its vision of a modern venereal disease control programme could be realized. Together with taking on the entrenched Japanese position that surveillance of prostitutes was the key to venereal disease control, it had to accommodate the view of US military commanders that only medical checks of prostitutes and streetwalkers could bring down high rates of venereal disease among their men. The neat symmetry between these positions was captured in Isamu Nieda's remark that Japanese police involvement in public health controls, rejected in principle by the PH&W, had been *reintroduced* by the US provost marshal in the form of 'vice squads', made up of American military police and native policemen. These issues merit some consideration before we move on to look at the details of the more broadly conceived venereal disease control system that began to emerge in the final years of Occupation.

As discussed by a number of historians, the Japanese government rapidly established the Recreation Amusement Association (RAA) – *Tokushu Ian Shisetsu Kyōkai* – at the end of August 1945 to channel the sexual needs of foreign troops into what Tanaka Yuki describes as a system of 'Japanese comfort women for the Allied forces'.[52] Reflecting a rather different set of concerns about the potentially disruptive effects of a venereal disease epidemic among his troops, MacArthur authorized SCAPIN 153 on 16 October 1945. This required syphilis, gonorrhoea and chancroid to be legally designated as reportable diseases, and called for individuals likely to spread sexually transmitted diseases to be tightly controlled under existing laws. SCAPIN 153 also called for the provision of adequate facilities for the effective diagnosis and treatment of patients and the establishment of minimum technical and administrative standards. Cognizant of the need for concerted action by both Japanese and American authorities, the Occupation for its part issued condoms to its soldiers, which many apparently neglected to use,[53] and set up 'prophylactic stations' in the vicinity of the brothel districts for their benefit. Nevertheless, the incidence of venereal disease among them began to rise alarmingly. The rate among American troops reached as high as 25 per cent by March 1946, the great majority of cases being gonorrhoea.[54]

According to John Dower, the scale of the venereal disease problem was the key motivation for the Occupation's order to abolish licensed prostitution (SCAPIN 642) on 21 January 1946, despite it being justified in terms of democracy and human rights.[55] In any case, it simply changed the context of venereal disease control rather than enhancing it. It brought the end of the RAA, but not the end of prostitution. As Kovner puts it, 'MacArthur's decree did not close the market in sexual services, nor did it free women from all forms of debt bondage. It merely deregulated the market.'[56] Changes in terminology masked striking continuities. 'Special eating and drinking shops' (*tokushu inshokuten*) appeared in what had been the 'licensed brothel districts' (*yūkaku*) – areas now designated on police maps by red lines (*akasen*). Entertainment districts newly associated with the sale of sexual services were marked by blue lines (*aosen*). These designations served as the natural correlates of the licensed and unlicensed areas of the past. 'Prostitutes' (*shōgi*) were now known as 'hostesses' (*settaifu*), who 'voluntarily' subjected themselves to medical examinations for venereal disease.[57]

As would be expected from the superficial nature of the changes brought about, the problem of high rates of venereal disease infection among GIs did not subside. Thus, the Occupation chose to attack the problem more vigorously – prohibiting servicemen from visiting establishments associated with the sale of sex by placing them 'off limits' in March 1946. According to Tanaka, this served to cast many impoverished women adrift from their moorings, compelling them to become 'streetwalkers' constantly soliciting for American custom. As a result, contact between these *Pan-Pan* as they became known and GIs became more likely, posing 'an enormous threat to the seemingly successful and orderly occupation'.[58] In response to the urgency of the problem, the Occupation resorted to harsher measures. They initiated the deployment of vice squads, consisting of Japanese police and American military police, which rounded up suspected streetwalkers and detained them in jail-like establishments for medical examination.

As already intimated, the importance of the perceived threat of high levels of venereal disease infection among tactical troops lies in the degree to which it overshadowed the PH&W's efforts to establish a modern system of venereal disease control for the benefit of the Japanese people. This is clear from reports from the field on control of sexually transmitted diseases, compiled initially by Oscar Elkins, the official responsible for venereal disease in the PH&W's preventive medicine division. For example, one such report for Chiba prefecture in October 1946 remarked that public health energies were directed at the routine examination of prostitutes. The rationale for this was ' "protection of our troops" by these periodic examinations and by occasional police raids'. Meanwhile, members of the public in need of treatment consulted with private doctors, who did not bother to report their infections. In short, there was 'no public program of venereal disease control' as required by SCAP directives.[59] In Saitama prefecture the military government health officer confessed to feeling 'restricted and limited by directives from higher authorities, to the establishment, supervision and other support of civilian clinics only in those areas where there are heavy troop concentrations'.[60] In May of the following year, Elkins highlighted the muddled thinking of the Occupation on venereal disease by stating in relation to Kyushu that nothing had been done to initiate a control programme for the general public *despite the concentration of US forces (19th Infantry Regiment) in Oita prefecture* (my italics).[61] A month later, now in Sendai, Elkins stated that the military government health officer was under pressure from higher authorities in tactical organization to direct his efforts away from the general public to the medical examination of prostitutes.[62] At the end of 1947, Elkins' successor (Philip Bourland) noted in relation to venereal disease control conferences convened in Tokyo, Yamagata and Kyoto the emphasis placed on a coordinated programme that encompassed the public as a whole rather than prostitutes as a separate group. Also stated was the principle of not issuing health cards or certificates for the purpose of prostitution, because the medical checks on which they were based were unreliable.[63]

These points were strongly reiterated by John Glismann, the able military government health officer for Kyoto, on 18 June 1948. He explained that the Kyoto public health department would no longer engage in the routine examination of cabaret girls and prostitutes and so would cease issuing health certificates on that basis. This was because such regular check-ups had been discredited as a method of venereal disease control 'all over the world', revealing an infection rate of only 5–8 per cent when the true one was 75–95 per cent. For this reason, certification was counter-productive as it encouraged sex with prostitutes who were likely to be still infected with venereal disease. Above all, Glismann wanted the energies and resources expended on this group of people to be redirected at the public at large.[64] Unfortunately, however, his views flew in the face of those of tactical commanders, who encouraged the deployment of Kyoto city vice squads. Not only did these perpetuate the practices that Glismann rejected as problematic in public health terms, they flouted the civil liberties of many Japanese women, who were hauled in and detained for invasive medical checks on the whim of a military policeman. Indeed, Glismann felt compelled to report two incidents he witnessed in February 1948 to a superior. One involved the arrest of seven girls brought into Heian Hospital late on 12 February, none of whom in his estimation were likely to be 'streetwalkers'. The other incident occurred in the early hours of the following morning when he observed a military police vice squad raiding houses while their residents slept. It was Glismann's opinion that these raids involving Japanese and military police were unlawful.[65]

Nieda's lengthy report on venereal disease control activities up to the end of 1949 captures the frustration felt by those like Glismann with a predominantly public health perspective, who were committed to establishing venereal disease clinics and hospitals accessible and freely used by the public. He refers to 'many reports from various sources relative to indiscriminate apprehension of innocent women in violation of their civil rights' and argues forcefully that the 'indignities forced upon these women and the injustice done to them' discredited the venereal disease programme in the eyes of the public. Contrary to the views of Nieda and his colleagues, that patients with venereal disease should be treated no differently from those with other diseases, the military were acting on their conviction that spreading venereal disease was a crime prejudicial to the security of the Occupation forces and thus should be prosecuted in the provost court. As a result of this policy of treating suspected carriers as criminals, venereal disease hospitals became jails, with barred windows, barbed wire fences and police guards. 'It is no wonder', Nieda complained, 'that our efforts to induce the general public to utilize the services of these hospitals have failed.'[66] In his memoir, Sams acknowledged 'pretty severe repercussions' arising from the military police's clumsy campaign of suppression. He recalled that much resentment was caused by the indiscriminate nature of these 'sweeps', and that even a female member of the Diet had found herself caught in one.[67]

The anger generated by this behaviour in Oita prefecture was such that a petition was sent to the commanding officer of Oita Military Government Team on 8 December 1948. Although it acknowledged that the military police's roundups had resulted in some infected women being treated, the petition argued that these successes did not adequately mitigate the injustices and the damage done to the cause of democracy. Evidence presented included the arrest and examination of 403 women between 17 November and 5 December, 283 of whom were free of venereal disease; the arrest of a bride on her honeymoon; the assumption that all women employed at restaurants, dance halls and hotels were prostitutes; and the reluctance of American military policemen to heed the advice of their Japanese colleagues.[68] Guinn Goodrich, the commanding officer of Oita Military Government Team, was sufficiently concerned about the military police's wholesale apprehension of girls and women to write to his superior at regional level, listing in detail many instances of 'serious disregard of democratic privileges'. Goodrich stated that only 10 per cent of 1,053 women apprehended between 1 January and 28 February 1949 were infected with venereal disease, and Japanese police estimated that only around one-quarter of them had been streetwalkers.

Therefore, '650–750 innocent girls and women [were] subjected to the humiliation of being displayed to the public as prostitutes while being taken to the police station in the MP open jeep.' They were 'further humiliated by being subjected to an examination for venereal disease'. A necessarily vague resolution, objecting to the 'unjust physical examinations of women', was passed by a communist-sponsored rally on 28 March 1949. This evidenced the damage done to the Occupation's reputation by the actions of its military police.[69] In a visit to Oita prefecture in May 1949, Nieda complained that despite Goodrich's exposure of military police misconduct, the situation had if anything deteriorated further, with military police now working alone rather than alongside Japanese police.[70] Whether it was Shiga prefecture in central Honshu, where the military police supervised the routine examination of cabaret dancers,[71] or Hokkaido, where weekly examination of the prostitutes was carried out at the behest of the commanding officer (11th Airborne Division),[72] Nieda constantly highlighted obstruction of more enlightened venereal disease prevention strategies by military elements. For him and others of a like mind, these episodes demonstrated the difficulties encountered in 'setting up a venereal disease control programme based upon modern public health principles'.[73]

Apart from focusing energies and resources on society at large rather than a very narrow section of it, the other 'modern' approaches towards venereal disease control that Nieda had in mind were early diagnosis and effective treatment. Reflecting on the US's record in stemming the spread of sexually transmitted diseases during the war years, a prominent American venereologist, J. R. Heller, identified the essential elements of venereal disease epidemiology as follows: finding infected people ('case finding'), recording them, holding them to full courses of treatment ('case holding'), and tracing their contacts to identify and eliminate additional infections ('contact tracing'). Only by these means was it possible to break the chain of infection. While Heller acknowledged that such initiatives were just as important in peacetime as during a war, he noted that military mobilization necessitated an intensification of these activities and a more vigorous approach generally. For example, the routine blood testing of Americans selected for military service represented an unprecedented attempt to reduce the reservoir of syphilis infection, estimated to be around three million people in the US. However, significant reductions depended on close liaison between military and civilian health authorities over sources of infection and contacts liable to spread disease. In 1942, Heller reported, the Office of the Surgeon General of the US Army had acknowledged the need for a standard method of reporting contacts and for an effective method of 'routing this information' to civilian services.[74] These experiences are important because they contextualize American reform efforts in Japan, and suggest that the US did not really grasp the nettle of venereal disease control until forced to do so by the exigencies of war. The resources necessary to trace contacts and ensure that patients complete lengthy treatment schedules presumably served as a disincentive to confront this particular disease menace until absolutely necessary.

The dilapidated state of much of Japan's medical infrastructure, the shortage of doctors, nurses and technicians, the inadequacy of many laboratories, and the dearth of modern drugs all combined to delay the development of a comprehensive venereal disease control programme until some years into the Occupation. Indeed, it was not until 1 September 1948 that the Venereal Disease Prevention Law, 'for the purpose of contributing to the improvement and promotion of public health', came into effect.

The new law called on the state and local government to educate the public about venereal disease prevention and treatment. It required doctors, on diagnosis, to reinforce these messages, to enquire about possible sources of the disease and subsequent contacts and to report cases to the director of the local health centre within 24 hours. Furthermore, they were expected to disclose any instances of failure to undergo treatment or to persevere with it for the allotted time. Adopting a more proactive approach, the law specified health examinations of pregnant women and couples prior to marriage as opportunities to gauge the incidence of venereal disease and to prevent its spread. The power to order reported contacts of venereal disease patients or those 'suspected to be habitual prostitutes' to submit to medical examination and treatment if necessary resided with the prefectural governor. Penal provisions were specified for prostitutes who wilfully infected others and less harsh ones for anyone else who acted in this way. As for the chief agencies of disease control, these were specified as venereal disease hospitals and clinics, the latter operating for the most part in the health centres (as defined in the law of September 1947).

As happened so often with the Occupation, the reality on the ground militated against the aspirations embodied in the new law. Rather like in the case of tuberculosis, the reports of PH&W officials from the field narrate a tale of slow, fitful progress. While they alluded to satisfactory levels of expertise, they frequently highlighted inadequate resources. Starting with the issue of diagnosis, the observations of Elkins and Nieda suggest that in this area at least, procedures were perhaps not as 'archaic' as generally implied. Time and again they refer to serological or blood serum tests for syphilis, commonly Murata or Ide tests, which generally passed muster. This was evidenced by the PH&W weekly bulletin for 2–8 May 1949, which revealed that quality checks by US Army 406th General Laboratory indicated that the Murata, Ide and Hokken (or Kitasato) tests, all obviously of Japanese derivation, were satisfactory but were more sensitive than the US Kahn test and so produced more false positive reactions. As a result, it was recommended that they be used as screening tests and positive or doubtful reactions should be confirmed by the more rigorous Wassermann test, originally developed in 1906.

During their travels and inspections of venereal disease facilities, Elkins and Nieda constantly referred to these tests as part of their survey of progress on the diagnostic front. Elkins toured Chiba, Tokyo and Saitama prefectures in 1946, and the following year visited Aichi (twice), Kyoto (twice), Osaka, Miyagi, Fukushima, Ibaraki, Tochigi, Gumma, Yamanashi and Kanagawa prefectures, together with the regions of Chugoku,[75] Shikoku and Kyushu. Between 1948 and 1949 Nieda ranged even more broadly, covering 41 of Japan's 46 prefectures (the few exceptions being Kagawa, Fukui, Nagano, Tokyo and Kanagawa). In

1950 M. D. Dickinson surveyed the Kanto region[76] and visited Aichi, Gifu, Mie, Osaka, Nara, Hyogo and Wakayama prefectures. In January 1947 Elkins described a laboratory in Nagoya with the necessary equipment to carry out all the serological and bacteriological examinations necessary for venereal disease control. These presumably encompassed the blood tests listed above, together with dark-field microscopes,[77] ethyl alcohol for Gram staining of smears for gonococci (*Neisseria gonorrhoea*),[78] equipment for culturing them and resources for mass serological examinations.

For the most part, however, observers from the PH&W noted deficiencies and limitations, frequently alluding to the inability of most health centre laboratories to carry out Wassermann tests and their consequent dependence on municipal or prefectural institutions to confirm their screening tests.[79] Moreover, only rarely did they catalogue adequate supplies of dark-field microscopes; there were very few mentions of culturing gonococci and staining of smears; and only occasional references to mass serological testing. The latter merit attention as they are suggestive of a more vigorous approach to case finding and provide some insight into the levels of infection throughout the general population. For example, in May 1948 Nieda reported that mass serological examinations of factory workers, among others, in Gunma prefecture had been conducted since March, and of 3,000 tests around 5 per cent were positive.[80] In July of the same year, Nieda referred to mass serological surveys of selected groups in Ibaraki prefecture that revealed syphilis levels of 9 per cent among prisoners, 5 per cent among coal miners and factory workers and 40 per cent among prostitutes.[81] In Hokkaido the public health authorities had performed 35,000 blood tests on factory workers, students, prisoners, office workers, government employees, pregnant women, farmers and fishermen and were still actively identifying cases of venereal disease in this way.[82] Of 1,013 factory workers tested in Matsuyama (Ehime prefecture) in October 1948, 4.4 per cent gave positive results. In 1949 Nieda reported mass serological campaigns only in Kanagawa, Niigata and Saga prefectures. In Kanagawa 20,000 employees of 23 factories had been tested, and in Niigata blood samples were taken from nearly 35,000. The combination of Murata and Wassermann tests revealed an infection rate of around 3 per cent.[83] Although these mass checks were conducted in only a few prefectures, they at least demonstrate a nascent sense of venereal disease as a social problem much broader than the related issue of prostitution. Such attitudes were reflected in another important element of case finding, namely effective public education to encourage citizens to volunteer themselves for diagnosis and treatment. Where this is mentioned in reports, it is described in fairly uniform, uncritical terms as involving posters, lectures, pamphlets, newspapers, exhibits, radio and movies.[84]

Vital to the challenge of case finding was contact tracing. This was a point made vigorously by Nieda to those responsible for venereal disease control in Shizuoka prefecture in May 1948. Observing that case finding here consisted mainly of weekly examination of prostitutes, biannual checks on food handlers, barbers, etc. and general educational activities, he explained that identifying and following up contacts represented 'the basis for controlling venereal disease by breaking the chain of infection'. Those on the receiving end of his instruction promised that it would soon be instituted.[85] In his reports for the remainder of 1948 Nieda very seldom praised health centres for effective work in the field. The one exception was Yamagata health centre, which impressed him with the energy and vigour of its 'contact tracing and case holding procedures'.[86] These activities were frequently lumped together as 'fieldwork', requiring health centre personnel to reach into communities to find cases of disease or to ensure that patients persevered with treatment until they were no longer infectious.

In some cases, contact tracing was not happening at all, and where it was being done it was often not being adequately followed up. Obviously the work was time consuming, and thus perhaps difficult to justify when there were shortages of personnel. For example, in Kyoto Nieda encountered a health centre where two nurses had investigated 20 contacts, finding only three infected cases. On 25 May 1948 he reported that contact tracing was no longer being done at one health centre he visited in Gunma prefecture, since the male investigator had resigned in February. His report on Ibaraki prefecture revealed that public health nurses were visiting contacts and merely 'advising' them to be examined for venereal disease. Where there were adequate resources, there was a greater likelihood of effective follow-up. In Osaka Nieda found 20 male investigators engaged in contact tracing, together with public health nurses. Letters were sent to those identified as possibly infected, and home visits were made to those who did not reply (around two-thirds of the contacts). Again, in Hyogo prefecture both male investigators and nurses were contacting those reportedly exposed to venereal disease infection.[87] Aichi prefecture was visited in both 1947 and 1948. On the first trip Elkins reported that contacts were reported but not adequately investigated, and the following year Nieda saw poor contact information and, more importantly, a shortage of public health nurses and bicycles as the chief impediments to success. Likewise, in Gifu and Miyagi prefectures fieldwork was precluded by a shortage of nurses and bicycles.[88]

While it was reported that public health nurses were not undertaking home visits in Aomori, Shimane, Tottori, Yamaguchi and Okayama prefectures, it was stated in relation to Hiroshima that public health nurses spent most of their time on tuberculosis control. Nieda may have been right to point out that their work should include venereal disease control in the field, but he could not have faulted them on their choice of priorities. Clearly, tuberculosis represented a much more serious hazard to public health than syphilis and gonorrhoea. The following year Nieda reported on venereal disease control activities in Fukui prefecture, again stating that public health nurses focused their home visits mostly on tuberculosis patients. He reminded them that their work in the community should include venereal disease contact tracing and case holding.[89]

A similarly mixed pattern of activity continued into 1949 and 1950, with some prefectures confronting the problem of venereal disease with much greater vigour than others.

However committed they were, their efforts were invariably hampered by competing priorities, low staffing levels or a lack of transport. For example, Nieda praised the efforts of staff in one health centre in Naruto city (Tokushima prefecture). They were seeing 100 patients per week and, despite transport being a major problem, four public health nurses were actively engaged in visiting homes to interview contacts and check up on patients. In contrast, Nieda found that contact tracing was either not being conducted at all or was undertaken half-heartedly in Ehime, Saitama, Yamanashi, Fukuoka, Nagasaki, Toyama and Ishikawa.[90] He found more cause for optimism with such examples as Kochi model health centre, which had developed an effective system of contact tracing whereby 25 public health nurses lived and worked in assigned districts. Like-wise, he reported that 15 public health nurses working out of Miyazaki model health centre included contact tracing and case holding in their home visits. Providing for model health centres generously was obviously vital if they were to succeed as prototypes.[91] Rather depressingly, Dr Dickinson surveyed venereal disease activities in the Kantō region during March 1950 and concluded that contact tracing was almost entirely restricted to contacts of Occupation forces. He seemed to be suggesting that the exercise was largely a waste of time and effort when he revealed that of 1,375 contact reports received between 1 November 1949 and 21 March 1950, only 30 women had been identified and just eight found to be infected. According to Dickinson's review of *hokenjo* venereal disease clinics, they all reported 'a few Japanese to Japanese contacts traced but there is no formal system. The tracing was due to the doctor's own initiative'.[92]

As for the other aspect of home visits for venereal disease control, 'case holding' attracts relatively few explicit references in the survey reports. However, enough is revealed to suggest that patients seldom completed treatment programmes. In early 1948 Fukushima venereal disease hospital – well-equipped and adequately supplied with drugs – seems to have provided something of a beacon in the surrounding gloom. Eighty per cent of its syphilis patients completed the prescribed course of treatment. This compared with a figure of 50 per cent for Hokkaido, where Nieda called for lapsed cases to be reported to the local health centre to be followed up by public health nurses. A similar figure was recorded for Shizuoka prefecture, and was attributed to the large number of fishermen interrupting their treatment to go back to work. More commonly, patients lost interest after symptoms subsided or were put off by high treatment fees. The extent of the problem was clear from the experience of Aichi model health centre, which opened on 17 July 1948 and by October was experiencing a dropout rate of around 80 per cent.[93]

Ultimately, the key to case holding and to venereal disease control more generally was the establishment of effective treatment programmes of short duration. In this vein, Heller noted that one of the greatest obstacles to effective disease control in the US during the war was the difficulty of ensuring that syphilis patients continued with treatment schedules until they were permanently non-infectious. This was not surprising, given that treatment involved 20 injections of an arsenical (mapharsen) and 20 injections of heavy metal (bismuth) over a period of around 40 weeks. 'Lapsing from treatment', Heller maintained, 'became the rule rather than the exception.' The solution to this problem was provided by the development of new types of therapy – sulfa drugs (sulfonamides) and penicillin

– that enabled patients to be hospitalized in rapid treatment centres (RTCs) and rendered them permanently non-infectious in less than two weeks. Heller stated that penicillin's place in the treatment of gonorrhoea was now established, and accurately predicted that in a few years it might provide that 'ideal quick treatment for syphilis'.[94] Unfortunately, the RTC model could not be applied to Japan due to inadequate supplies of penicillin, insufficient in-patient facilities and a lack of expertise among Japanese medical personnel. As a result, Occupation guidance dictated that syphilis patients receive a lengthy course of 40 arsenicals and 30 bismuth injections.[95] According to Nieda's summary report of 1949, Japanese doctors were advised to treat gonorrhoea with penicillin and/or sulfathiazole, syphilis with mapharsen and bismuth subsalicylate, and chancroid with sulfathiazole.[96] This remained the advice until penicillin could be produced cheaply enough to permit its generalized use in the treatment of venereal disease, which occurred towards the end of the Occupation.

The urgency with which penicillin, still in its experimental stage in Japan, was introduced by the Occupation largely derived from the rising problem of venereal disease among American servicemen. Dower contends that this accounts for the first patents for penicillin being sold to Japanese companies as early as April 1946.[97] The threat to the health of American soldiers was such that the Occupation authorities could not wait for the resumption or development of indigenous manufacturing capability as they did with other diseases. Thus, they targeted supplies of 'modern drugs', directing them towards hospitals and clinics engaged in venereal disease control in areas of troop concentration.

Limited quantities of penicillin, sulfonamides, mapharsen and bismuth subsalicylate were supplied from US Army stocks or imported until Japan could meet its own needs. Sulfathiazole had been manufactured in Japan during the war, but not in substantial quantities and, according to American commentators, of questionable quality.[98] Thus, Sams was exaggerating a little when he declared that 'clinical measures available for treatment [in Japan] were of pre-sulfonamide days'.[99] Still, it was not until 1948 that an ample quantity of sulfathiazole was being manufactured in Japan to meet all medical needs. As for penicillin, the official history of the Occupation describes the speed of development towards mass production as 'phenomenal', particularly during 1949 and 1950, when its price fell steeply.[100] The remarkable drop in venereal disease case rates, from 230.7/100,000 in 1949 to just 143.5 in 1950, was attributed by Sams and others to penicillin, which now represented an affordable, convenient and swift cure for early syphilis in the majority of cases. Its pervasive use and effectiveness 'reduced the reservoir of infected cases who could spread the disease'.[101]

Conclusion

There is no doubt that Japan benefited greatly from American advice and expertise in penicillin production.[102] The impact of this antibiotic on venereal disease control was perhaps comparable to that of streptomycin on tuberculosis – both represented striking advances in the face of entrenched underlying causes and very limited resources for time-consuming preventive strategies. The long-awaited cure for tuberculosis finally ended a culture of concealment, and penicillin inhibited the spread of venereal disease by quickly eliminating the infection. Indeed, the confidence invested in penicillin may even have encouraged prostitution and promiscuity in the sense that the risk of infection was now less of a deterrent. More significant than the parallels between tuberculosis and venereal disease during the Occupation, however, are the differences. Tuberculosis was the leading cause of mortality among Japanese until 1950, but had no public health implications for the Occupation itself; venereal disease was generally a much less pressing problem for the Japanese, but was of major significance for the health and efficiency of US troops.

As a result, there were divisions within the Occupation over the nature and purpose of venereal disease control. On the one hand, those concerned with reform rejected the narrow approach of the past that had placed undue emphasis on regular medical checks of prostitutes in licensed districts to the detriment of a more modern and effective approach that encompassed the whole of society. On the other hand, military commanders concerned about the number of US servicemen contracting venereal disease adopted a classical colonial perspective of the problem. They blamed Japanese prostitutes for infecting their men, and so targeted suspected streetwalkers in sweeps organized by the military police that subjected countless innocent women to detention and invasive medical checks. As late as 1950 the tactical commander responsible for Osaka ordered the provost marshal 'to see that street walkers were cleaned up', necessitating the use of night-time 'raids' that were generally viewed with disdain by those with a public health brief. Members of the PH&W and sympathetic medical officers in military government teams generally endeavoured to represent venereal disease in more progressive terms, as a disease like any other that could be easily diagnosed, treated and prevented. Their efforts undoubtedly contributed much to the development of modern systems of venereal disease prevention and treatment that, judging from reports from the field, many Japanese doctors and public health nurses embraced.

While Sams was justified in highlighting the shortcomings of Japan's historical record on venereal disease, he surely overstated his case when he claimed that 'Japanese physicians, with very few exceptions, were unfamiliar with the epidemiological and clinical manifestations of VD'.[103] As in other countries, venereal disease may have been relatively neglected by Japan's medical establishment, but the ready implementation of recommended case finding procedures, and some experience of sulfa drugs suggests that there was a reasonably solid foundation on which to build. In the case of tuberculosis, there was no question of a lack of expertise. The preventive strategies adopted by the PH&W, particularly the use of BCG, essentially endorsed established Japanese positions. Ultimately, chronic infectious diseases like venereal disease, tuberculosis and dysentery were rooted in particular environmental conditions and required active community engagement to bring them under control. The key agencies in this regard were the *hokenjo*. The degree to which they came to represent a new ethos of public health in Japan is the subject of the next chapter.

7   The health centre

The history of the *hokenjo* or health centre provides an ideal window to test the major arguments presented in the previous chapters. The health centre was created by the Health Centre Law in 1937, while the crucial revision to the law was made in 1947 under the Occupation. One can thus observe the two versions of the same institution: an old version created by the pre-war Japanese government and the new one guided into existence by the Occupation and PH&W. An obvious question is: what was the impact of Japan's defeat, the Occupation and the post-war drastic changes on the system and performance of health centres?

One way to answer the question is to examine the decision-making of the central government, concentrating on the post-war policy negotiations between the Welfare Ministry and the Occupation, and to investigate who created the post-war health centre and which was more important, the Japanese beginning or the American revision. Another way is to examine the problem at the local level of individual health centres. Since health centres are local institutions responsible for the health of the people in their district, one needs to go down to the level of the local and the individual health centres to get a more detailed and nuanced picture.[1] Local health centres also reveal the agency of the people of Japan during the period under examination: seen from the viewpoint of the sick in Japan, the health centre of their district was the most important governmental medium to coordinate their health-seeking behaviour. The history of the health centre is thus a classic subject of social history of medicine and health seen from the patients' point of view, as propagated by the late Roy Porter. Analysis of the negotiations among health high officials of the Japanese government and the officers of the Occupation is far from the only means for social historical understanding of the health centre and the people in Japan.

This chapter shall thus use not just records about the central government, but also evidence from individual health centres. Major sources are published ones: reports, newsletters and anniversary publications of the health centres, which cover the periods both before and after the war.[2] Many of these publications were local, ephemeral and sometimes difficult to find in a systematic way, but the Gordon A. Prange Collection now available at the National Diet Library on microfilm allows historians to study them in a systematic way for the Occupation period. There were also many articles or short notes, written often by the directors of the health centres about their institute's activities, published in medical journals. Weaving these materials from the local level with the records from the central agencies, this chapter will discuss the history of the health centre from an angle that is different from classic works on this subject, such as the 'official history' of the Welfare Ministry and Sugiyama Akiko's work, which concentrated on the policies of the central government.[3] The differences and continuities of the health centres will be examined at the local level, and the impact of the Occupation will be assessed at each individual health centre. The following sections are chronologically arranged: the first and second sections analyse the situation of pre-war health centres, while the third and fourth sections discuss the post-war development and continuities.

The new core of the people's health

Although evaluating the overall picture of old health centres established under the 1937 Health Centre Law is difficult, a sample of evidence shows enormous differences among them. Several health centres were very active and performing their duties vigorously. Active ones showed considerable difference in their activities between one another, due to their background, locations and the orientation of the directors. Many others, however, showed little sign of activity, and one suspects some existed only on paper.

Kisarazu Health Centre in Chiba was certainly one of the best health centres before the war, and its report is an eloquent testimony to its activities.[4] It was established in January 1938 for eight towns and 29 villages, with a total population of 136,000. In the latter half of 1938, it conducted about 4,000 health consultations. Since the majority of those who visited the health centre for consultation came from its immediate vicinity, an effort was made to reach residents who lived far away and check them with advanced equipment such as microscopes, centrifuge tubes and the devices to measure blood sedimentation rate. The consultation service in total discovered 644 patients with tuberculosis, and the three nurses home-visited more than one-third of them. Parasitological surveys of hookworms and ascaris was another focus of the centre's work, which found between one-fifth and one-third of the surveyed population to be infected. Vermifuge such as santonin was given to them. The living conditions of the rural population were surveyed in three villages. Wells were surveyed and chemical analysis of well-water was conducted. The content of school lunches was also examined.[5] The pattern of receiving medicine was a target of extensive survey in two villages, which found more than 80 per cent of medical expenditure was paid to doctors, and 12–14 per cent was for over-the-counter drugs. Eugenic consultation had three questions about marriage and tuberculosis, addressing marriage and venereal disease, family life and impotence. The centre also accepted medical students of Tokyo Imperial University for fieldwork in rural public health for four months. The Kisarazu health centre was a vigorously active institution, a textbook example of the new public health.

One prominent part of the centre's work was the control of venereal diseases.[6] They were the target of the most extensive and innovative measures, because the navy showed a keen interest in protecting the aerial division based at Kisarazu from contracting venereal disease. The questioner of the owners of brothel houses revealed a serious lack of knowledge on their part of the types of venereal disease, their early symptoms and preventive measures. With the help of the navy, the police and the military police (*kempei*), the brothel houses formed a union, while the prostitutes made a union for the improvement of health. Condoms paid for by the houses were used and prostitutes were taught how to use mercurial drugs. The women were to be subject to health checks three times per month, which the health centre admitted was 'not within the power of the health centre, which is an advisory institution'. As a result of these measures, the navy pilots were allowed to patronize the houses, and the rate of infection among them became much lower. This trespass of the boundary of administrative power was possible no doubt because of the strong influence of the navy on the policy of the district. In this instance, the health centre served as an outpost of the military.

Matsudo health centre in Chiba prefecture, responsible for a population of about 140,000, presented a somewhat different face. Its report for the year 1939 shows the health centre worked with other local organizations.[7] To cover the regions remote from the centre, it worked with Kōfūkai, a charitable NGO established in 1928 by the soy-sauce fermenters in Noda town. Kōfūkai worked with the local Medical Association (*Ishikai*) and midwives' association to provide a health consultation service. The health centre inherited this activity from Kōfūkai. It also collaborated with the employment agency in Ichikawa town to give aftercare for tuberculosis patients who had lost their jobs due to the disease. It was trying to integrate various local governmental offices and private organizations into a concerted force to improve health.

The health centre in Japan was thus envisioned as the core of various organizations related to public health and preventive medicine. To be active, a health centre should activate and work with other organizations. Sakai Kikuo, the head of the hygienic division for the city of Tokyo, expressed this view most clearly in his lecture in 1937.[8] He wrote that urban health consultation centres were doing a great job in reducing tuberculosis or vaccinating children against diphtheria. A health centre would organize such clinics and centres into a 'unified and melted whole'. Various other organizations would be included, such as medical associations, pharmacists' associations, hospitals, District Welfare Commissioners (*Homen Iin*), District Associations (*Chonaikai*) and Women's Associations (*Fujinkai*). Within such an organic system of public health, in which governmental and non-governmental organizations coexisted, the people would become healthy through self-government. This system of government, civil society and people would be equipped with urban amenities and the benefits of science and technology, which would affect every aspect of life, clothes, food and living: 'This will develop the self-government of the city in terms of urban public health. The self-government will enable the urban dwellers to enjoy the happiness of health.'[9] To this bright picture of health in cities through the integration of governmental and non-governmental organizations and self-government by the people, Sakai did not forget to add a nationalist ingredient: it would lead to a powerful state and Yamato race. The health centre was at the heart of this progressive project of reforming the health of society.

Rural health was conceptualized in a similar vein. The drive towards organizing rural public health into a system with a health centre at its core resonated with the idea of Yosano Hikaru (1902–92), who was the leading figure at the Institute of Rural Health at Tokorozawa. Yosano envisaged the health centre as the new hub of rural public health, replacing the old *eisei kumiai* under the control of the police:

> Public health administration in rural villages should be newly organized. Many heads of the health centres are able and earnest workers. Public health nurses should be more widespread. Rural villages only have the Hygiene Association under the Contagious Diseases Act, which has many inconveniences and should be replaced by a new system.[10]

Cooperation with other organizations was partly motivated by the lack of resources, and more importantly, the desire to achieve a more efficient society. Total war and the mobilization of the people necessitated the rational and efficient use of medical resources. In particular, expensive medical instruments such as X-ray machines should be used more efficiently. At present, various health organizations such as tuberculosis centres, health consultation centres by national health insurance, and health consultation centres for post office insurance existed with great regional variation: some regions had none of these institutions, while over 160 regions had several of them. Many of them had X-ray machines, and one region had several X-ray machines, which led to the waste of films and other resources. A health centre was expected to unify these institutions and create a network for efficient distribution of health resources.[11]

This vision of new public health and the health centre was understood within the context of the social change Japan had experienced since the Meiji period.[12] The head of Matsudo health centre, Seijō Minoru, had a clear historical vision about the mission of the health centre, which should replace control of disease by the police:[13]

> The policy for hygiene in our country developed as a branch of police administration and has been regarded by the people as such. Such an approach, however, has come to a dead end and no new development can be hoped for. The new national health policies for our country should be delivered by health centres whose control lies in the hands of medically educated administrators. If anybody thinks that only police can perform such work, that is an attempt to decivilize oneself and one's brethren.[14]

During the Meiji period, the argument went, the government had to *force* people into public health. The level of education had been low, knowledge of medicine, disease and the body was severely limited. Seijō characterized the situation succinctly: 'People avoided medicine and authority.' The view at the time was that people should be forced to conform to public health rules imposed by the government, and the police were the best means to enforce conformity. Seijō maintained, however, that things had changed. People now voluntarily sought medicine from the authorities. Local health officers often experienced people demanding preventive inoculation upon the outbreak of infectious diseases. Seijō himself experienced a flood of people asking for vaccination against smallpox. New priorities of the health centre were tuberculosis, syphilis, trachoma, helminthiasis and other parasitic diseases, whose diffusion was much slower and whose symptoms progressed in much more gradual ways. The profile of the diseases changed, and the relationship between people and the state shifted favourably for the new public health. The days of police-controlled public health had thus gone. The new public health should depend on people's initiatives.[15] Seijō's announcement here closely follows the progressive vision of Katsumata Minoru, an able administrator at the Office of Hygiene of the Home Ministry who insisted on the independence of public health administration from the police.[16] Indeed, Seijō's new vision of public health through newly created nonforceful civil institutions anticipated the reform of the health centre during the post-war period.

Behind this ambitious programme of the fundamental recasting and integration of the health administration and organizations lay an even more ambitious wartime vision of transforming the nation and the people. Medicine and health were less a strictly curative or preventive issue than a medium for transforming the people into a more desirable shape and achieving the new nation, state and region.[17] The families, particularly its women, were given special importance, because the family was the medium which connected the individual, the society and the nation. Sakai maintained the importance of the family, women and children:

> Female citizens protect the family and children. In total, women and children comprise about two-thirds of the entire nation. They should be integrated, organized, and mobilized in organic ways in order to implement successful public health. Without the integration of women and children, theories and advices are useless.[18]

Likewise, Shigeta Shin'ichi wrote succinctly: 'Families should be united into a large family of the state since families are the basic unit of the state, while the state and the region help the families to function properly.'[19] Through the members of the family, the local community received a strong infusion of the spirit of the state and the nation.[20] The rural hygiene movement was promulgated with a strong dose of ethics for peasants and villagers.[21] Teruoka Gitō, an authority on rural health, wrote that the rural health and hygiene movement should be guided by the three principles of labour, frugality and cooperation. Whereas labour and frugality were ethics of individuals, cooperation became possible only through communities of the village, the settlement or the neighbourhood, which provided the basis for various community hygiene activities such as community kitchens or day nurseries. Teruoka summarized: '[One] should follow. One should work with others. Co-operation is absolutely vital for rural hygiene.'[22] The language of autonomy and self-government thus coexisted with an emphasis on cooperation and community solidarity.

Failure of the old health centre system

The Welfare Ministry and active health centres expressed a progressive programme and an ambitious vision of integrating the society and people into health through the health centre. One doubts, however, to what extent these visions were achieved or even pursued outside the Ministry and a handful of active centres. The effort for the war, first with China and then with the US and Allied forces, might have fuelled the governmental policy talks and the propaganda, but it seriously hampered the actual construction and development of health centres.[23] Although the original plan was to build 550 health centres and 1,100 branches, the actual number constructed was only 187 by the end of 1941. By the end of 1943, the number was still 306, far behind the original plan, which was becoming increasingly impossible to achieve. In response to this situation, the Ministry simply changed the name and status of various health consultation institutions, designating them 'health centres', a procedure which they called 'integration'. By this cheating and cover-up, so to speak, the number of health centres jumped to 770 in 1944. Despite its failure to develop the health centre system effectively, the Ministry issued a number of new regulations and guidelines which put the health centre at the core of the national public health programme. In January 1939, the Welfare Ministry defined connections between health centres and the National Health Insurance Associations, enabling the latter to utilize the health facilities of the former, so that 'through the close connections of National Health Insurance and Health Center, the health measures on the first line in each district should be completed'.[24] In November 1941, the health centre was asked to act as a hub for the networks of health guidance organizations within a prefecture.[25] The revision of the National Physical Strength Law in February 1942 and the Elements of the Guidance of National Health in June 1942 also put the health centre at the core of public health policy.

Although the official history of the health centre praised the 'completion' of the network in 1944 and celebrated the progress of the laws, orders and guidelines, this is a serious misrepresentation, to say the least. The official history reveals that those who were responsible for the health centre were more interested in internal and external negotiation than in the real situation at the local level. If seen from the viewpoint of local health centres, the plan was a complete fiasco for many of them.

A few examples will suffice. Takigawa Health Centre in Hokkaido was established in 1944, as one of the 400 health consultation stations turned into a health centre. The building was the one used by the Health Consultation Centre of Simplified Postal Insurance of the town. Dr Isamu Eguchi, the director of the consultation centre, continued to direct the new health centre. He also retained the consultation centre's functions 'for the benefit of the clients', deciding to 'gradually change to the proper duties of a health centre'. Such language clearly shows that the health centre just carried on the previous works of the consultation centre.[26] Likewise, Obihiro Health Centre, which was also in Hokkaido, had a precarious existence before 1945. Unlike Takigawa Centre, Obihiro Health Centre benefited from a newly built office. The situation, however, was no more positive there. There was one doctor, one public health nurse, one midwife and three clerks. The doctor recalled that despite having no background in public health, he had left his job at the internist clinic of the Imperial University of Hokkaido to work for the health centre at the invitation of the local government. The main work for him was health consultation and finding those suffering from tuberculosis through X-ray examination. Direct exposure to X-rays apparently caused him to suffer from X-ray sickness and he had a difficult relationship with local medical practitioners. He withdrew from the health centre after two and a half years and returned to work at the internist clinic. The health centre could not find a stable replacement, hosting five directors over the next six years.[27] Nakatsu Health Centre in Oita prefecture also suffered from very limited human resources, even before the start of the war with the US. Its director wrote that for the entire fiscal year of 1940, the assistant doctor was called to war and he was the only doctor at the centre. A pharmacist was there for only five months, and two assistant technicians were a former policeman and former stretcher bearer for the army, neither of them capable of performing their duties and one of them at the centre for only seven months. Three public health nurses were often absent. With such serious personnel problems, the centre's priority of finding and preventing cases of tuberculosis relied almost entirely on doctors working for the local factories.[28]

It was this mixture of seriously under-staffed and under-funded institutions, propped up by grandiose orders and regulations, that existed at the end of the war, or even before the war with the US started. Damage by air-raids, although emphasized by the Welfare Ministry in its official history, was only a part of the problem of the old system. Despite some active health centres and celebrations by the Ministry, the system as a whole was not functioning effectively.

Post-war reform at the centre

The revision of the old Health Centre Law in 1947 clearly set the entire system into a new situation. Naturally the Japanese and Americans had different answers to the question of who was responsible for the dramatic improvement of the system. As we have encountered repeatedly throughout this book, the Americans were generally confident about their role as the saviour and civilizer of the enemy they defeated; they saw the question of the health centre in the same light. The Americans regarded the old health centre in Japan as inefficient, lacking rational structure and limited in its scope. They emphasized the revolutionary nature of the changes they effected to the health centre system. Crawford Sams, in typical fashion, wrote that the health centres under the old regime were mainly small and inefficient clinics for treatment, which resembled what the US had had two decades before. The 'two decades' might have been Sams' diplomacy, and he once said to the Japanese they were 'medieval', as one Japanese health officer recalled with bitterness.[29] His narrative was that GHQ started almost from scratch, fought with the vicious pre-war legacy and established a national system of health centres, which was the pride of the PH&W. Sams wrote that he and his team were proud of the establishment of the system, and he invited many doctors from the US and Britain to represent the health centres as his own achievement.

The Japanese saw and have seen the history of the health centre in a very different light, emphasizing the essential continuity between the old system established before the war and the new system. They readily admitted the deplorable condition of many health centres, which the Occupation army witnessed: their state immediately after the war was due to wartime scarcity or the damage wrought by US air-raids. When the worst of the situation had passed, they started to recover and develop the health centres. The new health centres of the 1947 Law were far from something given or imposed by GHQ, but rather what the Japanese asked them to authorize and materialize. The most eloquent story cast in this frame was told by Kusumoto Masayasu, one of the medical bureaucrats who worked at the Welfare Ministry and negotiated with GHQ over policy questions. Kusumoto's account begins by stressing GHQ's strong interest in the protection of US soldiers from infectious diseases. As we discussed in Chapter 3, the Occupation was anxious to control ravaging epidemics of acute infectious diseases immediately after the war. Another target of action was venereal diseases. Registered prostitutes were examined and treated at health centres. An expansion of venereal disease control at health centres to all Japanese patients was proposed by Lucius Thomas of the PH&W in February 1947. At his request, Kusumoto started a clever negotiation and replied that the Japanese government would implement the required policy if GHQ authorized an expansion of the health centres with larger resources, power and budgets. Kusumoto eventually persuaded Thomas, and at Kusumoto's request, Katsumata Minoru, the father of modern public health in Japan, who later became a Member of Parliament, persuaded Sams.[30] The memorandum was accordingly issued on 7 April 1947, which suggested radical expansion of the facilities of health centres. The revised Health Centre Law, which closely followed the memorandum, was passed in September 1947.

Kusumoto's reminiscences thus relate how the new system of health centres started from a Japanese idea, and was achieved through clever and patient negotiations with GHQ. The Welfare Ministry was the author of the new health centre, and bargained with GHQ for the realization of its plan. It is of little surprise that this story of Japanese achievement was incorporated into the official history of the health centre, compiled by the Welfare Ministry.[31] This story was also incorporated into *Kōseishō Gojūnenshi* [*Fifty Years of the History of the Welfare Ministry*], the official history of the Welfare Ministry.[32] Based on these accounts, Sugiyama Akiko's standard account of the health centre and public health during the Occupation period also followed Kusumoto's account, adding a twist that the American concern with emphasizing the welfare of the Japanese people also derived from their rivalry with the Soviet Union.[33]

This version also fits well with the newly dominant historiography of the development of health care under the welfare state in Japan. The new orthodox interpretation emphasizes the continuity in terms of health care policies before and after the war. Indeed, the rapid implementation of such key health care policies as the Health Centre Law (1937) and National Health Insurance Law (1938), which became the pillars of the post-war health care system, was exactly due to the massive mobilization of resources necessitated by total war.[34] Although further research into archives of the Welfare Ministry and GHQ will certainly give more nuances, there is little doubt that Kusumoto's 'official' version captures a certain core of truth: the new health centre was, basically, planned by the Welfare Ministry, not imposed by GHQ. The aims of the old and the new systems largely overlapped with one another. There existed a certain amount of continuity between the goals of the old system and the new one.

Building the new system

The new Health Centre Law of September 1947 was clearly distinct from the old one in many respects, as Sams, Kusumoto, Sugiyama and other have already pointed out. First, its power expanded to include administrative works. The new law gave the head of each health centre the power over 11 (or 12) items: (1) teaching and improving hygienic knowledge; (2) works related to vital statistics; (3) improvement of nutritional standards; (4) environmental hygiene; (5) social nurses; (6) improvement of public medicine; (7) maternal and infant health; (8) dental hygiene; (9a) public health testing; (9b) mental hygiene; (10) prevention of tuberculosis, venereal diseases and infectious diseases; (11) other works necessary for the improvement of public health in the district.[35] The health centre now had the power to administer these functions, while the old law had allowed the power of 'guidance' (*shidō*) only. This was exactly what the pre-war public health mandarins had demanded but achieved only to a limited extent.

The budget and the number of personnel increased drastically. While the old law allowed health centres to employ 8,600 people in total, the new law accorded the system of health centres much greater manpower. In January 1948, a budget was allocated for 14,671 persons working for the health centres. During the year, further allocations were made for 1,560 persons charged with pest control and 1,767 tasked with food and drink hygiene. In addition, an extra 5,000 temporary jobs were created mainly for the treatment of venereal diseases. In total, the new health centres were equipped with a workforce 2.7 times larger than the old centres.[36] The new workforce was not just more numerous, but also better trained. Doctors, technicians and nurses made up about two-thirds of the employees.[37] The Welfare Ministry was aware that a job at a health centre was not popular among doctors. Rightly or wrongly, health officials identified the cause of this unpopularity as the low standard of science and technology available at each centre:

In engaging in public health service, it is supposed that young medical practitioners have not discontentment only in their material treatment, but rather
have unrest in the fact that they cannot satisfy their aspiration after learning
and conscience as the technicians.[38]

To attract young and technologically oriented doctors, the health centre had to
have a lot of high-standard machines and apparatus for bacteriological examinations, chemical tests and X-ray analysis, together with library resources. Connections with universities and medical schools were sought, and official health
technicians were to hold the additional post of professor or lecturer of a medical
school. With better manpower in terms of number and quality, the new health
centre was much better prepared for the work it was going to tackle.

The severe lack of standardization, uniformity and association among health
centres, which was the major defect of the old system, was addressed from the
beginning. Initiatives for a more uniform and unified system of health centres
came from both the Japanese and the Occupation. The Japanese initiatives
started earlier than the materialization of the new system by the Welfare Ministry or GHQ. Indeed, it was an action from below, with heads of health centres in
Tokyo asking the Ministry, GHQ and the Tokyo Metropolitan Government for
help in improving their facilities. They first met on 9 October 1946, and issued a
resolution on 17 October, which was brought to the three governing bodies as a
petition from the Association of the Heads of the Health Centres in Tokyo. It
requested better technological equipment, better-trained personnel, more personnel and more administrative power for health centres.[39] The movement soon
spread to other prefectures, and in February 1947 the National Association of the
Heads of Health Centres started to be organized.[40] This initiative from below
preceded the discussion of reforming health centres by the central authorities,
which suggests the democratic fervour prevalent among public health doctors
and its contribution to the making of the new system.

GHQ was also concerned with the lack of uniformity and general standards
across the health centres in the country. As soon as the new system started in
January 1948, GHQ advised the Welfare Ministry to establish a 'model' health
centre in Tokyo, where health officers from around the country were summoned
and inducted into the new works of the health centre. Suginami Health Centre was
chosen as the model, and the training sessions started as soon as the centre opened
in April. Copying the Suginami model into local prefectures quickly followed, and
by the end of 1948 almost all prefectures had established their model prefectural
health centres. The National Institute of Public Health acted as the training centre
for the officers of the prefectural model health centres from June 1948 to March
1949. GHQ and the Welfare Ministry continued to guide and train officers of the
local health centres in 1950. On 25 February 1950, Lucius Thomas, the head of the
Preventive Medicine Division, summoned the representatives from prefectural
health departments and public works departments to hold a conference 'in order to
secure uniformity and plans and procedures' for projected health centres. Local
health and public works officers were to be familiarized into the overall programme

and to learn a single plan for the construction of health centres, their location, size, type of building and interior arrangements. Health centres were routinely evaluated by US military officers and their reports were sent back to GHQ.[41] The Welfare Ministry recognized the importance of national uniformity and standardization and a conference was held in March 1950 with 102 trainees.[42] The prefectural model health centres would, in turn, train health officers in their respective prefectures. Within a year or two of the start of the new system, GHQ and the Welfare Ministry had implemented a scheme which ensured the standard and the uniformity of every single health centre in the country.[43]

The strong initiative for uniformity flowing from the centre seems to have been smoothly effected at the local level. The guidance from the centre, however, occasionally conflicted with the idea of local autonomy. Early on in the establishment of new health centres, GHQ put them under scrutiny and intervened when necessary. They routinely and systematically conducted 'health center evaluations', by means of which activities, facilities and personnel were surveyed and listed. Occasionally, they found some health centres to be inefficient. For instance, in August 1949, Lucius Thomas and officers at the Welfare Ministry met to discuss deficiencies of public health programmes in the Shikoku area. The meeting was a very tough one, for Thomas wanted to fire two health department chiefs for the deficient nature of health centres in their prefectures:

> Recent staff visit to Shikoku Health Department: Chiefs of Kagawa and Kōchi are competent and aggressive. The public health programs in the two prefectures were found to be well-organized and their health centres were good. The chiefs of Ehime and Tokushima appeared to be disinterested and extremely inefficient and these prefectures have poor organization and programs. The inefficiency of the organization and neglect of the public health program appears to be due almost entirely to the lack of leadership and gross inefficiency of the chiefs.[44]

Despite such occasional forceful intervention from the centre and the Occupation, the new health centres expressed visible hope and vigour, which is entirely understandable. With vastly increased financial and human resources, each health centre did not have strong grounds to be dissatisfied with the new situation. Just a few years after the end of the war and a couple of years after the 1947 law, health centres were feeling confident about their achievement and potential. In 1951, Tatematsu Sōichi, the director of Yao Health Centre in Osaka prefecture, and other health officers petitioned GHQ about the administrative rights of the health centre. In the petition, they emphasized the enormous improvement of health they had experienced: 'No one can deny that after the war our country has developed and improved amazingly in the field of public health.' He wrote that 'We feel as if we are separated by an age' from the epidemics of typhus and smallpox immediately after the war. The vital statistics, a newly added responsibility, showed that their works were bearing fruit: 'The average span of life had been prolonged by ten years.'[45] Directors of health centres remembered the early years of the new system with enormous pride and told their heroic tales, such as halving infant mortality from 100 to 50/1,000 births in a couple of years or dramatically decreasing the infection rate of parasites in a year.[46]

No doubt the new health centre system was more efficient and successful. They were achieving what their predecessors could not before the Occupation due to the lack of resources and organizations, and the new medical technologies such as DDT or antibiotics. The crucial question is whether the new health centres subscribed to different principles or social philosophies in their pursuit of the health of the people. Were they pursuing the old goals with a new ethos, or were they playing the old game much better?

Several distinctively new ethoses were expressed clearly by the new health centres. The most prominent new principle was an article from the Constitution of Japan, which was promulgated in 1946. Article 25 of the Constitution, which granted all people 'the right to maintain the minimum standards of wholesome and cultured living', was repeatedly cited as if a mantra for the public health of the new era. Shigehara Health Centre of Chiba prefecture opened the first issue of *Hokenjo Nyūsu* with a quote from Article 25: 'If one demands healthy and cultural life, one needs to apply intelligence and hygienic science.' Likewise, Ueda Health Centre in Nagano titled their newsletter 'Bunka Ihō', meaning 'Culture and Medicine Newsletter'.[47] Military success or building a strong empire was no longer the major goal. Instead, 'culture' became the overarching theme of public health. The newsletter of Shizuki Health Centre in Hyogo Prefecture expressed its hope that Japan would develop as 'a country of high culture', so distancing itself from the strongly expressed military ambition of the pre-war state.[48] With all its complications and complexities, the new Constitution, according to John Dower, 'tapped into popular aspirations for peace and democracy in quite remarkable ways', and this was exactly what happened to the post-war health centres.[49] As a symbolic act, the emphasis on article 25 of the new Constitution as their core defining principle captures the direction and the aspirations of the new health centres. Nothing is further from the earlier vision of the healthy and strong nation that would rule Asia and be loyal to the Emperor.[50]

But one needs to be careful in understanding what health centres meant by 'culture', given its ambiguous and multivalent connotations. Rather than the means for personal fulfilment or happiness, it was regarded as an orderly march towards economic recovery. The head of Ueda Health Centre criticized the 'opera-house' view of culture and maintained that culture should be regarded as a complex of labour, production and social order. The aim of the health centre and public health was, according to him, to allow the people to acquire cultural status through the rationalization of everyday life and adoption of correct habits.[51] This view of 'culture' clearly resonated with the social medicine, which was propagated before or during the war.

Attitudes towards venereal disease also showed a new ethos, which tried to separate the disease from the sense of shame. As mentioned earlier, treatment of venereal diseases was the starting point of the new health centre. Although the function of the venereal disease clinic was originally proposed by GHQ and not emphasized by Japanese health officials, it turned out that its work was the most popular part of the health centres and overwhelmed other activities. GHQ expressed the dawn of a new age in the treatment of venereal diseases, most notably in a series of press conference on Radio Tokyo to publicize the activities of the new health centres from October 1948 to March 1949.

> True, in the past no venereal disease control program existed for the general public – only prostitutes received examination and treatment in the few scattered VD clinics and hospitals. But that was yesterday. Today, for the first time in the history of Japan, an efficient and effective program for all-out control of VD is conducted for the general public. [At the VD clinic which was located in each health centre], patients are received courteously, afforded every consideration, and are secure in the knowledge that all matters pertaining to their cases are treated confidentially.[52]

Perhaps echoing this 'new age' programme, the health centres started to frame the control of venereal disease in a new language. An article in *Hokenjo Jihō* [*Health Centre News*] of Shigehara Health Centre in Chiba prefecture contrasted the old culture of shame with the new, open one. Venereal diseases should no longer be regarded as a shameful disease, 'as one sows, so one shall reap' [*jigojitoku*] or 'hiding unpleasant realities' [*kusai mono ni futa*]. Such an approach would not eradicate the diseases. Rather, venereal disease should be treated as an ordinary disease. A newsletter from Iwauchi Health Centre in Hokkaido maintained that patients should not feel shameful about the disease, and society should not blame the patient, but encourage and help the patient from a broad viewpoint of the public's welfare.[53] A similar view was expressed in Ueda Health Centre's newsletter.[54]

Here, again, one needs to be cautious in emphasizing the novelty and openness of the new treatment of venereal diseases. There existed a large dose of pre-war identification of venereal disease with 'race poison' or *minzoku doku*. The rhetoric of 'the purification of the race' surrounded the new Venereal Diseases Prevention Law (1947), which was a close echo of the nationalist agenda for a strong army. *Nikutai no Akuma* [*The Devil of the Flesh*], an educational film about the dangers of venereal disease, was made from an earlier film composed by the navy.[55] Similar continuity characterized the issue of eugenics. Yao Health Centre in Osaka Prefecture laid strong emphasis on eugenics, sex education and reproductive health. As soon as the committee for the health centre was established, a new committee for implementing the Eugenic Protection Law was formed, headed by the director of the health centre. The newsletters contained a series of articles and advisory statements on eugenics.[56]

Conclusion

This chapter has sketched the continuities and changes of the health centre system. The accounts of Crawford Sams and Japanese health officials were both one-sided. It should be noted that the pre-war Japanese government envisaged the health centre as the core of a progressive public health which lay not in the enforcement of health measures but in the self-government of the people. To a certain extent, this ideal was pursued by some health centres. The post-war health centre system was not created and granted by GHQ from above. On the other hand, the situation varied enormously among 770 health centres that came into existence towards the end of the war. Many suffered from a fundamental lack of resources, and perhaps a great number of them were just nominal. The post-war reform, assisted by GHQ, infused many more resources and technological advances into the system. It also achieved uniformity across the centres and raised the general standard of the system. Equipped with this new infusion, the new health centres exhibited genuine vigour.

Conclusion

Whether they are predominantly benign or punitive, military occupations are first and foremost expressions of power. They involve a victorious nation invariably dictating terms to a vanquished foe, the unequal nature of the relationship often subtly reinforced by the occupier's careful management of information. The power to control information media enables it to represent its actions and reforms as advantageous to the nation under its control and to disguise the protection and promotion of its own interests, which may or not coincide with the desires and aspirations of those on the receiving end of its policies. Historians conventionally are drawn to those sites or subjects where the Occupation's exercise of power is most manifest or overt, usually in relation to security, constitutional and economic issues.

In the case of the Occupation of Japan, there has been a reluctance to explore such subjects as natural resources or public health, where reform seems much less politically loaded, perhaps even apolitical. It is the main contention of this book that, despite appearances to the contrary, the reform of public health in Occupied Japan was politically charged and was presented in such a way as to enhance the reputation of the principal Allied power, the US. Much was made of the immense scale of its achievements and its benign, humanitarian motivations with a view to harvesting the consequent fruits of Japanese goodwill. Here was an instance of the exercise of 'soft power', of winning hearts and minds through the promotion of beneficial reforms ostensibly inspired by the occupying power.

Of course, this approach required that Japan's past record be belittled. It was necessary to dismiss or disparage Japan's historical record on public health so as to highlight the contrast between the US, responsible for bestowing upon Japan 'modern' forms and systems of public health, and its recipient, apparently lacking in knowledge and expertise in this regard. This contrast was overdrawn, deliberately or otherwise, so as to underline the impressive impact of public health reform. In short, it was necessary to posit a sharp break with the past, for Occupations of a reformist nature are judged according to their success in transforming institutions and practices in line with modern democratic, progressive norms.

The argument presented in this book, that the role of the PH&W was much less significant than has conventionally been understood, revolves around four key issues. First, the nature and limitations of the Occupation, and the influence of Crawford Sams as propagandist for his section. Second, the degree to which the struggle to prevent and control epidemics of acute infectious diseases depended on public health interventions that were familiar to the Japanese. Third, the origins and impact of strategies adopted to tackle more intractable problems (e.g. malnutrition, dysentery, tuberculosis and venereal disease) and the strength of associated community engagement; and, finally, the legacy of the Occupation's reform initiatives, particularly with regard to the revamped *hokenjo* and the culture of public health that they represented. Each of these themes illuminates the contention advanced by this book that for the most part the Occupation's public health reforms were more familiar than alien to Japanese participants. Often it was a case of resuming practices interrupted by the war years. This much was clear from a promotional advertisement in 1948 for the *Journal of the American Medical Association – Japanese Edition*, the stated purpose of which was 'to recover from backwardness caused by the war, and to catch up to the international standard as swiftly as possible'.[1] In other words, there was general agreement among both American and Japanese medics as to how to confront the challenges they faced, a convergence of views that belies the dominant narrative of the imposition of reform according to a number of 'alien prescriptions'.

The politics of public health and the limits of Occupation

Despite their claims to the contrary, Sams and the PH&W were largely involved in rebuilding and restoring systems of public health established in Japan from the late nineteenth century rather than *creating them anew*. This situation reflected the realities of indirect Occupation, which assumed a functioning and reasonably effective Japanese government with sufficient power and reach to ensure that its instructions were acted on at prefectural and local levels. Moreover, the policy guidance that MacArthur received in late 1945 made it clear that the Japanese were expected to take responsibility for their plight and to make the most of the resources they could muster. Imports would only be justified to prevent disease and unrest that might endanger the Occupation's mission or those Americans working to carry it out. Only when famine threatened or typhus erupted with potentially disastrous consequences were US imports of food, DDT and typhus vaccine permitted, but only temporarily until indigenous supplies were assured. There were a few occasions when a vaccine, insecticide or medicine was developed or improved at American prompting, but for the most part the Japanese set about resuming or increasing production of established products to meet the needs of the time. In other words, indirect Occupation was premised on US confidence in the capability of the Japanese authorities to respond to disease threats adequately with minimal interference from the PH&W.

This, of course, is not the impression created by the large number of SCAP instructions or commands on public health emanating from the PH&W. These detailed what the Japanese government must do to confront the menaces of

epidemic disease and chronic infections, both exacerbated by the social dislocation brought about by war and defeat. However, for the most part these prescriptions were uncontroversial, readily adopted by those Japanese charged with
carrying them out. Usually, they accorded with medical opinion among native
doctors and scientists about how best to confront the threats they faced. This was
not surprising, given that they were no less committed to adopting modern, scientific approaches to problems of public health than their American counterparts.
The essential obstacle to achieving rapid progress against disease was not the
Japanese mindset, as Sams implied, but rather the dilapidated sanitary infrastructure and parlous state of hospitals, clinics and laboratories as a result of neglect
and incendiary bombing. As Japan's wartime prospects had deteriorated, so had
it become harder to sustain efforts to safeguard standards of public health.

Scenes of devastation greeted those like Sams, who came to Japan with a
mission of radical reform. The two were not compatible. For the first two years
of the Occupation, the head of the PH&W struggled with his Japanese counterparts to prevent epidemics from raging out of control. When it was possible by
around 1947 to direct attention to chronic infectious diseases, it was a case of
mitigating rather than eradicating the social conditions that served as their breeding ground. These problems seem even more insurmountable when one considers the handful of qualified Americans able to give them their undivided
attention. Moreover, most of the health officers in the military government teams
knew much less about programmes of public health than they did about hospital
medicine.[2] In short, they depended on Japanese energy and expertise to make
any progress in their prefectures.

Despite this, the relatively few historians who work on this subject tend to
emphasize American leadership and energy at the expense of Japanese experience and commitment. The principal reason for this must be the historical and
historiographical importance of Crawford Sams, the chief of the PH&W, who
looms large over contemporary accounts of public health during this period and
whose version of events has largely held sway since. The absence of a rigorous
critique is very surprising, given his personal stake in the enterprise, and his
patriotic sense of the need to burnish the reputations of MacArthur and the US in
Japan. Indeed, the recent work of Dower and others that examine the Occupation
through such lenses as race and gender might prompt readers of Sams' memoir
to locate it within a larger colonial discourse; one that posits a false dichotomy
of Japan as feudal, primitive, dirty and malnourished and the US as democratic,
hygienic, healthy and quintessentially modern. The absence of a counter-
narrative during the Occupation, largely as a result of censorship, seemed to
reinforce the validity of the official line. Interestingly, the colonial mentality of
Sams and his team was replicated in their Japanese colleagues, who blamed epidemics of cholera and typhus on Korean labourers.

However, alongside this colonial perspective was Sams' hard-edged anti-
communism that required the US's reputation be greatly enhanced by its record
in Japan. Thus, the chief of the PH&W always swiftly rebutted any suggestions
that the work of his section was failing to transform the landscape of public

health in Japan. Witness his skilful use of Japanese statistics to demonstrate progress. Moreover, his confident performance at the ACJ on 30 April 1947, when he presented the PH&W's record in overwhelmingly positive terms, was typical of his strident defence of the US against the USSR, represented in this case by General Derevyanko. He fully understood the importance of the Occupation for America's reputation and standing, and never missed an opportunity to improve his country's prospects in the Cold War. Such considerations influenced his backing for imports of DDT for typhus control and dry skim milk for the school lunch programme.

For Sams, the political side of his work, the public relations, was just as important as its more technical aspects. He felt a strong compulsion to present the Occupation-sponsored reforms as revolutionary. This meant denying Japanese agency in large part; such distortion was clearly justified by the propaganda advantages it would bring the US. It also derived from Sams' convictions and clear-sightedness, which inspired him to action but left no room for doubt or negotiation. In short, he seldom countenanced any criticism of the US, because he genuinely believed in the superiority of its values and institutions and strove to promote them in the face of the communist threat. His narrative of reform in Japan was coloured by these principles.

Acute and chronic infectious diseases: a collaborative approach

Throughout this book the analysis of public health in Japan has been centred on disease, distinguishing between acute infectious diseases like smallpox, cholera and diphtheria and chronic ones like tuberculosis and dysentery. It has traced the nineteenth-century advance of Japanese science, chiefly microbiology, in response to the threat posed to national strength by epidemics, and it has explored the efforts made to ameliorate the social and economic conditions, which fostered the spread of particular diseases. With Nagayo Sensai at the helm, the emerging nation state of Meiji Japan proved a quick study in disease control. It was not long before vaccination against smallpox was universally adopted, and cholera brought under control by means of a rigorous quarantine regime, an effective vaccine and strict regimens of isolation and disinfection. The very capable Japanese microbiologist, Kitasato, was at the forefront of the development of vaccines and antitoxins, working closely with leading scientists in Germany. Indeed, his close ties with the world-famous microbiologist, Robert Koch, captures the degree to which Japan was integrated into the world of modern science.

However, as the threat of acute infectious diseases receded in the face of these public health interventions, so the problem of such chronic conditions as tuberculosis and dysentery came to the fore. These reflected the social consequences of rapid industrialization and military development that caused the national interest to displace pressing issues of social import. The social ferment that resulted during the Taisho period (1912–26) produced not just political agitation but also a commitment on the part of middle-class social activists to work with government to improve standards of health, hygiene and sanitation. This lifestyle improvement movement identified inadequacies of dietary balance, clean water supply and sewage disposal. It highlighted the importance of community engagement and harnessing the power of an educated public for the work of hygienic modernization. Such considerations had caused pioneers of modern hygiene like Nagayo, Gotō and Mori to encourage a hygiene consciousness among the people, as well as ensuring the means for active monitoring and enforcement of public health regulations. While Sams chose to stress the history of compulsion – hygiene police (*eisei keisatsu*) – more vital was the tradition of *jichi eisei* or *jichi soshiki* (autonomous organization), represented by the hygiene associations (*eisei kumiai*). The hygiene consciousness that this evidenced would prove vitally important in the context of an indirect Occupation and a formal commitment on the part of American reformers to strip the police of their economic and public health functions.

In practice, the PH&W depended on the police, medical personnel and such established local organizations as *eisei kumiai* and neighbourhood associations to carry out vaccination campaigns against smallpox, cholera, typhus, typhoid, diphtheria, Japanese B encephalitis and tuberculosis. Despite a propensity to dismiss the quality of Japanese vaccine and vaccination technique, it is quite clear, for example, that the responsibility and credit for bringing the smallpox epidemic of 1946 under control lay with those Japanese that organized and implemented the vaccination drive. Similarly, claims about the introduction of a new and much improved typhoid vaccine or diphtheria toxoid have to be treated with caution, given the evidence for native production and use before 1945. Moreover, Sams' indictment of Japan's record on vector control in relation to enteric diseases takes little account of the evidence to the contrary, some of it in official US publications like the *Civil Affairs Handbook*. It is also difficult to square with the country's status as a global leader in the production of pyrethrum, used in and around Japanese homes and for control of agricultural pests, as well as being exported to the US, among other countries. While there is no doubt that DDT was brought in and extensively deployed by mainly Japanese teams to tackle the typhus epidemic in 1946, less persuasive is the contention that it supplanted pyrethrum in more routine insect control programmes. Evidence presented in this book shows that vector control in the communities across Japan continued to rely on domestically produced rat poisons and pyrethrum, which was preferred to DDT due to the delayed action of the latter.

When it came to more entrenched problems like dysentery and parasitical diseases, the PH&W expressed dissatisfaction with the lack of provision for clean, treated water, and the inadequate infrastructure for sewage disposal. They acknowledged limited Japanese advances in these areas, such as with regard to the development of the sanitary privy, and recommended more of the same. It was beyond the remit of the Occupation and obviously beyond the capabilities of the Japanese at this time to start designing and building a more modern sanitary infrastructure. Indeed, their chief concern was restitution of pre-war standards.

The limits of the Occupation's ambitions in this regard provide some context for the increasing incidence of dysentery from 1949. While the aetiology of this jump in cases remains obscure, it nevertheless undermined Sams' protestations of major improvements in environmental hygiene. A lack of resources often prevented effective action against chronic problems. In the case of parasitical diseases, for example, a deficit of chemical fertilizers made it difficult to reduce reliance on night soil and the shortage of vermifuges constrained the effectiveness of treatment programmes.

Similar considerations applied to the most serious public health problem affecting Japan at this time, namely the very high incidence of tuberculosis. There seems to have been agreement among American and Japanese parties that elevated rates of morbidity in part reflected nutritional deficiencies and could best be corrected by higher intake of animal protein. However, despite an avowed ambition to change nutritional patterns, there was no real prospect of rebalancing the Japanese diet away from its reliance on carbohydrates towards sources of animal protein in the near or medium term. Thus, the PH&W focused its energies on the provision of dry skim milk for school children, and may have helped to restore many to the stature of their pre-war counterparts. Much less persuasive is the claim that the school lunch programme inculcated new nutritional habits among the young.

As regards the more general assault on the problem of tuberculosis, the PH&W acknowledged that it could do little about the straitened socio-economic conditions that favoured its spread and so relied on the efforts of Japanese doctors and public health nurses to confront the problem as best they could. For the most part, they endeavoured to continue established programmes of tuberculin testing, BCG inoculation, X-ray examinations and blood tests in the face of deficient resources. Reports from the field highlighted the dilapidated state of the *hokenjo* in the wake of war and defeat. Also significant was the limited bed capacity in sanatoria for the isolation and treatment of infectious cases, although the large number of empty beds in these facilities indicated that misgivings about them had only been heightened by serious food shortages. In the circumstances, Japanese doctors and public health nurses worked to ensure more effective isolation and care of active cases in the home. Their work was made more difficult by the sense of shame and fatalism that many felt towards tuberculosis, causing a culture of concealment that served to exacerbate the problem. Only with the development of an effective cure for tuberculosis were Japanese able to tackle the problem openly and effectively. Despite a steep drop in deaths from the disease, however, morbidity levels remained high, reflecting the entrenched nature of many of the social problems besetting Japan.

Similarly, advances in treatment hugely benefited venereal disease control programmes that were hampered by insufficient resources for effective systems of case finding, contact tracing and case holding. The urgency with which penicillin was introduced by the Occupation highlights the priority accorded its own troops, among whom the incidence of venereal disease was rising rapidly. Interestingly, this military concern put the commanders of tactical troops in Japan on a collision course with members of the PH&W, who were trying to introduce modern, progressive systems of venereal disease control to the Japanese public. The latter were defined in opposition to the conventional forms of regulation, namely compulsory health checks on prostitutes and forced treatment programmes in secure hospitals. While the PH&W worked to encourage a culture of voluntary check-ups and treatment programmes at *hokenjo*, the US military police worked with Japanese police in 'vice squads' that targeted suspected streetwalkers and detained them for intrusive medical checks for venereal disease. Such divisions became less serious with the pervasive use of penicillin, which rapidly broke the chain of infection. Sams' claims about the ignorance of Japanese doctors regarding venereal disease diagnosis and treatment were an exaggeration, as was his assertion that there were virtually no sanitary engineers in Japan at the outset of the Occupation.

Legacies of Occupation

The generous sharing with Japan of American scientific advances in the form of penicillin and streptomycin undoubtedly made a great contribution to improving standards of public health. This much is clear from the drop in mortality from tuberculosis, which by 1951 was no longer the leading cause of death in Japan. At the same time the speed with which domestic production of these vital drugs was increased to meet domestic demand was testament to the expertise and commitment of Japanese producers. That is to say, the Japanese scientific community was sufficiently advanced in the production of medicines to make the most of expert American guidance and instruction. Here, then, was a positive legacy.

For the most part, however, Japanese scientists and doctors independently continued with the work of tuberculin testing, X-ray analysis, blood sedimentation tests, serological and bacteriological examinations, etc. BCG and other vaccines were administered to the Japanese public as before, and local organizations undertook routine operations against such disease vectors as flies, mosquitoes and rats. By acknowledging the contribution that the Japanese themselves made to disease control during the Occupation, this book does not mean to disparage the leadership and endeavours of those in the PH&W and military government, many of whom worked energetically and selflessly to assist their Japanese colleagues. Sams was clearly an inspirational figure, but he and his colleagues did not preside over a revolution in public health as he claimed. Rather, the opportunities presented by the Occupation enabled the more progressive approaches associated with the early interwar period and the collaborative initiatives of the Rockefeller Foundation to reassert themselves. As has been shown throughout this book, many Japanese officials, doctors and public health nurses embraced the prescriptions of the PH&W as a return to effective strategies of disease control. This was part of what Takemae characterizes as 'a powerful surge of creative energy "from below"'.[3]

The positive effects of this mutual collaboration were only too clear from Sams' fond memories and high praise for those Japanese who worked with him to bring tuberculosis under control. Likewise, he acknowledged the active and decisive role of all those who had struggled to prevent the outbreak of a cholera epidemic in 1946. However, the relationship between Sams and his Japanese colleagues was a very unequal one, with strong colonial overtones. This formally necessitated a pivotal role for the US and a subordinate one for Japan. The persistence of this narrative over the post-war decades can be explained by Sams' skills as a propagandist for the PH&W. It also reflects the appeal of an ideology of scientific progress powerfully conveyed by DDT and penicillin, the close ties that developed between the two countries after 1952, and the strong sense of gratitude among many Japanese for US food relief.

What light does this study shed on the nature of the Occupation more broadly? First, it illuminates the gravity of prevailing socio-economic conditions, and the dilapidated infrastructures of public health and sanitation, conducive to serious outbreaks of epidemic disease. Too often, this sense of social crisis is lost amid analyses of reform that tend to focus on what historians refer to as the 'revolution from above'. Second, this book highlights the limits of indirect Occupation. There was just a handful of Americans in GHQ SCAP with public health expertise, a small group of military government health officers spread thinly throughout Japan and a tendency to push for the resumption of pre-war practices rather than radical change, the resources for which were not available. Third, the upshot of this was a much greater need for Japanese expertise, participation and commitment than was and has been acknowledged. Occupation initiatives could only succeed when there was a ready constituency of energetic support and the required level of proficiency among those Japanese implementing them. Lastly, this study illuminates the split personality of the Occupation – the coexistence of progressive reform initiatives with the hard-edged realities of military rule. In a sense, Sams himself combined these conflicting attributes. He personified both a caring, benevolent Occupation and a harsh, colonial enterprise.

Notes

Introduction

1 Mark Gayn, *Japan Diary*, New York: William Sloane Associates, 1948, p. 1.
2 Letter from James S. Simmons to Crawford F. Sams, 23 April 1951, file 36, Box 4, Crawford F. Sams Collection, Hoover Institution Archives, copyright Stanford University.
3 E. Takemae, *Inside GHQ*, London: Continuum, 2002, pp. 426–33.
4 Ibid., p. 405.
5 An example of this is Christopher Aldous, *The Police in Occupation Japan: Control, corruption and resistance to reform*, London: Routledge, 1997.
6 M. E. Caprio and Y. Sugita, 'Introduction', in M. E. Caprio and Y. Sugita (eds), *Democracy in Occupied Japan: The US occupation and Japanese politics and society*, London: Routledge, 2007, p. 2.
7 C. Gluck, 'Entangling illusions: Japanese and American views of the Occupation', in W. I. Cohen (ed.), *New Frontiers in American–East Asian Relations: Essays presented to Dorothy Borg*, New York: Columbia University Press, pp. 175–7.
8 J. Dower, *Empire and Aftermath*, Cambridge, MA: Harvard University Press, 1979, p. 311.
9 *The Occupation of Japan: The Proceedings of a Seminar on the Occupation of Japan and its Legacy to the Postwar World*, Norfolk, VA: MacArthur Memorial, 1975. Lawrence H. Redford (ed.), *The Occupation of Japan: Impact of legal reform*, 1977; *The Occupation of Japan: Economic policy and reform*, 1980; Thomas W. Burkman (ed.), *The Occupation of Japan: Educational and social reform*, 1981; *The Occupation of Japan: The international context*, 1984; *The Occupation of Japan: Arts and culture*, 1988; William F. Nimmo (ed.), *The Occupation of Japan: The impact of the Korean War*, 1990; *The Occupation of Japan: The grass roots*, 1992.
10 Rinjirō Sodei, 'Keynote address' and Allen H. Meyer, 'Repatriation at the grass roots level', in William F. Nimmo (ed.), *The Occupation of Japan: The Grass Roots*, pp. 6, 105–7.
11 G. Daniels, 'The social history of Occupied Japan: some source and problems', *Japanese Studies*, STICERD (Suntory Toyota International Centre of Economics and Related Disciplines), LSE, 1990.
12 Gluck, 'Entangling illusions', p. 193.
13 Mark Metzler, 'The Occupation', in William M. Tsutsui (ed.), *A Companion to Japanese History*, Oxford: Blackwell, 2007, p. 266.
14 J. Dower, *Embracing Defeat: Japan in the wake of World War II*, New York: W. W. Norton, 1999.
15 See: Steven J. Fuchs, 'Feeding the Japanese: food policy, land reform, and Japan's economic recovery', pp. 26–47; Sayuri Guthrie-Shimizu, 'Occupation policy and the Japanese fisheries management regime, 1945–52', pp. 48–66; Yoneyuki Sugita, 'Uni-

versal health insurance: the unfinished reform of Japan's healthcare system',
pp. 147–77, in M. E. Caprio and Y. Sugita (eds), *Democracy in Occupied Japan: The
US occupation and Japanese politics and society*, London: Routledge, 2007.

16 This followed close on the heels of an article by Adam D. Sheingate and Takakazu
Yamagishi, 'Occupation politics: American interests and the struggle over health
insurance in postwar Japan', *Social Science History*, vol. 30, no. 1, 2006, pp. 137–64.

17 Ibid., p. 139.

18 A. Sugiyama, *Senryōki no iryō kaikaku*, Tokyo: Keisō Shobō, 1995.

19 Bernard J. Turnock, *Public Health: What it is and how it works*, 3rd edition, Boston,
MA: Jones and Bartlett, 2004, p. 96.

20 Charles-Edward A. Winslow was an important figure in the history of public health in
the US. C.-E.A. Winslow, 'The untilled fields of public health', *Science*, vol. 51,
1920, p. 30.

21 Monica Das Gupta, 'Public health in India: an overview', World Bank Research
Working Paper 3787, December 2005, p. 1.

22 Turnock, *Public Health*, pp. 12–13.

23 Ann Bowman Jannetta, 'From physician to bureaucrat: the case of Nagayo Sensai', in
Helen Hardacre (ed.), *New Directions in the Study of Meiji Japan*, Leiden: Brill, 1997,
p. 159.

24 *Kōseishō* is generally translated as Ministry of Health and Welfare or just Welfare
Ministry. The latter form will be used hereafter.

25 Supreme Commander of the Allied Powers (SCAP), Statistics and Reports Section,
History of the Non-Military Activities of the Occupation of Japan, Tokyo: SCAP,
1952. Consisting of a total of 55 volumes, volume 18 covers public welfare, volume
19 public health and volume 20 social security.

26 Studies of public welfare (*fukushi*) include Toshio Tatara, 'The Allied Occupation and
Japanese public welfare: an overview of SCAP activities during the early phase',
Donald V. Wilson, 'Social welfare personnel and social work education during the
Occupation of Japan, 1945–1948' and Nakamura Yūichi, 'The Occupation period and
after', all included in Thomas Burkman (ed.), *The Occupation of Japan: Educational
and social reform*, Norfolk, VA: MacArthur Memorial, 1981. In Japanese, see
Murakami Kimiko, *Senryōki no fukushi seisaku*, Tokyo: Keisō Shobō, 1987.

27 J. Hunter, 'Textile factories, tuberculosis and the quality of life in industrializing
Japan', in J. Hunter (ed.), *Japanese Women Working*, London: Routledge, 1993,
pp. 75–84.

28 George Rosen, 'What is social medicine? A genetic analysis of the concept', *Bulletin
of the History of Medicine*, vol. 21, 1947, p. 730.

29 Crawford F. Sams, *'Medic': The mission of an American military doctor in Occupied
Japan and wartorn Korea*, edited by Zabelle Zakarian, Armonk, NY: M. E. Sharpe,
1998, pp. 66–7.

30 William Johnston, *The Modern Epidemic: A history of tuberculosis in Japan*, Cambridge, MA: Harvard University Press, pp. 266–7, 275–8, 283.

31 See the *American Journal of Public Health and the Nation's Health*, vol. 42, 1952,
pp. 557, 565.

32 M. Metzler, 'The Occupation', in William M. Tsutsui (ed.), *A Companion to Japanese History*, Oxford: Blackwell, 2007, p. 273.

33 Turnock, *Public Health*, pp. 16–17.

34 Dower, *Embracing Defeat*, p. 407.

35 Sey Nishimura, 'Medical censorship in Occupied Japan, 1945–1948', *The Pacific Historical Review*, vol. 58, no. 1, 1989, pp. 1–21.

36 Takemae, *Inside GHQ*, pp. 117–18.

37 Sey Nishimura, 'Promoting health during the American Occupation of Japan: the
Public Health Section, Kyoto Military Government Team, 1945–49', *American
Journal of Public Health*, vol. 98, no. 3, 2008, pp. 424–34; 'Promoting health in

American-Occupied Japan: resistance to Allied public health measures', *American Journal of Public Health*, vol. 99, no. 8, 2009, pp. 1364–75.

38 From November 1949 Burma and Pakistan brought the number of countries represented on the Commission to 13.

39 Sams, *'Medic'*, p. 178.

40 Public Health and Welfare Section (PHW) fiche 01631–2, National Diet Library (NDL), Tokyo. Hereafter, citations of SCAP documents on fiche in the NDL will follow the abbreviated form of just section and fiche number (e.g. PHW 01631–2).

41 Watanabe Mikio, ' "DDT kakumei" to sono jidai', *Juntendō Igaku*, vol. 49, no. 2, 2003, pp. 260–1.

42 Large's review of Takemae's *Inside GHQ*, in *Journal of Japanese Studies*, vol. 29, no. 2, 2003, p. 438.

43 Nishimura, 'Promoting health during the American Occupation of Japan', p. 432.

44 Sams, *'Medic'*, pp. 3, 188, 267.

45 US Strategic Bombing Survey, Medical Division, *The Effects of Bombing on Health and Medical Services in Japan*, June 1947.

1 Confronting epidemics

1 Sams was addressing the Council on Medical Education on 27 February 1946 when he made these remarks. Quoted in E. Marui, 'Public health and "koshu-eisei" ', in T. Ogawa (ed.), *Public Health: Proceedings of the 5th International Symposium on the Comparative History of Medicine – East and West*, Osaka: Taniguchi Foundation, 1980, p. 102.

2 S. Sakai, *Nihon no Iryōshi* [*A History of Japanese Medicine*], Tokyo: Tokyo Shoseki, 1982, pp. 391–2.

3 R. Rogaski, *Hygienic Modernity: Meanings of Health and Disease in Treaty-Port China*, Berkeley, CA: University of California Press, 2004, p. 141.

4 Ann Bowman Jannetta, 'From physician to bureaucrat: the case of Nagayo Sensai', in H. Hardacre (ed.), *New Directions in the Study of Meiji Japan*, Leiden: Brill, 1997, p. 159.

5 Ban Tadayasu, *Tekijuku to Nagayo Sensai* [*Tekijuku and Nagayo Sensai*], Osaka: Sogensha, 1987, p. 156.

6 Rogaski, *Hygienic Modernity*, p. 145.

7 S. Burns, 'Constructing the national body: public health and the nation in nineteenth-century Japan', in T. Brook and A. Schmid (eds), *Nation Work*, Ann Arbor, MI: University of Michigan Press, 2000, p. 17.

8 W. Johnston, *The Modern Epidemic: A history of tuberculosis in Japan*, Cambridge, MA: Harvard University Press, 1995, pp. 179–80.

9 Comment made in the course of a lecture given in 1963. Quoted in Hiroshi Mizuno, 'Social development of hygiene in modern Japan', in Y. Kawakita, S. Sakai and Y. Ōtsuka (eds), *History of Hygiene: Proceedings of the 12th International Symposium on the Comparative History of Medicine – East and West*, Tokyo: Ishiyaku, 1991, p. 242.

10 Burns, 'Constructing the national body', p. 18.

11 G. Rosen, *A History of Public Health*, Baltimore, MD: Johns Hopkins University Press, 1993, p. 138.

12 Johnston, *Modern Epidemic*, p. 180.

13 H. Kasahara, ' "Eisei keisatsu" to "jichi eisei" no sōkoku – eisei gyōsei no mosaku no tenkan' [Conflict between 'hygiene police' and 'autonomous hygiene' – the switch of hygiene administration by trial and error] in H. Kasahara and K. Tamai (eds), *Nihon seiji no kōzō to tenkai* [*The Development of Japan's Political Structure*], Tokyo: Keio University Press, 1998, pp. 93–114.

14 Takeshi Nagashima, 'Meiji medical officials' international comparisons of administrative machinery and the historiography of public health', in S. Sakai, T. Sakai, C.

Oberlander and Y. Ichinokawa, *Transaction in Medicine and Heteronomous Modernization: Germany, Taiwan, Korea and Japan*, Tokyo: University of Tokyo Center for Philosophy, 2009, pp. 99–104.

15　Rogaski, *Hygienic Modernity*, p. 145.

16　Nagashima, 'Meiji medical officials' international comparisons', p. 97.

17　Jong-Chan Lee, 'Hygienic governance and military hygiene in the making of Imperial Japan, 1868–1912', *Historia Scientarium*, vol. 18, no. 1, 2008, p. 6.

18　E. Marui, 'Public health and "koshu-eisei" ', p. 103.

19　Burns, 'Constructing the national body', p. 26. For a useful summary of the origins of public health in Japan, see Kōzō Tatara, 'The origins and development of public health in Japan', in R. Detels, W. Holland, J. McEwen and G. Omenn (eds), *Oxford Textbook of Public Health*, 3rd edition, vol. 1, *The Scope of Public Health*, New York: Oxford University Press, 1997, p. 56.

20　Johnston, *The Modern Epidemic*, p. 174.

21　Tatara, 'The origins and development of public health in Japan', p. 57.

22　Johnston, *The Modern Epidemic*, pp. 174–5.

23　M. Fukuda, 'Public health in modern Japan: from regimen to hygiene', in D. Porter (ed.), *The History of Public Health and the Modern State*, Amsterdam: Rodopi, 1994, p. 390; Tatara, 'The origins and development of public health in Japan', p. 57.

24　Nagashima, 'Meiji medical officials' international comparisons', p. 98.

25　Fukuda, 'Public health in modern Japan', p. 391.

26　J. Wicentowski, *Policing Health in Modern Japan*, PhD dissertation, Department of History, Harvard University, May 2007, p. 27.

27　S. Obinata, *Kindai Nihon no Keisatsu to Chiiki Shakai* [*The Modern Japanese Police and Provincial Society*], Tokyo: Chikuma Shobō, 2000, p. 49.

28　Wicentowski, *Policing Health in Modern Japan*, p. 35.

29　Johnston, *The Modern Epidemic*, p. 176; S. Oguri, *Chihō Eisei Gyōsei no Sōritsu Katei* [*The Process of Establishing Local Hygiene Administrations*], Tokyo: Iryōtosho, 1981, pp. 169–71.

30　H. Saitō, 'The hygiene movement in Japan during the mid-Meiji period', in Y. Kawakita, S. Sakai and Y. Otsuka (eds), *History of Epidemiology: Proceedings of the 13th International Symposium on the Comparative History of Medicine – East and West*, Tokyo: Ishiyaku, 1993, p. 140.

31　Johnston, *The Modern Epidemic*, p. 178; Saitō, 'The hygiene movement in Japan', p. 143.

32　Lee, 'Hygienic governance', p. 8.

33　J. Bartholomew, 'Science, bureaucracy, and freedom in Meiji and Taisho Japan', in T. Najita and J. Koschmann, *Conflict in Modern Japanese History: The neglected tradition*, Princeton, NJ: Princeton University Press, 1982, p. 338.

34　S. Liu, *Medical Reform in Colonial Taiwan*, PhD thesis, Department of History, University of Pittsburgh, 2000, p. 70.

35　Rogaski, *Hygienic Modernity*, pp. 153–4.

36　Nagashima, 'Meiji medical officials' international comparisons', p. 98.

37　Quoted in R. Bowring, *Mori Ōgai and the Modernization of Japanese Culture*, Cambridge: Cambridge Univerity Press, 1979, p. 27.

38　M. Fujimura, *Nisshin Sensō* [*The Sino-Japanese War*], Tokyo: Iwanami Shoten, 1973, p. 184. Lee, 'Hygienic governance', p. 12.

39　Rogaski, *Hygienic Modernity*, p. 159.

40　Lee, 'Hygienic governance', p. 13.

41　W. G. Locher, 'Max von Pettenkofer (1818–1901) as a pioneer of modern hygiene and preventive medicine', *Environmental Health and Preventive Medicine*, vol. 12, 2007, p. 244.

42　P. Weindling, *Epidemics and Genocide in Eastern Europe 1890–1945*, Oxford: Oxford University Press, 2000, p. 21.

43 Bartholomew, 'Science, bureaucracy, and freedom', p. 312.
44 Ibid., pp. 300–3.
45 Ilza Veith, 'Mutual indebtedness of Japanese and Western medicine', *Bulletin of the History of Medicine*, vol. 52, 1978, p. 400.
46 Fukuda, 'Public health in modern Japan', p. 397.
47 T. Kawakami, *Gendai Nihon Iryōshi* [*A History of Modern Medicine in Japan*], Keiso Shobo: Tokyo, 1965, p. 131.
48 See Johnston, *The Modern Epidemic*, pp. 198–206.
49 Bartholomew, 'Science, bureaucracy, and freedom', pp. 307–14.
50 L. Seaman, *The Real Triumph of Japan*, London: Appleton, 1906, pp. 5–7, 11–13, 117, 119, 255. This triumphalist narrative has been contested by Claire Herrick, who argues that its resonance reflected concerns in Britain and the US about the medical failures of their own armies. See '"The conquest of the silent foe": British and American military medical reform rhetoric and the Russo-Japanese War', in R. Cooter, M. Harrison and S. Sturdy, *Medicine and Modern Warfare*, Amsterdam: Rodopi, 1999, pp. 99–117.
51 C. Oberlander, 'The rise of Western "scientific medicine" in Japan: bacteriology and beriberi', in M. Low (ed.), *Building a Modern Japan: Science, technology and medicine in the Meiji era and beyond*, New York: Palgrave Macmillan, 2005, pp. 31–2.
52 K. Aoki, 'Short history of epidemiology for non-infectious diseases in Japan. Part 1: selected diseases and related episodes from 1880 through 1944', *Journal of Epidemiology*, vol. 17, no. 1, 2007, p. 6.
53 Oberlander, 'The rise of Western "scientific medicine" in Japan', pp. 21–3, 27–8.
54 Bartholomew, 'Science, bureaucracy, and freedom', p. 302.
55 For a detailed, meticulously researched and thoroughly engaging study of the introduction of Jennerian vaccination to Japan, see Ann Jannetta, *The Vaccinators: Smallpox, medical knowledge and the 'opening' of Japan*, Stanford, CA: Stanford University Press, 2007.
56 Ann Jannetta, 'Jennerian vaccination and the creation of a national public health agenda in Japan, 1850–1900', *Bulletin of the History of Medicine*, vol. 83, 2009, p. 131.
57 Ibid., p. 133.
58 Ibid., pp. 135–8.
59 Nihon Tōkei Kyōkai [Japan Statistics Association] ed., *Nihon chōki tōkei sōran* [*Historical Statistics of Japan*], vol. 5, Tokyo: Nihon Tōkei Kyōkai, 1987, p. 144. Hereafter *NCTS*.
60 S. Yamamoto, 'Introduction of the Western concept and practice of hygiene to Japan during the 19th century', in Y. Kawakita, S. Sakai and Y. Ōtsuka (eds), *History of Hygiene: Proceedings of the 12th International Symposium on the Comparative History of Medicine – East and West*, Tokyo: Ishiyaku, 1991, p. 188.
61 Burns, 'Constructing the national body', p. 20.
62 A. Suzuki and M. Suzuki, 'Cholera, consumer, and citizenship: modernisations of medicine in Japan', in H. Ebrahimnejad (ed.), *The Development of Modern Medicine in Non-Western Countries*, London: Routledge, 2009, p. 186.
63 S. Yamamoto, 'Cholera in Japan', in T. Ogawa (ed.), *Public Health: Proceedings of the 5th International Symposium on the Comparative History of Medicine – East and West*, Tokyo: Saikon, 1981, p. 170.
64 Yamamoto, 'Introduction of the Western concept and practice of hygiene', p. 181.
65 Suzuki and Suzuki, 'Cholera, consumer and citizenship', p. 188.
66 Ibid., 189. Yamamoto, *Nihon Korera-shi*, pp. 407–584.
67 Ibid., pp. 600–7.
68 Bartholomew, 'Science, bureaucracy, and freedom', p. 314.
69 Yamamoto, 'Cholera in Japan', pp. 177–8.
70 Ibid., p. 178.

71 Sensitized vaccines were made by combining the living cholera microorganisms with the useful constituents of immune serum.

72 Rokuro Takano, Itsuya Ohtsubo and Zenjuro Inouye, *Studies of Cholera in Japan*, Geneva: League of Nations Health Organisation, 1926, p. 43.

73 Ibid., p. 2.

74 Yamamoto, 'Introduction of the Western concept and practice of hygiene', p. 183.

75 Yamamoto, 'Cholera in Japan', pp. 170–86.

76 *NCTS*, pp. 144–5.

77 Takano *et al.*, *Studies of Cholera in Japan*, p. 42.

78 *NCTS*, p. 144.

79 Crawford F. Sams, *'Medic': The mission of an American military doctor in Occupied Japan and wartorn Korea*, edited by Zabelle Zakarian, Armonk, NY: M. E. Sharpe, 1998, p. 93.

80 T. Nagashima, 'Sewage disposal and typhoid fever: the case of Tokyo 1912–1940', *Annales de Démographie Historique*, vol. 108, 2004, pp. 109, 115.

81 *NCTS*, pp. 144–5.

82 Nagashima, 'Sewage disposal and typhoid fever', p. 110.

83 Ann Jannetta, *Epidemics and Mortality in Early Modern Japan*, Princeton, NJ: Princeton University Press, 1987, p. 145.

84 K. Shiga, 'The trend of prevention, therapy and epidemiology of dysentery since the discovery of its causative organism', *New England Journal of Medicine*, vol. 215, no. 26, 1936, pp. 1205, 1209–11.

85 Ibid., p. 1207.

86 Jannetta, *Epidemics and Mortality*, p. 150.

87 Jannetta, 'Jennerian vaccination', p. 132, fn 18.

88 The louse as vector for epidemic typhus was established by Charles Nicolle in 1909, enabling the Japanese authorities to target their disinfection measures.

89 *NCTS*, p. 146.

90 T. Nagashima, 'Exposure to infectious disease in modern Japan: a case study. The typhus epidemic of 1914', paper presented to the International Economic History Congress, Helsinki, August 2006.

91 M. Watanabe, 'Taishō ni okeru hasshin chifusu dairyūkō ni tsuite – bōeki gyōseimen kara ikkōsatsu' [Concerning the typhus epidemic of 1914 in Tokyo – a study from the perspective of epidemic prevention], *Nihon Ishigaku Zasshi*, vol. 48, no. 4, 2002, p. 607.

92 J. N. Hays, *The Burdens of Disease*, New Brunswick, NJ: Rutgers University Press, 2002, p. 251.

93 E. K. Tipton, *Modern Japan: A social and political history*, London: Routledge, 2002, p. 59.

94 *NCTS*, p. 147.

95 J. Bartholomew, 'Science, bureaucracy, and freedom', p. 314.

96 G. Rosen, *A History of Public Health*, Baltimore, MD: Johns Hopkins University Press, 1958, p. 313.

97 J. Lewis, 'The prevention of diphtheria in Canada and Britain 1914–45', *Journal of Social History*, vol. 20, No. 1, 1986, p. 163.

98 Shiga, 'The trend of prevention, therapy and epidemiology of dysentery, p. 1209.

99 US Strategic Bombing Survey, *The Effects of Bombing on Health and Medical Services in Japan*, hereafter *USSBS*, Medical Division, June 1947, p. 169.

100 Lewis, 'The prevention of diphtheria', pp. 164, 168, 170.

101 Ibid., pp. 166, 168. Accidents had occurred in countries other than Britain and Canada. See H. J. Parish, *A History of Immunization*, Edinburgh: E. S. Livingstone, pp. 151–3.

102 G. Rosen, *A History of Public Health*, p. 314. See also Ann Hardy, *The Epidemic Streets*, Oxford: Clarendon Press, 1993, pp. 80–109. Hardy puts more store in the immunization campaigns:

If antitoxin serum assisted a natural decline in the virulence of the disease, the eventual disappearance of diphtheria as a serious threat to the lives of children in the twentieth century was due to the immunization campaigns launched in the years after 1923.

(p. 109)

103 Hardy, *The Epidemic Streets*, pp. 56, 79.
104 *NCTS*, pp. 146–7.
105 G. W. Rice and E. Palmer, 'Pandemic influenza in Japan, 1918–19: mortality patterns and official responses', *Journal of Japanese Studies*, vol. 19, no. 2, 1993, p. 413. This article is the source for the remainder of this paragraph and the one that follows.
106 Ibid.
107 Ibid., p. 389.

2 The limits of disease prevention

1 R. Narita, 'Women and views of women within the changing hygiene conditions of late nineteenth- and early twentieth-century Japan', trans. Gretchen Jones, *US–Japan Women's Journal*, English supplement, vol. 8, 1995, p. 64.
2 M. B. Jansen, *The Making of Modern Japan*, Cambridge, MA: Harvard University Press, 2002, p. 548.
3 S. Garon, *Molding Japanese Minds*, Princeton, NJ: Princeton University Press, 1998.
4 W. Johnston, *The Modern Epidemic: A history of tuberculosis in Japan*, Cambridge, MA: Harvard University Press, 1995, p. 34.
5 J. Hunter, 'Textile factories, tuberculosis and the quality of life in industrializing Japan', in J. Hunter (ed.), *Japanese Women Working*, London: Routledge, 1993, p. 74.
6 *Kōshū Eisei*, vol. 55, no. 5, 1937, pp. 350–4.
7 Johnston, *The Modern Epidemic*, pp. 38–40.
8 According to M. E. Teller, 'the diagnosis of incipient tuberculosis was a challenge even to the best clinician'. *The Tuberculosis Movement*, New York: Greenwood, 1988, p. 86.
9 As stated in Chapter 1, the notifiable diseases at this time were cholera, smallpox, typhoid, dysentery, typhus, diphtheria, plague and scarlet fever.
10 Nihon Tōkei Kyōkai [Japan Statistics Association] ed., *Nihon chōki tōkei sōran* [*Historical Statistics of Japan*], vol. 5, Tokyo: Nihon Tōkei Kyōkai, 1987, pp. 144, 146, 148, 154. Hereafter *NCTS*.
11 M. Fukuda, 'Public health in modern Japan: from regimen to hygiene', in D. Porter (ed.), *The History of Public Health and the Modern State*, Amsterdam: Rodopi, 1995, p. 395.
12 *NCTS*, pp. 154–5.
13 US Strategic Bombing Survey, *The Effects of Bombing on Health and Medical Services in Japan*, hereafter *USSBS*, Medical Division, June 1947, p. 215.
14 Hunter, 'Textile factories', pp. 77–8.
15 Ibid., pp. 78, 85–9. Ishihara's research was published in 1913, an article on mill girls and tuberculosis ('Jokō to kekkaku') appearing in *Kokka Igakkai Zasshi* in November of that year.
16 Johnston, *The Modern Epidemic*, p. 95.
17 Kōseishō Imukyoku, *Isei Hyakunenshi* [*A Hundred Year History of the Medical System*], Tokyo: Gyōsei, 1976, pp. 141–2; Y. Murakami, *20 Seiki no Nihon (9) Iryō* [*Twentieth Century Japan (9): Medicine*], Tokyo: Yomiuri Shimbunsha, 1996, p. 50; M. Powell and M. Anesaki, *Health Care in Japan*, London: Routledge, 1990, p. 44.
18 G. J. Kasza, 'War and welfare policy in Japan', *The Journal of Japanese Studies*, vol. 61, no. 2, 2002, pp. 418–20.

19 Johnston, *The Modern Epidemic*, p. 101.
20 Ibid., pp. 234–6, 239–41, 246–54, 258–9.
21 M. Fukuda, 'Public health in modern Japan', p. 394.
22 Johnston, *The Modern Epidemic*, pp. 259–60; A. Takahashi, *The Development of the Japanese Nursing Profession*, London: Routledge, 2004, p. 131.
23 Yamada Masao, *Guntai ni okeru hai-kekkaku rokumakuen no yobō ni kansuru shiryō*, Rikugun-shō, 1932, p. 8. Referred to in W. Johnston, *Disease, Medicine and the State: A social history of tuberculosis in Japan, 1850–1950*, PhD thesis, Harvard University, 1987, p. 128.
24 The statement was made by J. B. Grant of the Rockefeller Foundation. Quoted in Takahashi, *Japanese Nursing Profession*, p. 154.
25 A. Sugaya, *Nihon Shakai Seisaku Shiron* [*An Essay on Japanese Social Policy*], Tokyo: Nihon Hyōronsha, 1990, p. 83.
26 K. Cwitertka, *Modern Japanese Cuisine*, London: Reaktion, 2006, p. 121.
27 T. Saiki (ed.), *Progress of the Science of Nutrition in Japan*, Geneva: League of Nations Health Organisation, 1926, p. 5.
28 Cwiertka, *Modern Japanese Cuisine*, pp. 122, 135.
29 Ibid., pp. 77–8, 82.
30 S. B. Hanley, *Everyday Things in Premodern Japan*, Berkeley, CA: University of California Press, 1999, pp. 165–6.
31 I. Taeuber, *The Population of Japan*, Princeton, NJ: Princeton University Press, 1958, p. 289.
32 Johnston was head of the Foods Branch, Price and Rationing Division, Economic and Scientific Section, GHG SCAP.
33 B. F. Johnston with Mosaburō Hosoda and Yoshio Kusumi, *Japanese Food Management in World War II*, Stanford, CA: Stanford University Press, pp. 90–1.
34 For an insightful study of these campaigns, see S. Garon, *Molding Japanese Minds: The state in everyday life*, Princeton, NJ: Princeton University Press, 1998.
35 *Shiba shiritsu eiseikai kaihō*, vol. 12, 1902, p. 2. Quoted in R. Narita, 'Women and views of women', *US–Japan Women's Journal*, English supplement, vol. 8, 1995, p. 68.
36 'Densenbyō ni tsuite', *Fujin eisei zasshi*, vol. 146, p. 18, Quoted in R. Narita, 'Women and views of women', p. 67.
37 Garon, *Molding Japanese Minds*, p. 129.
38 S. Partner, 'Taming the wilderness: the lifestyle improvement movement in rural Japan, 1925–65', *Monumenta Nipponica*, vol. 56, no. 4, 2001, p. 491.
39 Garon, *Molding Japanese Minds*, p. 82.
40 R. Takano, 'Bacteriological and parasitological study of night soil disposal in Japan', *Journal of the Japan Public Health Association*, December 1927. Quoted in *Civil Affairs Guide, Water Supply and Sewage Disposal in Japan*, War Department Pamphlet no. 31–61, 70 [PHW 00896].
41 *Civil Affairs Guide, Water Supply and Sewage Disposal* [PHW 00895].
42 Ibid.
43 S. R. Johansson and C. Mosk, 'Exposure, resistance and life expectancy: disease and death during the economic development of Japan, 1900–1960', *Population Studies*, vol. 41, 1987, pp. 230–1.
44 Japan International Cooperation Agency, *Japan's Experiences in Public Health and Medical Systems*, 2005, pp. 263–4.
45 K. F. Kiple (ed.), *The Cambridge Historical Dictionary of Disease*, Cambridge: Cambridge University Press, p. 231.
46 Narita, 'Women and views of women', p. 69.
47 Hunter, 'Textile factories', p. 75.
48 'Legal and social measures against trachoma in Japan', *British Journal of Ophthalmology*, vol. 19, no. 6, 1935, pp. 323–5.

49 John Farley, *To Cast Out Disease: A history of the International Health Division of the Rockefeller Foundation (1913–1951)*, Oxford: Oxford University Press, 2004, pp. 245–6; Takahashi, *Japanese Nursing Profession*, pp. 145–8.

50 Ibid., p. 146.

51 *Kōshū Eisei*, vol. 55, no. 5, pp. 350–4.

52 Irene Taeuber identifies an upward trend until 1918, after which it was downward, with 'episodic interruptions'. While the rate was 169 in 1919–20, it was 84 in 1941. Taeuber presents data for infant mortality by prefecture, 1919–20 to 1953. See *The Population of Japan*, Princeton, NJ: Princeton University Press, 1958, pp. 301–2.

53 S. Fruhstuck, *Colonizing Sex: Sexology and social control in modern Japan*, Berkeley, CA: University of California Press, 2003, p. 24.

54 M. Powell and M. Anesaki, *Health Care in Japan*, London: Routledge, 1990, p. 38.

55 S. Burns, 'Constructing the national body: public health and the nation in nineteenth-century Japan', in T. Brook and A. Schmid (eds), *Nation Work*, Ann Arbor, MI: University of Michigan Press, 2000, pp. 33–4.

56 S. Garon, 'The world's oldest debate? Prostitution and the state in Imperial Japan, 1900–1945', *The American Historical Review*, vol. 98, no. 3, 1993, p. 712.

57 Ibid., p. 721.

58 Y. Kusama, *Kindai Kasō Minshū Seikatsu Shi [A Narrative of the Lives of the Modern Poor]*, vol. 2, Tokyo: Akashi Shoten, 1987, pp. 1072, 1075.

59 Narita, 'Women and views of women', pp. 75–6.

60 Garon, 'The world's oldest debate?', p. 727.

61 *Army Services Forces Manual M 354-13*, Civil Affairs Handbook Japan Section 13: Public Health and Sanitation, 10 February 1945, 69. The total number of recorded cases was 12,640 in 1914, 11,605 in 1920, 7,888 in 1925 and 6,920 in 1930. Of the cases recorded in 1930, 942 were syphilis, 1,116 chancroid and 4,862 gonorrhoea. The division of cases was similar for the other years. The figure for 1938 comes from K. Yoshimi (ed.), *Baishō no Shakai Shi [Social History of Prostitution]*, Tokyo: Yūzankaku, 1984, p. 173.

62 Fruhstuck, *Colonizing Sex*, pp. 26–7, 38–40.

63 M. Anesaki, 'History of public health in modern Japan: the road to becoming the healthiest nation in the world', in M. J. Lewis and K. L. Macpherson, *Public Health in Asia and the Pacific*, Abingdon: Routledge, 2008, p. 59.

64 H. E. Wildes, *Typhoon in Tokyo: The Occupation and its aftermath*, London: Macmillan, 1954, p. 218.

65 Fruhstuck, *Colonizing Sex*, p. 42.

66 J. Dower, 'The useful war', in *Japan in War and Peace: Essays on history, race and culture*, London: Harper Collins, 1995, p. 10.

67 G. M. Berger, *Parties out of Power in Japan, 1931–41*, Princeton, NJ: Princeton University Press, 1977.

68 Dower, 'The useful war', p. 23.

69 K. Tsuneishi, 'C. Koizumi: as a promoter of the Ministry of Health and Welfare and originator of the BCW research program', *Historia Scientiarium*, vol. 26, March 1984, pp. 107–8.

70 Kasza, 'War and welfare policy in Japan', p. 423.

71 Y. Sugita, 'Universal health insurance: the unfinished reform of Japan's healthcare system', in M. E. Caprio and Y. Sugita (eds), *Democracy in Occupied Japan*, London: Routledge, 2002, p. 149.

72 Ibid., p. 150.

73 Kasza, 'War and welfare policy in Japan', p. 424.

74 *Isei Hyakunen Shi [A Hundred Year History of the Medical System]*, pp. 290–1, 331–2; Takahashi, *Japanese Nursing Profession*, pp. 132–3; T. Havens, *Valley of Darkness: The Japanese People and World War Two*, Lanham, MD: University Press of America, 1986, pp. 47–8; Taeuber, *Population of Japan*, 284–5; F. Ohtani,

One Hundred Years of Health Progress in Japan, Tokyo: International Medical Foundation of Japan, 1971, pp. 64–5.
75 Takahashi, *Japanese Nursing Profession*, pp. 135, 156.
76 Havens, *Valley of Darkness*, p. 48.
77 *Isei Hyakunen Shi*, p. 236; Ohtani, *One Hundred Years of Health Progress*, p. 66.
78 Johnston, *The Modern Epidemic*, p. 275.
79 Fukuda, 'Public health in modern Japan', pp. 395–6.
80 Ibid.; Johnston, *The Modern Epidemic*, pp. 280–4.
81 Fukuda, 'Public health in modern Japan', p. 397.
82 R. A. Pape, 'Why Japan surrendered', *International Security*, vol. 18, no. 2, 1993, p. 164.
83 *USSBS*, p. 219.
84 S. H. Yamashita, *Leaves from an Autumn of Emergencies*, Honolulu: University of Hawaii Press, 2005, pp. 85, 127.
85 Ibid., pp. 237–8, 243, 259.
86 Hanley, *Everyday Things in Premodern Japan*, p. 81.
87 *USSBS*, p. 44; J. B. Cohen, *Japan's Economy in War and Reconstruction*, Minneapolis, MN: University of Minnesota Press, 1949, p. 370.
88 *USSBS*, pp. 54, 56.
89 Owen Griffiths, 'Need, greed, and protest in Japan's black market, 1938–49', *Journal of Social History*, vol. 35, No. 4, 2002, p. 828.
90 Havens, *Valley of Darkness*, p. 116.
91 Cwiertka, *Modern Japanese Cuisine*, p. 129; Havens, *Valley of Darkness*, p. 131.
92 Johnston, *Japanese Food Management*, p. 162.
93 Griffiths, 'Need, greed, and protest in Japan's black market', p. 828.
94 Cohen, *Japan's Economy*, p. 378.
95 Yamashita, *Leaves from an Autumn of Emergencies*, p. 173.
96 *USSBS*, pp. 58, 89–90.
97 Yamashita, *Leaves from an Autumn of Emergencies*, pp. 265–6.
98 *NCTS*, p. 145.
99 *USSBS*, p. 111.
100 Summary of report of sanitary engineering activity [PHW 01143].
101 Havens, *Valley of Darkness*, p. 147.
102 *USSBS*, pp. 102, 111, 120, 162.
103 Havens, *Valley of Darkness*, 176–7; Pape, 'Why Japan surrendered', p. 164.
104 A. Hardy, *The Epidemic Streets*, Oxford: Clarendon Press, 1993, p. 191.
105 *NCTS*, p. 147; K. Shimizu, *Nihon kōshū eisei-shi: Shōwa zenki hen* [*History of Public Hygiene in Japan: early Showa edition*], Tokyo: Fuji Shuppun, 1989, p. 42.
106 *NCTS*, p. 145. The number of patients increased from 287 in 1939 to 575 and 654 in 1940 and 1941, respectively. The number then fell to 385 in 1942, rose again to 546 in 1943, before dropping to 311 the following year.
107 Shimizu, *Nihon kōshū eisei-shi*, pp. 52–3.
108 Yamashita, *Leaves from an Autumn of Emergencies*, pp. 243–6.

3 'Controlling wildfire diseases'

1 Crawford F. Sams, 'Japan's new public health program', *Military Government Journal*, September–October 1948, p. 9.
2 Chapter 8 of Sams' memoir, *'Medic'*, edited by Zabelle Zakarian, identifies smallpox, typhus and cholera as 'wildfire diseases'.
3 SCAP, *Political Reorientation of Japan, September 1945 to September 1948*, vol. II, Washington, DC: US Government Printing Office, 1949, pp. 413, 425.
4 Ibid., p. 436.
5 Ibid., p. 425.

6 Crawford F. Sams, *'Medic': The mission of an American military doctor in Occupied Japan and wartorn Korea*, edited by Zabelle Zakarian, Armonk, NY: M. E. Sharpe, 1998, pp. xiii–xiv; E. Takemae, *Inside GHQ: The Allied Occupation of Japan and its Legacy*, London: Continuum, 2002, p. 191.

7 Sams, 'Japan's new public health program', pp. 9–14.

8 R. Shimazaki-Ryder and Shigeno Ōishi, *Sengo Nihon no Kango Kaikaku [Nursing Reform in Postwar Japan]*, Tokyo: Nihon kango kyōkai shuppankai, 2003, pp. 249, 283. The comment about Japan being an 'underdeveloped country' was made during the interview, the reference to 'modern concepts' in a letter to Ms Ryder, 16 November 1981. Sams also refers to Japan as an 'underdeveloped country' on p. 66 of his memoir (*'Medic'*).

9 Ibid., p. 249 (letter to Ms Ryder, 16 November 1981).

10 F. Bowers, 'Discussion', in Burkman (ed.), *The Occupation of Japan: Arts and Culture*, Norfok, VA: MacArthur Memorial, 1988, pp. 203–4.

11 J. Dower, *Embracing Defeat: Japan in the wake of World War II*, New York: W. W. Norton, 1999, pp. 209–11.

12 Takemae, *Inside GHQ*, p. 192.

13 M. Schaller, *Douglas MacArthur: The Far Eastern general*, New York: Oxford University Press, 1989, p. 121.

14 Shimazaki-Ryder, *Sengo Nihon no kango kaikaku*, p. 251 (letter to Ms Ryder, 11 January 1982).

15 Ibid., pp. 252, 287. The comment about Cohen being a communist is made during the interview and the remark about communist infiltration occurs in a letter to Ms Ryder, 11 January 1982.

16 Dower, *Embracing Defeat*, pp. 406–11. The subject is skilfully analysed in chapter 14, 'Censored democracy: policing the new taboos', pp. 405–40.

17 'Decline of epidemics verified by SCAP', *Nippon Times*, 7 January 1946; 'Starvation claim voiced in Nippon denied by SCAP', *Nippon Times*, 23 December 1945.

18 US Army Service Forces HQ, *Civil Affairs Handbook: Japan, Section 13: Public Health and Sanitation*. Hereafter referred to as *CAH*.

19 Takemae, *Inside GHQ*, pp. 190–1.

20 Analysis of population, military and police strength by prefecture, 29 August 1947 [G-2 02776].

21 Takemae, *Inside GHQ*, p. 405.

22 *Nippon Times*, 7 January 1946.

23 SCAP, *History of the Non-Military Activities of the Occupation of Japan*, monograph 19: public health (hereafter *HNMA*), appendix 11, p. 52.

24 Nihon Tōkei Kyōkai [Japan Statistics Association] ed., *Nihon chōki tōkei sōran [Historical Statistics of Japan]*, vol. 5, Tokyo: Nihon Tōkei Kyōkai, 1987, pp. 145, 147. Hereafter *NCTS*.

25 SCAP, *Summations of Non-Military Activities*, vol. 4, pp. 249, 258.

26 SCAP Allied Translator and Interpreter Service (ATIS), press translations, social series 273, item 2, 'Smallpox in Yamaguchi-ken', *Bocho Shimbun* (Yamaguchi), 15 February 1946. As the references that follow all conform to the above pattern of 'social series' and 'item', these descriptors will be omitted and the abbreviated form 273:2 used.

27 211:1, 'Smallpox'.

28 *The Mainichi*, 14 March 1946. The outbreak of the disease in Chiba on 31 January was likewise attributed to 'prisoners sent from Ashiya prison in Hyogo prefecture'.

29 184:6, 'A case of smallpox found in the south western area of Tokyo', *Mainichi Shimbun*, 21 January 1946; 192:4, 'Smallpox case in Akita', provincial paper *Kahoku Shimpō* (Sendai), 20 January 1946; 207:1, 'Smallpox in Tokushima ken', *Tokushima Shimbun*, 23 January 1946; 209:1, 'Smallpox case in Sendai', *Kahoku Shimpō*, 24 January 1946; 218:1, 'Smallpox', *Hyūga Nichi Nichi*, 27 January 1946;

223:2, 'Smallpox in Kagawa and Ehime prefectures', *Kochi Shimbun*, 29 January 1946.

30 245:2, 'Smallpox on Hirado', *Nagasaki Shimbun*, 5 February 1946; 241:2, 'Prevention of smallpox in Tokyo', *Tokyo Shimbun*, 8 February 1946.

31 272:3, 'Smallpox', *Jiji Shimpō*, 19 February 1946; 277:3, 'Typhus and smallpox', *Asahi Shimbun*, 21 February 1946.

32 306:6, 'Smallpox throughout Japan', *Hokkoku Mainichi Shimbun*, 28 February 1946.

33 290:3, 'Smallpox', *Niigata Nippō*, 24 February 1946.

34 345:4, 'Prevention of smallpox and typhus', *Yomiuri Hochi*, 16 March 1946.

35 'Smallpox epidemic has passed its peak', *Nippon Times*, 10 May 1946.

36 241:2, 'Prevention of smallpox in Tokyo'.

37 'Careful report is compiled of infectious diseases here', *Nippon Times*, 17 February 1946.

38 289:6, 'Smallpox'.

39 303:2, 'Typhus and smallpox', 2 March 1946.

40 421:3, 'Smallpox and typhus cases', *Asahi Shimbun*, 10 April 1946.

41 Concern about US servicemen being exposed to smallpox turned out to be justified. One source records the deaths from smallpox of three Americans, stationed in Kobe. It transpired that the men had not been properly vaccinated. See the short piece by G. B. Robinson, 'Questions and reflections: smallpox 1945–smallpox 1996', *Pharos*, vol. 59, no. 2, 1996, p. 42.

42 *HNMA*: 19, appendix 11, p. 52.

43 191:1, 'Smallpox in Yamaguchi ken', *Bōchō Shimbun*, 15 January 1946; 207:1, 'Smallpox in Tokushima ken', *Tokushima Shimbun*, 23 January 1946.

44 229:1, 'Smallpox in Tokushima', *Tokushima Shimbun*, 31 January 1946.

45 292:4, 'Smallpox and vaccinations', *Tokushima Shimbun*, 21 February 1946.

46 272:3, 'Smallpox', *Jiji Shimpō*, 19 February 1946.

47 241:2, 'Prevention of smallpox in Tokyo', *Tokyo Shimbun*, 8 February 1946.

48 277:3, 'Typhus and smallpox', *Asahi Shimbun*, 21 February 1946.

49 289:6, 'Smallpox', *Asahi Shimbun*, 26 February 1946.

50 See, for example, 259:1, 'Smallpox and typhus cases', *Nippon Sangyō Keizai*, 14 February 1946, in which it is stated that the epidemic prevention division is recommending that citizens be vaccinated against smallpox.

51 315:2, 'Smallpox vaccination in Yamaguchi ken', *Bōchō Shimbun*.

52 305:4, 'DDT and disease', *Asahi Shimbun*.

53 334:3, 'Anti-typhus and small pox measures', *Asahi Shimbun*.

54 *Mainichi*, 14 March 1946.

55 345:4, 'Prevention of smallpox and typhus', *Yomiuri Hōchi*.

56 308:3, 'Smallpox and typhus', *Mainichi Shimbun*, 4 March 1946. See 313:2, 'Smallpox and typhus vaccinations', *Yomiuri Hōchi*, 5 March 1946.

57 309:4, 'Vaccination', *Tokyo Shimbun*, 5 March 1946.

58 Sams, *'Medic'*, pp. 81–2.

59 *Nippon Times*, 10 May 1946; Sams, *'Medic'*, p. 83.

60 *Mainichi*, 27 April 1946.

61 Much of this section on the typhus epidemic of 1946 draws on research conducted by Chris Aldous in 2005, published as 'Typhus in Occupied Japan (1945–6): an epidemiological study', *Japanese Studies*, vol. 26, no. 3, 2006, pp. 318–33.

62 The USA Typhus Commission was established by Executive Order No. 9285 on 24 December 1942 as a joint undertaking of the army, navy and US Public Health Service, under the supervision and direction of the Secretary of War. The Executive Order stated that it was 'to formulate and effectuate a program for the study of typhus fever and the control thereof, both within and without the United States, when it is, or may become a threat to the military population.' Its first overseas field headquarters was established in Cairo on 7 January 1943, and from then until 30

June 1946, when it was dissolved, it was involved in the investigation and control of typhus in areas where it posed a public health menace to American forces.

63 According to *The Merck Manual of Diagnosis and Therapy* (1966), Rickettsia are 'small cocci or coccobacilli which occupy a position between the viruses and the bacteria.... Rickettsias differ from bacteria in that they require the presence of living cells for growth.'

64 H. Zinnser, *Rats, Lice and History*, Boston, MA: Bantam, 1935, p. 180.

65 Ibid.

66 C. A. Winslow, *The Conquest of Epidemic Disease*, New York: Hafner, 1967, p. 359.

67 K. Shimizu, *Nihon kōshū eiseishi: Shōwa zenki hen*, Tokyo: Fuji Shuppan, 1989, pp. 40–2.

68 M. Weiner, *Race and Migration in Imperial Japan*, London: Routledge, 1994, p. 198.

69 Sams, *'Medic'*, p. 85.

70 Shimizu, *Nihon kōshū eiseishi*, p. 42.

71 Weiner, *Race and Migration*, p. 200.

72 J. B. Cohen, *Japan's Economy in War and Reconstruction*, Minneapolis, MN: University of Minnesota Press, 1949, p. 161.

73 *HNMA*: 19, p. 28.

74 Report of AFPAC Headquarters of USA Typhus Commission [NDL: PHW 00843].

75 As occurred, for example, with the Naples epidemic of 1943–44.

76 Sams, *'Medic'*, p. 88.

77 Ibid.

78 SCAP, *Summations*, vol. 2, November 1945, p. 159.

79 SCAP, *Summations*, vol. 5, February 1946, p. 260.

80 A. Scoville, 'Epidemic typhus fever in Japan and Korea', in F. R. Moulton (ed.), *Rickettsial Diseases of Man*, Washington, DC: American Association for the Advancement of Science, 1948, pp. 32–4.

81 Ibid., p. 31. A short section on Nagasaki in an extensive report of the USA Typhus Commission (25 May 1946) noted clusters of cases in two coal mines in the area, but stated that 'the origin of the outbreak was directly traceable to Osaka' [PHW 00843].

82 F. Cartwright and M. Biddiss, *Disease and History*, 2nd edition revised, Stroud: Sutton, 2000, p. 85.

83 ATIS trans., roll no. 11, Press trans., editorial series 5 April–20 April 1946. Editorial series: 741, item 1, 'The prevention of eruptive typhus'.

84 Dower, *Embracing Defeat*, pp. 90, 93.

85 Takemae, *Inside GHQ*, p. 406.

86 Sams, *'Medic'*, p. 59.

87 E. Seidensticker, *Tokyo Rising: The city since the Great Earthquake*, New York: Alfred A. Knopf, 1990, p. 156.

88 'Return prohibited to crowded cities', *Nippon Times*, 11 March 1946.

89 'Osaka to be dusted with DDT repeatedly', *Mainichi*, 20 March 1946.

90 'Entry to Tokyo banned', *Nippon Times*, 2 April 1946.

91 Memo for: Executive Officer, USA Typhus Commission; subject: Typhus fever in Tokyo; date: May 1946; from: Addison B. Scoville [PHW 02166].

92 DDT is the acronym for dichlorodiphenyltrichloroethane.

93 Quoted in E. Russell, *War and Nature*, Cambridge: Cambridge University Press, 2001, p. 176.

94 From Armed Forces Pest Management Board, Office of the Deputy Under Secretary of Defence, 'Delousing procedures for the control of louse-borne diseases during contingency operations, 6 March 2002, 13, Appendix C 'Review of methods of controlling body louse infestations'. See www.afpmb.org/pubs/tims/TG6/TG6.pdf.

95 Russell, *War and Nature*, p. 127.
96 *HNMA*: 19, p. 213.
97 Russell, *War and Nature*, p. 150.
98 Memo for Executive Officer, USA Typhus Commission; subject: Report of typhus outbreak in Osaka, Honshu; dated: 3 February 1946; from: T. Berge [PHW 00171].
99 Memo for: Executive Officer, USA Typhus Commission; subject: Typhus in Osaka; dated: 29 April 1946; from: F. Blanton [PHW 00170].
100 As Sams explains, it depended on the multiplication of rickettsia in the living tissue of unhatched chick embryos.
101 According to Sams (*'Medic'*, p. 85), 5.3 million Japanese were inoculated between September 1945 and 1 July 1946.
102 Memo for: Executive Officer, USA Typhus Commission; subject: Typhus in Osaka; dated: 29 April 1946; from: F. Blanton [PHW 00170].
103 Ibid.
104 Y. Igarashi, *Bodies of Memory: Narratives of war in postwar Japanese culture, 1947–70*, Princeton, NJ: Princeton University Press, p. 67.
105 Report of AFPAC Headquarters of USA Typhus Commission [PHW 00843].
106 Memo for record, 4 November 1946; subject: Article for magazine press conference, Radio Tokyo [PHW 02166].
107 Report of AFPAC Field HQ USA Typhus Commission, 25 May 1946 [PHW 00843].
108 Ibid. The limited use of typhus vaccine in Japan prior to 1946 is suggested by a comment in the *Asahi Shimbun* on 21 February, that preventive vaccination was 'rare in Japan until now'.
109 *Summations*, vol. 7, April 1946, p. 246.
110 'Typhus threat here said under control', *Nippon Times*, 12 April 1946.
111 Report of AFPAC Field HQ USA Typhus Commission, 25 May 1946 [PHW 00843]. The report states that 'all case-finding, vaccination, and dusting teams were instructed, *in so far as possible*, by US Army personnel'.
112 The monthly summation for May 1946 stated that 'Ten thousand hand dusters for applying DDT powder have been manufactured and instructions issued for the production of an additional 10,000'. Regarding DDT, it reported that 'approximately 375 tons of 10% dusting powder were produced during May. The 100% DDT concentrate was furnished to Japanese manufacturers from US stocks since no concentrate is available in Japan' (p. 218).
113 US Army Service Forces HQ, *Civil Affairs Handbook: Japan, Section 13: Public Health and Sanitation*, 10 February 1945, p. 17.
114 Sams, *'Medic'*, p. 89.
115 *HNMA*: 19, pp. 91–2.
116 *Summations*, vol. 7, April 1946, p. 249.
117 Memo for Imperial Japanese Government, 6 April 1946; Subject: Quarantine procedures for cholera in repatriates [PHW 00813].
118 GHQ SCAP, memo 6 April 1946; subject: Quarantine procedures for cholera in repatriates [PHW 00813].
119 Sams, *'Medic'*, p. 91. GHQ SCAP, memo July 1946; subject: prevention of introduction of cholera into Japan.
120 *NCTS*, p. 145.
121 ATIS press translations, social series 490, item 2, 'Food situation on cholera infected ships', *Asahi Shimbun*, 26 April 1946.
122 Social series 496, item 2, 'The repatriation ships at Uraga, *Asahi Shimbun*, 28 April 1946.
123 Uraga cholera story (query of Col. Sams), 1 May 1946 [PHW 00814].
124 Ibid. This is the source for the remainder of this paragraph.
125 The exposed position of the harbour hampered operations during this period.

126 ATIS press translations, 524:3, 'Cholera cases decreasing at Uraga', 4 May 1946.
127 Memo for record, 4 November 1945; subject: Conference with Dr Otsubo, Tokyo Health Dept; to: Chief, Public Health and Welfare Section; from Wilson C. Williams, Lt. Colonel, Medical Corps, Chief, Preventive Medicine Sub-Section [PHW 00814].
128 Sams, *'Medic'*, pp. 90–1.
129 GHQ, AFPAC, memo for G-3, 24 June 1946; subject: Visit to reception centre at Sasebo, Kyushu [GIII 00291].
130 Memo for record, 16 April 46; subject: Laboratory facilities for detection of cholera carriers at Uraga repatriation port. It was noted that 'more technical help and a larger laboratory space, properly screened against flies, should be made available' [PHW 00814].
131 Memo for record, 15 June 1945; subject: Spread of cholera form Hakata reception centre [PHW 00813].
132 432:6, 'Cholera at Uraga', *Tokyo Shimbun*, 14 April 1946. Mention is also made of Morita in 428:7, 'Cholera at Uraga', *Yomiuri Hōchi*, 12 April 1946.
133 Memo 8 April 1946 [PHW 00814].
134 Memo for record, 10 April 1946; subject: Cholera in repatriates at Uraga [PHW 00814].
135 Memo for record, 10 June 1946; subject: Cholera control, release of fishing quarantine on Tokyo Bay [PHW 00813].
136 451:3, 'Combating cholera'.
137 Memo for record, 15 April 1946 [PHW 00814].
138 523:8, 'Anti-epidemic measures'.
139 Memo for record, 16 July 1946; subject: Cholera control in Tokyo [PHW 00813].
140 Ministry of Health and Welfare, 3 September 1946 [PHW 00812].
141 *HNMA*: 19, pp. 42–3.
142 *Summation*, vol. 9, pp. 261–3.
143 *HNMA*: 19, p. 43.
144 Sams, *'Medic'*, p. 102.
145 PHW 01632. Attached to the record of his verbal summary is a lengthy report, 30 April 1947, in which it is stated that 'The Japanese had never used toxoid for immunisation.'
146 *Summations*, vol. 3 (December 1945), p. 161.
147 Memo for record, 11 December 1946; subject: Conference with Welfare Ministry (Diphtheria Toxoid etc.) [PHW 02103].
148 Memo for record, 28 July 1947; subject: Diphtheria immunization program [PHW 02103].
149 See statistics in *NCTS*, pp. 146–7.
150 GHQ SCAP, Public Health and Welfare Section, *Public Health and Welfare in Japan, 1945–48*, p. 26.
151 Sams, *'Medic'*, p. 102.
152 S. Nishimura, 'Promoting health during the American Occupation of Japan: the Public Health Section, Kyoto Military Government Team, 1945–1949', *American Journal of Public Health*, vol. 98, no. 3, 2008, p. 430.
153 Letter 7 February 1949 [PHW 02107].
154 H.E. Wildes, *Typhoon in Tokyo*, London: George Allen, 1954, p. 215.

4 'We're cleaning up Japan'

1 K. Holliday, 'We're cleaning up Japan', *New Leader*, vol. 34, no. 8, 1951, pp. 12–14.
2 The Allied Council for Japan examined 'the state of public health in Japan' at its

thirty-first meeting on 30th April 1947, when Sams responded to a number of questions posed by Derevyanko, the Soviet delegate.

3   PHW 01631.
4   H. E. Wildes, *Typhoon in Tokyo*, New York: Macmillan, p. 214.
5   G. H. Stuart, *Public Health in Occupied Japan*, PhD thesis, London School of Hygiene and Tropical Medicine, April 1950, p. 38.
6   Typhoid fever monthly cases Japan, 1900–1947 [PHW 92491].
7   Eiji Marui, 'The American and Japanese experience with vital statistics reform in the early days of the Occupation', in Yoshio Kawakita, Shizu Sakai and Yasuo Ōtsuka, *History of Epidemiology: Proceedings of the 13th International Symposium on the Comparative History of Medicine – East and West*, Ishiyaku: Tokyo, 1993, p. 200.
8   PHW 01631.
9   Crawford F. Sams, *'Medic': The mission of an American military doctor in Occupied Japan and wartorn Korea*, edited by Zabelle Zakarian, Armonk, NY: M. E. Sharpe, 1998, pp. 93–5.
10   US Army Service Forces HQ, *Civil Affairs Handbook: Japan, Section 13: Public Health and Sanitation*, p. 65. Hereafter referred to as *CAH*.
11   J. S. Simmons, T. F. Whayne, G. W. Anderson and H. M. Horack, *Global Epidemiology: A geography of disease and sanitation*, vol. 1, Philadelphia: J. B. Lippincott, 1944, p. 137. Simmons was Sams' mentor.
12   During the First World War, paratyphoid A and B strains were combined with the typhoid vaccine to constitute the so-called triple vaccine, i.e. TAB vaccine, aimed to protect subjects from typhoid and paratyphoid. For more details about the history of prophylactic inoculation against typhoid, see R. L. Huckstep, *Typhoid Fever and other Salmonella Infections*, Edinburgh: E & S Livingstone, 1962, pp. 7–8, 110.
13   *Summations*, vol. 3, December 1945, p. 161.
14   SCAP, *History of the Non-Military Activities of the Occupation of Japan*, monograph 19: public health (hereafter *HNMA*: 19), p. 41.
15   Memo for Record, 25 March 1948; subject: Typhoid fever control [PHW 02102].
16   *HNMA*: 19, pp. 41–2.
17   J. Felsen, *Bacillary Dysentery, Colitis and Enteritis*, Philadelphia and London: Saunders, 1945, p. 16.
18   C. F. Sams, 'American public health administration meets the problems of the Orient in Japan', *American Journal of Public Health and the Nation's Health*, vol. 42, no. 5 (pt 1), 1952, p. 564.
19   Nihon Tōkei Kyōkai [Japan Statistics Association] ed., *Nihon chōki tōkei sōran* [*Historical Statistics of Japan*], vol. 5, Tokyo: Nihon Tōkei Kyōkai, 1987, p. 147. Hereafter *NCTS*.
20   *HNMA*: 19, pp. 33–4, 38.
21   *NCTS*, p. 151.
22   *HNMA*: 19, p. 35. For a detailed analysis of malaria epidemics in Occupied Japan, see S. Tanaka, S. Sugita and E. Marui, 'Sengo senryōki ni okeru mararia ryūkō no niruikei', *Nippon Eiseigaku Zasshi*, vol. 64, no. 1, 2009, pp. 3–13.
23   E. Sydenstricker, 'The epidemic outbreak in Japan', *Public Health Reports*, vol. 39, no. 50, 1924, p. 3125.
24   J. S. Simmons *et al.*, *Global Epidemiology*, p. 137.
25   J. R. Paul, *A History of Poliomyelitis*, New Haven, CT and London: Harvard University Press, 1971, pp. 168–74.
26   Paul, *History of Poliomyelitis*, pp. 174–5.
27   *Summations*, vols 2 (November 1945), p. 159; 3 (December 1945) p. 163; 5 (February 1946), p. 266; 6 (March 1946), p. 231; 9 (June 1946), p. 259; 10 (July 1946), p. 230; 16 (January 1947), p. 240; 24 (September 1947), p. 249; 31 (April 1948), p. 285; 35 (August 1948), p. 255.

28 *HNMA*: 19, pp. 36–7. *NCTS*, p. 147. The latter records the number of cases in 1948 as 4,757, much fewer than the 7,208 stated in the *HNMA*.
29 Sams, *'Medic'*, p. 93. *HNMA*: 19, p. 68.
30 E. Takemae, *Inside GHQ*, London: Continuum, 2002, p. 409.
31 Environmental sanitation section, Development of sanitary conditions in Japan, 1946–1949 [PHW 01143]. See also Central Sanitary Bureau, Home Ministry, *The Sanitary Laws of Japan*, 1911.
32 *HNMA*: 19, p. 68.
33 *CAH*, p. 89.
34 Memo for record, 19 April 1946; subject: Supplies for mosquito and fly control program [PHW 03661].
35 Memo from Warren Bradlee, Preventive Medicine Division [PHW 04547].
36 W. Grunge, 'Japan's pyrethrum position threatened', *Far Eastern Survey*, vol. 8, no. 9, 1939, p. 110. Natural Resources Section (NRS) report no. 78, *Pyrethrum in Japan*, 1947 [NRS 02104].
37 NRS report, *Pyrethrum in Japan*.
38 Summary, Conference on Rodent and Insect Control, 22–27 April 1946 [PHW 04544].
39 *Operations Manual for Field Use of DDT in Medical and Sanitary Entomology* [PHW 04547].
40 Y. Igarashi, *Bodies of Memory: Narratives of War in Postwar Japanese Culture, 1945–70*, Princeton, NJ: Princeton University Press, 2000, p. 69.
41 B. Kushner, *The Thought War: Japanese Imperial Propaganda*, Honolulu: University of Hawai'i Press, 2006, p. 188.
42 Holliday, 'We're cleaning up Japan', p. 14.
43 Y. Murakami, *Iryō – kōrei shakai e mukatte, 20 seiki no Nippon (9)*, Tokyo: Yomiuri Shimbunsha, 1996, pp. 60–4.
44 Memo for record, 14 August 1946; subject: Sanitation, insect and rodent control in Kyushu [PHW 01694].
45 E. P. Russell, 'The strange career of DDT: experts, federal capacity, and environmentalism in World War II', *Technology and Culture*, vol. 40, no. 4, 1999, pp. 777–80.
46 Editorial, reprinted in *Soap and Sanitary Chemicals*, April 1944.
47 J. Perkins, 'Reshaping technology in wartime: the effect of military goals on entomological research and insect-control practices', *Technology and Culture*, vol. 19, no. 2, 1978, pp. 169–71.
48 Russell, 'The strange career of DDT', p. 784.
49 R. Carson, *Silent Spring*, London: Penguin, 1962, pp. 23, 25.
50 Ibid. This was the title of chapter 10, pp. 142–57.
51 Memo for the Chief of Staff [PHW 04540].
52 Memo from NRS to PH&W and Office of Chief Surgeon, 21 April 1946.
53 Russell, 'The strange career of DDT', p. 789.
54 Ibid., p. 795.
55 A memo of May 1946, addressed to Commanding General 8th Army, subject: 'Control of insect and rodent-borne diseases', stated that 'Japanese equipment and supplies will be utilized to the utmost in carrying out the necessary programs' [PHW 03661].
56 *HNMA*: 19, p. 213.
57 Check sheet, 22 May 1946; from: PH&W; to: ESS; subject: Petroleum products for mosquito and fly control program [PHW 03661].
58 Memo for record, 19 April 1946; subject: Supplies for mosquito and fly control program [PHW 03661].
59 Memo for record, 23 August 1946; subject: Production of pyrethrum emulsion for mosquito and fly control program [PHW 02329].

60 *Summations*, vol. 11, August 1946, p. 230.
61 *Summations*, vol. 7, April 1946, p. 247; *HNMA*: 19, p. 213.
62 Memo for record, 19 April 1946; subject: Supplies for mosquito and fly control program [PHW 03661].
63 Memo for record; from: E. A. Turner, sanitary engineer; subject: Conference on insect and rodent control materials [PHW 04547].
64 *Summations*, vol. 22, July 1947, p. 262; vol. 23, August 1947, p. 290.
65 Memo for record, 17 September 1946; subject: Meeting reference increase in growth of pyrethrum flowers [PHW 02329].
66 NRS report no. 78 [NRS 02104].
67 *Summations*, vol. 25, October 1947, p. 274.
68 *Summations*, vol. 27, December 1947, p. 309; vol. 32, May 1948, p. 366; vol. 33, June 1948, p. 296; vol. 34, July 1948, p. 312.
69 Proposal of abolishing distribution control of pyrethrum flowers, 16 May 1949 [PHW 02329].
70 Memo for record, 8 July 1949; subject: Pyrethrum emulsion [PHW 02329].
71 *HNMA*: 19, p. 217.
72 Memo for record, 22 August 1949; from: Lerdy M. Martine, Supply Division [PHW 04065]; subject: Distribution and use of DDT products.
73 G. McLaughlin, 'History of pyrethrum', in J. Cassida (ed.), *Pyrethrum the Natural Insecticide*, New York: Academic Press, 1973, p. 9. He states that after 1945 'Japan never regained any large proportion of pyrethrum export capacity'. The key players are now Kenya, Tanzania and Ecuador.
74 Sams, Report on sanitary teams, 1948 [PHW 01693].
75 Takemae, *Inside GHQ*, p. 410.
76 *HNMA*: 19, pp. 63, 69.
77 Memo for record, 14 August 1946; subject: Sanitation, insect and rodent control in Kyushu [PHW 01694].
78 M. Hashimoto, *Kōshū eisei to soshiki katsudō*, Tokyo: Seishin-Shobō, 1955, pp. 101–4.
79 S. Garon, *Molding Japanese Minds: The state in everyday life*, Princeton, NJ: Princeton University Press, 1998, p. 150.
80 E. A. Turner, Summary report of sanitary engineering activity in Japan (September 1945–December 1949) [PHW 01143].
81 Ibid.
82 Memo for record, 28 December 1948; from: Lucius G. Thomas, Chief, Preventive Medicine Division; subject: Corporations developing sanitary interest [PHW 04553].
83 Welfare Ministry, Imperial Japanese Government, Sanitary Association (district) – Reasons which call for compulsory membership [PHW 04554].
84 Sams, Report on sanitary teams, 1948 [PHW 01693].
85 Sams, *'Medic'*, p. 94.
86 E. A. Turner, Summary report of sanitary engineering activity in Japan (September 1945–December 1949) [PHW 01143].
87 Memo for record, 19 April 1946; subject: Supplies for mosquito and fly control program [PHW 03661].
88 Control of insect and rodent borne diseases in Japan, 30 April 1946; from PH&W, through G-4, to AG [PHW 03661].
89 Memo for record, 14 August 1946; subject: Sanitation, insect and rodent control in Kyushu [PHW 01694].
90 *Summations*, vol. 12, September 1946, p. 207.
91 *Summations*, vol. 22, July 1947, p. 262; vol. 23, August 1947, p. 290.
92 *HNMA*: 19, p. 214.
93 PHW 01143.

94 *HNMA*: 19, p. 69.
95 HQ, 8th Army, Plan for civil information activities on sanitation and insect control, 28 May 1948 [CIE(B) 01358].
96 PHW 04543.
97 *HNMA*: 19, p. 74.
98 William Tsutsui, 'Landscapes in the dark valley: toward an environmental history of wartime Japan', *Environmental History*, vol. 8, no. 2, 2003, p. 8.
99 C. L. W. Swanson, 'Preparation and use of composts, night soil, green manures, and unusual fertilizing materials in Japan', *Agronomy Journal*, vol. 41, no. 7, 1949, p. 278 [Natural Resources Section NRS 02325].
100 Swanson, 'Preparation and use of composts', p. 278.
101 Tsutsui, 'Landscapes in the dark valley', p. 8.
102 Takemae, *Inside GHQ*, p. 412.
103 Sams, *'Medic'*, p. 92.
104 Plan for civil information activities on sanitation and insect control, HQ US Army, 28 May 1948 [Civil Information and Educations Section CIE (B) 01358]. A report by E. A. Turner, Chief of the Sanitary Engineering Branch, Preventive Medicine Division, PH&W Section, covering the period September 1945 to December 1949, stated that 27 per cent of Japanese were 'fortunate enough to live in areas served by muncipal supplies' [PHW 01143].
105 *CAH*, pp. 92–3.
106 Memo for record, 28 August 1947. Attached is Kanai's plan itself [PHW 02109].
107 Memo for: representatives attending fertiliser conference; subject: Summary of discussion on increased use of night soil and other waste products for fertiliser; March 1946 [PHW 00898].
108 Memo for record, 14 March 1946; subject: Japanese studies of the sanitary treatment of human excreta [PHW 00898].
109 R. P. Dore, *City Life in Japan: A study of a Tokyo ward*, London: Routledge and Kegan Paul, 1958, p. 65.
110 Ibid.
111 Committee on Sanitation, Resources Council, ESB, report dated August 1950 [PHW 01695].
112 An interim report on progress of work, study group no. 3, Committee on Sanitation, Resources Council, August 1950 [PHW 01695].
113 *HNMA*: 19, p. 70.
114 PHW 00895.
115 Suggestions to the Ministry of Health for the Improvement of Sanitary Conditions, 6 December 1945 [PHW 01694].
116 *HNMA*: 19, p. 71.
117 ATIS translation, 'New water supply plans', *Asahi Shimbun*, 21 February 1946, summary [CHS(B) 01181].
118 *Summations*, vol. 9 (June 1946), p. 259.
119 *Summations*, vol. 2 (November 1945), 158; *HNMA*: 19, p. 71.
120 ATIS translation, 'Tokyo suffers water shortages', *Asahi Shimbun*, 23 July 1946, full translation [CHS(B) 01181].
121 *Summations*, vol. 2 (November 1945), p. 158; *HNMA*: 19, p. 71.
122 *Stars and Stripes*, 21 November 1945.
123 *Summations*, vol. 8 (May 1946), p. 224.
124 *HNMA*: 19, p. 71; *Summations*, vol. 11 (August 1946), p. 234.
125 *HNMA*: 19, p. 71.
126 *Stars and Stripes*, 1 September 1949 and 5 September 1949 [CHS(B) 01181].
127 C. F. Sams, *'Medic'*, p. 92.
128 W. M. Tsutsui, 'Landscapes in the dark valley', p. 305.
129 Conference on rodent and insect control, April 1946 [PHW 04545].

130 R. Tren and R. Bate, *Malaria and the DDT Story*, London: Institute of Economic Affairs, 2001, p. 40.

5 Nutrition and disease

1 Crawford F. Sams, *'Medic': The mission of an American military doctor in Occupied Japan and wartorn Korea*, edited by Zabelle Zakarian, Armonk, NY: M. E. Sharpe, 1998, p. 54.
2 B. F. Johnston with Mosaburō Hosoda and Yoshio Kusumi, *Japanese Food Management in World War II*, Stanford, CA: Stanford University Press, p. 3.
3 Sams, *'Medic'*, p. 67.
4 Ann Jannetta, *Epidemics and Mortality in Early Modern Japan*, Princeton, NJ: Princeton University Press, 1987, p. 175.
5 Memo for record, 16 October 1947; subject: Information requested for United States food drive [PHW 01245].
6 F. B. Smith, *The Retreat of Tuberculosis*, London: Croom Helm, 1988, p. 19.
7 Paper on 'Mass vaccination under postwar conditions in Japan', Folder: Personal, 1 August 1955–, Box 7, Crawford F. Sams collection, Hoover Institution Archives, copyright Stanford University.
8 SCAP, *History of the Non-Military Activities of the Occupation of Japan*, monograph 19: public health (hereafter *HNMA*: 19), Table 28 'Death rates per hundred thousand – ten selected causes', p. 65.
9 Johnston, *Japanese Food Management*, pp. 91, 164.
10 US Strategic Bombing Survey, *The Effects of Bombing on Health and Medical Services in Japan* (hereafter *USSBS*), p. 59.
11 Johnston, *Japanese Food Management*, p. 92.
12 K. Cwitertka, *Modern Japanese Cuisine*, London: Reaktion, 2006, pp. 117, 122.
13 *USSBS*, pp. 47–8.
14 Ibid., p. 135. A Natural Resources Section memo of 27 October 1945 likewise referred to surveys of caloric and protein intake carried out by the National Nutrition Laboratory in some cities in June 1945, which identified soy beans as a key source of protein [NRS 11393].
15 Memo for record; from: Warren Leonard, head of the agricultural division [NRS 11393].
16 Memo for record, 2 November 1945; subject: Comments on studies by SWNCC [NRS 11393].
17 Memo 14 October 1946; subject: Information of general application pertaining to SCAPIN 422; 11 December 1946; from: R. G. Hersey, Asst Adj. Gen.; subject: 'Nutritional surveys of civilian population' [NRS 11393].
18 Cwiertka, *Modern Japanese Cuisine*, p. 135.
19 *Summations*, vol. 3 (December 1945), p. 164.
20 Public Health and Welfare Section, *Public Health and Welfare in Japan* (September 1945–December 1948), p. 163.
21 Ibid., Chart 28, p. 167; *HNMA*: 19, p. 120, appendix 1 G (average daily food consumption, May 1946–November 1950: selected cities and rural areas). A memo of 14 October 1946 (Information of general application pertaining to Directive Number SCAPIN 422, 11 December 1946, subject: 'Nutritional surveys of civilian population') suggests a slightly slower process of development but the data presented in monthly and annual accounts confirms the sequence stated [NRS 11393].
22 *Public Health and Welfare in Japan* (September 1945–December 1948), p. 165; *Summations*, vol. 32 (May 1948), p. 375; vol. 34 (July 1948), p. 319.
23 Vitamin chart compiled by T. K. Hibbert [PHW 02183].
24 Ministry of Health and Welfare, *A Brief Report on Public Health Administration in Japan*, 1951, p. 21.

25 *Summations*, vol. 16 (January 1947), p. 242. A map of Japan identified the sites of these surveys and produced runs of data from the May, August and November nutrition studies. Graphs also recorded daily consumption of various foods among families of these workers (p. 245), average daily caloric intake (p. 246), consumption of fats, proteins and carbohydrates (p. 247) and symptoms associated with nutritional deficiencies (p. 249). Coverage of these groups continued in later issues during 1947 (April, June and October) but ceased in 1948.

26 Memo for Secretary of Agriculture, Secretary of State, 28 March 1946; subject: Final report of food situation in Japan [ESS(C) 00095].

27 Outgoing message; from: SCAP; to: WARCOS [ESS(C) 00095]. The message begins with the statement 'Please pass following message to Anderson, Secretary of Agriculture, and Clayton, Assistant Secretary of State, from Harrison.'

28 Hoover was considered an expert on nutrition and food relief, having been instrumental in famine relief after the First World War. For more details on the work of the Famine Emergency Committee, see Amy Bentley, *Eating for Victory: Food rationing and the politics of domesticity*, Chicago, IL: University of Illinois Press, 1998, pp. 142–53.

29 Japanese food situation 1946, prepared for Herbert Hoover and members of his committee, 1 May 1946 [NRS 023310]. This is the source for the remainder of this paragraph and the following ones unless otherwise stated.

30 Transmittal sheet, 26 August 1946; from: chief, subsistence branch, supply division; to: military planning division, requirements branch, civilian supply section; subject: Information on military government diets for Japan [NRS 11393].

31 Public Health and Welfare Section, *Public Health and Welfare in Japan, 1945–48*, p. 166. According to the July 1946 issue of the monthly summations (p. 234), non-delivery of rations was 'a device adopted by the local ration officials as a substitute for reducing the size of the official ration in any period of low reserves'.

32 J. Dower, *Embracing Defeat: Japan in the wake of World War II*, New York: W. W. Norton, 1999, p. 262.

33 GHQ, United States Armed Forces Pacific; Public Relations Office; For immediate release, 20 May 1946: General MacArthur today issued the following statement which warns against demonstrations and disorders by mass mobs [G-2 00244].

34 Dower, *Embracing Defeat*, p. 266.

35 Johnston, *Japanese Food Management*, p. 215.

36 Acccording to the October 1946 issue of the *Summations* (vol. 13), the release of imported food for July and August amounted to 174,708 and 213,314 tons respectively. The bulk of this was cereals (157,435 and 163,371 tons), but it also included canned goods (17,273 and 49,943 tons), p. 182.

37 *Summations*, vol. 13 (October 1946), p. 182.

38 *Summations*, vol. 10 (July 1946), p. 233. See also J. B. Cohen, *Japan's Economy in War and Reconstruction*, Minneapolis, MN: University of Minnesota Press, 1949, p. 477. Cohen contends that the figure for rural areas was 2,022 calories.

39 *HNMA*: 19, p. 120.

40 Public Health and Welfare Section, *Public Health and Welfare in Japan, 1945–48*, pp. 166–7.

41 *Summations*, vol. 10 (July 1946), p. 234; vol. 11 (August 1946), p. 234.

42 *Summations*, vol. 10 (July 1946), pp. 232–3.

43 Public Health and Welfare Section, *Public Health and Welfare in Japan, 1945–48*, p. 166.

44 HNMA: 19, Appendix 1.

45 This was a joint War, State and Agriculture mission that undertook its work in Japan 2–27 February 1947, according to 'invitational and formal orders of the Secretary of War dated January 24, 1947'.

46 Report on food and fertiliser situation in Japan, Korea and the Ryukyus by Joint War,

State and Agricultural Mission, 4 April 1947 [PHW 01246]. This is the source for the following paragraphs unless otherwise stated.

47 Captain Kittredge was assigned responsibility for investigating the nutritional status of the Japanese and Korean populations; Mr Tuck the collection, distribution and rationing systems; Colonel Harrison and Mr Koenig the indigenous production of food and fertilizer and import requirements respectively; and Mr Whitman payment for imports by exports.

48 Summary of Harrison Mission Findings, 4 April 1947 [PHW 01246].

49 *Summations*, vol. 34 (July 1948), pp. 319, 323–4.

50 Public Health and Welfare Section, *Public Health and Welfare in Japan, 1945–48*, p. 169.

51 *Summations*, vol. 25 (October 1947), p. 257.

52 *Summations*, vol. 29, p. 266.

53 *Summations*, vol. 10 (July 1946), p. 234.

54 Report on food and fertiliser situation in Japan, Korea and the Ryukyus by Joint War, State and Agricultural Mission, 4 April 1947 [PHW 01246]. This is the source for the bulk of the following paragraph.

55 Hearing called for 1400 hours, 11 February 1947, at the Tokyo residence of PM Yoshida [PHW 02843].

56 *Summations*, vol. 9 (June 1946), p. 88.

57 Telegram, the Political Adviser in Japan (Atcheson) to the Secretary of State Tokyo, 18 January 1947; *Foreign Relations of the United States*, 1946, p. 165.

58 Aide-memoire to Norwegian Embassy, Washington, 9 June 1947, *Foreign Relations of the United States*, 1946, p. 222.

59 *HNMA*: 19, p. 122; Yasuhiro Matsumura, 'Nutrition trends in Japan', *Asia Pacific Journal of Clinical Nutrition*, vol. 10 (supplement), 2001, S41.

60 Nihon Tōkei Kyōkai [Japan Statistics Association] ed., *Nihon chōki tōkei sōran* [*Historical Statistics of Japan*], vol. 5, Tokyo: Nihon Tōkei Kyōkai, 1987, pp. 118–19. Hereafter *NCTS*.

61 *HNMA*: 19, appendices 1BB, 1FF.

62 Ibid., p. 197d.

63 Simon Partner, 'Taming the Japanese wilderness: the lifestyle improvement movement in rural Japan, 1925–1965', *Monumenta Nipponica*, vol. 56, no. 4, 2001, pp. 504–6. *HNMA*, Public Health, appendix 1BB.

64 Ibid., p. 505.

65 Report on food and fertiliser situation in Japan, Korea and the Ryukyus by Joint War, State and Agricultural Mission, 4 April 1947 [PHW 01246].

66 Review of the School Lunch Programme by Kinki Military Government Team, January 1949 [PHW 02191].

67 T. Azuma (Director of Physical Education Bureau, Education Ministry), Report on the outline of school lunch program in Japan [PHW 02191].

68 UNICEF school lunch demonstration course in Japan [PHW 04077].

69 Memo for record, 12 May 1950; subject: Current status of school lunch – nursery school program [PHW 02193].

70 Letter, 1 May 1947 [PHW 02185].

71 Memo for record, 15 October 1946; from: Nelson Neff, Chief of Welfare Division of PHW; subject: School lunches for Japanese school children [PHW 02186].

72 T. Azuma, Report on the outline of school lunch program in Japan [PHW 02191].

73 Memo for record, 15 October 1946; from: Nelson Neff, Chief of Welfare Division of PHW; subject: School lunches for Japanese school children [NDL: PHW 02186].

74 Memo for record, 8 November 1946; from: Nelson Neff; subject: School lunch program [NDL; PHW 02186].

75 Civil Historical Section, *History of the Non-military Activities*, Monograph 35: *Price and Distribution Stabilization: Food Program*, p. 136 (hereafter *HNMA*: 35).

76 Memo for record, 12 December 1947; from: Nelson Neff; subject: Conference regarding first anniversary of school lunch program [PHW 02185].
77 Memo for record, 10 June 1948; subject: School lunch program requirements for third quarter 1948 [PHW 02183].
78 Memo for record, 21 July 1949; from: Nelson Neff; subject: School lunch program reorganisation [PHW 02188].
79 Memo for record, 19 July; from: Nelson Neff; subject: School lunch programming [PHW 02188].
80 Review 11 January 1949, for the Commanding General, 8th Army [PHW 02191].
81 Memo for record, 12 May 1950; subject: Current status of school lunch – nursery school program [PHW 02193].
82 UNICEF school lunch demonstration course in Japan [PHW 04077].
83 *HNMA*: 35, pp. 138–9.
84 Memo for record, 12 May 1950; subject: Current status of school lunch – nursery school program [PHW 02193].
85 Memo for record, 12 October 1948; subject: School lunch program [PHW 02183].
86 Memo for record, 29 March 1947; subject: School lunch program [PHW 02185].
87 T. Nishi, *Unconditional Democracy*, Stanford, CA: Hoover Institution Press, 1982, p. xxv.
88 A. Ehara, 'School meals and Japan's changing diet', *Japan Echo*, August 1999, pp. 57–8.
89 Memo for record, 12 May 1950; subject: Current state of school lunch – nursery school program [PHW 02193].
90 Education Ministry, 'Growth of pupils in the city of Sendai in recent years and the effect of the school lunch program' [PHW 02193].
91 PHW 04079.
92 *NCTS*, p. 155.
93 *HNMA*: 19, p. 125.
94 Cwiertka, *Modern Japanse Cuisine*, p. 130.
95 Letter from Sams to Miss Jane C. Ebbs, Nutritional Adviser, Dept of Army, 21 December 1949 [PHW 02039].
96 W. Insull, T. Oiso and K. Tsuchiya, 'Diet and nutritional status of Japanese', *The American Journal of Clinical Nutrition*, vol. 21, no. 7, 1968, pp. 753–67.
97 Ibid., p. 767.
98 R. A. Leiby, *Public Health in Occupied Germany 1945–1959*, PhD, University of Delaware, 1984, p. 172.
99 PHW 01246.

6 Chronic infectious diseases

1 Presentation to ACJ, 30 April 1947 [PHW 01632].
2 H. E. Wildes, 'Post-war public health developments', *Contemporary Japan*, vol. 21, 1953, p. 589.
3 Crawford F. Sams, *'Medic': The mission of an American military doctor in Occupied Japan and wartorn Korea*, edited by Zabelle Zakarian, Armonk, NY: M. E. Sharpe, 1998, p. 110.
4 Paper on 'Mass vaccination under postwar conditions in Japan', Folder: Personal, 1 August 1955–, Box 7, Crawford F. Sams collection, Hoover Institution Archives, copyright Stanford University.
5 Ibid.
6 Yoji Obayashi, *Dried BCG Vaccine*, World Health Organisation Monograph Series, No. 28, Geneva: WHO, 1955, p. 7.
7 Paper on 'Mass vaccination under postwar conditions in Japan', Sams collection.
8 Letter to Sams from Alice Fordyce of National Health Education Committee, 31

July 1957. Folder: personal, 1956–July 1957, Box 7, Crawford F. Sams collection collection, Hoover Institution Archives, copyright Stanford University.

9 'Why have we not accepted BCG vaccination? Report by the Medical Advisory Committee of Research Foundation', *Journal of the American Medical Association*, vol. 164, no. 9, 1957.

10 Letter to Sams, 30 September 1969, Folder: personal, 1967, Box 7, Crawford F. Sams collection, Hoover Institution Archives, copyright Stanford University.

11 W. Johnston, *The Modern Epidemic: A History of Tuberculosis in Japan*, Cambridge, MA: Harvard University Press, 1995, p. 287.

12 Ibid., p. 284.

13 C. F. Sams, 'Experiences in immunization against TB with BCG in Japan', 13 November 1953, folder: no title, Box 3, Crawford F. Sams collection, Hoover Institution Archives, copyright Stanford University.

14 Ibid.

15 Memo for record, all by Albert Knight: 8 November 1947, TB control survey in Miyagi prefecture; 26 November 1947, survey of work in TB control Kyoto prefecture; 1 December 1947, survey of facilities for TB control in Hyogo prefecture; 1 December 1947, survey of TB control in Shiga prefecture; 23 December 1947, survey trip in Shizuoka prefecture; 22 March 1948, survey for TB control in Wakayama prefecture; 1 April 1948, survey of TB in Nara prefecture; 1 April 1948, TB survey in Osaka prefecture; 20 May 1948, TB survey in Saga prefecture [PHW 00164–00165].

16 S. Nishimura, 'Promoting health during the American Occupation of Japan: the Public Health Section, Kyoto Military Government Team, 1945–1949', *American Journal of Public Health*, vol. 98, no. 3, 2008, p. 427.

17 'Experiences in immunization against TB with BCG in Japan', 13 November 1953, folder: no title, Box 3, Crawford F. Sams collection, Hoover Institution Archives, copyright Stanford University.

18 T. Shimao, 'Tuberculosis and its control: lessons from the past and future prospect', *Kekkaku*, vol. 80, no. 6, 2005, pp. 481–9.

19 SCAP, *History of the Non-Military Activities of the Occupation of Japan*, monograph 19: public health (hereafter *HNMA*: 19), p. 60; 'Experiences in immunization against TB with BCG in Japan', 13 November 1953, CFS collection.

20 Memo for record, 6 June 1950; subject: Visit to Osaka [PHW 00165].

21 Memo for record, 30 December 1950; subject: Staff visit by Dr. A. P. Knight. Prefecture and city visited: Kanagawa, Yokohama [PHW 00165].

22 Memo for record, 6 March 1951; subject: Staff visit by Albert P. Knight [PHW 00166].

23 Memo for record, 30 June 1951; subject: Staff visit to Iwate, Aomori and Hokkaido [PHW 00167].

24 Ibid.

25 'Experiences in immunization against TB with BCG in Japan', 13 November 1953, CFS collection.

26 Memo for record, 3 December 1947; subject: Summary of survey trip through Toyama, Ishikawa, Shiga, Hyogo and Kyoto prefectures [PHW 00164].

27 Memo for record, 23 December 1947; subject: Survey trip on Shizuoka prefecture [PHW 00164].

28 Memo for record, all by Albert Knight: 8 November 1947, survey in Tochigi prefecture; 8 November 1947, TB control survey in Miyagi prefecture; 25 August 1947, TB survey at Tokushima prefecture; 7 November 1947, survey of work in TB in Iwate prefecture [PHW 00164–5].

29 Memo for record, all by Albert Knight: 8 November 1947, survey of Ibaraki prefecture regarding TB control; 8 November 1947, survey in Tochigi prefecture; 26 November 1947, survey of work in TB control Kyoto prefecture; 28 November

1947, survey of TB control in Toyama prefecture; 1 December 1947, survey of facilities for TB control in Hyogo prefecture; 1 December 1947, survey of TB control in Shiga prefecture [PHW 00164–5].
30 *HNMA*: 19, p. 58; 'Experiences in immunization against TB with BCG in Japan', 13 November 1953, CFS collection.
31 Memo for record, 26 November 1947; subject: Survey of work in TB control Kyoto prefecture [PHW 00164].
32 Memo for record, 6 June 1950; subject: Visit to Osaka [PHW 00164].
33 Sams, *'Medic'*, p. 110.
34 *HNMA*: 19, p. 60.
35 Memo for record, 6 June 1950; subject: Visit to Osaka [PHW 00164].
36 Memo for record: Tokushima, 25 August; Ibaraki, 8 November; Fukushima, 8 November; Kyoto, 26 November [PHW 00164–5].
37 Memo for record: Matsuyama, 15 August 1947; Fukushima, 8 November 1947; Toyama, 28 November 1947 [PHW 00164–5].
38 PHW 00164.
39 Memo for record, 5 July 1950; from Albert Knight; subject: Staff visit to Kyushu civil affairs region [PHW 00165].
40 Memo for record, 25 August 1947; subject: TB survey at Tokushima prefecture [PHW 00165].
41 Memo for record, 20 May 1948; subject: TB survey in Shimane prefecture [PHW 00164].
42 Memo for record, 5 July 1950; subject: Staff visit to Kyushu civil affairs region [PHW 00165].
43 Nihon Tōkei Kyōkai [Japan Statistics Association] ed., *Nihon chōki tōkei sōran* [*Historical Statistics of Japan*], vol. 5, Tokyo: Nihon Tōkei Kyōkai, 1987, p. 155. Hereafter *NCTS*.
44 Johnston, *The Modern Epidemic*, pp. 98–9.
45 Sams, *'Medic'*, p. 111.
46 Letter from Knight to Sams, 9 January 1954, folder: personal file, Box 5, 1 January 1954–31 March 1954, Crawford F. Sams collection collection, Hoover Institution Archives, copyright Stanford University.
47 Johnston, *The Modern Epidemic*, p. 287.
48 *HNMA*: 19, pp. 209–12; *Public Health and Welfare in Japan: Annual Summary – 1949, vol. 1*, p. 27.
49 *NCTS*, p. 155.
50 Selman A. Waksman, *The Conquest of Tuberculosis*, Berkeley, CA: University of California Press, 1964, p. 205.
51 Summary report [PHW 01141].
52 Y. Tanaka, *Japan's Comfort Women: Sexual slavery and prostitution during World War II and the US Occupation*, London: Routledge, 2002. See also Sarah Kovner, 'Base cultures: sex workers and servicemen in Occupied Japan', *The Journal of Asian Studies*, vol. 68, no. 3, 2009, pp. 777–804; Y. Fujime, 'Japanese feminism and commercialised sex: the union of militarism and prohibitionism', *Social Science Japan Journal*, vol. 9, no. 1, 2006, pp. 33–50; John Lie, 'The state as pimp: prostitution and the patriarchal state in Japan in the 1940s', *The Sociological Quarterly*, vol. 38, no. 2, 1997, pp. 251–63; Mire Koikari, 'Gender, power and US imperialism: the Occupation of Japan, 1945–52', in T. Ballantyne and A. Burton (eds), *Bodies in Contact: Rethinking Colonial Encounters in World History*, Durham and London: Duke University Press, 2005, pp. 342–62.
53 S. Nishimura, 'Promoting health in American-Occupied Japan: resistance to Allied public health measures', *American Journal of Public Health*, vol. 99, no. 8, 2009, p. 1366.
54 Tanaka, *Japan's Comfort Women*, p. 161.

55 J. Dower, *Embracing Defeat: Japan in the wake of World War II*, New York: W. W. Norton, 1999, p. 130.
56 Kovner, 'Base cultures', p. 777.
57 Fujime, 'Japanese feminism', p. 38; Kovner, 'Base cultures', pp. 789–91; Lie, 'State as pimp', p. 258.
58 Koikari, 'Gender, power and US imperialism', p. 350.
59 Memo for record, 23 October 1946; from: Oscar Elkins, consultant, VD control; subject: VD control inspection trip to facilities in Chiba prefecture [PHW 00188].
60 Memo for record, 1 November 1946; from: Oscar Elkins; subject: VD inspection trip to Saitama prefecture [PHW 00188].
61 Memo for record, 2 May 1947; subject: Inspection of civilian VD facilities in Kyushu [PHW 00188].
62 Memo for record, 2 June 1947; subject: VD control inspection trip: Miyagi, Fukushima, Ibaraki, Tochigi and Gunma prefectures [PHW 00188].
63 Memo for record, 12 December 1947; subject: VD control conferences [PHW 00187].
64 Memo for Kyoto post command VD council [PHW 00187].
65 To: Colonel Devine, Kinki Military Government Region; subject: Operation of Kyoto city vice-squads [PHW 00187].
66 Summary report [PHW 01141].
67 Sams, *'Medic'*, p. 106.
68 Petition signed by S. Yamashita, Chief, Oita Liaison and Coordination Office; subject: Petition concerning the control of prostitution [PHW 00189].
69 Memo, 1 April 1949; subject: Military police activities in Beppu City, Oita Prefecture; through: commanding officer, Kyushu Military Government Region; to: commanding general, 8th Army. Interestingly, the commanding officer at regional level did not forward the memo to HQ at Yokohama, crossing out the 'thru' and replacing it with 'to'. Presumably he felt it best to deal with this rather explosive matter at the regional level.
70 Memo for record, 10 June 1949; subject: Staff visit by Dr I. Nieda to Oita Prefecture, Oita City, Beppu City [PHW 00189].
71 Memo for record, 24 June 1948; subject: VD inspection trip to Kyoto, Shiga and Nara prefectures [PHW 00187].
72 Memo for record, 31 August 48; subject: VD inspection trip to Hokkaido [PHW 00187].
73 Summary report [PHW 01141].
74 J. R. Heller, 'Venereal disease epidemiology in wartime', *American Journal of Public Health and the Nation's Health*, vol. 35, no. 11, 1945, pp. 1210–16.
75 Chūgoku included the prefectures of Yamaguchi, Hiroshima, Shimane, Tottori and Okayama.
76 Kantō was made up of ten prefectures: Niigata, Nagano, Gunma, Yamanashi, Saitama, Tochigi, Kanagawa, Tokyo, Chiba, Ibaraki.
77 In order for the bacterial spirochete of syphilis (*Treponema pallidum*) to be visible, it was necessary to use a dark-field condenser, which causes the image to appear bright against a dark background.
78 Gram staining or Gram's method, developed in 1884, serves to differentiate between Gram-positive and Gram-negative groups of bacteria. *Nisseria gonorrhoea* or gonococci are Gram-negative, bean-shaped bacteria.
79 For examples, see: memo from Nieda, 1 July 1948, VD inspection trip to Ibaraki prefecture. While Nieda noted lab facilities for smears and Murata serological examinations in 11 of 15 health centres, only two laboratories in the prefecture were suitably equipped to undertake Wassermann tests. In his surveys of Osaka and Wakayama, reported on 6 August 1948, he likewise stated that Wassermann tests were performed at the prefectural laboratory only. On 8 November he reported a

similar pattern in Miyagi and Yamagata prefectures and no facilities for Wassermann tests in Aomori prefecture [PHW 00187]. On 9 April 1949, in relation to
Niigata, Nieda recorded the usual division between screening tests in health centre
labs and Wassermann tests confined to a single, presumably well-equipped prefectural laboratory, and in Fukuoka (28 April 1949) found no capacity for the confirma-
tory tests [PHW 00189].

80 Memo for record, 25 May 1948; subject: VD control inspection trip to Gunma prefecture [PHW 00187].
81 Memo for record, 1 July 1948; subject: VD inspection trip to Ibaraki prefecture
[PHW 00187].
82 Memo for record, 31 August 1948; from: Nieda; subject: VD inspection trip to
Hokkaido [PHW 00187].
83 Memo, 26 January 1949 regarding Ehime; 14 March 1949 for Kanagawa; 9 April
1949 for Niigata; 2 May for Saga prefecture [PHW 00189].
84 Two examples include Nieda's memo of 1 July 1948 on Ibaraki prefecture [PHW
00187] and his memo of 14 July 1949 on Ishikawa prefecture [PHW 00189].
85 Memo for record, 21 May 1948; subject: VD control inspection trip to Shizuoka prefecture [PHW 00187].
86 Memo for record, 8 November 1948; subject: VD control visit to Yamagata prefecture [PHW 00187].
87 Memo, 24 June 1948, inspection trip to Kyoto, Shiga and Nara prefectures; 25 May
1948, VD control inspection trip to Gunma prefecture; 1 July 1948, VD inspection
trip to Ibaraki prefecture; 6 July 1948, trip to Osaka, Wakayama and Hyogo prefectures; 8 November 1948, VD control field visit to Yamagata prefecture [PHW
00187].
88 Memo, 19 September 1947, civilian VD control facilities in Aichi prefecture; 15
October 1948, VD inspections – Aichi, Gifu and Mie prefectures; 8 November 1948,
VD control field trip to Miyagi prefecture [PHW 00187].
89 Memo, 8 November 1948, VD control trip to Aomori prefecture; 14 December 1948,
trip to Shimane prefecture; 14 December 1948, trip to Hiroshima prefecture; 14
December 1948, trip to Tottori prefecture; 15 December 1948, trip to Yamaguchi;
15 December 1948, trip to Okayama [00187]; 14 July 1949, Fukui prefecture, Fukui
city [PHW 00189].
90 Memo, 25 January 1949, visit to Tokushima city, Naruto city; 26 January 1949, visit
to Ehime prefecture; 9 February 1949, visit to Saitama prefecture; 16 February 1949,
visit to Yamanashi prefecture; 28 April, visit to Fukuoka prefecture; 2 May 1949,
visit to Nagasaki prefecture; 11 July 1949, Toyama prefecture; 14 July 1949,
Ishikawa prefecture [PHW 00189].
91 Memo, 12 February 1949, visit to Kochi city; 17 June 1949, Miyazaki city [PHW
00189].
92 Memo, 4 April 1950, staff visit to Kanto, 20–24 March 1950 [PHW 00188].
93 Memo, 19 February 1948, VD control inspection trip to Fukushima prefecture; 31
August 1948, VD inspection trip to Hokkaido; 21 May 1948, VD control inspection
trip to Shizuoka prefecture; 24 June 1948, VD inspection trip to Kyoto, Shiga and
Nara prefectures; 15 October 1948, VD inspections – Aich, Gifu and Mie prefectures [PHW 00187].
94 Heller, 'Venereal disease epidemiology in wartime', pp. 1213–14.
95 Principles of VD control, 1947 [PHW 01141].
96 VD control activities in Japan, October 1945–December 1949 [PHW 01141].
97 Dower, *Embracing Defeat*, p. 130.
98 *HNMA*: 19, p. 212.
99 Sams, '*Medic*', p. 106.
100 *HNMA*: 19, pp. 203–4.
101 Sams, '*Medic*', p. 107.

212   *Notes*

102 VD control activities in Japan, October 1945–December 1949 [PHW 01141].
103 Sams, *'Medic'*, p. 106.

7 The health centre

1 A vast amount of works emphasize the importance of the local level in the Anglo-American history of public health. See, among others, Dorothy Porter, *Health, Civilization and the State: A history of public health from ancient to modern times*, London: Routledge, 1999; Simon Szreter, 'The importance of social intervention in Britain's mortality decline c.1850–1914: A reinterpretation of the role of public health', *Social History of Medicine*, vol. 1, 1988, pp. 1–37.

2 My search for these materials depended on the annual bibliographies listed in *Nihon Shakai Eisei Nenkan* [*Annual Index of Social and Hygienic Works in Japan*], published by the Kurashiki Institute of Labour Science, now available in reprints.

3 The Health Centre Section, Welfare Ministry, *Hokenjo Sanjūnen Shi* [*Thirty Years of the Health Centre*], Tokyo: Nihon Kōshūeisei Kyōkai, 1971; Sugiyama Akiko, *Senryōki no Iryōkaikaku* [*Medical Reform during the Occupation Period*], Tokyo: Keisō Shobō, 1995.

4 *Chibaken Kisarazu Hokenjo Jigyō Hōkoku* [*A Report of the Kisarazu Health Centre of Chiba Prefecture*] vol. 1, 1939.

5 Similar surveys were conducted in Katsuyama Health Centre in Fukui Prefecture, Mikkaichi Health Centre in Toyama Prefecture, and Ueda Health Centre in Nagano Prefecture. See Honda Yūgorō, 'Nōson hoken taisaku ni tsuite', [On rural health measures] *Nihon Igaku Oyobi Kenkō Hoken* [*Japanese Medicine and Health Insurance*], vol. 3278, 1942, pp. 832–3; vol. 3279, 1942, pp. 893–5; vol. 3280, 1942, p. 947; vol. 3281, 1942, pp. 1002–3; vol. 3282, 1942, pp. 1056–7.

6 *A Report of the Kisarazu Health Centre of Chiba Prefecture*, pp. 63–5.

7 *Chibaken Matsudo Hokenjo Jigyō Hōkoku* [*A Report of Matsudo Health Centre in Chiba Prefecture*] vol. 1, 1940.

8 Sakai Kikuo, 'Daitoshi ni okeru kōshūeisei jigyō' [*Public health enterprises in large cities*], *Tōhoku Igaku Zasshi* [*Journal of Tokoku Medicine*], vol. 20, no. 3, 1937, pp. 255–65.

9 Sakai, 'Public health enterprises in large cities', p. 265.

10 Yosano Hikaru, 'Nōson hoken mondai ni tsuite' [On rural health], *Ikai Shūhō* [*Medical Weekly*], vol. 342, 1941, pp. 29–30.

11 Niimi Masayoshi, 'Hoken shidōmō no genjō ni tsuite' [The present state of the network of health advice], *Kōshū Eisei* [*Public Health*], vol. 60, no. 6, 1942, pp. 308–14.

12 'New public health' is a concept now under debate by historians and sociologists. See Alan Peterson and Deborah Lupton, *The New Public Health: Health and self in the age of risk*, London: Sage Publications, 1996; Nikolas Rose, *Powers of Freedom: Reframing political thought*, Cambridge: Cambridge University Press, 1999; Signild Vallgårda, 'Appeals to autonomy and obedience: continuity and change in governing technologies in Danish and Swedish Health Promotion', *Medical History*, vol. 55, 2011, pp. 27–40.

13 Seijō Minoru later became an influential health administrator, responsible for leprosy control, TB control and the investigation of Minamata disease. See *Seijō-san no Omoide* [*The Reminiscences of Dr Seijō*], Tokyo: Sankō Publication, 1993.

14 *A Report of Matsudo Health Centre in Chiba Prefecture*, p. 1.

15 Katō Kanjirō, 'Nōgyosanson no eisei tōjisha ni' [To those who are responsible for hygiene in agricultural, fishing, and mountainous villages], *Kōshū Eisei* [*Public Health*], vol. 51, no. 4, 1937, pp. 232–9.

16 *Kindai Koshūeisei no Chichi Katsumata Minoru* [*Katsumata Minoru, the Father of Modern Public Health*], Tokyo: Japan Public Health Association, 1970.

17 Kawauchi Atsushi, 'Senjiki iryō no keiken: Kenkō Aomoriken no seiritsu to tenkai' [The experience of wartime medicine: The establishment and development of Health Aomori Movement] in Namikawa Kenji and Kawanishi Hidemichi (eds), *Chiiki Nettowāku to Shakai Hen'yō* [*The Regional Network and Social Transformation*], Tokyo: Iwata Shoten, 2008, pp. 427–57.

18 Sakai, 'Public health enterprises in large cities', p. 260.

19 Shigeta Shin'ichi, 'Toshi kōseishisetsu no chiiki soshiki ni tsuite', [On the regional organization of urban health facilities], *Nihon Igaku Oyobi Kenkō Hoken* [*Japanese Medicine and Health Insurance*], vol. 3307, 1942, pp. 2366–7; vol. 3308, 1942, pp. 2412–19; vol. 3309, 1942, pp. 2473–4; vol. 3310, 1942, pp. 2521–2. The quotation is from p. 2417.

20 Kawauchi Atsushi, 'Chiiki iryō to fasizumu' [Local medicine and fascism], in Namikawa Kenji, David Howell and Kawanishi Hidemichi (eds), *Shūhenshi kara Zentaishi e* [*From Peripheral History to Total History*], Osaka: Seibundō, 2009, pp. 323–56.

21 There existed subtle difference in nuance between urban and rural public health ethics. Public health in cities should be provided through controlled cooperation of the public and private organizations. It will make urban people enjoy the happiness of modern life through the promotion of the most pleasurable state of health. Taniguchi Masahiro, 'Hōmon hokenfu jigyō ni tsuite' [On visiting nurses], *Iryō Kumiai* [*Medical Union Journal*], vol. 3, no. 12, 1939, pp. 5–6.

22 Teruoka Gitō, 'Hoken eisei ni tsuite' [On health and hygiene], *Hoken Kyōiku* [*Health Education*], vol. 5, no. 3, 1941, pp. 40–1.

23 This paragraph is based on the official history of the health centre: Kōseishō Hokenjo-ka [The Health Centre Section, Welfare Ministry], *Hokenjo Sanjūnen Shi* [*Thirty Years of the Health Centre*], Tokyo: Nihon Kōshūeisei Kyōkai, 1971, pp. 71–107.

24 *Sha-hatsu* vol. 45, 28 January 1939, Development and Present Situation of Health Center in Japan, Prepared, Translated by Welfare Ministry, Japanese Government [PHW 00804].

25 *Hatsu-jin* vol. 101, 29 November 1941. The National Health Physical Strength Law established powerful programmes to secure a nation with health and strength.

26 *Hokkaido Takigawa Hokenjo Jūnen no Ayumi* [*The First Ten Years of Takigawa Health Centre in Hokkaido*] (n.p., n.d.), p. 3.

27 *Obihiro Hokenjo Gojūnen Shi* [*Fifty Years of Obihiro Health Centre*], Obihiro: Obihiro Hokenjo, 1991.

28 Sumida Shigenobu, 'Waga hokenjo ni okeru jissaiteki hoken shidō' [Practical health guidance at our health centre], *Nihon Igaku Oyobi kenkōhoken* [*Japanese Medicine and Health Insurance*], vol. 3289, 1942, pp. 1418–19.

29 *Tokyo-to Hokenjo Jūgonen Shi* [*Fifteen Years of Health Centres in Tokyo*], Tokyo, n.p., 1965, p. 62. This remark is from a memoir of Tsukahara Kunio, who joined the first model health centre at Suginami and taught Public Health at the University of Tokyo.

30 Katsumata's role in the making of the modern public health administration is told by dozens of his 'disciples' in the Welfare Ministry. See *Katsumata Minoru, the Father of Modern Public Health*. At a roundtable by a group of public health bureaucrats, they remembered a very close relationship between Katsumata and Sams, especially the latter's trust of the former. See ibid., pp. 203–41.

31 *Thirty Years of the Health Centre*, pp. 113–16.

32 Koseishō Gojūnenshi Henshū Iinkai, *Kōseishō Gojūnenshi*, Tokyo: Kōseimondai Kenkyūkai, 1988, p. 722.

33 Sugiyama, *Medical Reform during the Occupation Period*, pp. 163–9.

34 Works on total war and the welfare health policies are now vast. Takaoka Hiroyuki, *Sōryokusen Taisei to Fukushi Kokka* [*The Total Ware Regime and the Welfare State*], Tokyo: Iwanami Shoten, 2011; Mima Tatsuya, 'Gunkokushugi jidai: Fukushikokka

no kigen' [The period of militarism and the origin of the welfare state], in Satō Jun'ichi and Kuroda Kōichirō (eds), *Iryō Sinwa no Shakaigaku* [*Sociology of the Myths of Medicine*], Tokyo: Sekaishisōsha, 1998, pp. 103–26.

35 *Hokenjohō*, 1947.9.5. Law no. 101, art. 2.
36 *Thirty Years of the Health Centre*, pp. 121–3.
37 Ibid., p. 122. The figure is for October 1948.
38 *Development and Present Situation of Health Centre in Japan*, prepared and translated by the Welfare Ministry [PHW 00804].
39 Tokyoto Hokenjo Shochōkai [Association of the Heads of Health Centres in Tokyo], *Tokyoto Hokenjo Jūgoshūnen Kinenshi* [*Fifteen Years of the Association of the Heads of Health Centres in Tokyo*], Tokyo: n.p., 1965, pp. 64–7.
40 *Thirty Years of the Health Centre*, pp. 125–30.
41 For local health centres, the visit of and remarks by the US officers were important. The newsletter of Shigehara Health Centre noted a very positive remark of Col. Hester with obvious pride. Shigehara Health Centre, *Hoken Nyūsu*, [*Health Centre Newsletter*] No. 3, 28 February 1949.
42 PHW 02078.
43 *Thirty Years of the Health Centre*, pp. 130–7.
44 Conference with the Chief, Public Sanitarians Bureau, Welfare Ministry, re: Deficiencies of Public Health Programs in Certain Prefectures and Suggested Remedial Measures [PHW 02078].
45 Retention by Health Centres of Administrative Functions: Petition [PHW 02078].
46 Kashima Hokenjo, *Jūnen no Ayumi* [*Ten years of Kashima Health Centre*], n.p., 1955, p. 116.
47 *Bunka Ihō* was published by Ueda Health Centre, and issues between vol. 15 (January 1948) and vol. 31 (July 1949) are available in the Prange Collection.
48 Shizuki Hokenjo, *Atarashii Eisei* [*New Hygiene*], vol. 1, no. 1, 1948, p. 1.
49 For the complex meanings of the Constitution of Japan, see J. Dower, *Embracing Defeat: Japan in the wake of World War II*, New York: W. W. Norton, 1999, pp. 346–404. The quotation is from p. 347.
50 In *Bunka Ihō*, one doctor, Isaka Naoichi, emphasized the bad effect of marriage between close relatives, and cited the instances of emperors who became insane: *Bunka Ihō* [*Cultural Medicine Newsletter*], vol. 16, 1948.
51 *Bunka Ihō* [*Cultural Medicine Newsletter*], vol. 15, 1948.
52 Press conference for 9 November 1948 [PHW 02079].
53 *Iwauchi Hokenjo Renraku Hō* [*Newsletter of Iwauchi Health Centre*], vol. 3, 1949, p. 3.
54 *Bunka Ihō*, vol. 16, 1948.
55 The Diet's Welfare Committee discussed the issue of the film. Proceedings of the National Diet, Shūgi'in, 6 April 1949.
56 *Yao Hokenjo Jihō* [*Yao Health Centre Newsletter*], vol. 1, nos. 3, 5, 6, 1949, included articles on Eugenics Protection Law, sex education and family planning.

Conclusion

1 S. Nishimura, 'The US medical occupation of Japan and the history of the Japanese language edition of *JAMA*', *Journal of the American Medical Asssociation*, vol. 274, no. 5, 1995 p. 438.
2 Elkins noted in relation to VD control in June 1947 that few of the military government health officers he encountered had expected to be doing public health work and it was rare that any of them had paid much attention to this field in medical school. Memo for record, 2 June 1947; subject: VD control inspection trip – Miyagi, Fukushima, Ibaraki, Tochigi and Gunma prefectures [PHW 00188].
3 E. Takemae, *Inside GHQ*, London: Continuum, 2002, pp. xl.

Bibliography

National Diet Library, Tokyo

SCAP records on microfiche

Civil Historical Section – CHS(B) 01181
Civil Information and Education Section – CIE(B) 01358–9
Economic and Scientific Section – ESS(B) 15981–2, ESS(C) 00095
Far Eastern Commission – FEC(B) 1540–1
Natural Resources Section – NRS 02104, 02114, 02325, 02331–2, 07911–12, 07914, 11392–3

Public Health and Welfare Section

PHW 00164–7, 00170–3, 00187–9, 00268–9, 00804, 00811–14, 00817–21, 00843, 00895–6, 00898, 01115, 01137–8, 01140, 01141–2; 01143–4, , 01245–7, 01631–2, 01693–5, 02039, 02078–9, 02102–4, 02106–7, 02109–10, 02166–9, 02175, 02183, 02185–8, 02191–3, 02220–3, 02329, 02491–3, 02843–4, 03660–1, 03810, 04065, 04076–8, 04079, 04225, 04231–2, 04539–40, 04543–5, 04547–8, 04553–4, 05512, 92491

Journals

Iwauchi Hokenjo, *Iwauchi Hokenjo Renraku Hō* [*Newsletter of Iwauchi Health Centre*].
Kisarazu Hokenjo, *Chibaken Kisarazu Hokenjo Jigyō Hōkoku* [*A Report of the Kisarazu Hokenjo of Chiba Prefecture*].
Matsudo Hokenjo, *Chibaken Matsudo Hokenjo Jigyō Hōkoku* [*A Report of Matsudo Health Centre in Chiba Prefecture*].
Ōhara Rōdōkagaku Kenkyūjo, *Nihon Shakai Eisei Nenkan* [*Annual Index of Social and Hygienic Works in Japan*].
Shigehara Hokenjo, *Hokenjo Nyūsu*, [*Health Centre Newsletter*].
Shizuki Hokenjo, *Atarashii Eisei* [*New Hygiene*].
Ueda Hokenjo, *Bunka Ihō* [*Cultural Medicine Newsletter*].
Yao Hokenjo, *Yao Hokenjo Jihō* [*Yao Health Centre Newsletter*].

Hoover Institution Archives, Stanford University

Crawford F. Sams Collection (16 boxes). Box 3, folder: no title; Box 4, file 36; Box 5, folder: personal file, 1 January 1954–31 March 1954; Box 7, folder: personal, 1 August 1955–; folder: personal, 1967.

Sheffield University Library, UK

ATIS (Allied Translator and Interpreter Series) translations.
Social series: item – 184:6, 191:1, 192:4, 207:1, 209:1, 211:1; 218:1, 223:2; 229:1, 241:2; 245:2, 259:1, 272:3, 273:2, 273:3, 277:3, 289:6, 290:3, 292:4, 293:3, 295:3, 303:2, 305:4, 306:6, 308:3, 309:4, 313:2, 315:2, 323:6, 326:3, 334:3, 345:4, 421:3, 428:7, 432:6, 490:2, 496:2, 523:8, 524:3.
Editorial series: item – 741:1.

SCAP printed sources

General Headquarters, Supreme Commander for the Allied Powers (GHQ, SCAP), Public Health and Welfare Section, *Public Health and Welfare in Japan, Summary, 1945–48*; *Public Health and Welfare in Japan, Annual Summary – 1949, vol. 1*; *Annual Summary – 1950.*

GHQ, SCAP, *History of the Non-Military Activities of the Occupation of Japan*, Tokyo, Historical Section, 1950–1, volumes 18 (*Public Welfare*), 19 (*Public Health*), 35 (*Price and Distribution Stabilization: Food Program*).

GHQ, SCAP, *Summations of Non-Military Activities in Japan*, nos 1–35 (September/October 1945–August 1948).

SCAP, *Political Reorientation of Japan, September 1945 to September 1948*, vol. II, Washington, DC: US Government Printing Office, 1949.

Official US sources

US Army Service Forces HQ, *Civil Affairs Handbook: Japan, Section 13: Public Health and Sanitation*, 10 February 1945.

US Strategic Bombing Survey, *The Effects of Bombing on Health and Medical Services in Japan*, Medical Division, June 1947.

Official Japanese sources

Central Sanitary Bureau of the Home Department, *The Sanitary Laws of Japan*, 1911.

Welfare Ministry Japan, *A Brief Report on Public Health Administration in Japan*, 1951.

Nihon Tōkei Kyōkai [Japan Statistics Association], ed., *Nihon Chōki Tōkei Sōran*, vol. 5. *Nihon Tōkei Kyōkai [Health and Medical Care]*, Tokyo, 1987, pp. 115–209.

Shūgi'in Gijiroku [Proceedings of the House of Representatives].

Articles

Aldous, C., 'Contesting famine: hunger and nutrition in Occupied Japan, 1945–52', *Journal of American–East Asian Relations*, vol. 17, no. 3, 2010, pp. 230–56.

Aldous, C., 'Transforming public health? A critical view of progress made against enteric diseases during the American-led Occupation of Japan (1945–52)', *Nihon Ishigaku Zasshi* [*Journal of Japanese History of Medicine*], vol. 54, no. 1, 2008, pp. 3–17.

Aldous, C., 'Typhus in Occupied Japan (1945–46): an epidemiological study', *Japanese Studies*, vol. 26, no. 3, 2006, pp. 317–33.

Anesaki, M., 'History of public health in modern Japan: the road to becoming the healthiest nation in the world', in M. J. Lewis and K. L. Macpherson (eds), *Public Health in Asia and the Pacific*, Abingdon: Routledge, 2008, pp. 55–72.

Aoki, K., 'Short history of epidemiology for non-infectious diseases in Japan. Part 1: selected diseases and related episodes from 1880 through 1944', *Journal of Epidemiology*, vol. 17, no. 1, 2007, pp. 1–18.

Bartholomew, J., 'Japanese Nobel candidates in the first half of the twentieth century', *Osiris*, vol. 13, 1998, pp. 238–84.

Bartholomew, J., 'Science, bureaucracy, and freedom in Meiji and Taisho Japan', in T. Najita and J. Koschmann (eds), *Conflict in Modern Japanese History: The Neglected Tradition*, Princeton, NJ: Princeton University Press, 1982, pp. 295–341.

Berlin, R. B., 'Impressions of Japanese medicine at the end of World War II', *Scientific Monthly*, vol. 64, 1947, pp. 41–9.

Berry, J. C., 'Medicine in Japan: its development and present status', in George H. Blakeslee (ed.), *Japan and Japanese–American Relations*, New York: G. E. Stechert, 1912, pp. 136–60.

Beukers, H., 'The fight against smallpox in Japan; the value of Western medicine proved', in H. Beukers, A. M. Luyendijk-Elshout, M. E. van Opstall and F. Vos (eds), *Red-Hair Medicine: Dutch–Japanese Medical Relations*, Amsterdam: Rodopi, 1991.

Bowers, J. Z., 'The adoption of German medicine in Japan: the decision and the beginning', *Bulletin of the History of Medicine*, vol. 53, 1979, pp. 57–80.

Burns, S., 'Constructing the national body: public health and the nation in nineteenth-century Japan', in T. Brook and A. Schmid (eds), *Nation Work: Asian Elites and National Identities*, Ann Arbor, MI: University of Michigan Press, 2000, pp. 17–49.

Burns, S., 'Bodies and borders: syphilis, prostitution, and the nation in Japan, 1860–1890', *US–Japan Women's Journal*, English supplement, vol. 15, 1998, pp. 3–29.

Conde, D., 'The Korean minority in Japan', *Far Eastern Survey*, 26 February 1947, pp. 41–5.

Cullather, N., 'The foreign policy of the calorie', *The American Historical Review*, vol. 112, no. 2, 2007, pp. 1–26.

Daniels, G., 'The social history of Occupied Japan: some sources and problems', *Japanese Studies*, STICERD, LSE, 1990.

Das Gupta, M., 'Public health in India: an overview', World Bank Research Working Paper 3787, December 2005.

Doull, J. A. and Sandidge, R. P., 'Is the prophylactic use of diphtheria antitoxin justified?', *Public Health Reports*, vol. 39, no. 7, 1924, pp. 283–94.

Ehara, A., 'School meals and Japan's changing diet', *Japan Echo*, August 1999, pp. 56–60.

Fuchs, S. J., 'Feeding the Japanese: food policy, land reform, and Japan's economic recovery', in M. Caprio and Y. Sugita (eds), *Democracy in Occupied Japan: The US Occupation and Japanese politics and society*, London: Routledge, 2007, pp. 26–47.

Fujime, Y., 'Japanese feminism and commercialized sex: the union of militarism and prohibitionism', *Social Science Japan Journal*, vol. 9, no. 1, 2006, pp. 33–50.

Fukuda, M. H., 'Public health in modern Japan: from regimen to hygiene', in D. Porter (ed.), *The History of Public Health and the Modern State*, Amsterdam: Rodopi, 1994, pp. 385–402.

Garon, S., 'The world's oldest debate? Prostitution and the state in Imperial Japan, 1900–1945', *The American Historical Review*, vol. 98, no. 3, 1993, pp. 710–32.

Gluck, C., 'Entangling illusions: Japanese and American views of the Occupation', in W. I. Cohen (ed.), *New Frontiers in American–East Asian Relations*, New York: Columbia University Press, 1983, pp. 169–236.

Griffiths, O., 'Need, greed, and protest in Japan's black market, 1938–1949', *Journal of Social History*, vol. 35, no. 4, 2002, pp. 825–58.

Grunge, W. H., 'Japan's pyrethrum position threatened', *Far Eastern Survey*, vol. 8, no. 9, 1939, pp. 109–10.

Guthrie-Shimizu, S., 'Occupation policy and the Japanese fisheries management regime, 1945–1952', in M. Caprio and Y. Sugita (eds), *Democracy in Occupied Japan: The US Occupation and Japanese politics and society*, London: Routledge, 2007, pp. 48–66.

Hanley, S. B., 'Urban sanitation in preindustrial Japan', *Journal of Interdisciplinary History*, vol. 18, no. 1, 1987, pp. 1–26.

Hashimoto, M., 'Forty years of my public health study', *Bulletin of the Institute of Public Health*, vol. 33, no. 1, 1984, pp. 1–15.

Herrick, C., '"The conquest of the silent foe": British and American military medical reform rhetoric and the Russo-Japanese War', in R. Cooter, M. Harrison and S. Sturdy (eds), *Medicine and Modern Warfare*, Amsterdam: Rodopi, 1999.

Holliday, K., 'We're cleaning up Japan', *New Leader*, vol. 34, no. 8, 1951, pp. 12–14.

Honda, G., 'Differential structure, differential health: industrialization in Japan, 1868–1940', in R. H. Steckel and R. Floud, *Health and Welfare during Industrialization*, Chicago, IL: University of Chicago Press, 1997.

Honda, Yūgorō, 'Nōson hoken taisaku ni tsuite', [On rural health measures], *Nihon Igaku Oyobi Kenkō Hoken* [*Japanese Medicine and Health Insurance*], vol. 3278, 1942, pp. 832–3; vol. 3279, 1942, pp. 893–5; vol. 3280, 1942, p. 947; vol. 3281, 1942, pp. 1002–3; vol. 3282, 1942, pp. 1056–7.

Hunter, J., 'Textile factories, tuberculosis and the quality of life in industrializing Japan', in J. Hunter (ed.), *Japanese Women Working*, London: Routledge, 1993, pp. 69–97.

Insull, W., Oiso, T. and Tsuchiya, K., 'Diet and nutritional status of Japanese', *The American Journal of Clinical Nutrition*, vol. 21, no. 7, 1968, pp. 753–77.

Jannetta, A., 'Jennerian vaccination and the creation of a national public health agenda in Japan, 1850–1900', *Bulletin of the History of Medicine*, vol. 83, no. 1, 2009, pp. 125–40.

Jannetta, A., 'From physician to bureaucrat: the case of Nagayo Sensai', in H. Hardacre (ed.), *New Directions in the Study of Meiji Japan*, Leiden: Brill, 1997, pp. 151–60.

Johannson, S. R. and Mosk, C., 'Exposure, resistance and life expectancy: disease and death during the economic development of Japan, 1900–1960', *Population Studies*, vol. 41, 1987, pp. 207–35.

Kasahara, H., '"Eisei keisatsu" to "jichi eisei" no sōkoku: eisei gyōsei no mosaku no tenkan' [Conflict between 'hygiene police' and 'autonomous hygiene': the switch of hygiene administration by trial and error], in H. Kasahara and K. Tamai (eds), *Nihon Seiji no Kōzō no Tenkai* [*The Development of Japan's Political Structure*], Tokyo: Keio University Press, 1998, pp. 93–114.

Kasza, G. J., 'War and welfare policy in Japan', *The Journal of Asian Studies*, vol. 61, no. 2, 2002, pp. 417–35.

Katō, Kanjirō, 'Nōgyosanson no eisei tōjisha ni' [To those who are responsible for hygiene in agricultural, fishing, and mountainous villages], *Kōshū Eisei* [*Public Health*], vol. 51, no. 4, 1937, pp. 232–9.

Kawata, C., 'A historical view of people's involvement in health care in modern Japan', in Yoshio Kawakita, Shizu Sakai and Yasuo Otsuka (eds), *History of Hygiene*, Tokyo: Ishiyaku Euro America, 1991, pp. 247–64.

Kawauchi, Atsushi, 'Chiiki iryō to fashizumu' [Local medicine and fascism], in Namikawa Kenji, David Howell and Kawanishi Hidemichi (eds), *Shūhenshi kara Zentaishi e* [*From Peripheral History to Total History*], Osaka: Seibundō, 2009, pp. 323–56.

Kawauchi, Atsushi, 'Senjiki iryō no keiken: Kenkō Aomoriken no seiritsu to tenkai' [The experience of wartime medicine: the establishment and development of Aomori Health Movement] in Namikawa Kenji and Kawanishi Hidemichi (eds), *Chiiki Nettowāku to Shakai Hen'yō* [*The Regional Network and Social Transformation*], Tokyo: Iwata Shoten, 2008, pp. 427–57.

Kiikuni, K., 'The development of hospitals and clinics in Japan', in T. Ogawa (ed.), *Public Health: Proceedings of the Fifth International Symposium on the Comparative History of Medicine – East and West*, Tokyo: Saikon, 1981, pp. 1–11.

Kobayashi, K., 'Trends in national nutritional survey of Japan', *Nutrition and Health*, vol. 8, 1992, pp. 91–6.

Koikari, M., 'Gender, power and US imperialism: the Occupation of Japan, 1945–52', in T. Ballantyne and A. Burton (eds), *Bodies in Contact: Rethinking colonial encounters in world history*, Durham and London: Duke University Press, 2005, pp. 342–62.

Kovner, S., 'Base cultures: sex workers and servicemen in Occupied Japan', *The Journal of Asian Studies*, vol. 68, no. 3, 2009, pp. 777–804.

Lee, Jong-Chan, 'Hygienic governance and military hygiene in the making of Imperial Japan, 1868–1912', *Historia Scientiarum*, vol. 18, no. 1, 2008, pp. 1–23.

Lewis, J., 'The prevention of diphtheria in Canada and Britain 1914–1945', *Journal of Social History*, vol. 20, no. 1, 1986, pp. 163–76.

Lie, J., 'The state as pimp: prostitution and the patriarchal state in Japan in the 1940s', *The Sociological Quarterly*, vol. 38, no. 2, 1997, pp. 251–63.

Locher, W. G., 'Max von Pettenkofer (1818–1901) as a pioneer of modern hygiene and preventive medicine', *Environmental Health and Preventive Medicine*, vol. 12, 2007, pp. 238–45.

Marui, E., 'The American and Japanese experience with vital statistics reform in the early days of the Occupation', in Y. Kawakita, S. Sakai and Y. Ōtsuka (eds), *History of Epidemiology: Proceedings of the 13th International Symposium on the Comparative History of Medicine – East and West*, Tokyo: Ishiyaku Euro-America, 1993, pp. 191–225.

Marui, E., 'Public health and "koshu eisei" ', in T. Ogawa (ed.), *Public Health: Proceedings of the 5th International Symposium on the Comparative History of Medicine – East and West*, Osaka: Taniguchi Foundation, 1980, pp. 99–107.

Metzler, M., 'The Occupation', in W. M. Tsutsui (ed.), *A Companion to Japanese History*, Oxford: Blackwell, 2007, pp. 265–80.

Meyer, A. H., 'Repatriation at the grass roots', in W. Nimmo (ed.), *The Occupation of Japan: The Grass Roots*, Norfolk, VA: MacArthur Memorial, 1992, pp. 101–15.

Mima, Tatsuya, 'Gunkokushugi jidai: fukushikokka no kigen' [The period of militarism and the origin of the welfare state], in Satō Jun'ichi and Kuroda Kōichirō (eds), *Iryō Sinwa no Shakaigaku* [*Sociology of the Myths of Medicine*], Tokyo: Sekaishisōsha, 1998, pp. 103–26.

Miyashita, S., 'Legal and social measures against trachoma in Japan', *British Journal of Ophthalmology*, vol. 19, 1935, pp. 323–5.

Mizuno, H., 'A historical perspective on the social development of "hygiene" in modern Japan', in Y. Kawakita, S. Sakai and Y. Ōtsuka (eds), *History of Hygiene: Proceedings of the 12th International Symposium on the Comparative History of Medicine – East and West*, Tokyo: Ishiyaku EuroAmerica, 1991, pp. 227–45.

Morris-Suzuki, T., 'An act prejudicial to the Occupation forces: migration controls and Korean residents in post-surrender Japan', *Japanese Studies*, vol. 24, no. 1, 2004, pp. 5–28.

Nagashima, T., 'Meiji medical officials' international comparisons of administrative machinery and the historiography of public health', in *Transactions in Medicine and Heteronomous Modernization*, Tokyo: University of Tokyo Center for Philosophy, 2009, pp. 97–106.

Nagashima, T., 'Exposure to infectious disease in Modern Japan: a case study of the typhus epidemic of 1914', 2006, pp. 1–13.

Nagashima, T., 'Sewage disposal and typhoid fever: the case of Tokyo 1912–1940', *Annales de Demographie Historique*, vol. 108, no. 2, 2004, pp. 105–17.

Narita, R., 'Women and views of women within the changing hygiene conditions of late nineteenth- and early twentieth-century Japan', trans. Gretchen Jones, *US–Japan Women's Journal*, English supplement, vol. 8, 1995, 64–86.

Niimi, Masayoshi, 'The present state of the network of health advice' [Hoken shidōmō no genjō ni tsuite], *Kōshū Eisei* [*Public Health*], vol. 60, no. 6, 1942, pp. 308–14.

Nishimura, S., 'Promoting public health during the American Occupation of Japan: Resistance to allied public health measures, 1945–1952', *American Journal of Public Health*, vol. 99, no. 8, 2009, pp. 1364–75.

Nishimura, S., 'Promoting public health during the American Occupation of Japan: the Public Health Section, Kyoto Military Government Team, 1945–49', *American Journal of Public Health*, vol. 98, no. 3, 2008, pp. 424–34.

Nishimura, S., 'The US medical occupation of Japan and history of the Japanese-language edition of *JAMA*', *Journal of the American Medical Association*, vol. 274, no. 5, 1995, pp. 436–56.

Nishimura, S., 'Medical censorship in Occupied Japan, 1945–48', *The Pacific Historical Review*, vol. 58, no. 1, 1989, pp. 1–21.

Oberlander, C., 'The rise of modern "scientific medicine" in Japan: bacteriology and ber-iberi', in M. Low (ed.), *Building a Modern Japan: Science, technology and medicine in the Meiji era and beyond*, New York: Palgrave Macmillan, 2005, pp. 13–36.

Pape, R. A., 'Why Japan surrrendered', *International Security*, vol. 18, no. 2, 1993, pp. 154–201.

Partner, S., 'Taming the Japanese wilderness: the lifestyle improvement movement in rural Japan, 1925–1965', *Monumenta Nipponica*, vol. 56, no. 4, 2001, pp. 487–520.

Perkins, J. H., 'Reshaping technology in wartime: the effect of military goals on entomo-logical research and insect-control practices', *Technology and Culture*, vol. 19, no. 2, 1978, pp. 169–86.

Rice, G. W. and Palmer, E., 'Pandemic influenza in Japan, 1918–19: mortality patterns and official responses', *Journal of Japanese Studies*, vol. 19, no. 2, 1993, pp. 389–420.

Rosen, G., 'What is social medicine? A genetic analysis of the concept', *Bulletin of the History of Medicine*, vol. 21, 1947, pp. 674–732.

Russell, E. P., 'The strange career of DDT: experts, federal capacity, and environmental-ism in World War II', *Technology and Culture*, vol. 40, no. 4, 1999, pp. 770–96.

Ryder, R., 'Nursing reorganisation in Occupied Japan, 1945–52', *Nursing History Review*, vol. 8, 2000, pp. 71–94.

Saito, H., 'The hygiene movement in Japan during the mid-Meiji period: the ideological structure of the early movement', in Y. Kawakita, S. Sakai and Y. Ōtsuka (eds), *History of Epidemiology: Proceedings of the 13th International Symposium on the Comparative History of Medicine – East and West*, Tokyo: Ishiyaku Euro-America, 1993, pp. 137–60.

Sakai, Kikuo, 'Daitoshi ni okeru kōshūeisei jigyō' [Public health enterprises in large cities], *Tōhoku Igaku Zasshi* [*Journal of Tohoku Medicine*], vol. 20, no. 3, 1937, pp. 255–65.

Sams, C. F., 'American public health administration meets the problems of the Orient in Japan', *American Journal of Public Health and the Nation's Health*, vol. 42, no. 5, 1952, pp. 557–65.

Sams, C. F., 'Japan's new public health program', *Military Government Journal*, September–October 1948, pp. 9–14.

Scoville, A. B., 'Epidemic typhus fever in Japan and Korea', in F. R. Moulton (ed.), *Rickettsial Diseases of Man*, Washington, DC: American Association for the Advancement of Science, 1948, pp. 28–35.

Sheingate, A. and Yamagishi, T., 'Occupation politics: American interests and the struggle over health insurance in postwar Japan', *Social Science History*, vol. 30, no. 1, 2006, pp. 137–64.

Shiga, K., 'The trend of prevention, therapy and epidemiology of dysentery since the discovery of its causative organism', *New England Journal of Medicine*, vol. 215, no. 26, pp. 1205–11.

Shigeta, Shin'ichi, 'Toshi kōseishisetsu no chiiki soshiki ni tsuite' [On the regional organization of urban health facilities], *Nihon Igaku Oyobi Kenkō Hoken* [*Japanese Medicine and Health Insurance*], vol. 3307, 1942, pp. 2366–7; vol. 3308, 1942, pp. 2412–19; vol. 3309, 1942, pp. 2473–4; vol. 3310, 1942, pp. 2521–2.

Sugita, Y., 'Universal health insurance: the unfinished reform of Japan's healthcare system', in M. Caprio and Y. Sugita (eds), *Democracy in Occupied Japan: The US Occupation and Japanese Politics and Society*, London: Routledge, 2007, pp. 147–77.

Sumida, Shigenobu, 'Waga hokenjo ni okeru jissaiteki hoken shidō' [Practical health guidance at our health centre], *Nihon Igaku Oyobi Kenkō Hoken* [*Japanese Medicine and Health Insurance*], vol. 3289, 1942, pp. 1418–19.

Suzuki, A., 'Medicine, state and society in Japan, 500–2000', in W. F. Bynum and H. Bynum (eds), *Dictionary of Medical Biography*, vol. 1, Westport, CT: Greenwood Press, 2007, pp. 79–89.

Suzuki, A. and Suzuki, M., 'Cholera, consumer, and citizenship: modernisation of medicine in Japan', in H. Ebrahimnejad (ed.), *The Development of Modern Medicine in Non-Western Countries*, London: Routledge, 2009, pp. 184–203.

Szreter, Simon, 'The importance of social intervention in Britain's mortality decline c.1850–1914: A reinterpretation of the role of public health', *Social History of Medicine*, vol. 1, 1988, pp. 1–37.

Tanami, Y. and Yamamoto, J., 'The venereal disease problem in Japan', *Bulletin of the World Health Organisation*, vol. 19, 1958, pp. 519–29.

Taniguchi, Masahiro, 'Hōmon hokenfu jigyō ni tsuite' [On visiting nurses], *Iryō Kumiai* [*Medical Union Journal*], vol. 3, no. 12, 1939, pp. 5–6.

Tatara, K., 'The origins and development of public health in Japan', in R. Detels, W. Holland, J. McEwen and G. Omenn (eds), *Oxford Textbook of Public Health*, 3rd edition, vol. 1, *The Scope of Public Health*, New York: Oxford University Press, 1997, pp. 55–72.

Teruoka, Gitō, 'Hoken eisei ni tsuite' [On health and hygiene], *Hoken Kyōiku* [*Health Education*], vol. 5, no. 3, 1941, pp. 40–1.

Tsuneishi, K., 'C. Koizumi: as a promoter of the Ministry of Health and Welfare and an Originator of the BCW research program', *Historia Scientiarum*, vol. 26, 1984, pp. 95–113.

Tsutsui, W., 'Landscapes in the dark valley: toward an environmental history of wartime Japan', *Environmental History*, vol. 8, no. 2, 2003, pp. 294–311.

Vallgårda, Signild, 'Appeals to autonomy and obedience: continuity and change in governing technologies in Danish and Swedish health promotion', *Medical History*, vol. 55, 2011, pp. 27–40.

Veith, I., 'On the mutual indebtedness of Japanese and Western medicine', *Bulletin of the History of Medicine*, vol. 52, 1978, pp. 383–409.

Watanabe, Mikio, ' "DDT kakumei" to sono jidai', *Juntendō Igaku*, vol. 49, no. 2, 2003, pp. 260–1.

Watanabe Mikio, 'Taishō san nen, Tokyo ni okeru hasshin chifusu dairyūkō ni tsuite': bōeki gyōseimon kara ikkōsatsu' [Concerning the typhus epidemic of 1914 in Tokyo: a study from the perspective of epidemic prevention], *Nihon Ishigaku Zasshi* [*Journal of Japanese History of Medicine*], vol. 48, no. 4, 2003, pp. 597–615.

Wildes, H. E., 'Post-war public health development', *Contemporary Japan*, vol. 21, nos 10–12, 1953, pp. 573–92.

Yamamoto, S., 'Introduction of the Western concept and practice of hygiene to Japan during the 19th century', in Y. Kawakita, S. Sakai and Y. Ōtsuka (eds), *History of Hygiene: Proceedings of the 12th International Symposium on the Comparative History of Medicine – East and West*, Tokyo: Ishiyaku EuroAmerica, 1991, pp. 175–92.

Yamamoto, S., 'Cholera in Japan', in T. Ogawa (ed.), *Public Health: Proceedings of the Fifth International Symposium on the Comparative History of Medicine – East and West*, Tokyo: Saikon, 1981, pp. 169–89.

Yosano, Hikaru, 'On rural health' [Nōson hoken mondai ni tsuite], *Ikai Shūhō* [*Medical Weekly*], vol. 342, 1941, pp. 29–30.

Books

Aldous, C., *The Police in Occupation Japan: Control, corruption and resistance to reform*, London: Routledge, 1997.

Ban, T., *Tekijuku to Nagayo Sensai* [*Tekijuku and Nagayo Sensai*], Osaka: Sogensha, 1987.

Bentley, A., *Eating for Victory: Food rationing and the politics of domesticity*, Urban, IL and Chicago, IL: University of Illinois Press, 1998.

Berger, G. M., *Parties out of Power in Japan, 1931–41*, Princeton, NJ: Princeton University Press, 1977.

Bowers, J. Z., *When the Twain Met: The rise of Western medicine in Japan*, Baltimore, MD: Johns Hopkins University Press, 1980.

Burkman, T. W. (ed.), *The Occupation of Japan: Educational and social reform*, Norfolk, VA: MacArthur Memorial, 1981.

Caprio, M. and Sugita, Y. (eds), *Democracy in Occupied Japan: The US Occupation and Japanese politics and society*, London: Routledge, 2007.

Cartwright, F. and Biddiss, M., *Disease and History*, 2nd edition revised, Stroud: Sutton, 2000.

Cohen, J. B., *Japan's Economy in War and Reconstruction*, Minneapolis, MN: University of Minnesota Press, 1949.

Cohen, T., *Remaking Japan: The American Occupation as New Deal*, New York: Free Press, 1987.

Cwiertka, K., *Modern Japanese Cuisine: Food, power and national identity*, London: Reaktion, 2006.

Dore, R. P., *City Life in Japan: A study of a Tokyo ward*, London: Routledge and Kegan Paul, 1958.

Dower, J., *Embracing Defeat: Japan in the wake of World War II*, London: W. W. Norton, 1999.

Dower, J., *Japan in War and Peace: Essays on history, race and culture*, London: Harper Collins, 1995.

Dower, J., *Empire and Aftermath: Yoshida Shigeru and the Japanese experience, 1878–1954*, Cambridge, MA: Harvard University Press, 1988.

Farley, J., *To Cast Out Disease: A History of the International Health Division of the Rockefeller Foundation (1913–1951)*, Oxford: Oxford University Press, 2004.

Fisch, A. G., *Military Government in the Ryukyu Islands 1945–50*, Washington, DC: Center of Military History, 1988.

Francks, P., *The Japanese Consumer: An alternative economic history of modern Japan*, Cambridge: Cambridge University Press, 2009.

Fruhstuck, S., *Colonizing Sex: Sexology and social control in modern Japan*, Berkeley, CA: University of California Press, 2003.

Fujikawa, Y., *Japanese Medicine*, New York: Paul B. Hoeber, 1934.

Fujimura, M., *Nisshin Sensō [The Sino-Japanese War]*, Tokyo: Iwanami Shoten, 1973.

Fujino, Y., *Nihon Fashizumu to Iryō [Japanese Fascism and Medicine]*, Tokyo: Iwanami Shoten, 1993.

Garon, S., *Molding Japanese Minds: The State in Everyday Life*, Princeton, NJ: Princeton University Press, 1997.

Gayn, M., *Japan Diary*, New York: William Sloan, 1948.

Hanley, S. B., *Everyday Things in Premodern Japan*, Berkeley, CA: University of California Press, 1999.

Hardy, A., *The Epidemic Streets: Infectious Disease and the Rise of Preventive Medicine, 1856–1900*, Oxford: Clarendon, 1993.

Harris, S. H., *Factories of Death: Japanese Biological Warfare, 1932–45, and the American Cover-up*, London: Routledge, 1994.

Harrison, M., *Disease and the Modern World*, Cambridge: Polity, 2004.

Havens, T. R. H., *Valley of Darkness: The Japanese People and World War Two*, Lanham, MD: University Press of America, 1986.

Hays, J. N., *The Burdens of Disease*, New Brunswick, NJ: Rutgers University Press, 2003.

Ienaga, S., *The Pacific War: World War II and the Japanese, 1931–1945*, New York: Pantheon, 1978.

Igarashi, Y., *Bodies of Memory: Narratives of war in postwar Japanese culture, 1945–1970*, Princeton, NJ: Princeton University Press, 2000.

Jannetta, A., *The Vaccinators: Smallpox, Medical knowledge and the 'opening' of Japan*, Stanford, CA: Stanford University Press, 2007.

Jannetta, A., *Epidemics and Mortality in Early Modern Japan*, Princeton, NJ: Princeton University Press, 1987.

Jansen, M. B., *The Making of Modern Japan*, Cambridge, MA: Harvard University Press, 2002.

Japan International Cooperation Agency (JICA), *Japan's Experiences in Public Health and Medical Systems*, Tokyo: JICA, 2005.

Johnston, B. F., *Japanese Food Management in World War Two*, Stanford: Stanford University Press, 1953.

Johnston, W., *The Modern Epidemic: A History of Tuberculosis in Japan*, Cambridge, MA: Harvard University Press, 1995.

Johnston, W., *Disease, Medicine and the State: A social history of tuberculosis in Japan, 1850–1950*, PhD thesis, Harvard University, 1987.

Kashima Hokenjo, *Jūnen no Ayumi* [*Ten years of Kashima Health Centre*], n.p., 1955.

Katsumata, Minoru, *Kindai Kōshūeisei no Chichi Katsumata Minoru* [*Katsumata Minoru, the Father of Modern Public Health*], Tokyo: Japan Public Health Association, 1970.

Kawakami, T., *Gendai Nihon Iryōshi* [*A History of Modern Medicine in Japan*], Tokyo: Keiso Shobo, 1965.

Kawakita, Y., Sakai, S. and Otsuka, Y. (eds), *History of Hygiene: Proceedings of the 12th International Symposium on the Comparative History of Medicine – East and West*, Tokyo: Ishiyaku, 1991.

Kiple, K. F. (ed.), *The Cambridge Historical Dictionary of Disease*, Cambridge: Cambridge University Press, 2003.

Kōseishō Gojūnenshi Henshū I'inkai [Welfare Ministry Fifty-Year History Editorial Committee], *Kōseishō Gojūnen Shi* [*A Fifty-Year History of the Welfare Ministry*], Tokyo: Kōseimondai Kenkyūkai, 1988.

Kōseishō Hokenjo-ka [The Health Centre Section, Welfare Ministry], *Hokenjo Sanjūnen Shi* [*Thirty Years of the Health Centre*], Tokyo: Nihon Kōshūeisei Kyōkai, 1971.

Kōseishō Imukyoku, *Isei Hyakunenshi* [*A Hundred Year History of the Medical System*], Tokyo: Gyōsei, 1976.

Kōseishō Nijūnenshi Henshū I'inkai [Welfare Ministry Twenty-Year History Editorial Committee], ed., *Kōseishō Nijūnen Shi* [*A Twenty-Year History of the Welfare Ministry*], Tokyo: Kōseimondai Kenkyūkai, 1960.

Kusama, Y., *Kindai Kasō Minshū Seikatsu Shi* [*A Narrative of the Lives of the Modern Poor*], vol. 2, Tokyo: Akashi Shoten, 1987.

Macfarlane, A., *The Savage Wars of Peace: England, Japan and the Malthusian Trap*, Oxford: Palgrave Macmillan, 2003.

McWilliams, W., *Homeward Bound: Repatriation of Japanese from Korea after World War 2*, Hong Kong: Asian Research Service, 1998.

Miyajima, M., *Robert Koch and Shibasaburo Kitasato*, Geneva: Sonor, 1931.

Morris, J., *The Phoenix Cup: Some notes on Japan in 1946*, London: Cresset, 1947.

Murakami, K., *Senryōki no Fukushi Seisaku*, Tokyo: Keisō Shobō, 1987.

Murakami, Y., *20 Seiki no Nihon 9: Iryō* [*Twentieth Century Japan, vol. 9: Medicine*], Tokyo: Yomiuri Shimbunsha 1996.

Nakashima, Y., *Byōki Nihonshi* [*Disease in Japanese History*], Tokyo: Yuzankaku, 1982.

Nimmo, W. F. (ed.), *The Occupation of Japan: The Grass Roots*, Norfolk, VA: MacArthur Memorial, 1992.

Nishi, T., *Unconditional Democracy: Education and politics in Occupied Japan, 1945–1952*, Stanford: Hoover Institution Press, 1982.

Nishimura, S., *Nihonjin no Inochi o Mamotta Otoko: GHQ Samusu Junsho no Tatakai* [*The Man who Saved Japanese Lives: The struggle of GHQ's Brigadier General Sams*], Tokyo: Kodansha, 2002.

Obayashi, M., *Josampu no Sengo* [*Midwifery in the Postwar Period*] Tokyo: Keisō Shobō, 1989.

Obinata, S., *Kindai Nihon no Keisatsu to Chiiki Shakai* [*The Modern Japanese Police and Provincial Society*], Tokyo: Chikuma Shobō, 2000.

Ogawa, T. and Sakai, S. (eds), *Matsumoto Jun Jiden to Nagayo Sensai Jiden*, Tokyo: Heibonsha, 1980.

Oguri Shirō, *Chihō Eisei Gyōsei no Sōritsu Katei* [*The Process of Establishing Local Hygiene Administrations*], Tokyo: Iryōtosho, 1981.

Ohtani, F., *One Hundred Years of Health Progress in Japan*, Tokyo: International Medical Foundation of Japan, 1971.

Ono, Y., *Seiketsu no kindai* [*Modernization and Cleanliness*], Tokyo: Kodansha, 1997.

Peterson, Alan and Lupton, Deborah, *The New Public Health: Health and self in the age of risk*, London: Sage Publications, 1996.

Porter, Dorothy, *Health, Civilization and the State: A history of public health from ancient to modern times*, London: Routledge, 1999.

Powell, M. and Anesaki, M., *Health Care in Japan*, London: Routledge, 1990.

Ranger, T. and Slack, P. (eds), *Epidemics and Ideas: Essays on the historical perception of pestilence*, Cambridge: Cambridge University Press, 1992.

Rogaski, R., *Hygienic Modernity: Meanings of Health and Disease in Treaty-Port China*, Berkeley, CA: University of California Press, 2004.

Rose, Nikolas, *Powers of Freedom: Reframing political thought*, Cambridge: Cambridge University Press, 1999.

Rosen, G., *A History of Public Health*, Baltimore, MD: Johns Hopkins University Press, 1993.

Russell, E. P., *War and Nature*, Cambridge: Cambridge University Press, 2001.

Sakai, S., *Nihon no Iryōshi* [*A History of Japanese Medicine*], Tokyo: Tokyo Shoseki, 1982.

Saiki, T., *Progress of the Science of Nutrition in Japan*, Geneva: League of Nations Health Organisation, 1926.

Sams, C. F., *'Medic': The mission of an American military doctor in Occupied Japan and wartorn Korea*, edited by Zabelle Zakarian, Armonk, NY: M. E. Sharpe, 1998.

Seaman, L., *The Real Triumph of Japan: The conquest of the silent foe*, London: Sidney Appleton, 1906.

Seidensticker, E., *Tokyo Rising: The city since the Great Earthquake*, New York: Alfred A. Knopf, 1990.

Seijō, Minoru, *Seijō-san no Omoide* [*The Reminiscences of Dr Seijō*], Tokyo: Sankō Publication, 1993.

Shimazaki-Ryder, R. and Ōishi, S., *Sengo Nihon no Kango Kaikaku* [*Nursing Reform in Postwar Japan*], Tokyo: Nihon kango kyōkai shuppankai, 2003.

Shimizu, K., *Nihon Kōshū Eisei Shi: Shōwa Zenki Hen* [*History of Public Hygiene in Japan: Early Showa edition*], Tokyo: Fuji Shuppan, 1989.

Stuart, G. H., *Public Health in Occupied Japan*, PhD dissertation, University of London, April 1950.

Sugaya, A., *Nihon Shakai Seisaku Shiron* [*An Essay on Japanese Social Policy*], Tokyo: Nihon Hyōronsha, 1987.

Sugaya, A., *Nihon Iryō Seisakushi* [*History of Japan's Medical Policy*], Tokyo: Nihon Hyōronsha, 1977.

Sugaya, A., *Nihon Iryō Seidōshi* [*History of Japan's Medical System*], Tokyo: Sanyōsha, 1976.

226   *Bibliography*

Sugiyama, Akiko, *Senryōki no Iryōkaikaku* [*Medical Reform during the Occupation*], Tokyo: Keisō Shobō, 1995.

Taeuber, I. B., *The Population of Japan*, Princeton, NJ: Princeton University Press, 1958.

Takahashi, A., *The Development of the Japanese Nursing Profession*, London: Routledge Curzon, 2004.

Takano, R., Ohtsubo, I. and Inouye, Z., *Studies of Cholera in Japan*, Geneva: League of Nations Health Organisation, 1926.

Takaoka, Hiroyuki, *Sōryokusen Taisei to Fukushi Kokka* [*The Total War Regime and the Welfare State*], Tokyo: Iwanami Shoten, 2011.

Takemae, E., *Inside GHQ: The Allied Occupation of Japan and its Legacy*, trans. Robert Ricketts and Sebastian Swann, London: Continuum, 2002.

Takemae, E., *C. F. Samusu, DDT Kakumei: senryōki no iryō fukushi seisaku o kaisō suru* [*DDT Revolution: Reflecting on the reform of medicine and welfare policy during the Occupation*], Tokyo: Iwanami Shoten, 1986.

Takigawa Hokenjo, *Hokkaido Takigawa Hokenjo Jūnen no Ayumi* [*The First Ten Years of Takigawa Health Centre in Hokkaido*], n.p., n.d.

Tanaka, Y., *Japan's Comfort Women: Sexual slavery and prostitution during World War II and the US Occupation*, London: Routledge, 2002.

Tipton, E. K., *Modern Japan: A social and political history*, London: Routledge, 2002.

Tokyo-to Hokenjo Jūgonen Shi [*Fifteen Years of Health Centres in Tokyo*], Tokyo, n.p., 1965.

Tokyo-to Hokenjo Shochōkai [Association of the Heads of Health Centres in Tokyo], *Tokyoto Hokenjo Jūgoshūnen Kinenshi* [*Fifteen Years of the Association of the Heads of Health Centres in Tokyo*], Tokyo: n.p., 1965.

Tracy, H., *Kakemono: A sketch book of postwar Japan*, London: Methuen, 1950.

Tsurumi, E. P. (ed.), *The Other Japan: Postwar realities*, Armonk, NY: M. E. Sharpe, 1988.

Turnock, B., *Public Health: What it is and how it works*, 3rd edition, Boston, MA: Jones and Bartlett, 2004.

Van Staaveren, J., *An American in Japan, 1945–48: A civilian view of the Occupation*, Seattle, WA: University of Washington Press, 1994.

Vernon, J., *Hunger: A modern history*, Cambridge, MA: Harvard University Press, 2007.

Watts, S., *Disease and Medicine in World History*, London: Routledge, 2003.

Watts, S., *Epidemics and History: Disease, power and imperialism*, New Haven, CT: Yale University Press, 1997.

Weindling, P. J., *Epidemics and Genocide in Eastern Europe 1890–1945*, Oxford: Oxford University Press, 2000.

Weiner, M., *Race and Migration in Imperial Japan*, London: Routledge, 1994.

Wicentowski, J., *Policing Health in Modern Japan*, PhD dissertation, Department of History, Harvard University, May 2007.

Wildes, H. E., *Typhoon in Tokyo*, New York: Macmillan, 1954.

Winslow, C. A., *The Conquest of Epidemic Disease*, New York: Hafner, 1967.

Yamamoto, S., *Nihon Korera Shi* [*A History of Cholera in Japan*], Tokyo: Tokyo University Press, 1982.

Yamashita, S. H., *Leaves from an Autumn of Emergencies*, Honolulu: University of Hawai'i Press, 2005.

Yoshimi, K. (ed.), *Baishō no Shakaishi* [*Social History of Prostitution*], Tokyo: Yūzankaku, 1984.

Zinnser, Hans, *Rats, Lice and History*, Boston, MA: Bantam, 1935.

Index